Effective Collaboration for Educating
the Whole Child

This book is dedicated to our students who have moved into professional roles and are exercising leadership every day to provide collaborative services to address the needs of the whole child. Their impact on the field and on children and youth are the true measure of our work. We also dedicate this work to the parents of students with complex needs who struggle daily to negotiate the maze of services distributed among multiple agencies. They are accidental "service coordinators," and from them we have so much to learn if we listen.

Effective
Collaboration
for Educating
the
Whole
Child

Carol A. Kochhar-Bryant
with Angela Heishman

A Joint
Publication

CORWIN
A SAGE Company

For information:

Corwin
A SAGE Company
2455 Teller Road
Thousand Oaks, California 91320
(800) 233-9936
Fax: (800) 417-2466
www.corwin.com

SAGE Ltd.
1 Oliver's Yard
55 City Road
London EC1Y 1SP
United Kingdom

SAGE Pvt. Ltd.
B 1/I 1 Mohan Cooperative
  Industrial Area
Mathura Road, New Delhi 110 044
India

SAGE Asia-Pacific Pte. Ltd.
33 Pekin Street #02-01
Far East Square
Singapore 048763

Printed in the United States of America

Library of Congress Cataloging-in-Publication Data

Kochhar-Bryant, Carol A.
Effective collaboration for educating the whole child / Carol A. Kochhar-Bryant, Angela Heishman.
    p. cm.
"A Joint Publication With the National Staff Development Council."
Includes bibliographical references and index.
ISBN 978-1-4129-6527-9 (pbk.)

  1. Children with social disabilities—Education—United States. 2. Multicultural education—United States. 3. Group work in education—United States. 4. School environment—United States. I. Heishman, Angela. II. Title.

LC4091.K63 2010
371.91—dc22   2009053419

This book is printed on acid-free paper.

10 11 12 13 14   10 9 8 7 6 5 4 3 2 1

Acquisitions Editor:	Jessica Allan
Associate Editor:	Joanna Coelho
Editorial Assistant:	Allison Scott
Production Editor:	Veronica Stapleton
Copy Editor:	Paula L. Fleming
Typesetter:	C&M Digitals (P) Ltd.
Proofreader:	Wendy Jo Dymond
Indexer:	Sheila Bodell
Cover Designer:	Scott Van Atta

Contents

Preface

An overarching goal of education is to promote the highest possible level of academic development for each child who arrives at the school door. However, academic development alone is insufficient for preparing today's 21st-century citizen. As school professionals become increasingly concerned with the academic performance of students, they are more aware of the need for educating the *whole child*—attending to cognitive, social-emotional, physical, and ethical development. Furthermore, emerging research related to the developing brain and new knowledge about child resilience makes it imperative that school personnel pay close attention to how the school, family, and community environments impact students' healthy development and school achievement.

Educating the whole child requires that teaching and learning embrace all dimensions of student development. Achieving these goals for each student requires collaboration among professionals within the school and in the community. This challenge raises several questions. How do professionals from different disciplines work together and blend their skills and talents to address the developmental needs of students? How do professionals work across the institutional boundaries of schools and community agencies? What attitudes and beliefs about collaboration are needed to work together effectively to create school environments for children who are healthy—socially, emotionally, and developmentally? Who takes responsibility for the collaborative process, and who intervenes when the process breaks down? This book describes the characteristics of effective collaborative teams for educating the whole child and how to create them.

It has long been recognized that schools alone cannot provide all the supports that children and their families need. *Shared responsibility* for a community's children has recently become a watchword for educators and human service personnel. The notion of shared responsibility implies working across school-community agency boundaries to create a well-coordinated service system to meet the holistic (whole-child) needs of students. This book, therefore, is concerned with connecting systems—within schools and between schools and communities—and the extraordinary communication and cooperation it takes to accomplish it.

This book also emphasizes the important transitions in the course of development and progress from elementary years through high school and into the adult world. The transition from one level to another (e.g., kindergarten to first grade, elementary to middle, middle to high school, and high school to higher education or employment) can be an exciting time, but it is daunting for many children and their parents. Recent research indicates that one-third of all children demonstrate mild to serious difficulties with such transitions, which can interfere with learning and development. Well-coordinated and supported transitions can make the difference between success and chronic struggle as children move from one level in the education system to the next. A *developmentally healthy environment* reflects the careful attention of professionals to these transitions.

Finally, this book centers on the role of collaboration and coordination as central to problem solving and change in classrooms, schools, and school-community systems. Collaboration and coordination are essential to change in relationships among people, which leads to change in practices, which ultimately leads to healthy development and academic progress in students. Often both the successes and the difficulties with the collaborative process can be traced to problems in professional and personal relationships. Likewise, the cornerstones of coordinated interagency relationships are the personal relationships of the individuals involved. The quality of these relationships depends on the team skills and beliefs and attitudes of the people involved. The chapters that follow address how professional collaboration and coordination work, who takes responsibility for the process, and how it ultimately can affect student outcomes.

INTRODUCTION TO THE CHAPTERS

Chapter 1, What Does It Mean to Educate the Whole Child? introduces the issues and challenges that professionals face in responding to the wide range of developmental needs of children and youth in schools. This chapter presents a picture of the conditions for children and youth today that greatly affect their educational participation, engagement, progress, and ultimate life outcomes—and that warrant a call to action. The chapter explores the challenges of educating children—*both with and without identified disabilities*—who develop at greatly differing rates. It examines the connection between children's environment and learning and defines collaboration as being essential in schools' responses to serving the whole child. The chapters in the balance of this book address *how* collaboration and coordination work for educating the whole child and who takes responsibility for the process.

Chapter 2, What Is a Developmentally Healthy School Environment? defines the characteristics of a healthy school environment, the factors that promote it, and those that undermine it. The chapter discusses the connections between school environment and learning and between social and emotional health and learning, the impacts of key transition points on learning, and the importance of professional collaboration in attending to the range of developmental domains of students. The chapter also explores the special needs of students, both with and without disabilities, who need extra support in the school environment, including those who do not meet criteria for special education. It addresses factors that are associated with school safety and violence prevention, school dropout prevention, and reduction in placement into alternative education settings, and it discusses the role of families.

Chapter 3, What Laws Promote Collaboration for the Whole Child Initiative? traces the history of our concern about the relationship between the school environment and children's development. It outlines the history of perspectives on the role of schools in addressing the needs of the whole child and introduces the emergence of strength-based approaches and the impact of the positive youth development movement. This chapter discusses policy makers' recognition of the importance of school-linked services and interagency collaboration in promoting students' academic success and general developmental progress through schooling. This chapter also provides an overview of the laws that promote developmentally healthy school environments, including the Individuals with Disabilities Education Improvement Act (IDEIA) of 2004, the No Child Left Behind Act (NCLB) of 2001, Safe and Drug-Free Schools legislation, and emerging mental health legislation at the state and federal levels.

Chapter 4, How Do Schools Create Developmentally Responsive Environments? discusses the roles, responsibilities, and interconnections among a variety of professionals who collaborate to create developmentally healthy school environments. These professionals include teachers, administrators, counselors, school psychologists, speech and language therapists, occupational therapists, and other related support service specialists in the school community. Their roles in developing strengths-based developmental approaches through collaboration are explored, with voices of professionals incorporated throughout the chapter.

Chapter 5, How Do Professionals Collaborate to Educate the Whole Child? discusses the essential relationships and skills needed for effective communication, collaboration, and coordination to take place and describes the characteristics of effective collaborative teams. It explores why intraschool collaboration and interagency service coordination have been so difficult to accomplish within the field of education. The chapter introduces models and strategies for collaboration, stages in the development of collaborative teams, barriers to collaboration, and principles and professional standards for collaboration. Examples of professional collaboration are presented.

Chapter 6, What Is the Role of Community Agencies? explores strategies to support developmentally healthy school environments through coordinated services between schools and community agencies. Models for coordination, stages in the development of school-agency relationships, development of interagency agreements, and whole-school approaches to coordination are introduced. Whole-school approaches and interagency coordination are illustrated with case examples.

Chapter 7, How Does Cultural and Linguistic Diversity Affect Professional Collaboration? explores the question of how cultural and linguistic diversity affects professional collaboration among educators and other professionals and how educators can improve collaboration and coordination of services for culturally and linguistically diverse students and families. The chapter introduces principles for professional collaboration with culturally and linguistically diverse students and parents, and it discusses barriers to communication and collaboration associated with diversity and presents strategies for overcoming them.

Chapter 8, Celebrating Our Work: The Benefits and Positive Impacts of Professional Collaboration, explores what is working in local schools to create developmentally healthy environments. It discusses the signs of success and describes methods of measuring the impact of collaboration on schools and student achievement. A tool for self-assessment of professional collaboration is presented.

WHAT IS THE AUTHORS' RELEVANT EXPERIENCE?

Throughout our professional lives, we have collaborated with teachers, counselors, school psychologists, speech and language specialists, and related services personnel to promote collaboration in their preparation and in their practice. We have learned three important lessons over the years: (1) across the nation, students preparing to work in schools in the fields of counseling, school psychology, and related professions are not adequately prepared in their training to collaborate with teachers, particularly in regard to students with special learning needs; (2) teachers in training across the nation are not adequately prepared to collaborate with other school professionals; and (3) school personnel and researchers confirm that the need for such collaboration is growing in every school district across the United States. Furthermore, few professionals are prepared for school settings in which social, emotional, and behavioral disorders are becoming more prevalent.

The book is also based on over 30 years' experience developing, managing, and studying school and community agency coordination, at the local, state, and national levels, for children and youth who are at risk of failing to thrive socially or academically in general education. The material in the book reflects our experiences working with schools, school systems, and states to improve collaboration and coordination among agencies. The chapters have also been shaped by years of research and countless interviews with teachers, school administrators, counselors and school psychologists, speech-language specialists, local and state coordinators, parents, students, and others involved in making collaboration and coordination work.

Finally, Carol Kochhar-Bryant's perspective has been deeply enriched by the experience of being a parent of a young adult who has needed specialized and supportive services from a variety of agencies and professionals through most of his life. He is now navigating the tumultuous passage of transition into young adulthood, gradually gaining ground in his daily struggle to overcome multiple challenges from within. Together over the years, he and his mother have negotiated services from five different agencies to provide the combination of supports he has needed. Together, they have learned just how important the parent is in the collaboration and coordination process, and just how unpredictable the journey.

FOR WHOM WAS THIS BOOK WRITTEN?

This book is designed for a variety of professionals who want to improve school collaboration and the coordination of services to address the needs of the whole child. The book is useful for any professional concerned with children—*both with and without identified disabilities*—who receive services that require professional collaboration within the school or among schools and community agencies. The material is appropriate for those preparing for professional roles in a variety of education and human services fields, including as general educators, special educators, administrators, school counselors, psychologists, speech-language therapists, parents and parent advocates, guidance counselors, school counselors and mental health workers, and professional development coordinators.

Acknowledgments

We would like to acknowledge the significant contributions of our editors, who were at once encouraging, supportive, and patient as they shepherded us through this process. Also, we express deep appreciation for our external review panel, whose comments, suggestions and critiques have greatly improved this work. Finally, we thank our colleagues who contributed anecdotes, stories, cases, and perspectives that added richness and depth to the landscape of this book.

Corwin gratefully acknowledges the contributions of the following individuals:

Charlotte Y. Alverson, Transition Specialist
Eugene, OR

Elizabeth Evans Getzel, VCU-RRTC Director of Postsecondary Education Initiatives
Virginia Commonwealth University
Richmond, VA

Deborah Long, Mentor Coordinator
Merced Union High School
Merced, CA

Amanda McKee, Math Teacher
Johnsonville High School
Johnsonville, SC

Maria Mesires, Seventh-Grade Life Science Teacher, Chair & Intermediate SAR for STANYS
Northcentral Case Middle School
Watertown, NY

Cathy Riggs, Director of Special Education and Pupil Services
Rocky Hill Public Schools
Rocky Hill, CT

Sancta Sorenson, Special Education Teacher
Omaha Public Schools
Omaha, NE

Pattie Thomas, Principal
Raymond L. Young Elementary School
Talladega, Al

Kathy Tritz-Rhodes, Principal
Marcus-Meriden-Cleghorn Schools
Marcus, IA

Kim Vogel, Principal
Parkdale Elementary School
Parkdale, OR

About the Author

 **Carol A. Kochhar-Bryant**, EdD, is Professor of Special Education at The George Washington (GW) University, Washington, D.C. She has developed and directed graduate and doctoral leadership development programs in special education and conducts evaluations for public school districts, state departments of education, and federal agencies to improve educational services for all learners. Trained in special education and psychology, Dr. Kochhar-Bryant has directed residential services for individuals with disabilities and community service coordination/case management services and has worked in in-patient psychiatric services. Her research interests focus on educating adolescents with complex learning needs in general and in alternative education settings, mental health concerns and system coordination, effective transition of youth to adult life, and preparation of leadership to assist at-risk youth. She collaborated for 10 years with the Hamilton Fish Institute on School and Community Violence at the GW University, conducting research on alternative pathways through education for youth. Her recent relevant publications on these subjects include *Pathways to Successful Transition for Youth with Disabilities* (coauthored with Gary Greene, 2nd edition, 2008); *Collaboration and System Coordination for Children with Special Needs: From Early Childhood to the Postsecondary Years* (2007); *Expelling Violent Students: The Alternative Is Education;* "Alternative Education as a Quality Choice for Youth: Preparing Educators for Effective Programs" (coauthored with Renee Lacey); "Caring Alternatives: Interagency Collaboration to Improve Outcomes for Students With Mental Health Needs"; and *Profiling Success in Alternative Education.* Dr. Kochhar-Bryant is past president of the Division on Career Development and Transition of the Council for Exceptional Children. She lives in Reston, Virginia, with her husband and is a mother of four.

ABOUT THE CONTRIBUTOR

 **Angela Heishman** is a Nationally Certified School Psychologist, a Certified School Psychologist in Pennsylvania, and a Licensed Professional Counselor. She holds a Diplomate in School Neuropsychology from the American Board of School Neuropsychology. She is currently a school psychologist and Student Assistance Coordinator at the Big Spring School District in Newville, Pennsylvania. In her previous employment at Teenline at Holy Spirit Hospital in Camp Hill, she served as a mental health liaison, program consultant, and crisis responder for several Student Assistance Teams across central Pennsylvania. She was also a lead trainer on the Student Assistance Program (SAP) model as endorsed by the Commonwealth Approved Training System through the Pennsylvania Department of Education's Division of Safe and Drug Free schools. In addition to her experiences as an outpatient counselor, she has also worked extensively with adults with disabilities in residential services. She is currently a doctoral candidate in special education at George Washington University, Washington, D.C. She lives with her husband and twin children, Ian and Ava.

What Does It Mean to Educate the Whole Child?

This is not a tidy tale; collaboration is an untidy business, full of uncharted territories, ambiguities, and institutional complexities.

—Marilyn Johnston, 1997, p. 3

To the doctor, the child is a typhoid patient; to the playground supervisor, a first baseman; to the teacher, a learner of arithmetic. At times, he may be different things to each of these specialists, but too rarely is he a whole child to any of them.

—From the 1930 report of the White House
Conference on Children and Youth

CHAPTER TOPICS

- Collaboration Makes Pioneers of Us All
- Dance of Development: The Paradox of Educating Children Who Develop at Different Rates
- What Does It Mean to Educate the Whole Child?
- What Is Collaboration, and Why Is It Important for Educating the Whole Child?
- What Is Developmentally Responsive Practice?
- How Do Environment and Health Status Affect Learning and Development?
- How Does Social-Emotional Health Affect Learning and Development?
- How Does Participation in High-Risk or Illegal Behavior Affect Learning and Development?
- What Is the Family's Role in Promoting the Development of the Whole Child?

INTRODUCTION: THE NEW FACE OF DIVERSITY

Educational professionals today expect highly diverse groups of students in their schools. Most deeply appreciate the value of such diversity for the learning communities that a school and classroom represent. What many may not be prepared for is the profound nature of the life experiences many students have faced or are facing that form the basis from which they will try to frame their futures. Many of the diverse faces in the classroom have grown up in circumstances that make them highly vulnerable, that can undermine their ability to learn and progress in school, or that make them unable to connect with adults and peers. This may not be news to a teacher who has worked to pull a struggling student back from the brink of failure. But it is a very timely subject for communities across the nation that face staggering social and economic costs resulting from the growing numbers of children and youth with highly complex barriers to learning.

Children of Poverty

Vulnerable children and youth include those in chronic poverty and victims of domestic violence and community unrest for whom daily survival is the primary goal. They are the children whose families and homes are threatened by crushing economic circumstances beyond their control. They include the orphans and foster children and others who are wards of the State.

Exploited and Refugee Children From Other Nations

This new face of diversity is a growing population that includes a wide range of exploited, refugee, and abandoned children from around the world who have come to the United States, often with the support of U.S. and international aid, relief, and protection agencies. They include the 10-year-old Sudenese boy whose family recently fled from a nation in conflict, having had no time to grieve the slaying of his brother and sister. They are the 15-year-old girl from Afghanistan who did not continue her education beyond elementary school because her high school was located 12 challenging miles on the other side of a mountain. They are the 8-year-old Namibian boy who has lost both parents to HIV; before he was rescued by his uncle, he had been raising his six brothers and sisters alone after his grandmother died. They are the daughter of a Guatemalan widow who is in the United States to earn what she can to send home to her family. They are the children of a Bosnian restaurant owner who managed to escape the occupation of his town and entered the United States under asylum. They are the 5-year-old orphan brothers from the Ukraine who were adopted by an American family after three years in an institution. They are the son of a 17-year-old Indonesian mother who was illegally trafficked into the United States and escaped with the help of a U.S. Department of State victim protection program.

These are the faces of trauma, deep emotional pain, survival, and struggle—but also often of great hope. They may come with little experience with schooling, and in most cases, they have substantial social and emotional needs.

Children of Divorce, Family, and Community Violence

Children of divorce and family violence now represent over half of all children in the United States. Research reveals that children from divorced families, or who live with family violence, are more likely to have academic problems than those in intact families, more likely to get into trouble with school authorities and police, and more likely to have social and emotional problems. In terms of grades, standardized test scores, and dropout rates, children whose parents divorce generally have poorer results (Jeynes, 2002).

Children With Health and Mental Health Disparities

The population of children with health and mental health disparities is on the rise. Health disparities directly and indirectly affect students' motivation and ability to learn. Reducing educationally related health disparities can favorably influence education outcomes and help close the achievement gap (Basch, 2009). Six educationally relevant health factors—vision, asthma, teen pregnancy, aggression and violence, physical activity, and nutrition/breakfast—disproportionately affect the urban minority youth population, and each affects educational outcomes. To this should be added diabetes, a growing problem that disproportionately affects the health of African American children and adults (Peek, Cargill, & Huang, 2007). According to Basch, healthier students make better learners, yet health issues mostly have been neglected in school reform.

Children in Families in Financial Crisis

A recently expanding population of children are those whose families are losing their homes due to foreclosure and bankruptcy and their jobs due to layoffs. The current economy has transformed many families from working or middle class to poor. The most vulnerable are children who

- have families directly impacted by economic difficulties.
- have parents working for financial institutions directly affected by the current economic situation.
- have suffered a personal loss from economic problems and/or other stressful events.
- live in communities seriously impacted by economic problems and/or other stressful events.
- suffer from mental health challenges (National Association of School Psychologists [NASP], 2008).

The sense of confusion and uncertainty experienced by many adults in these circumstances can be transmitted to children. Therefore, professionals should be alert to indications of stress in children under their care.

Children With Special Learning Needs

Finally, we add the children who learn differently or at a pace that is different from their typical peers, whether they need more time or less time to achieve developmental levels or proficiency in academic subjects. They include the talented child who appears bored, alienated, and silent in class and dreams only of getting home to create the music that has been the center of his attention since he can remember; the intensely gifted teen who can complete all of the mathematics problems before his peers but must wait for others to catch up; the child who cannot organize and focus on her work or sit quietly for any length of time without distracting her peers; and the student who is plagued with anxieties, the source of which he does not understand.

Children who come to school from dramatically unequal circumstances often leave school with similarly unequal skills and abilities (Neuman, 2009). However, many such children have been strengthened by their experiences and are mature beyond their years. Their success in the traditional school setting depends upon the sensitivity of professionals: educators who understand the child's unique experiences, appreciate the aspects of development that need special nurturing, and find a way to integrate the child into the social as well as academic community of learners.

As school professionals become increasingly concerned about student achievement, they also recognize that academic development and performance are intertwined with many other aspects of development that *must be nurtured*. They recognize the need to educate the *whole child*—attending to cognitive, social, emotional, physical, and talent development of children and youth from widely diverse backgrounds. The future of our nation depends on the healthy development of our children, and the development of our children depends on the readiness and dedication of qualified professionals dedicated to working with all children. Today's professionals appreciate diversity in learners and understand that no dimension of development is outside their role or concern. They likewise appreciate diversity in their colleagues and accept that the work of building the future cannot be done in isolation but only in collaboration with all who share the common mission.

COLLABORATION MAKES PIONEERS OF US ALL

As we read the litany of challenges and barriers to learning that children, families, and professionals face, it may be easy to become discouraged. But with us or without us, these children, youth and families face their challenges every day. Like parents, we professionals may feel the problem pile is too big for us. Parents, however, don't have the option to throw in the towel. Our discouragement is usually born out of a sense that we are too far behind to make improvements. We are too small to attack a Goliath of obstacles that seem to grow every day, and we feel very alone in the task. But *this is where we are—and it is where we must begin.* Like parents, professionals are on a journey that continues one step at a time. We attack each new challenge not alone but together, reaching out for support, and we make a difference one student at a time. Each act of collaboration forces us to see the world anew, rethink our traditional roles, and create new relationships with our peers that can help us work differently together on behalf of children and families. We all become pioneers on the frontier of our own making.

This chapter presents a picture of the conditions for children and youth today that greatly affect their educational participation, engagement, progress, and ultimate life outcomes—and that warrant a call to action. The chapter explores the challenges of educating children who develop at greatly different rates, examines the connection between children's environment and learning, and defines the collaboration essential in schools' responses to serving the whole child. The chapters in the balance of this book address *how* collaboration and coordination work to educate the whole child and who takes responsibility for the process. The primary goal is to explore the possibilities and potential of professional collaboration and interagency coordination for improving the education of all students with complex needs—both with and without identified disabilities. How our schools support children through different developmental paths reflects our nation's understanding of child development—and our commitment to students' long-term success.

DANCE OF DEVELOPMENT: THE PARADOX OF EDUCATING CHILDREN WHO DEVELOP AT DIFFERENT RATES

While tension will always exist between standardized education and individualized education, all educators agree on one thing: children and youth develop at very different rates cognitively, socially-emotionally, physically, and in language development. Until the late 1980s, most research examining life transitions and adjustments as students moved from elementary to middle school and from middle through high school was guided by the theory that problems with coping during development were caused by rapid cognitive, physical, and social-emotional changes. While grade progression occurs in lockstep fashion for all students, the developmental process for children does not occur in a step-by-step linear fashion. Rather, it zigzags, or dances, side to side and forward and backward but with a net movement forward, like the child who skips in small circles as he winds his way slowly down the street. Development is a gradual process, not an event, though children are often expected to force-fit their individual dance of development into the straight lines of grade progression and one-size-fits-all developmental expectations.

If we view educational environments as well-choreographed routines and students whose "dance" of development varies widely, then only a very few might actually dance "correctly." Most of the others will either be force-fit with some partial degree of success, or they may never fit at all. Yet the educational enterprise continues to offer standard routines unless the student has a legally required Individualized Education Program. Keeping with the metaphor, dance experts recommend that if a routine is for a group, then the dance instructor should gauge each person's flexibility and ability to follow through. Additional supports are provided for those who need extra time or preparation. Thus it is—or should be—with education.

Beyond the Metaphor: Research Confirms the Dance of Development

Humans develop in stages and in a variety of domains—physical, cognitive, emotional, social, and moral. Each domain develops in the context of all others and cannot be separated. Each affects the others in important ways. Development in these multiple, interacting domains can be viewed as passing thorough specific stages, with transitions to each new stage being influenced by, or contingent upon, accomplishments attained in previous stages. Just as children's language or mental capabilities develop as a result of maturation and experience, so too do children's development in other domains, such as social, emotional, and ethical. Development in the multiple domains varies somewhat for each child and is affected by both internal (biological predispositions, within-child abilities) and external (physical and social environment) influences (Brett, Smith, Price, & Huitt, 2003; Case & Okamoto, 1996).

Individual variation in development has at least two dimensions: (1) the inevitable variations around the average or typical path of development and (2) the uniqueness of each person developing in a unique social and community environment. Each child possesses an individual pattern and timing of growth, as well as individual personality, temperament, physical constitution, learning style, family, and experiential background. All children have unique strengths, talents, and interests, and for some children, special or atypical learning and developmental needs require special responses from the educational community.

As professionals recognize that individual variation is not only to be expected but also *valued,* they realize that decisions about curriculum and adults' interactions with children must be as individualized and as **developmentally responsive** as possible (National Association for the Education of Young Children [NAEYC], 2009). Development and learning result from the interaction of biological maturation and the environment, which includes both the physical and social worlds in which children live. Children are results of both predetermined heredity and environmental influences that affect maturation. Neither perspective alone is sufficient to explain individual learning or development; development is viewed as the result of an interactive, transactional process between the growing, changing individual and his or her experiences in the social and physical worlds (Butcher & Plomin, 2008; NAEYC; Petrill, Pike, Price, & Plomin, 2004). For example, a child's physical condition at birth may predict healthy growth, but family poverty and chronic malnutrition in early years may affect long-term outcomes and trigger a variety of developmental disabilities. Similarly, a child's unique temperament creates personality characteristics that can make a child cautious about the world, or outgoing, which in turn shapes his or her experiences and social environment.

WHAT DOES IT MEAN TO EDUCATE THE WHOLE CHILD?

The purpose of education has been debated for centuries. Many educators and child development experts argue that the overarching goal of education is to promote the highest possible levels of cognitive, social, emotional, physical, and ethical development for each child. The whole-child movement is based on the proposition that education must move beyond preparing children to become "well-educated" citizens who are productive participants in the economic system. Education must also cultivate in young people spirituality, reverence for the natural environment, and a sense of social justice. Education must inspire children's creativity, imagination, compassion, self-knowledge, social skills, and emotional health. In this way, the term *holistic education* simply means cultivating the whole person and helping individuals live more consciously within their communities and natural ecosystems (Miller, 2005).

More recently, educational psychologists have proposed that holistic education is aimed at helping students be the most that they can be, or what Maslow (1954) referred to as "self-actualization." Education with a holistic perspective is concerned with the development of every person's intellectual, emotional, social, physical, artistic, creative, and spiritual potentials. It seeks to engage students in the teaching/learning process and encourages personal and collective responsibility on the part of professionals charged with students' development.

The quest for holistic education requires that educational experiences and environments be adapted to the developmental path of the individual, rather than the individual adapted to the environment. In today's economy—and an era of standardization of curriculum, student assessments, educational environments, and expected grade-level progress—schools find little incentive for individualization based on the needs and postschool goals of the student. Having high expectations for all children is important, but expectations that are cast as rigid group norms do not reflect what is known about real differences in individual development and learning during the early years. Too many children and youth who cannot adapt to the standards are being left behind.

What Are the Core Qualities of Holistic Education?

Ron Miller (2008), a leading proponent of holistic education, defined it as follows:

Holistic education is an effort to cultivate the development of the whole human being. Where conventional schooling traditionally reflects the view of the child as a passive receiver of information and rules, or at most as a computer-like processor of information, a holistic approach recognizes that to become a full person, a growing child needs to develop—in addition to intellectual skills—physical, psychological, emotional, interpersonal, moral and spirited potentials. The child is not merely a future citizen or employee in training, but an intricate and delicate web of vital forces and environmental influences. (p. 5)

Miller identified four core qualities that characterize a holistic education:

1. *It encourages experiential learning.* There is more discussion, questioning, experimentation, and active engagement in a holistic learning environment and a noticeable absence of grading, testing, labeling, and comparing. Learning is more meaningful and relevant to students—it matters to their lives.

2. *Personal relationships are considered to be as important as academic subject matter.* These learning environments strive to cultivate a sense of community and belonging and qualities of safety, respect, caring, and even love.

3. *There is concern for the interior life of children; that is, for the feelings, aspirations, ideas, and questions that each student brings to the learning process.* Education is no longer viewed as the transmission of information; instead it is a journey inward as well as outward into the world.

4. *Holistic education expresses an "ecological consciousness."* It recognizes that everything in the world exists in context; that is, in relationship to inclusive communities. This involves a deep respect for the integrity of the biosphere, if not a sense of reverence for nature. It is a worldview that embraces diversity, both natural and cultural.

O'Hara (2006) explained that our current educational goals and practices are insufficient to the level of complexity of our world; they cannot deal with the uncertainty, flexibility, creativity, dialogue, understanding, and wisdom being asked of the 21st-century journeyer. What is being called for is the "cultivation of levels of consciousness and habits of mind that go way beyond the mental capacities canonized in the Western industrialized world" (p. 111).

What Does Educating the Whole Child Look Like?

The boxed text presents the experience of a full-service school that incorporates whole-child strategies.

A FULL-SERVICE SCHOOL FULFILLS ITS PROMISE

Positive Outcomes of a Whole-Child Approach (1999–2008)

In the late 1990s, teachers and administrators here at Thomas Edison Elementary School in Port Chester, New York, could see that the struggles of neighborhood families were affecting students' safety and well-being. They were also contributing to low academic achievement.

Although Port Chester is surrounded by affluent areas of Westchester County, our community is far from wealthy. More than 80 percent of Thomas Edison's students receive free or reduced-price lunch, and nearly 50 percent are English language learners. The majority of our families are recent immigrants. They struggle to afford adequate housing, child care, nutrition, and health care. They also face the stresses that accompany immigration: worry about legal status, the difficult process of acculturation, language barriers, frequent moves and disrupted schooling, separation from family members, and school expectations very different from those in their home countries. These factors all contributed to low academic performance at Edison: in 1999, only 19 percent of Edison's fourth graders passed New York State's English language arts assessment, and only 75 percent passed the state mathematics assessment.

Divining Community Concerns

That year, Edison began the process of becoming a full-service community school. First, Edison faculty and community stakeholders sought a deeper understanding of the conditions that were influencing student learning. We conducted focus groups, individual interviews, and surveys in which we asked school practitioners, parents, students, and representatives of community-based organizations what concerns they had about Edison's students' lives and schooling.

Teachers' frustrations included the fact that parents sent children to school sick—expecting the school nurse to provide primary health care—and the difficulty of communication with parents. Parents, in turn, expressed needs for child care, help overcoming language barriers, and guidance on school involvement. Community groups recognized how often emotional and physical stresses were handicapping students.

We drew on these concerns to design a school where the school district and community-based organizations combined resources to meet students' needs. We created a community-school advisory board that represented key constituents and met once a month during our first year, planning and putting in place the community-school framework and developing goals and measurable objectives. We hired a community-school coordinator to help secure funds, coordinate partnership activities, and serve as a liaison between Edison and the partner agencies.

Partnerships in Action

Our School-Based Health Center

A review of the school's health records confirmed teachers' observations that many students were coming to school sick. We discovered that less than 23 percent of Edison students had health care coverage. The school shared these data with the Open Door Medical Center, an organization providing medical care to poor and underserved families in Port Chester, and initiated a partnership with them. Open Door secured federal grants and other funding to establish a school-based health center.

At the health center, the Edison school nurse and the Open Door nurse practitioner coordinate health care initiatives involving students and their families. The nurse practitioner provides primary care to students at the school. Common colds and other illnesses, which were previously often left untreated, now receive prompt medical attention, reducing the number of student absences. A weekly visit from Open Door's dentist provides much-needed dental care for Edison's students.

All Edison students can receive health care at the center, including screenings, vaccinations, and prescription medication. During these procedures, the staff has uncovered more serious illnesses, such as diabetes, which might have remained undetected until serious symptoms or complications appeared. We refer students needing more complex medical care to Open Door's main medical facility in the community. And in addition to providing medical services, Open Door staff members provide nutrition and wellness education to parents and help families obtain federally funded medical insurance.

As a result of the health center's services, 94 percent of Edison's students are now medically insured and receive ongoing medical and dental care. The success of this model has led the district and Open Door to expand this kind of program to other schools.

Therapy and Family Casework

To complement the work of teachers and health center staff in addressing the developmental needs of the whole child, Edison set up a partnership with the Guidance Center, a local mental health facility. A bilingual family caseworker meets with families in crisis and helps parents realize their roles as their children's first teachers and primary advocates. The caseworker also supports the general parent population at the school, sometimes by facilitating communication between school staff and parents who do not speak English and by providing new families with school supplies and clothing, if needed. A social worker provides therapeutic counseling for students in crisis and teams up with the family caseworker to ease the stresses on students' families. These services help Edison establish links with the families that are hardest to reach.

Parent Education and Capacity Building

For the past six years, Edison has hosted the weekly bilingual gathering La Segunda Taza de Café ("A Second Cup of Coffee") for parents at the school, facilitated by the caseworker from the Guidance Center. At these gatherings, parents participate in workshops, seminars, and discussion groups about topics of interest to them. These topics include state standards and assessments, parents' rights and responsibilities in schools, strategies to help their children learn, and information on citizenship and naturalization. One goal behind this parent program is to develop parents' leadership capacity. Edison's immigrant parents are now visible in the school and active with the Parent Teacher Association.

Afterschool Enrichment

Services, Education, and Resources of Westchester, a nonprofit organization, was instrumental in creating Edison's afterschool program. This program now serves 130 students daily and meets the twin needs of homework help and child care that parents and teachers identified in our initial community survey. Through professional and nonprofessional staff members, including many bilingual workers, we both support students' growth in English and offer them enrichment experiences in their native languages—martial arts, photography, chess, tennis, computer-assisted instruction, and the opportunity to produce a literary magazine. We strive to validate the richness of our students' Hispanic heritage by bringing in artists to teach arts and crafts reflecting the culture and styles of indigenous Hispanic peoples. We also invite students to join a folk dance troupe that performs frequently.

Partnership With Manhattanville College

Edison's long-standing professional development relationship with Manhattanville College is an important resource for improving teaching and learning. Edison hires many teachers trained at Manhattanville (30 percent of our teachers are alumni), which provides us with qualified teachers willing and prepared to work in a school confronting the conditions of poverty.

(continued)

(Continued)

The majority of our new teachers from Manhattanville have participated in structured preservice learning experiences at Edison, ranging from facilitating small-group instruction to student teaching. All our new hires participate in a two-year induction program coordinated by the college liaison, with Edison teachers serving as mentors. This formal guidance has increased the school's retention of new teachers. In addition, veteran teachers continue to refine their practice by taking courses in English as a second language, literacy, and content-area instruction at the college for free or at reduced cost.

Results: Ten Years of Whole-Child Education

The changes we made in becoming a community school have led to dramatic achievement gains for our students. In 2008, these are our results:

- *In 2008, 70 percent of fourth graders scored proficient or better on the New York State's English language arts assessment (compared to 19 percent passing in 1999).*
- *In 2008, 94 percent of fourth graders scored proficient or better on the New York State's mathematics assessment (compared to 75 percent passing in 1999).*
- *Of our students, 94 percent are now medically insured (compared with less than 23 percent in 1999).*
- *Of our families, 75 percent now participate in schoolwide events.*

The New York State Education Department has recognized Thomas Edison for its innovative practices and achievement gains. Through 10 years of growing into a full-service community school, Edison has had some insights. A key feature of our design is the fact that community-based partners provide services on the school site and that it cultivates interagency cooperation. Reshaping ourselves as a community school has enabled our faculty to focus more on teaching and learning, has given families direct access to resources that improve their lives, and has expanded our partners' ability to reach children and families. We are now educating the whole child at Edison.

Source: Santiago, Ferrara, & Blank, 2008. Used with permission.

How did the school fulfill its promise and address the range of children's needs that affects academic progress? Who was involved in the whole-school change process?

How Do We Prepare Students for Life?

The Association for Supervision and Curriculum Development (ASCD; Commission on the Whole Child, 2007) has initiated a political movement to address this question: How do we equip today's students with 21st-century skills necessary for success? ASCD proposes a whole-child approach to provide the foundation for success in school, the workplace, the community, and life. This approach is supported by extensive research on six out-of-school factors (OSFs) common among the poor that significantly affect the health and learning opportunities of children and, accordingly, limit what schools can accomplish on their own:

1. Low birth-weight and nongenetic prenatal influences on children

2. Inadequate medical, dental, and vision care, often a result of inadequate or no medical insurance

3. Food insecurity

4. Environmental pollutants

5. Family relations and family stress

6. Neighborhood characteristics

These OSFs are related to a host of poverty-induced physical, sociological, and psychological problems that children often bring to school, ranging from neurological damage and attention disorders to excessive absenteeism, linguistic underdevelopment, and oppositional behavior. A seventh OSF, extended learning opportunities such as preschool, afterschool, and summer school programs, can help to mitigate some of the harm caused by the first six factors (Berliner, 2009).

The definition of a whole-child approach evolved from the work of ASCD's Commission on the Whole Child, especially the Commission's report *The Learning Compact Redefined: A Call to Action* (2007). ASCD leaders argue that educational institutions currently focus on students' success in reading and math, two vital subjects, but the educational experience should be made up of more than just these two subjects. The specific assumptions and challenges for practice upon which the initiative is based include the following:

- Healthy kids make better students. What can we do to ensure that all kids arrive at school healthy and ready to learn?
- Students who are scared have trouble concentrating. What can we do to ensure students feel safe and secure, both physically and emotionally, in their schools?
- Academic engagement is critical for success. How can schools and communities engage students in ways that are relevant and tied to the broader community beyond the classroom?
- Students who are supported by caring adults are most likely to excel. What elements are critical for student support, both inside and outside the classroom, to ensure high success? What does support for students mean, and how can we ensure all students have it?
- Students must be prepared for life outside of school. What must we do to provide a challenging, rigorous curriculum that prepares today's students for success in the workplace and higher education (McCloskey, 2007)?

According to the Commission on the Whole Child (2007), the whole child is

- intellectually active;
- physically, verbally, socially, and academically competent;
- empathetic, kind, caring, and fair;
- creative and curious;
- disciplined, self-directed, and goal oriented;
- free;
- a critical thinker;
- confident; and
- cared for and valued (p. 10).

ASCD (2008) further proposes that adults in the school's surrounding community need to be accountable for ensuring that students are safe; healthy; engaged; supported; and challenged with access to a broad curriculum that includes art, music, foreign languages, history, and social studies. These factors are defined below.

How Does Safety Affect Learning?

Students learn at high levels when they feel safe and secure. Safety also impacts attendance and cognitive development. Students who are fearful, bullied, or distracted by fights and other disruptive behavior are unlikely to do well academically. For example, only 38 percent of U.S. students always feel safe at school, and 30 percent rarely or never feel safe (School Health Policies and Program Study, 2007). About two-thirds (62 percent) of high school dropouts say their schools should have done more to enforce classroom discipline (Bridgeland, DiIulio, & Morison, 2006). Contributing to these conditions, only 20 percent of students report that they take part in making rules at their school (School Health Policies). In the school year 2003–2004, 1 in 10 teachers in the nation's city schools was threatened with injury or physically attacked. In-school threats and injuries were almost twice as prevalent in cities as in suburbs and towns or rural areas. In cities, public school teachers were six times more likely to be threatened with injury than private school teachers (12 percent versus 2 percent) and five times more likely to be physically attacked (5 percent versus 1 percent).

How Does Health Affect Learning?

Students learn at high levels when they are healthy. Students who are sick, who come to school hungry, who can't breathe because of asthma, who can't see the blackboard because of poor vision, or who can't concentrate because of pervasive toothaches or depression are unlikely to do well academically. ASCD recommends, at a minimum, the following (Commission on the Whole Child, 2007):

- A school health advisory council with students, family, and community members
- Routine screening for immunizations and vision, hearing, dental, and orthopedic concerns
- Physical education and health classes that emphasize sustaining healthy behaviors over a lifetime
- Making healthy food choices available at school

How Does Being Engaged Affect Learning?

It makes sense that for students to learn at high levels, they must first be motivated to learn and interested in their studies. Students who are bored by their classes, who don't feel motivated to achieve, and who don't see the connection between what they are learning in school and their real-world goals are unlikely to do well academically. One of every three high school students drops out of school—one in two for African American and Hispanic students (Swanson, 2008). Of these, nearly 7 in 10 (69 percent) say they weren't inspired or motivated to work hard, and 66 percent say they would have worked harder if they'd been challenged more (Bridgeland et al., 2006). Also, 7 in 10 employers say high school graduates don't have a strong work ethic, and nearly 4 in 10 say they have poor teamwork skills (Olson, 2007). To ensure that all students are adequately engaged, ASCD (2008) recommends, at a minimum, the following:

- Students participate in a wide array of extracurricular activities.
- Schools provide opportunities for community-based apprenticeships, internships, or projects.
- Teachers use active learning strategies, such as cooperative learning and project-based learning.

How Does Feeling Supported Affect Learning?

It makes sense that for students to learn at high levels, they must first feel supported by caring, qualified adults. Students who don't have access to adult role models, advisors, mentors, counselors—or to teachers who understand their social and emotional development—are unlikely to do well academically. Too few teachers have learned about child development as part of their preparation or ongoing professional development. Experts recommend one counselor for every 250 students across all grade levels, but the current average ratio is 1:488, with several states exceeding 1:700 (American School Counselor Association, 2004). Also, 15 million struggling students need mentors but don't have them (ASCD, 2008). To ensure that all students are adequately supported, ASCD recommends, at a minimum, that every student has an adult advisor or mentor and that students have access to school counselors or other student support systems.

How Does Feeling Challenged Affect Learning?

It makes sense that for students to learn at high levels, they must have access to a 21st-century curriculum that both challenges and inspires them. Students who spend most of their day being lectured and drilled in reading and math only, and who don't have access to courses in the arts, music, social studies, civics, and other broadening subjects, are more likely to tune out and are less likely to do well in school. Too many children don't have access to a 21st-century series of courses. For example, only one-third of U.S. middle and high school students and 5 percent of elementary students study a foreign language (Committee for Economic Development, 2006). The Partnership for 21st Century Skills (2009) says that schools are falling short in teaching such "emerging essential content" as global awareness; financial, economic, and entrepreneurial literacy; civic literacy; health and wellness; and life skills (Kay, 2009). However, 6 in 10 members of the public want students to take a wide variety of courses beyond "the basics" (Rose & Gallup, 2006), and 89 percent believe that arts should be taught in the public schools (Americans for the Arts, 2009). To ensure that all students are academically challenged with a well-balanced curriculum, the Association for Supervision and Curriculum Development (2008) recommends, at a minimum, the following:

- Schools provide a well-rounded curriculum for all students.
- Students have access to rigorous programs in arts, foreign languages, and social studies.
- Schools maintain flexible graduation requirements.

A child simply cannot learn at his or her best if he or she is not healthy, safe, engaged, supported, and challenged. As Miller (n.d.) observed, there is no best way to accomplish the goal of providing a holistic education to children.

> There are many *paths to learning* and the holistic educator values them all; what is appropriate for some children, in some situations, in some historical and social contexts, may not be best for others. The art of holistic education lies in its responsiveness to the diverse learning styles and needs of evolving human beings. . . . While few public schools are entirely committed to holistic principles, many teachers try hard to put many of these ideas into practice. By fostering collaboration rather than competition in classrooms, teachers help young people feel connected. By using real-life experiences, current events, the dramatic arts and other lively sources of knowledge in place of textbook information, teachers can kindle the love of learning. (Miller, ¶ 2–3)

WHAT IS COLLABORATION, AND WHY IS IT IMPORTANT FOR EDUCATING THE WHOLE CHILD?

> *My daughter could not have finished her 10th grade without a lot of support from her teachers and school counselor. After her father passed away, she needed extensive tutoring in reading and mathematics and group counseling services for an anxiety disorder. Without the collaboration among teachers and school professionals, we would not be here.*
>
> —Mother of a high school student with emotional disabilities

The idea of shared responsibility for a community's children has recently become a watchword for educators and human service personnel. The overarching goal of education is to promote the highest possible levels of academic, social, and career-vocational achievement for all children who enter the school doors. Achieving these goals depends on how professionals collaborate with one another to bridge the different and separate worlds of family and school, academic disciplines, professional roles, school and community, and community agencies. The notion of shared responsibility also implies working across agency boundaries to create a well-coordinated service system to meet the holistic needs of students. Coordination and collaboration are about connecting people within systems and the extraordinary commitment that is required to accomplish this goal.

What Is Collaboration?

The concepts of collaboration and coordination are not simply pleasing abstractions—they represent effective practices that affect student outcomes. A definition of collaboration can be drawn from the Latin roots meaning "to work" (*laborare*) "together" (*com*) (Merriam-Webster's Collegiate Dictionary, 2003). Therefore, collaboration, most simply, can be defined as work done jointly with others. The term *collaboration* is used widely today in education and human service fields.

We commonly refer to collaboration among different groups of people within and outside the schools—among teachers, between teachers and parents, among teachers in different schools, among teachers and related services personnel (e.g., speech therapist, audiologist, counselor, psychologist, reading specialist), and among teachers and community agency personnel. *Collaboration* is generally defined as a process of participation through which people, groups, and organizations form relationships and work together to achieve a set of agreed-upon results (Kochhar-Bryant, 2008). At the heart of effective and long-lasting school collaboration are effective relationships among professionals. Collaboration in special education and human services involves a range of relationships among people in different roles and disciplines within schools and among schools and with human service agencies in the community that serve children and families. The terms *collaboration* and *coordination* represent the following:

- *Ideas* about how people can work together to improve teaching and learning, student development and achievement, and the engagement of community service agencies
- *Philosophies* about how creative change blends or synthesizes a variety of perspectives and values among people to make things possible for students, families, professionals, schools, and systems

- *Practical strategies and processes* through which people can effect change, solve problems, or improve practices
- *Commitment* to working together constructively and embracing new ideas

Collaboration can be thought of as the "people" part and *system coordination* as the "organizational," or broader system, part. However, collaboration and system coordination are inextricably linked—collaborative relationships are essential for system coordination to occur. Results of collaboration may affect an individual student (collaboration on an Individual Education Program team or child study team), a group of professionals (co-teaching team), or a whole organization (school improvement team). Collaboration has also been defined recently in a variety of other ways.

- The process of shared creation between two or more individuals with complementary skills interacting to create a shared understanding that none had previously possessed or could have come to on their own. Collaboration creates a shared meaning about a process, a product, or an event (Montiel-Overall, 2005).
- A style of interaction professionals use in order to accomplish a goal they share, often emphasized in inclusive schools. Collaboration emphasizes common goals, relationships, and mutual interdependence and is a way to build community as well as being a way of life within a community (Friend & Cook, 2009).
- The sharing of resources among school community stakeholders toward accomplishing goals and objectives or solving problems (Midura & Glover, 2003)
- Team-building activities that develop mutual trust and promote collaborative decision making that meets the diverse needs of the school community (Lambert, 2003)
- Communities of practice, which are are groups of people who share a concern or a passion for something they do and who interact regularly to learn how to do it better (Wenger, McDermott, & Snyder, 2002)
- Relationships that provide opportunities for mutual benefit and results beyond what any single organization or sector could realize alone (Peter F. Drucker Foundation for Nonprofit Management, 2002)
- Planning, deciding, and acting jointly but also *thinking* together. There is a commitment to shared resources, power, and talent (John-Steiner, Weber & Minnis, 1998).

Six common themes arise from these definitions, indicating that collaboration

1. involves new *relationships* among people.
2. involves *sharing of resources* (human or other).
3. involves *trust* among people working together in peer (nonhierarchical) relationships.
4. involves *joint responsibility* for outcomes.
5. involves *joint decision making* and actions.
6. is aimed at achieving specific *results* or change.

Expectations for collaborative practices are a centerpiece of the No Child Left Behind Act of 2001 (NCLB), the Safe and Drug Free Schools Act, the Individuals with Disabilities Education Improvement Act of 2004, and related education and disability laws discussed in Chapter 3.

What Is the Difference Between Collaboration, Consultation, and Interagency Service Coordination?

Collaboration can be distinguished from *consultation* and *interagency service coordination*. Consultation, a form of collaboration, typically refers to one-time or short-term services that teachers and other professionals offer or receive from one another or offer to parents. It involves a request for a service or an advisory opinion. Consultation can also involve problem-solving relationships in which peer professionals share their unique skills and provide group recommendations to improve a situation for a child or group of children or to solve an organizational problem (Chrispeels, Strait, & Brown, 1999; Dettmer, Dyck, & Thurston, 2005).

Collaboration can also be distinguished from interagency service coordination. As mentioned previously, collaboration refers to the relationships among people working together (e.g., special education teachers and general education teachers), and system coordination refers to the organizational or institutional relationships among agencies that are linked in their efforts to educate and support students and their families (e.g., the school counseling unit and the community mental health service agency). However, collaboration and interagency coordination are inextricably linked—collaborative relationships are essential for interagency coordination to occur.

The field of children's mental health services in the United States has embraced the philosophy of systems of care over the past few decades, leading to the development of improved interagency coordination and more comprehensive services to children and families. Learning from the mental health field, schools are increasingly recognizing that the educational performance of all children, particularly those who are at risk, will not improve unless efforts are made to remove the barriers to learning that begin outside the classroom walls. Linking students and schools to integrated health and human services is one strategy. Collaboration across agency lines and among public and private providers is one of the most significant—yet challenging—developments in human services in recent years.

Why Collaborate?

Recent arguments for strengthening professional collaboration and for implementing coordinated school-linked services rests on six basic premises. These premises could serve as a point of discussion among school faculty and staff as they define their roles in student-centered support teams.

1. All facets of a child's well-being impact his or her potential for academic success, career development, and long-term independence.

2. A growing number of American school-age children can be considered at risk for school failure and other social problems, such as substance abuse and incarceration (Centre for Educational Research and Innovation, 1998; Cuban & Usdan, 2002; Hodgkinson, 2006).

3. Prevention is more cost-effective for society than correction or remediation. For example, Hodgkinson (2003) reported that an established relationship exists between dropping out of school and the probability of committing a crime and that dropout prevention is cheaper in the long run than the cost of incarceration.

4. Children who are at risk for school failure come to school with multiple problems that cut across conventional health, social, and education systems boundaries, and

schools are ill-equipped to handle such problems alone (Cuban & Usdan, 2002; Kirst & Jehl, 1995).

5. The current system of child-related service delivery is fragmented and in need of coordination, since many children fall through the cracks and fail to get the services they need.

6. Because schools have sustained long-term contact with children, they are the logical gateway for providing a spectrum of services to address the needs of children that affect academic progress (Adelman & Taylor, 2007b; Kirst & Jehl, 1995).

All children have unique strengths, talents, and interests, and for some children, atypical learning and developmental needs require differentiated and individualized responses from the educational community.

WHAT IS DEVELOPMENTALLY RESPONSIVE PRACTICE?

Because developmental domains are interrelated, educators can organize children's learning experiences in ways that help them to develop optimally in all areas and that make meaningful connections across domains (Bredekamp & Copple, 1997). More recently, however, researchers are asking—due to widely varying developmental differences—if some factors not centered in the child or adolescent but rather associated with the school environment may create stress. They have begun looking at the structure of classes, student decision making (or lack thereof), increased school size, greater departmentalization, ability grouping, increased use of competition as a motivator, and increased rigor in grading and testing. Studies have suggested that as students mature, they want more autonomy and opportunity for self-management and personal decision making (Bremer, Kachgal, & Schoeller, 2003; Deci & Ryan, 2008; Doll, Sands, Wehmeyer, & Palmer, 1996; Eisenman & Chamberlin, 2001; Field, Hoffman, & Spezia, 1998; J. E. Martin, Marshall, & De Pry, 2002; Wehmeyer, Abery, Mithaug, Powers, & Stancliffe, 2003).

The term *developmentally appropriate practice* (DAP) has been part of the educational lexicon for decades, particularly in reference to the education of young children. Developmentally appropriate practice is a perspective within early childhood education in which a teacher or caregiver nurtures a child's social/emotional, physical, and cognitive development by basing all practices and decisions on (1) theories of child development, (2) the individually identified strengths and weaknesses of each child, and (3) the child's family and cultural background (Bredekamp & Copple, 1997; NAEYC, 2009). In a DAP environment, individualization becomes a key component in making sure the needs and interests of each child are focused on.

For very young children, developmental milestones mean a set of functional skills or age-specific tasks that most children being to do within a certain age range. The pediatrician uses milestones to monitor how a child is developing. Although each milestone has an age level, the actual age when a typically developing child reaches that milestone can vary quite a bit: again, every child is unique (American Academy of Pediatrics, Committee on Children with Disabilities, 2001).

DAP emphasizes learning as a socially interactive process. Teachers prepare the classroom environment for children to learn through active exploration and interaction with adults, other children, and materials. Nondevelopmentally appropriate practices include overuse of individual drill and other practice techniques that can stifle interest, creativity, and curiosity and lead to boredom in children. Such techniques stress memorization of facts and do not prepare children to adapt to different situations. In non-DAP programs, adult attitudes are not informed by an understanding of how children learn and develop, and non-DAP programs lack appropriate training and support systems for teachers.

Developmentally appropriate practices are based on extensive research about child development and learning; what is known about the unique needs, strengths, and interests of each child; and what is known about the cultural and social environments in which each child lives—in other words, looking at the whole child (NAEYC, 2009). Children learn when they feel secure and accepted and are encouraged and respected as people who can initiate decisions, make judgments, and take responsibility. Classroom practices that are developmentally appropriate tend to be child initiated, and they have been shown to be associated with higher levels of cognitive functioning, social skills development, and creativity in comparison to traditional didactic teaching methods. Learning activities and materials are concrete and relevant to children's lives (Bredekamp & Copple, 1997; Clements, Reynolds, & Hickey, 2004). This topic is discussed in greater depth in Chapter 2.

What Is Developmentally Responsive Practice for Adolescents?

Developmentally responsive practice is as important for preadolescent and adolescent students as it is for young children. Building on the DAP concept for young children, the term *developmentally responsive* was introduced for adolescents by the National Middle School Association (George & Lawrence, 1982). Early adolescence is a period of great variability in development among youngsters of the same gender and chronological age (Anfara & Andrews, 2003). The changes and variability have implications for middle school teachers and counselors seeking to foster the growth, development, and learning of early adolescents (Mertens, Anfara, & Caskey, 2007).

Youth Development Framework

The youth development framework incorporates developmentally responsive practices for adolescents. The youth development approach prepares young people to meet the challenges of adolescence and adulthood through a coordinated, progressive series of activities and experiences that help them to become socially, emotionally, physically, and cognitively competent. The positive youth development movement has emerged as a reaction to the problematic assumptions around deficit models of development. Approaching development as a healing of "maladaption" has proven to be an ineffective as well as an uninspirational approach to a young person and to building human potential.

A positive youth development framework views youth with the glass half full—seeing what can go right with youth, rather than what can go wrong. Rather than seeing young people as problems, it views them as capable of building on their strengths and talents and contributing to their communities. Rather than asking, "What's wrong with these kids?" professionals ask, "What is right with these teens? What is working in their lives? What are their special talents and interests?" The National Youth Development Information Center (n.d.-a) defined *youth development* as a process that prepares young people to meet the challenges of adolescence and adulthood through a coordinated, progressive series of activities and experiences that help them to become cognitively, socially, emotionally, physically, and ethically competent.

Personal and social development is a fundamental part of the curriculum for all students, because society is concerned with children's all-round development as persons living in society. Secondly, such development is important as of the foundation for other types of learning and for lifelong learning. The youth development framework is based on the following assumptions for effective programs:

- Focus on strengths, capabilities, and developmental needs rather than on problems, risks, and vulnerabilities
- Appreciative, health-based approaches
- Belief that young people can make successful transitions to adulthood and gain lifelong resilience
- Appropriate and positive supports from adults and peers
- Building self-determination skills

Effective youth development programs are characterized by the following:

- Promoting comprehensive and flexible youth development
- Engaging youth in planning for the future
- Integrating multiple developmental domains: academic, social-psychological, and career
- Including a curriculum that blends school-based and community-based approaches
- Designing programming as part of a larger developmental space linked to other settings
- Designing programs to be intensive during middle to high school transition years, in Grades 9 to 12 and through age 21 if needed
- Accounting for variation in the development of adolescents and their needs for long-range planning and services before age 16
- Focusing Individualized Education Program (IEP) post-secondary goals to help students move away from home, establish a social life, become lifelong learners, and work a part- or full-time job
- Designing individual programming around a coordinated set of activities and systematic approach, as required by the Individuals with Disabilities Education Improvement Act of 2004

Programming for youth, therefore, becomes part of a larger developmental space and should be intentionally linked to other settings in which young people grow and develop, particularly post-secondary settings. Meaningful participation of young people in their own educational and future planning is considered a key youth development practice and promotes healthy development and learning (Roth & Brooks-Gunn, 2003; Sagawa, 2003). Meaningful participation means activities through which young people have opportunities to make significant decisions, develop and practice leadership skills, and experience a sense that they belong or matter to others.

HOW DO ENVIRONMENT AND HEALTH STATUS AFFECT LEARNING AND DEVELOPMENT?

Each child who enters the school represents a unique mosaic of individual, family, and community experiences that affect how they engage with their teachers and their peers each day. A variety of factors shape the child or youth's potential for creativity and critical thinking, including prenatal care, health status, food insecurity, poverty, family structure and absence of one or both parents, physical environment in the home, environmental pollutants, neighborhood characteristics, and participation in high-risk or illegal behaviors (Berliner, 2009). When these impacts on children are understood, the urgency with which educational and related professionals must reassess school priorities becomes clear.

How Does Child Poverty Affect Learning and Development?

The child poverty rate is perhaps the most widely used measure to identify the health and well-being of children. Conditions of poverty have been associated with crime, physical abuse, and learning and emotional problems. Measures of poverty status, secure parental employment, and food security offer insight into the material well-being of children and factors that affect their health and development. While the number of poor children living in families totally dependent on welfare has fallen in the past two decades, the number of poor children living in families earning an income (no income from public assistance) increased from 4.4 million in 1976 to 6.9 million in 2000. Currently, 13.3 million children live below the official poverty level (Annie E. Casey Foundation, 2009; Wertheimer & Atienza, 2006). Despite the wealth in the United States, the rate of poverty among children is higher than in any other developed country. Elders (2002) observed that children of the "Five-H Club"—hungry, healthless, homeless, hugless, and hopeless—have difficulty concentrating on schoolwork, which often leads them to mask learning difficulties by exhibiting acting-out behaviors.

SOBERING STATISTICS ON POVERTY

In 2007, 18 percent of children ages 0 to 17 lived in poverty, up from 17 percent in 2006. The poverty rate for younger children was higher than for older children. About 21 percent of children under 6 years and 16 percent of children 6 to 17 years lived in poverty in 2006. The poverty rate was higher for Black children and for Hispanic children than for White, non-Hispanic children. In 2007, 10 percent of White, non-Hispanic children lived in poverty, compared with 35 percent of Black children and 29 percent of Hispanic children. Poverty among related children varies greatly by family structure. In 2007, children living in families with a female head with no husband present continued to experience a higher poverty rate (43 percent) than children living in married-couple families (9 percent).

A family's food security is its access at all times to enough food to ensure active, healthy lives for all family members. In some food insecure households, only adults are affected, but in most such households, children are also affected to some extent. About 17 percent of children (12.4 million) lived in households that were food-insecure at times in 2007.

Source: Federal Interagency Forum on Child and Family Statistics, 2009.

What Health Disparities Are Facing Children and Youth?

Healthier students make better learners, yet health issues have been mostly neglected in school reform issues, observed Charles Basch (in press). Children's health is influenced by their genetic makeup and biology, social and physical environment, and behaviors, as well as the availability of services. However, a track record now demonstrates that certain programs and policies favorably influence these factors and, since educationally relevant health disparities directly and indirectly affect students' motivation and ability to learn, help close the achievement gap. In the short term, schools may be the best hope for addressing the physical health and social-emotional needs of urban minority youth and for helping them to succeed academically and in life. While most schools in the United States implement some programs or policies that address health, the extent and quality of these programs is by and large limited and insufficient to meet the needs of youth facing the greatest educational and health challenges.

Basch (2009) described six educationally relevant health factors—vision, asthma, teen pregnancy, aggression and violence, physical activity, and nutrition—that should be priorities for schools serving urban minority youth: each disproportionately affects that population, there is strong evidence that each affects educational outcomes, and the feasibility of school-based policies and programs that address them has been demonstrated. All are interrelated synergistically.

1. **Vision affects learning.** An estimated one in five school-age youths has a vision problem. Less than half of the states require that teachers be notified of the results of vision screening. In a nationally representative sample of more than 48,000 youths, poor minority youths appear to be underdiagnosed and undertreated for eye-care problems. In another national sample of more than 14,000 children with special health care needs, Black, Hispanic, and multiracial children were two to three times more likely than Whites to have unmet vision care needs (Heslin, Casey, Shaheen, Cardenas, & Baker, 2006).

SOBERING STATISTICS ON ASTHMA

"In 2006, 9 percent of children had current asthma. This included children with active asthma symptoms and those with well-controlled asthma. This percentage had not significantly changed since 2001. The incidence of asthma in children differs by race/ethnicity: in 2006, the highest rates of current asthma were reported among Black, non-Hispanic children (13 percent) and Puerto Rican children (26 percent), compared with the lowest rates of asthma among White, non-Hispanic children (9 percent) and Asian children (6 percent). In 2006, nearly 6 percent of all children had suffered one or more asthma attacks in the previous 12 months."

Source: Federal Interagency Forum on Child and Family Statistics, 2009.

2. **Asthma affects learning.** Asthma is a leading chronic disease among children, and rates of childhood asthma have remained at historically high levels since the 1990s. Compared with children who do not have asthma, children who do are more likely to

have disturbed sleep. Nocturnal asthma is associated with greater severity of the disease, but even youth with "stable asthma" experience considerably more sleep problems than children who do not have asthma. In a recent review of all studies examining asthma and school attendance, virtually every study found a positive association between the disease and school absenteeism (Stranges, Merrill, & Steiner, 2008).

SOBERING STATISTICS ON TEEN BIRTH

In 2007, the adolescent birth rate was 22.2 per 1,000 adolescents ages 15 to 17 (140,640 births, according to preliminary data), up from the 2006 rate of 22.0 per 1,000. A long-term decline had begun in 1991–1992. However, this was the second consecutive year of increase, possibly showing an interruption in what had been a positive trend.

Compared with women who delay childbearing until age 30, teen mothers' education is estimated to be two years shorter. Teen mothers are 10 to 12 percent less likely to complete high school, and they have 14 to 29 percent lower odds of attending college.

Sources: Federal Interagency Forum on Child and Family Statistics, 2009; Hofferth, Reid, & Mott, 2001.

3. **Teen births affect learning.** Teens who become pregnant are less likely to complete high school or college. Teens who have one pregnancy are at increased risk of having another. Children born to teen mothers are more likely to become teen mothers themselves. In all likelihood, an unmarried teen mother and her child will live in poverty, further perpetuating a cycle of poverty and subsequent nonmarital teen births. Even small changes in the rate of nonmarital teen births would have substantial effects on the numbers of children living in poverty. Most students receive some kind of sex education programs, but those with the greatest needs are least likely to receive these kinds of programs.

Besides poverty, consequences of teen parenting are infant low birth weight and a high risk of child maltreatment. Low birth weight (LBW) is an important risk factor for future health conditions, disability, and death. The percentage of infants born LBW has increased for more than two decades. A number of factors may have contributed to this increase: the increases in multiple births, which are more likely to result in LBW infants than single births (though single LBW has also increased); obstetric interventions such as induction of labor and cesarean delivery; infertility therapies; and delayed childbearing.

SOBERING STATISTICS ON LOW BIRTH WEIGHTS

In 2006, 14 percent of Black, non-Hispanic infants were born LBW; even when maternal age was taken into account, this percentage continued to be higher than that of any other racial or ethnic group. Of all infants, the trend has been upward: 7.0 in 1990, 8.1 in 2004, 8.2 in 2005, and 8.3 percent in 2006.

Source: Federal Interagency Forum on Child and Family Statistics, 2009.

Child maltreatment includes physical, sexual, and psychological abuse, as well as neglect (including medical neglect), and it is associated with a number of negative outcomes for children. In 2006, there were 12 substantiated child maltreatment reports per 1,000 children ages 0 to 17 (U.S. Department of Health and Human Services, 2007). Younger children were more frequently victims of child maltreatment than older children. These children enter the school system with several strikes against them. Maltreatment affects typical brain development and undermines development of peer and adult relationships.

4. **Physical activity and nutrition affect learning.** The percentage of overweight children is a public health challenge. Physical activity affects metabolism and all major body systems, exerting powerful positive influences on the brain and spinal cord and, consequently on emotional stability, physical health, and ability to learn (Maddison et al., 2009). Over the past few decades, a steady and dramatic increase in obesity has occurred throughout the U.S. population, particularly among children and youth. Currently, one-third of American children and youth are either obese or at risk of becoming obese. The National Governors Association (2003), representing all 50 of the nation's governors, reported that the prevalence of obesity among U.S. students contributes to poor academic performance, increases health and education costs, and threatens to constrain state budgets and economic growth. Children with chronic health conditions can also be limited in their ability to participate fully in age-appropriate activities.

SOBERING STATISTICS ON OBESITY

In 1976–1980, only 6 percent of children ages 6 to 17 were overweight. By 1988–1994, this percentage had risen to 11 percent, and it continued to rise to 15 percent in 1999–2000. In 2005–2006, 17 percent of children ages 6 to 17 were overweight. While there was an increase in overweight among U.S. children between 1988–1994 and 2003–2004, the percentage of overweight children did not significantly change between 2003–2004 and 2005–2006.

Over the past 30 years, the obesity rate has nearly tripled for children ages 2 to 5 years (from 5 to 14 percent) and youth ages 12 to 19 years (from 5 to 17 percent), and it has quadrupled for children ages 6 to 11 years (from 4 to 19 percent) . In 2006, 9 percent of children were reported by parents as having activity limitation due to chronic conditions. This rate has remained stable since 2001.

Source: Federal Interagency Forum on Child and Family Statistics, 2009.

Many school districts are challenged to create healthy environments because of the prevalence of unhealthy food choices in schools, the elimination of health education and physical education classes, and the abandonment of recess. For instance, nearly 79.1 percent of elementary schools provide daily recess for all grades. Furthermore, 77.0 percent of middle schools and 91.3 percent of high schools offered students opportunities to participate in at least one interscholastic sport, and 29.1 percent of these schools provided transportation home for participating students (Centers for Disease Control and Prevention [CDC], 2006).

Nutritional health has been associated with children's memory development and ability to learn. Animal studies have shown that a diet rich in high levels of saturated fat

(French fries, donuts, hamburgers) can hinder brain function associated with memory. Even though some fat is important for health, rats fed diets in which approximately 40 percent of daily calories came from saturated fats performed poorly on tests of memory and learning. Human studies have also reported negative results of high-fat diets (Society for Neuroscience, 2003b).

SOBERING STATISTICS ON ENVIRONMENTAL POLLUTANTS

Child exposure to air pollution, as established by the Primary National Ambient Air Quality Standards, has improved recently. In 1999, 65 percent of children lived in counties in which one or more air pollutants rose above allowable levels; in 2006, the percent was 55, still more than half. The ozone standard is exceeded most often. Ozone can cause respiratory problems and aggravate diseases such as asthma. Particulate matter can have these effects as well. About 13 percent of children in 2006 lived in counties that exceeded the annual allowable level for fine particulate matter (smog). The percentage of children served by community drinking water systems that did not meet all applicable health-based standards has fluctuated between 5 and 12 percent during the period 1999–2006; it was 10 percent in 2006.

Source: Federal Interagency Forum on Child and Family Statistics, 2009.

5. **Physical environment of home and school affects learning.** Children's physical environments should support their healthy development and keep them safe from hazardous conditions. Indicators of physical environment and safety include exposure to air pollutants, drinking water contaminants, and lead, as well as measures of housing problems and deaths from injury.

SOBERING STATISTICS ON HOMELESS CHILDREN

"In 2005, 40 percent of U.S. households (both owners and renters) with children had one or more of three housing problems: physically inadequate housing, crowded housing, or a housing-cost burden of more than 30 percent of household income. Cost burdens have driven significant increases in the incidence of problems since 2003, when 37 percent of households had one or more such housing problems. Severe cost burdens—housing costs exceeding 50 percent of income—are especially prevalent among the lowest-income renters, affecting 45 percent of very-low-income renters with children in 2005" (Federal Interagency Forum on Child and Family Statistics, 2009). "For the 2006–07 school year, 78 percent of local education agencies (LEAs) across the nation enrolled more than 679,000 homeless students" (Bowman, Burdette, & Julianelle, 2008).

6. **Housing and homelessness affect learning.** Inadequate, crowded, or costly housing can pose serious problems to children's physical, psychological, and material well-being.

Primary nighttime residence is defined as the type of residence (e.g., shelter, hotel, doubled-up in the home of a relative or friend) where a homeless child or unaccompanied youth is staying at the time of enrollment or the type of residence where a currently enrolled child or youth is staying when he or she is identified as homeless (Bowman, Burdette, & Julianelle, 2008). Families experiencing homelessness are not a static group. As a result of catastrophic events such as hurricanes, job loss, or death of a parent, families fall into homelessness every day. Many states (34 percent) have difficulty maintaining accurate data counts of homeless children and youth enrolled in local education agencies (LEAs).

When homeless children also need special education services, the problems are compounded for families. Social and educational services must be designed to be supportive of homeless children and families, and collaboration and coordination across educational and human service systems are essential for meeting these challenges.

HOW DOES SOCIAL-EMOTIONAL HEALTH AFFECT LEARNING AND DEVELOPMENT?

Emotional and affective development occurs in specific stages, with transitions to new stages dependent upon accomplishments attained in earlier stages. Just as children's language and mental capabilities develop as a result of maturation and experience, so too does children's affective development. Affective development is impacted by both internal (biological predispositions, within-child abilities) and external (physical and social environment) influences (Brett et al., 2003).

SOBERING STATISTICS ON EMOTIONAL AND BEHAVIORAL DISABILITIES

"In 2006, 5 percent of parents reported that their child had definite or severe difficulties with emotions, concentration, behavior, or being able to get along with other people. The rate at which boys were reported as having such difficulties (7 percent) was twice the rate for girls (3 percent). Among parents of children with serious difficulties, 84 percent reported that they had contacted a health care provider or school staff about their child's difficulties, 49 percent reported that medications were prescribed for their child, and 44 percent reported that their child received treatment other than medication" (Federal Interagency Forum on Child and Family Statistics, 2009).

Mood disorders are common among children and adolescents (Davis et al., 2005; Guetzloe, 2003; Wood, 2007). At least 1 in 10, or about 6 million people, have a serious emotional disorder that requires professional intervention (S. Foster, Rollefson, Doksum, Noonan, & Robinson, 2005; U.S.DHHS, 2007). Furthermore, the U.S. General Accountability Office (GAO, 2003) found that in six states, an estimated 12,700 parents gave up custody of their children in 2001 to obtain the mental and behavioral health services the children needed but could not obtain in schools. Between 10 and 15 percent of the child and adolescent population exhibits some symptoms of depression (GAO, 2007).

The affective domain involves complex information processing that is integrally related to all other domains of human development (Brett et al., 2003; Plutchik, 2001). The affective domain is seen as contributing to social interactions through a concept often referred to as social-emotional learning (SEL) skills. SEL can be defined as the process through which people learn to recognize and manage emotions, care about others, make good decisions, behave ethically and responsibly, develop positive relationships, and avoid negative behavior (Fredericks, 2003). Parents' reports of their children's serious emotional and behavioral difficulties are a crucial first step so that medical professionals can be alerted and needed mental health services obtained.

Although Individuals with Disabilities Education Improvement Act (IDEIA) of 2004 requires that schools integrate children with diagnosed emotional disabilities, many more go undiagnosed and may receive punitive treatment (for "bad conduct") rather than the therapeutic or educational interventions that they need. A primary contributor to this problem is the fragmentation of needed diagnostic and intervention services and supports and the inability of schools and community agencies to collaborate to provide them. The adult and child mental health systems have embraced the philosophy and collaborative practices of "systems of care" or "wraparound" services over the past 20 years. However, these models are only recently being adopted in education. It is important for school professionals to be aware of the kinds of supportive service models and professional collaboration in use in schools across the United States that are demonstrating positive outcomes for students.

What Does Brain Research Reveal About Social-Emotional and Behavioral Disorders?

An increasing proportion of the general school population has mental health and behavioral disorders and is at risk of academic failure, school dropout, incarceration, suicide, and extended dependence in adulthood (Koller, 2007; Seltzer, Greenberg, Floyd, & Hong, 2004). In any given year, nearly 10 percent of the U.S. population suffers from a mood disorder; depressive disorders, anxiety disorders, and substance abuse often co-occur (National Institute of Mental Health [NIMH], 2008). The U.S. Department of Health and Human Services (2000) estimated that 21 percent of young people in the United States ages 9 to 17 (about 15 million children, or one in five) have diagnosable emotional or behavioral health disorders.

More than half of all cases of adult mental illnesses begin in the teenage years, and when untreated, depression and other mental health problems set up a child for a potentially difficult transition into adulthood (Bostic & Miller, 2005). Medical researchers studying depression are pointing to chemical imbalances in the brain as a likely cause (Alloy et al., 2001; Brosse, Sheets, Lett, & Blumenthal, 2002; Lewis, Lamm, Segalowitz, Stieben, & Zelazo, 2006; Ratner, 2004).

Brains Are Plastic Through Childhood and Adolescence

Recently neuroscientists have made great strides in understanding the brain, using increasingly sophisticated imaging techniques. Although great emphasis has been placed on the first three years of development, the enormous dynamic activity that occurs in the brain's biology between ages 3 and 16 has been less well studied. For decades, neuroscientists believed that our brains are hardwired after childhood, but recently, through the use of brain-imaging technology, they are reaching the conclusion that the human brain is capable of profound and permanent alterations throughout the life span. New studies graphically reveal that the brain's center of reasoning and problem solving is one of the last areas to mature and that higher-order brain centers, such as the prefrontal cortex, don't fully develop until young adulthood (Giedd, 2004; Gogtay et al., 2007; Lenroot & Giedd, 2006). The brain is also understood to be a good deal more plastic (able to reorganize neural pathways based on new experiences) than once thought (Geidd; Gogtay et al.). The findings have tremendous implications for understanding thinking, motivation, and behavior in adolescents and young adults as they navigate middle and high school and transition to adulthood.

Teens Process Emotions Differently

MRI studies are also shedding new light on how teens may process emotions differently than adults (Immordino-Yang & Damasio, 2007; Lucas & Baird, 2004). Recent advances in neuroscience highlight connections among emotions, social functioning, and decision making that have the potential to revolutionize our understanding of the role of affect in learning. Until recently, emotions were not viewed as having a brain basis, and their central role in governing behavior and rational thought had been overlooked (A. R. Damasio, 2005). Today, through studies of individuals with brain lesions, researchers can map emotional processes and atypical responses to specific areas of the brain (H. Damasio, 2005; Davis et al., 2005). In particular, the neurobiological evidence suggests that the aspects of cognition that we engage most heavily in schools—learning, attention, memory, decision making, and social functioning—are profoundly affected by and subsumed within the processes of emotion (Bechara, 2005; A. R. Damasio, 2005; Goswami, 2006; Hauser, 2006; Immordino-Yang, 2008; Immordino-Yang & Damasio). The study of emotions, and of the relationship between early and continuing social development and learning, requires greater collaboration among neuroscientists, psychologists, and educators.

What Effect Does Child Abuse Have on the Brain?

Child abuse occurs in families of every socioeconomic level, ethnic background, and religion. Only recently have researchers begun to attend to the potential influence of childhood traumatic experiences on adult disease, preferring to look for genetic causes of disease and pure biochemical factors without considering experiential influences (McCollum, 2006). Children who are physically abused are more likely to exhibit problem behaviors that require discipline than those children who do not experience abuse. These students have difficulty forming relationships with their peers and exhibit physically aggressive behaviors and social skills deficits.

Two major types of abuse are typically identified—emotional and physical (Menard, Bandeen-Roche, & Chilcoat, 2004). Emotional abuse has been defined as excessive demands placed on children by parents, peers, or siblings and the failure of parents to provide an emotional support system (Thompson & Kaplan, 1999). Students who have experienced emotional abuse may exhibit a low self-esteem, suicidal thoughts, depression, antisocial behaviors, and difficulty initiating and maintaining relationships with adults and peers. Deficits in cognitive functioning are greater in students who are abused than in those who are not (DHHS, 2007).

Recent brain research indicates that while physical wounds typically heal over time, maltreatment at an early age can create an enduring, harmful influence on a child's developing brain (McCollum, 2006; Society for Neuroscience, 2003a). A growing body of research has linked childhood experiences of maltreatment with a host of physical conditions that can emerge in adolescence or adulthood. Maltreatment disrupts early sensitive periods of growth and creates lifelong challenges for social, emotional, and cognitive development, as well as physical health. Many health problems—including panic disorder/posttraumatic stress disorder, chronic fatigue syndrome, depression, some autoimmune disorders, suicidal tendencies, abnormal fear responses, preterm labor, chronic pain syndromes, and ovarian dysfunction—can be understood, in some cases, as the result of childhood maltreatment (De Bellis, 2005; McCollum).

How Does Social-Emotional Health Fit in With Curriculum Standards?

The growing population of students with social-emotional and behavioral difficulties that interfere with learning represents a major challenge to achieving the goals of No Child Left Behind (NCLB). New state data reveal unanticipated consequences of the high-stakes accountability system mandated by the NCLB (Center on Education Policy, 2006). Students with social-emotional and behavioral difficulties are particularly at risk. There is a disconnect between standards-based educational environments on one hand and the highly variable cognitive, social, and emotional development of children and youth on the other, including the learning preferences, interests and talents, and rapid physical changes that occur during early adolescence (Takanishi, 1997). Critics of highly standardized education claim that states have crafted standards that are too narrow and do not allow educators to include nonacademic learning objectives such as those that focus on social and behavioral skills, career-vocational development, physical and health development, and functional skills (Izzo, Hertzfeld, Simmons-Reed, & Aaron, 2001).

As school curriculum and instruction are increasingly driven by academic tests, there is evidence in the states of gaps that prevent students from accessing a rich and broad curriculum because of reduced attention to subjects such as social studies, art, music, drama, physical education, sports, and many extracurricular and afterschool activities (National Education Association, 2009). These activities are a source of satisfaction for many students and keep them engaged in school. For example, the arts connect many students' interests and talents to the learning environment and can combat alienation. There is an urgency for professionals to understand the relationships among elements of the curriculum, students' interests and talents, and student engagement in learning. The boxed text presents one teacher's perspective on why students need access to a comprehensive curriculum.

COMPREHENSIVE CURRICULUM

In my school, the staff is so worried about closing the achievement gap for the students, it is becoming the norm to have academic afterschool groups. On rotating days, the students stay for one-and-a-half hours to review and learn math and reading skills. The idea looks good on paper, but it has cut into our arts programs, limiting the music, art, and drama groups to only a few students. For chorus or band, this is not a good thing.

It seems to the children who are in the afterschool math and reading groups that they will never measure up to the other students who are in the chorus. The performing groups have become the elite bunch in the school.

For many of the slower achievers, the arts are what keep them interested in coming to school. It may be just the motivation they need to stay in school and succeed in other areas. We had a student who was labeled as "troubled" from his elementary school, and he was placed in the school chorus his first year in the middle school. His behavior changed both in school and at home. His mother got more involved in his academic education, and the student went on to the high school and was very popular and successful.

> *With NCLB, pulling students from arts classes should not be a remedy for making sure all students learn together. The problem with NCLB is that all children do not achieve at the same time. They are not all on the same page when it comes to learning. All students will learn what they need to become successful, but they will do it at their own pace. NCLB must make sure all students start at the same level in order to achieve what needs to be done. We must all make sure the resources are in place for the development of the whole child. To lose any of our classes just to ensure that one program works the way the government wants it to is not an option.*
>
> *Leave the education to the ones who are in the trenches and work every day with the students who need them. We do know what we are doing, and we can help all students become smart, successful, productive citizens for the future.*
>
> *Ina Allen, Music Teacher, Evanston District #65, Chicago*

What Are the Outcomes for Disconnected Youth?

There is a sizable group of highly disadvantaged young people whose risks are multiplied because they are not productively engaged in either school or work and, therefore, are not likely to become financially independent (Lippman, Atienza, Rivers, & Keith, 2008). The Bureau of Labor Statistics refers to them as "disconnected youth." Approximately 8 percent of young people in the United States between the ages of 16 and 19 are not in school and are not employed (Federal Interagency Forum on Child and Family Statistics, 2009). BLS indicates that these groups include the following:

- Youth in lower-income households
- Youth whose parents are Black
- Youth who live with just one biological parent
- Youth whose parents are unemployed and have less education (Hair & Moore, 2007)

In addition, young people were more likely to be disconnected later in life if their physical health was reported as less than "very good" and if their friends belonged to gangs, were truant, smoked, drank heavily once or more a month, and used illegal drugs. In contrast, young people who participated in job training programs, job search programs, or school-to-work programs during high school were less likely to become disconnected. This research suggests that improving physical health, avoiding negative peer groups and risk behaviors, and participating in programs that facilitate employment can reduce youth alienation and dropout.

Reconnecting Youth

Young people who drop out of high school are typically encouraged to earn their GED credential. While those who earn a GED have higher hourly wages and finish more years of high school than do people who drop out and do not earn a GED, they also have lower levels of work-related skills, such as perseverance, dependability, and consistency (Heckman & Rubinstein, 2001). Employers look for job-specific skills and personal qualities that suggest a person will be a dependable worker, rather than looking only at high school educational credentials (Kerckhoff, 2002). Building and assessing work-related skills in addition to, or as part of, a GED course can help dropouts succeed in the job market after obtaining their GED. Having effective job assistance programs available in the community for youth who have dropped out of high school might help these youth avoid low-wage first jobs and attain higher-quality employment.

HOW DOES PARTICIPATION IN HIGH-RISK OR ILLEGAL BEHAVIORS AFFECT LEARNING AND DEVELOPMENT?

The participation of young people in high-risk or illegal behaviors can have severe, long-term consequences for our youth and our society. These behaviors include cigarette smoking, drinking alcohol, using illicit drugs, engaging in sexual activity, and participating in violent crimes. The information presented in the following sections should sound an alarm to all adults concerned about the long-term success of our children and should make professional collaboration a priority.

How Do Drugs and Alcohol Affect Learning?

In contrast to the more positive outlook for smoking, the illegal use of drugs and alcohol and abuse of prescription drugs among adolescents is on the rise nationwide (Volkow, 2005). Even after aggressive substance abuse education, the use of drugs and alcohol has not decreased. Early onset of heavy drinking (five or more alcoholic beverages in a row during a single occasion in the previous two weeks) may be especially problematic, potentially increasing the likelihood of serious health, cognitive, and emotional outcomes.

SOBERING STATISTICS ON DRUG AND ALCOHOL USE

Heavy drinking has been declining among preteens and teens from 1995 to 2007: from 15 to 10 percent of 8th graders, from 24 to 22 percent of 10th graders, and from 30 to 26 percent of 12th graders. Recent illicit drug use, defined as using within the past 30 days, has also undergone a long-term decline from 1995 to 2007: from 15 to 7 percent of 8th graders, from 23 to 17 percent of 10th graders, and from 26 to 22 percent of 12th graders. However, illicit drug use held steady from 2006 to 2007.

Source: Federal Interagency Forum on Child and Family Statistics, 2009.

Students who abuse substances have a difficult time keeping up with their peers academically. Substance abuse not only affects students' academic achievement but also may result in poor attendance, difficulty concentrating, apathy, impulsivity and disordered behavior, and sleeping in class, all of which greatly impact cognition and thinking patterns (SAMHSA Office of Applied Studies, 2006).

How Does Smoking Affect Learning?

Cigarette smoking has serious health consequences; it is estimated that more than 6 million of today's underage smokers will die of tobacco-related illnesses (Federal Interagency Forum on Child and Family Statistics, 2009). On the positive side, cigarette smoking rates among adolescents are on the decline.

SOBERING STATISTICS ON SMOKING

The percent of students who smoke has been declining, as measured by the number who report smoking in the previous 30 days. Among 8th graders, 10 percent smoked in 1996, 4 percent in 2006, and 3 percent in 2007. Among 10th graders, 7 percent smoked daily in 2007, 18 percent in 1996. Among 12th graders, 12 percent smoked daily in 2007, 25 percent in 1997.

Source: Federal Interagency Forum on Child and Family Statistics, 2009.

How Does Early Sexual Activity Affect Learning?

Early sexual activity is associated with emotional and physical health risks that can undermine educational progress or lead to school dropout. Youths who engage in sexual activity are at risk of contracting sexually transmitted infections (STIs) and becoming pregnant. The percentage of students in Grades 9 through 12 who reported ever having had sexual intercourse declined from 54 percent in 1991 to 46 percent in 2001 and remained stable from 2001 to 2005. In 2005, 18 percent of students in Grades 9 through 12 who had sexual intercourse in the past three months reported that they or their partner had used birth control pills before their last sexual intercourse, and 63 percent reported condom use (up from 46 percent in 2001) (Hallfors, Waller, Bauer, Ford, & Halpern, 2005; Meier, 2007).

How Does Youth Violence Affect Learning?

Violence among children and youth contributes to disruptions in the educational process, including in-school and out-of-school suspension, school dropout, incarceration, or placement in alternative education programs. Serious violent crimes include aggravated assault, rape, robbery (stealing by force or threat of violence), and homicide.

Child and adolescent violence in schools requires early assessment and positive interventions that involve collaborative and coordinated school and human service responses.

SOBERING STATISTICS ON YOUTH VIOLENCE

In 2005, the rate of serious violent crime offenses was 17 crimes per 1,000 juveniles ages 12 to 17, compared with 52 crimes per 1,000 juveniles in 1993. In 2005, injury deaths among adolescents ages 15 to 19 were 50 deaths per 100,000 adolescents, a decrease from 51 deaths per 100,000 in 2004. However, deaths among adolescents due to homicides increased in 2005 for the first time since 1993. The homicide rate among Black males is particularly high and increased from 55 deaths per 100,000 adolescents ages 15 to 19 in 2004 to 60 deaths per 100,000 in 2005. Firearms account for the majority of homicides; 2005 also marked the first increase in the firearm homicide rate since 1993.

Source: U.S. Department of Justice, Bureau of Justice Statistics, 2005.

How Does Increased Placement in Alternative Education Affect Learning?

Changes in the No Child Left Behind Act of 2001, the Individuals with Disabilities Education Improvement Act of 2004 (IDEIA), Safe and Drug-Free Schools legislation, Gun-Free Schools Act, and state laws on student discipline make alternative in-school and out-of-school settings more likely options for a growing number of students who may be experiencing academic failure or subject to disciplinary violations. The role of school professionals is affected by these policies. IDEIA 2004 and NCLB allow greater discretion for local school personnel to remove students, including students with disabilities, who violate codes of conduct (IDEA, § 665). States are experiencing a dramatic rise in the proportion of public school students who are voluntarily or involuntarily enrolled in alternative educational programs. In the past two decades, public concern about violence, weapons, drugs, and a climate of disrespect among students in elementary and secondary schools has contributed to an expansion of state policy options for students being "pushed out" due to poor academic progress and test scores, resulting in the exclusion of children at high school, middle school, and even elementary levels.

Most states have responded by revising their state discipline policies, allowing local schools to use suspension options for a wider range of behaviors and school code violations (Kochhar-Bryant, 2008; Lehr, Lang, & Lanners, 2004; White & Kochhar-Bryant, 2005). Together, these laws increase school personnel's emphasis on policies and practices oriented toward safety, security, management of student behavior, and consequences for rule breaking. Because of the dramatic growth of school exclusion policies and alternative educational placements across the United States, there is increased scrutiny of these programs and policies. In other industrialized countries (e.g., United Kingdom, Canada, Australia), a rights-based approach to childhood social exclusion is being promoted in which exclusion is viewed as a consequence of education systems that do not systematically allow children access to the critical capabilities they need to integrate into society (Kochhar-Bryant & Stephenson, 2007).

The good news is that school districts that have made great progress in reducing student push-out or expulsion to alternative education through professional collaboration, coordinated support, and prevention services.

WHAT IS THE FAMILY'S ROLE IN PROMOTING THE DEVELOPMENT OF THE WHOLE CHILD?

Educational research has provided evidence that the participation of parents and other family members is the most crucial factor in a child's potential to benefit from education and related services. The success of the collaborative process in schools is closely linked to the quality of teacher–family relationships.

As children age, important changes in parent–child relationships affect learning. The strength of school–family partnerships declines with each grade level, beginning with kindergarten, and show the most dramatic decrease at the point of transition into the middle grades (Elias, 2001; Henderson & Raimondo, 2002). Preadolescents (ages 9–12) begin to push their parents away, and peers take on greater important in their lives. For example, in the elementary years, the student may have been proud to have his mother or father as a school volunteer. But now, in middle school, having his mother's presence in the school may be "embarrassing" or viewed as "spying" or undermining his independence. Students want their parents to be less visible and less active in school settings.

As a result, students often discourage their parents from volunteering to help in school and sometimes even from attending parent-teacher conferences (Billig, 2001; Brookmeyer, Fanti, & Henrich, 2006; Sadowski, 2003; Sanders & Epstein, 2000). While many parents would like to maintain their involvement during the middle school years, only a small percentage receives adequate guidance from schools on how to help their children. Families need timely information on courses, curriculum choices, grading procedures, and testing and assessments throughout elementary, middle, and high school.

Communication between schools and families during middle and high school years should not be one-way—from the school to the family—or only after the child has been in trouble for some time. When students face social, academic, and personal problems, a coordinated effort is needed among families, school professionals, and community agencies to address the problems (Hines, 2001; Swaim, 2003). Coordination between professionals and families can mean that clear messages are received and that adequate help is provided before the problem grows too large.

AN IMPERATIVE TO CELEBRATE OUR WORK

The challenges presented in this chapter are sobering, and the urgency to address them is palpable in the school hallways and classrooms. Teachers and related professionals are under pressure to examine and improve their practices and gain new knowledge and skills. However, all too often, the emotional side of our work is unattended. What occurs within the school walls to grow young minds and bodies is among the most important work of a society. It is therefore imperative that those who work with children and youth have opportunities to celebrate their work and to renew their commitment and dedication. The low retention rate of too many professionals demonstrates that we have not yet found a way to integrate renewal processes into professional development. This topic will be discussed more in Chapter 8.

CLOSING

Collaboration and coordination are essential to change in relationships among people, which leads to change in practices, which ultimately leads to change and progress in students. The development of collaborative relationships among professionals does not develop in a tidy, step-by-step, linear fashion. Instead, it is messy, complex, and unpredictable. New patterns of relationships typically emerge that are very different from the traditional isolation and independent work that has been characteristic of teachers, administrators, school professionals, and parents. A developmentally healthy school environment reflects a vision of professional collaboration that is focused on nurturing the whole child.

SUMMARY OF KEY POINTS

- Educating the whole child means attending to cognitive, social, emotional, physical, and talent development of children and youth from widely diverse backgrounds.
- School professionals today must be prepared to understand the extraordinary nature of the life experiences of many children in schools today.
- While grade progression and performance expectations occur in lockstep fashion for all students, the developmental process for children is nonlinear and variable.

- Environmental conditions, poverty, and health status affect learning and development.
- Social-emotional health affects learning and development and children's long-term outcomes.
- Participation in high-risk behaviors affects short-term and long-term learning, development, and life outcomes for students.

KEY TERMS AND PHRASES

- Whole child
- Holistic education
- System coordination
- System theory
- Broader definition of achievement
- Strategic collaboration
- Developmental variability
- Ecological theory
- Developmental perspective
- Developmentally responsive practice

- Youth development framework
- Transitions
- Health disparities
- Social-emotional health
- Child poverty
- High-risk behaviors
- Disconnected youth and development
- Alternative education
- Shared responsibility

2

What Is a Developmentally Healthy School Environment?

Angela Heishman

A child's life is like a piece of paper on which every passerby leaves a mark.

—Chinese proverb

The development of human resiliency is none other than the process of healthy human development.

—Bonnie Bernard, 2004, p. 9

CHAPTER TOPICS

- What Is the Relationship Between Social and Emotional Health and Learning?
- What Are the Characteristics of a Developmentally Healthy School Environment?
- Ten Strategies That Promote a Developmentally Responsive School Environment
- What Models and Initiatives Exist for Creating a Developmentally Responsive School Environment?

INTRODUCTION

Despite widely differing opinions about the role and responsibilities of school systems, many young people rely on schools to serve as de facto institutions to provide medical, social work, and psychological services as families struggle to meet their children's basic nutritional, health, and safety needs (Hoagwood & Johnson, 2003). Although schools may focus on students' success in reading and math, the children who walk through our schools' hallways are not oblivious to the events occurring in their outside world.

In my work in student assistance, for example, I recall a referral of a student described as being inattentive, a daydreamer, and unmotivated. She vividly described the process of "playing old tapes" of her dad beating her mom and being worried each day that her mom would be dead when she came home from school. Although the student indicated a strong desire to do well in her classes, these thoughts and related fears infiltrated every aspect of her life. Other students spend their days praying and hoping that by some miracle their parents will stop drinking. Many of these students cannot appreciate the relevance of classroom lessons in their lives. Also sitting in our classrooms are children with grumbling stomachs, infected wounds, untreated asthma, aching teeth, and other health concerns that impede their ability to concentrate on instruction. Growing numbers of children spend limited time in physical activity during the school day or outside of school, and their food choices and eating behaviors only exacerbate the incidence of obesity. There are students who cannot see beyond their present life circumstances to envision a future . . . or one that they really desire to attain.

With the growing consensus that a wide range of factors within children's environments could have a significant impact on their learning and long-term outcomes, it could be argued that school professionals have an ethical obligation to examine current practices, policies, and school settings to ensure that they are appropriately meeting the developmental needs of children and adolescents. Children cannot reach their fullest potential or at least sufficiently learn until their basic psychological, social, health, physical, and emotional needs are adequately met. Given the high expectations placed upon our children and our schools during a time of excessive stress and economic uncertainty, the time is now to collaborate and create school environments that truly address the developmental needs of the whole child to ensure opportunities for success. The goal of this chapter is to examine the relationship between social and emotional health and learning and investigate the characteristics of a developmentally responsive, healthy school environment that meets the full range of developmental needs of children.

WHAT IS THE RELATIONSHIP BETWEEN SOCIAL AND EMOTIONAL HEALTH AND LEARNING?

Social-Emotional Well-Being

In contrast to emphasizing reactive and punitive practices that focus on aberrant and negative behaviors of children, renewed attention is being paid to strengths-based approaches that incorporate social-emotional wellness into educational programming (Bear, 2008). While the term *mental health* often evokes negative images of individuals with mental illness and limited life outcomes, the term *social and emotional well-being* tends to be associated with positive qualities and opportunities (Bernard, Stephanou, & Urbach, 2007). While it continues to be important for specialized staff to meet the complex needs of students identified with significant mental health issues, educators are becoming more aware of the necessity to incorporate prevention and intervention models into the general school curriculum, especially within subgroups of vulnerable children (Bernard et al.). They also recognize the importance of social and emotional development across all grade levels.

Although each child has his or her own developmental path, some individuals need direct instruction in certain social skills sets in order to become successful in meeting specific social and academic expectations. For example, some children develop emotional intelligence naturally, while others are developmentally delayed in understanding and managing their behaviors and emotions. **Emotional intelligence,** which has been found to be positively linked to overall life success, refers to the awareness of and ability to monitor one's own and others' feelings and emotions, to discriminate among them, and to use this information to guide one's thinking and actions (Goleman, 1995; Salovey & Grewal, 2005). When children do not understand their own feelings or those of others, they are likely to respond inappropriately and in maladaptive ways (Kam, Greenberg, & Kusche, 2007). These individuals are vulnerable to being ridiculed or ostracized by their peers and misinterpreted by their teachers and other adults. Difficulty in understanding the emotions of others, in regulating behaviors and emotions, and in the ability to form friendships with others affect students' overall social and emotional well-being (Blair, 2003; Kam et al.). Social-cognitive skills assist children in accurately understanding the emotional context of a situation and regulate their emotional arousal so they can free their cognitive powers to think through a problem (Pellegrini, 2005). Teaching a researched-based affective (social-emotional) education as part of the core curriculum can have a positive influence in reducing stress, building positive social relationships, and assisting students with learning strategies that regulate their emotional arousal systems (Hoagwood & Erwin, 1997; Huang et al., 2005; Kam et al.).

Resilience

Related to the topic of social and emotional well-being is the term *resilience*. Resilience can be associated with social and emotional well-being, as it involves the person's ability to deal with particular challenges that contribute to the maintenance or realignment of internal and external assets (Response Ability, 2005). Simply stated, *resilience* is defined as "the innate human ability to rebound from adversity with even greater strength to meet future challenges" (Brendtro & Larson, 2006, p. 33). Resilience has been studied since the 1960s and 1970s by theorists striving to understand the etiology of mental illness and the consequences that trauma and threat have on human development (Masten, 2007). Leaders in resiliency science recognize from a developmental perspective the importance of certain qualities that aid vulnerable individuals in recovering from significant trauma in their lives (Masten). Within the past several decades, significant research has investigated the specific qualities that are believed to reduce the risk of the most vulnerable populations.

Developmental Assets: The Positive Building Blocks

Previously, it was hypothesized that only a few individuals possessed the personality traits needed to overcome significant vulnerability, but research indicates that resilience is in fact the norm (Benson, Scales, Hamilton, & Sesma, 2006a). Studies of children at risk show that 60 percent eventually made positive adjustments into adulthood (Werner, 2004). Researchers have since identified various "positive building blocks" that are needed for children and adolescents to succeed. One of most widely used approaches to cultivating positive youth development is the Search Institute's (2007) Framework of Developmental Assets. This framework was introduced in 1990 and has been revisited and updated to its current form of 40 developmental assets. According to the Search

Institute, all children and adolescents need and deserve the range of "developmental nutrients" identified in the framework of developmental assets (see Table 2.1).

Table 2.1   Developmental Assets for the Middle Child and Adolescent

Asset Type	Asset Name and Definition	
	External Assets	
Support	Family support	Family life provides high levels of love and support.
	Positive family communication	Young person and her or his parent(s) communicate positively, and young person is willing to seek advice and counsel from parent(s).
	Other adult relationships	Young person receives support from three or more nonparent adults.
	Caring neighborhood	Young person experiences caring neighbors.
	Caring school climate	School provides a caring, encouraging environment.
	Parent involvement in schooling	Parent(s) are actively involved in helping young person succeed in school.
Empowerment	Community values youth	Young person perceives that adults in the community value youth.
	Youth as resources	Young people are given useful roles in the community.
	Service to others	Young person serves in the community one hour or more per week.
	Safety	Young person feels safe at home, at school, and in the neighborhood.
Boundaries and Expectations	Family boundaries	Family has clear rules and consequences and monitors the young person's whereabouts.
	School boundaries	School provides clear rules and consequences.
	Neighborhood boundaries	Neighbors take responsibility for monitoring young people's behavior.
	Adult role models	Parent(s) and other adults model positive, responsible behavior.
	Positive peer influence	Young person's best friends model responsible behavior.
	High expectations	Both parent(s) and teachers encourage the young person to do well.
Constructive Use of Time	Creative activities	Young person spends three or more hours per week in lessons or practice in music, theater, or other arts.
	Youth programs	Young person spends three or more hours per week in sports, clubs, or organizations at school and/or in community organizations.
	Religious community	Young person spends one hour or more per week in activities in a religious institution.
	Time at home	Young person is out with friends "with nothing special to do" two or fewer nights per week.

Asset Type	Asset Name and Definition	
Internal Assets		
Commitment to Learning	*Achievement motivation*	Young person is motivated to do well in school.
	School engagement	Young person is actively engaged in learning.
	Homework	Young person reports doing at least one hour of homework every school day.
	Bonding to school	Young person cares about her or his school.
	Reading for pleasure	Young person reads for pleasure three or more hours per week.
Positive Values	*Caring*	Young person places high value on helping other people.
	Equality and social justice	Young person places high value on promoting equality and reducing hunger and poverty.
	Integrity	Young person acts on convictions and stands up for her or his beliefs.
	Honesty	Young person "tells the truth even when it is not easy."
	Responsibility	Young person accepts and takes personal responsibility.
	Restraint	Young person believes it is important not to be sexually active or to use alcohol or other drugs.
Social Competencies	*Planning and decision making*	Young person knows how to plan ahead and make choices.
	Interpersonal competence	Young person has empathy, sensitivity, and friendship skills.
	Cultural competence	Young person has knowledge of and comfort with people of different cultural/racial/ethnic backgrounds.
	Resistance skills	Young person can resist negative peer pressure and dangerous situations.
	Peaceful conflict resolution	Young person seeks to resolve conflict nonviolently.
Positive Identity	*Personal power*	Young person feels he or she has control over "things that happen to me."
	Self-esteem	Young person reports having a high self-esteem.
	Sense of purpose	Young person reports that "my life has a purpose."
	Positive view of personal future	Young person is optimistic about her or his personal future.

Resilience and the Brain

Resiliency research has drawn primarily from the fields of social and behavioral science, although from the beginning, scientists theorized that neurobiological (brain biology) and genetic influences played an important role in young people's ability to adapt positively to significant trauma in their lives (Masten, 2007). Because of advances in technology and ongoing interest in educational neuroscience, a growing body of research is promoting our understanding of the neurobiological foundations of resilience and resilient adaptation (Curtis & Cichetti, 2003, 2007a, 2007b; Luthar & Brown, 2007). Research on psychobiological stress reactivity, self-regulation systems, the neuroscience of attachment relationships, neural plasticity, and the development of executive functioning skills have highlighted the importance of protective factors in the development of the whole child (Masten).

Neural plasticity, the ability of the brain to change, has been clearly established as a phenomenon that needs to be considered in studies of resiliency, based on the hypothesis that the environment may contribute to structural and functional reorganization of the brain (Luthar & Brown, 2007). Specifically, the quality of interactions and experiences that the child has with the environment influences whether connections are formed or eliminated during the process of synaptic pruning (Huttenlocher, 2002; Pally, 2007). In more recent years, it has been found that the malleability and overall development of the brain and interacting systems continues beyond one's early life experiences. Major physiological reorganization of the brain has been found to be significant during adolescence, when the brain continues to be influenced by the environment (Curtis & Cicchetti, 2007a; Silk et al., 2007).

To deepen their understanding of the impact that the environment has on brain plasticity, educational leaders must consider the role that the ecology of the school setting plays in development. One of the most important premises of resiliency research models is the belief that environments can be improved to support brain development and the developmental needs of children at risk (Benson et al., 2006a).

> *Educators themselves often don't make the link between health and education. They see their role as producing kids who are excited about learning, and giving them strong academic and life skills. But educators sometimes don't make the connection that health is a huge contributor to success in life. The irony is that as we've increased academic expectations, we've neglected the health and wellness side of things—which is a total contradiction.*
>
> —Gene Wilhoit (in Action for Healthy Kids, 2008, p. 22)

WHAT ARE THE CHARACTERISTICS OF A DEVELOPMENTALLY HEALTHY SCHOOL ENVIRONMENT?

Over the past two decades, with current curriculum heavily focused on students' academic progress, less attention has been paid to other significant domains essential to the developmental needs of our children. Students spend less time in physical education and at recess. In recent years, educational reformers have implored school administrators to lead the development and implementation of school models that attend to the range of developmental processes that facilitate learning. Creating a developmentally responsive school is as complex as the needs of a child. It requires an integration of practices that addresses the social, emotional, physical, and cognitive development of each child within an environment that is healthy, safe, engaging, challenging, and supportive.

Comprehensive Health: A Holistic View of Well-Being

The concerns of school professionals often reach far beyond providing students with high-quality instruction. Many students suffer from undiagnosed or poorly managed health concerns that affect their school attendance and interfere with their ability to learn; the latter may be due to frequent visits to the nurse's office or inability to engage fully in the classroom. The difficulty of affording good health care prevents families from providing their children with the services needed to treat serious health concerns. Children are not taken to the doctor until they become significantly ill, and such delays can have significant implications in the recovery process. School nurses serve as the only source of medical care for some children.

To minimize the impact of health concerns on learning, engagement, and academic success, school wellness advocates have identified the need to incorporate preventative strategies into the curriculum that encompass a holistic view of health. Such programs examine all aspects necessary for good health among children, including preventive health, medical intervention, physical activity, good nutrition, and social and emotional wellness. Although critics may argue that addressing the health needs of children is beyond the purview of schools, a strong case can be made that the health of children clearly influences their academic achievement and overall success in school.

How Does School Wellness Affect Student Achievement?

In response to the rising rates of childhood obesity in the nation, Congress and the federal government created the "Healthy States Initiative" as part of the Child Nutrition and WIC (Women, Infants and Children) Reauthorization Act of 2004. Wellness programs were designed based on the findings of two key determinants behind the increasing rate of overweight children: (1) poor nutrition habits and (2) more sedentary lifestyles (Council of State Governments, 2007). Research reveals that only 1 percent of children have diets that are consistent with the federal guidelines, while 64 percent do not participate in physical activity at the recommended level (CDC, 2005; Muñoz, Krebs-Smith, Ballard-Barbash, & Cleveland, 1997). Despite the attention that has been directed toward obesity's impact on children's overall wellness, many educational leaders have yet to recognize the significance that health, physical activity, and nutrition have for learning. Instead, recess, physical education, and health education are often viewed as ancillary portions of the school day (Pellegrini, 2005).

Studies have supported the link between school success and physical health and nutrition. Research conducted by the California Department of Education, for example, found programs that encouraged their students to become more physically active and fit also boosted academic performance (National Association for Sports and Physical Education, 2002). In a recent study, researchers found that among 11,000 children ages 8 and 9, those who had more than 15 minutes of recess a day showed better behavior in the classroom than those who had less time or none (Barros, Silver, & Stein, 2009).

The more physical fitness tests children passed, the better they did on academic tests (Chomitz et al., 2009). *The Learning Connection: The Value of Improving Nutrition and Physical Activity in Our Schools* (Action for Healthy Kids, 2004) reviewed and summarized the research linking the relationship between academic achievement and nutrition, physical activity and weight. The researchers found the following:

- Children who are well nourished tend to be better students in comparison to poorly nourished students, who exhibited weaker academic performance and lower scores on standardized achievement tests.
- Poor nutrition and hunger imply an inadequate intake of the vitamins, minerals, fats, and proteins that are necessary for optimal cognitive functioning.
- Physical activity and fitness are correlated with improved cognitive functioning, stronger achievement, increased concentration, and better test scores.
- Obesity and poor nutrition are associated with reduced achievement and a greater number of behavioral problems, which may be due to higher rates of absences, social stigmatization, or poor self-image.

Recess: A Necessity, Not an Option

A recent report, *Progress or Promises? What's Working For and Against Healthy Schools* (Action for Healthy Kids, 2008), identified several gaps in educators' attempts to create healthy and active school environments. One gap that was particularly noteworthy involves schools' failure to meet the National Association for Sport and Physical Education recommendations that children engage in at least 60 minutes of age-appropriate physical activity most days or every day. Districts have reported that insufficient funding, scheduling conflicts, and staffing issues prevent them from meeting this requirement. In addition, the traditional minimum of one hour a day of recess for children has been steadily decreasing over the past decade. Anyone working in an elementary school recognizes that denying a child recess is one of the most prevalent consequences used to address behavioral issues or incomplete schoolwork. It has become common practice to reduce recess periods to provide additional instruction time to students, especially to students falling below benchmark standards.

Advocates for school wellness have made significant efforts in explaining the importance of a "respite" during the school day for children. Recess, playtime, and time spent outside have been described as necessary not only for physical health and development but also for cognitive development and learning. Children both with and without attention deficit/hyperactivity disorder (ADHD) have shown improvements in their attention and ability to concentrate when provided with the opportunity to spend some time outdoors during the school day (Kuo & Faber-Taylor, 2004). It is important to recognize the mental energy required to learn—the long hours paying direct attention required for children to complete work, read, and take tests. Even the most attentive and persistent of students are likely to fatigue at some point. Involuntary attention—that is, attention that is usually associated with distraction—is believed to provide the brain with an opportunity to rest (Gumenyuk, Korzyukov, Alho, Escera, & Näätänen, 2003). Recess allows students to use other areas of the brain and provides an opportunity for the neurobiological components responsible for direct attention to rest. The child will then be able to return to coursework with renewed energy and attention (Chomitz et al., 2009; Pellegrini, 2005). The boxed text provides a perspective on recess from a student whose high level of energy interferes with his attention in class.

A CASE FOR RECESS

In elementary school my teachers considered me the "troublemaker," the "class clown," the "bad one." I remember trying really hard to listen, at least for a few minutes, but would become distracted . . . easily, by anything and everyone. I recall being yelled at almost constantly to put all four legs of the chair on the floor, to sit down in my seat, to stop tapping my pencil, to keep my eyes on the paper or on the board or at the teacher, and to "Shut up." I liked making the other students laugh, but I don't know if it was ever my intention to do so. It just sort of happened. Although I do have a few happy moments I can share from those years, I primarily remember feeling loathed by my teachers. It seemed that no matter what I did, I was being punished. The most devastating moments were doing those many occasions when my classmates would walk past my desk to go to recess as I sat there at my desk and was told to keep my head down. On a few of those occasions, I cried and I can still recall the heat on my face as the teachers scolded me for my bad behavior. As the day progressed, I remember feeling frustrated and anxious as I struggled to keep my attention. I remember wanting to run down the hallway, and many times I did, because I just had this energy that I could not control. Since then, I was diagnosed with ADHD and have been taking medication ever since. I am graduating from high school this year, and I plan to become a gym teacher. I still have some difficulty sitting still, but I have learned strategies to keep me focused. The one thing that I do know is that I do better with frequent breaks and opportunities to get "fresh air." Based on my experiences as a child with ADHD, I hope that I can help kids with similar experiences. I also hope to help other adults understand our need to "release" our energy.

Adolescent Health: Its Unique Characteristics

Adolescent health needs become more complex, as teens are more likely to be exposed to risky behaviors involving substance abuse, driving under the influence, smoking, and engaging in sexual activity, as well as other behaviors that could have deleterious short-term and long-term effects on their social, emotional, cognitive, and physical development (Bearman, Moody, Stovel, & Thalji, 2004). Adolescents are particularly at risk, as their level of independence increases but their ability to cope effectively with new responsibilities may be tenuous. Recognizing the vulnerability and needs of adolescents, the The Carnegie Corporation of New York established the Carnegie Council of Adolescent Development in 1986. For over two decades, the Council has examined the challenges of adolescents through various task forces, working groups, meetings and seminars, and commissioned studies. The Council synthesized its data and reported a set of strategies in *Great Transitions: Preparing Adolescents for a New Century* (1995). It also outlined six basic concepts of adolescence, presented in the boxed text.

THE CARNEGIE COUNCIL'S SIX BASIC CONCEPTS ABOUT ADOLESCENCE

1. The years from ten through fourteen are a crucial turning point in life's trajectory. This period, therefore, represents an optimal time for interventions to foster effective education, prevent destructive behavior, and promote enduring health practices.

2. Education and health are inextricably related. Good health facilitates learning, while poor health hinders it, each with lifelong effects. Commensurately, a positive educational experience promotes the formation of good health habits, while academic failure discourages it.

(continued)

(Continued)

3. Destructive, or health-damaging, behaviors in adolescence tend to occur together, as do positive, health-promoting, behaviors.

4. Many problem behaviors in adolescence have common antecedents in childhood experience. One is academic difficulty; another is the absence of strong and sustained guidance from caring adults.

5. Preventive interventions are more likely to be successful if they address underlying factors that contribute to problem behaviors.

6. Given the complex influences on adolescents, the essential requirements for ensuring healthy development must be met through the joint efforts of a set of pivotal institutions that powerfully shape adolescents' experiences. These pivotal institutions must begin with the family and include schools, health care institutions, a wide array of neighborhood and community organizations, and the mass media.

Source: Used with permission from the Carnegie Council, 437 Madison Avenue, New York, NY 10022, USA. Tel: (212) 371-3200, Fax: (212) 754-4073. Retrieved December 20, 2009, from www.carnegie.org/sub/pubs/reports/great_transitions/gr_intro.html.

Although adolescents are closely approaching adulthood and have gained significant self-efficacy in many areas, they are still experiencing significant growth and continue to need support to become productive adults. When designing school wellness policies, it is imperative for school personnel to recognize the unique needs of adolescents and to ensure that resources are distributed throughout the higher grade levels.

SAFE AND SECURE SCHOOLS

I was in my car thinking about a training I was to provide on the subject of resiliency to school professionals when I first heard the news broadcast across the radio about the massacre occurring at an affluent public school in Colorado. Like many of us working within the school setting, the images of that day continue to be embedded in my mind. As I have collaborated with hundreds of people, I have frequently heard comments referencing that our perfect view of schools as safe havens were shattered that very day. As we grieved over this tragedy, we continued to be confronted by other widely publicized incidents of young people shooting and killing their classmates, teachers, and principals. In response to these unfathomable events, law enforcement, school personnel, and mental health professionals were quickly tutored in the latest research on threat assessments and the design of safe and secure school environments.

In response to tragic situations, schools are called upon to assess their physical environments and to develop or revise their safety plans. Initiatives emerge that emphasize the development of comprehensive bullying prevention programs, zero-tolerance programs, threat assessments, and school safety plans with the aim of providing students with safe and secure environments in which to learn. Although a great deal has been learned about the potential for bullying, intimidation, and teasing, questions persist as to whether certain approaches to minimize the risk of violence may be counterproductive. For example, have schools' efforts to create a safe environment impeded our ability to provide a comforting and welcoming atmosphere? Have parents and grandparents been shut out because it is now more difficult for them to visit their loved ones' classrooms? Have we taken away important protective variables necessary for the "high-risk" child to be successful by expelling him for violating the school's zero-tolerance policy and introducing him to the juvenile justice system? It is important that school administrators continue to ask, "What makes a school environment healthy, and are we appropriately meeting the developmental needs of all children and adolescents?" (See boxed text.)

Healthy School Environment: The physical and aesthetic surroundings and the psychosocial climate and culture of the school. Factors that influence the physical environment include the school building and the area surrounding it, any biological or chemical agents that are detrimental to health, and physical conditions such as temperature, noise, and lighting. The psychological environment includes the physical, emotional, and social conditions that affect the well-being of students and staff.

Source: Used with permission from the Centers for Disease Control and Prevention. Retrieved December 20, 2009, from www.cdc.gov/HealthyYouth/CSHP/.

Physical and Social Environment: Safe, Clean, and Caring

There is little doubt that young people are influenced by the overall atmosphere and climate of classrooms and buildings. Creating a safe, clean, and caring environment is an important investment for schools in view of the significance that positive settings and safety have on the success of young people (Luthar & Brown, 2007). The physical quality of a school environment can shape the attitudes of students, teachers, and staff. For example, the brightness of lights, temperature of the room, color of the walls, and sound quality have all been examined and found to have some impact on learning, attitude, and behavior (Boman & Enmarker, 2004; Higgins, Hall, Wall, Woolner, & McCaughey Higgins, 2005). All of these factors are intertwined when examining how best to meet the needs of each and every child in the school setting (M. A. Berry, 2002).

Beyond nutrition and physical health, our young people are also exposed to various other health risks in their daily lives. Research conducted by the National Center for Education Statistics (2000) found that nearly half of the schools studied had at least one environmental factor considered to be unsatisfactory. Factors of concern included acoustics or noise control, ventilation, indoor air quality, heating, and ventilation. In one study investigating air quality in schools, it was found that volatile organic compounds, bioaerosols, dust mites, animal allergens, excessive levels of carbon dioxide, and inadequate violations were common (Daisey, Angell, & Apte, 2003; Frumkin, 2006). Researchers believe environmental conditions such as these present both short-term and long-term effects on young people's health and learning (Frumkin). To address these concerns, it is important for school personnel to employ staff with expertise in environmental risks and who understand their relationship to health and learning, then to engage them in schoolwide reform initiatives to improve the quality of the school environment.

How Does School Climate Affect Resilience?

Resiliency research suggests that one of the most important factors to consider when examining the quality of the school environment is whether it projects a sense of warmth and welcome. Schools can use multiple strategies to send the message that the school is a safe and caring place where bullying, victimization, indifference, and intolerance will not be accepted. Respect and kindness are required (M. Berry, 2002). The boxed text contains a summary of a variety of common traits that were found in schools that were seen as comfortable, safe, and radiating a "sense of well-being" (M. Berry).

THE HEALTHY SCHOOL ENVIRONMENT

Characteristics

- Provides adequate space and opportunities for students and teachers to spread out, reflect, interact, exchange information, and examine and test ideas
- Appearance is inviting.
- Students, teachers, and community want to be there.
- Adequate natural lighting enhances productivity.
- School strives for student-friendly conditions.
- Is inviting to good teachers and supports their retention (i.e. strike issues)
- Designed to reduce stress (i.e. comfortable, manages noise, consistent temperature)
- Is clean and sanitary
- Adverse health effect is small.

Classroom Conditions

- Lighting
- Classroom size
- Cleanliness
- Shows caring in maintaining classroom
- Safety (i.e. surveillance)

Source: Adapted from M. Berry, 2002.

How Does School Size Affect Learning?

Possibly one of the most pressing concerns reported by teachers and parents is classroom size. In communities across the nation, state governors, community leaders, and school leaders are debating whether and how to merge smaller school districts into larger districts as a means of addressing economic distress; particularly enaged are those who are concerned about inequality in school funding (Buchanan, 2004). Parents' concerns about the formation of these "mega-districts" is understandable. School consolidations can lead to greater sharing of support personnel (e.g., psychologists, counselors, speech and hearing specialists) among buildings as leaders pursue cost savings. In a system that is data driven and highly focused on improving test scores, teachers could easily miss opportunities to get to know their students in the classroom. Students with significant concerns could easily be overlooked. Furthermore, students' opportunities to participate in extracurricular activities are often reduced, as competition in academic and extracurricular activities increases. Many parents have expressed concern about their "average" kids being lost in schools filled with overachieving and gifted students.

> *As a former mental health liaison to several different schools, my colleagues were often surprised at the higher number of referrals for mental health assessments that I received in my smaller, more rural schools when compared to districts with thousands of more students. One important factor that affected rates of referrals for mental health assessments was teachers' opportunity to know their students. The better they knew their students, the more immediately they could identify the red flags.*

Studies have demonstrated that smaller classrooms facilitate opportunities for the development of a positive school climate, particularly due to more personal and timely connections with students and parents (Achilles, 1996, 1997; Finn, 1998; Watt, 2003). Wynne and Walberg (1995) found that smaller schools offer a more intimate educational experience. This is not to say that larger schools cannot offer this type of experience. For example, larger schools can provide a more personal environment by having students spend most of their day with the same group of teachers and students. Creating an intimate classroom environment involves more than just student–teacher ratio and classroom space; it also requires establishing conditions that contribute to the feeling of belonging to the school.

How Does School Membership Affect Learning?

School pride has long been thought to promote positive school climate. On the other hand, several factors have been found to influence the climate of the school deleteriously and therefore impede young people's ability to develop positive feelings of school membership (Benninga, Berkowitz, Kuehn, & Smith, 2006). Such factors are pervasive in schools and have been found to foster incidents of bullying, substance abuse, lower school performance, and school dropout rates. Examples include the following:

- Lack of connection
- Tolerance for disrespectful behaviors
- Inequitable discipline
- Inflexible culture
- Pecking order among students
- Code of silence prevailing among students

Regardless of the size of the school, unsupervised hallways, locker areas, bus stops, and bathrooms hold the potential for bullying, intimidation, and harassment (Menard, Grotpeter, Gianola, & O'Neal, 2008). Being bullied has both short-term and long-term effects on people, as they see themselves as outcasts. To reduce the rates of bullying and to intervene as necessary, it is imperative for schools to invest in the systematic formation of healthy school environments that promote pride in school membership.

Healthy or successful schools have been supported in the research as those that create a sense of membership and pride for all individuals, including those considered at-risk. Membership depends on social bonding; in other words, the ability to have meaningful and satisfying relationships with others in the school setting (Hagborg, 1998; Wehlage, Rutter, Smith, Lesko, & Fernandez, 1989). The next section further examines the importance of trusting and high-quality relationships.

> *Students who engage in bullying behaviors seem to have a need to feel powerful and in control.... Studies indicate that bullies often come from homes where physical punishment is used, where the children are taught to strike back physically as a way to handle problems, and where parental involvement and warmth are frequently lacking. In contrast to prevailing myths, bullies appear to have little anxiety and to possess strong self-esteem. There is little evidence to support the contention that they victimize others because they feel bad about themselves.*
>
> —R. Banks, 1997, ¶ 4

Quality Relationships: Key to Student Development

One of the most significant findings gathered from resiliency research is the impact that positive and healthy relationships between children and adults have in the development of individual resilience (Luthar & Brown, 2007). Educators employed within developmentally healthy schools are those who strive to provide positive mentors and role models to all children. As Weissbourd (1996) described, it is difficult to "exaggerate the importance of anchors in their lives—children and adults outside their families who are caring and attentive over time" (p. 63). Research has provided evidence that teachers can serve as protective resources in children's social and emotional adjustment and academic success (B. Berry, Johnson, & Montgomery, 2005; Raver, Garner, & Smith-Donald, 2007). Positive social relationships also play a role in improving students' outcomes and in buffering the harmful effects of prolonged stress and living in adverse environments (Gunnar & Fisher, 2006; Luthar & Brown).

In examining the needs of older school-age children, the forming of positive relationships with peers must also be considered when designing comprehensive prevention/intervention programs that address the needs of the whole child. The neural systems involved in reactivity to stress and emotional processing are believed to be significantly affected by environment stressors and the impact of social influences (Essex, Klein, Cho, & Kalin, 2002; Silk et al., 2007). In reviewing this literature, school personnel need to examine the damage that can occur when segregating or excluding students considered at risk from their mainstream peers (K. Dodge, Dishion, & Lansford, 2006). Such segregation reduces students' exposure to and reinforcement for displaying positive and adaptive behaviors. Resiliency research suggests that the adolescent brain holds a great deal of potential when provided with positive learning experiences and opportunities (Casey, Giedd, & Thomas, 2000; Curtis & Cicchetti, 2003; Luthar & Brown, 2007). Attention to the development of healthy and nurturing peer and adult relationships throughout children's educational career is a key component of education reform for developmentally healthy schools.

How Does Behavioral Engagement Affect Student Outcomes?

Research on at-risk youth has identified disengagement in school as a significant precursor to school failure. In *The Silent Epidemic: Perspectives of High School Dropouts* (Bridgeland et al., 2006), researchers found the explanation for school dropout rates to be complex, involving various individual, family, teacher, school, community, and societal factors (see also Rumberger, 2004). The respondents did indicate that, among a variety of factors, a lack of connection to the school environment, a belief that school was boring, a lack of motivation, and academic challenges significantly influenced their ultimate decision to drop out of school. There is evidence that students' significant disengagement occurs somewhere between one to three years prior to their withdrawal from school. These individuals typically demonstrate a disinterest in school, have poor attendance and low grades, have trouble getting out of bed in the morning, skip classes, and take extra long lunches (Bridgeland et al.). Excessive absenteeism has been found to be particularly indicative of student disengagement and a risk factor for dropping out (Bridgeland et al.; Rumberger).

As engagement and academic challenge have been promoted as essential qualities necessary for the development of the whole child, it is important to understand the dynamics related to positive learning conditions. Positive or ideal learning conditions involve sustained and frequent opportunities for students to engage in learning (Downer, Rimm-Kaufman, & Pianta, 2007). In such environments, teachers are typically sensitive toward children's needs and modify lessons to fit the emotional and academic needs of the individuals in the classroom, establish routines, monitor students to keep them engaged, and manage behaviors through a proactive approach (Downer et al.). Students instructed in these environments are likely to be engaged at a variety of levels, including cognitive engagement (e.g., thoughtfulness), emotional engagement (e.g., emotional connection to school), and academic achievement (Downer et al.; J. Fredericks, Blumenfeld, & Paris, 2004; Greenwood, Horton, & Utley, 2002; Pianta, LaParo, Payne, Cox, & Bradley, 2002). Creating a high-quality environment with conscientious teachers is invaluable in addressing the needs of vulnerable students.

TEN STRATEGIES THAT PROMOTE A DEVELOPMENTALLY RESPONSIVE SCHOOL ENVIRONMENT

Creating a developmentally responsive school environment does not necessarily require "giving up" on services and programs already in place. Schools seeking to create developmentally healthy school environments benefit from simultaneously using a bottom-up and top-down approach. They develop implementation teams that include a variety of representatives, including school leaders, school nurses, school counselors, school psychologists, food service directors; school grounds and building supervisors; physical education and health teachers; regular education and special education teachers; mental health, drug alcohol, and health care liaisons representing collaborative agencies; nutritionists; and intervention specialists. There are a variety of models and programs that can assist schools in implementing new models and programs (Doll & Cummings, 2008). Since systemic change in education is highly complex and challenging to implement, school personnel and related stakeholders may benefit in reviewing the literature on scaling up evidence-based practices (SEP) when attempting to transform our educational institutions into developmentally healthy schools (Fixsen, Blasé, Horner, & Sugai, 2009; see also www.fpg.unc.edu/~sisep/). Listed below are a variety of strategies to assist school teams in improving the quality of their school environments.

Strategy 1

Develop and implement school policies and programs that adopt a holistic view of health. School personnel need to design school policies and develop strategies specifically to examine the social, emotional, mental, physical, and overall well-being of children. School leaders can begin by designating a school health coordinator and formulating a school health council consisting of representatives from a variety of disciplines. It should consist of students, school staff, parents, and community members. Goals of this committee include assessing the school's policies and developing strategies to create and maintain a healthy school community. The Centers for Disease Control and Prevention (2008) advocates a systematic, schoolwide approach that addresses eight components that strongly influence health and learning:

1. Health education
2. Physical education
3. Counseling, psychological, and social services
4. Health services
5. Nutrition services
6. Healthy school environment
7. Parent/community involvement
8. Staff wellness

For school wellness programs to be successful, they must be integrated as essential components of the curriculum (Action for Healthy Kids, 2008). Resources to assist schools in forming such committees are listed in the boxed text.

RESOURCES IN FORMING SCHOOL HEALTH COUNCILS

Action for Healthy Kids: *Game On! The Ultimate Wellness Challenge* (www.actionforhealthykids .org/school-programs/our-programs/game-on/)

National Center for Chronic Disease Prevention and Health Promotion (www.cdc.gov/ chronicdisease/index.htm)

Healthy Youth! *Make a Difference: Key Strategies to Prevent Obesity; Build a Strong Foundation* (www.cdc.gov/HealthyYouth/KeyStrategies/build.htm)

National Center for Health Education: *Youth, Parents, and Communities: Establishing a Community-School Health Council* (www.nche.org/ypc_school_communityschoolhealthcouncil.htm)

American Cancer Society (Karen Shirer, principal author; Patricia P. Miller, editor): *Promoting Healthy Youth, Schools, and Communities: A Guide to Community-School Health Councils* (www.cancer.org/downloads/PED/Guide_to_Community_School_Health_Councils.pdf)

Physical and Health Education Canada: *Quality School Health: Make It Happen* (www.cahperd .ca/eng/health/qsh_happen.cfm)

Strategy 2

Identify resources and develop strategies to ensure that a continuum of health and medical services is available to all children and adolescents. Based on the significant role that health has on child development and learning, it is imperative for children to be provided with a continuum of health and medical services. Preventive health strategies should be considered an essential component in school health and wellness programs. The boxed text provides a summary of research-based policies that have been found to work to prevent disease.

PREVENTING DISEASE: RESEARCH-BASED POLICIES

- *Promote healthy eating.* Policies that give kids healthier food choices at school can help curb rising rates of youth obesity. Ensuring that every neighborhood has access to healthy foods will improve the nutrition of many Americans.

- *Get people moving.* Policies that encourage more physical activity among kids and adults have been proven to reduce rates of obesity and to help prevent other chronic diseases.

- *Discourage smoking.* Policies that support comprehensive tobacco control programs—those that combine school-based, community-based, and media interventions—are extremely effective at curbing smoking and reducing the incidence of cancer and heart disease.

- *Encourage prevention coverage.* Policies that encourage health insurers to cover the costs of recommended preventive screenings, tests, and vaccinations that are proven to increase the rates of people taking preventive action.

- *Promote health screenings.* Policies that promote—through worksite wellness programs and media campaigns—the importance of health screenings in primary care settings are proven to help reduce rates of chronic disease.

- *Protect kids' smiles.* Policies that promote the use of dental sealants for kids in schools and community water fluoridation are proven to reduce oral disease dramatically.

- *Require childhood immunizations.* Requiring immunizations for school and child care settings reduces illness and prevents further transmission of those diseases among children. Scientific, economic, and social concerns should be addressed when policies to mandate immunizations are considered.

- *Encourage immunizations for adults.* Policies that support and encourage immunizations of adults, including college students and health care workers, reduce illness, hospitalizations, and deaths.

- *Make chlamydia screenings routine.* Screening and treating chlamydia, the most common sexually transmitted bacterial infection, will help protect sexually active young women against infertility and other complications of pelvic inflammatory disease (PID) that are caused by chlamydia.

- *Promote routine HIV testing.* Making HIV testing part of routine medical care for those ages 13 to 64 can foster earlier detection of HIV infection among the quarter of a million Americans who do not know they are infected.

Source: Adapted from Council of State Governments, 2007.

Schools may strive toward developing a comprehensive health programs (CHPs) or develop a hybrid approach that allows for collaboration between schools and health clinics to meet the medical, dental, and overall health needs of all children and adolescents, regardless of their financial status.

Strategy 3

Implement school wellness policies and practices that promote physical activity and good nutrition K–12. Incorporating physical activity throughout the school day, particularly for younger children, and ensuring that the food choices made available to students are healthy and tasty are two essential components in fostering healthy child development and learning. As schools attempt to incorporate activities into the school day and improve nutritional options for school breakfasts, lunches, snacks, and parties, it is important to invite students, families, and community members to share their ideas. School personnel can utilize the expertise of nutritionists and physical fitness experts to help reduce obesity among students, while also considering the health needs of students with asthma and other conditions that may affect their level of physical activity. Examples of strategies that have been generated by one school wellness committee and elementary students are presented in the boxed text.

EXAMPLES OF SMALL STEPS TO SCHOOL WELLNESS

- *Snack and school parties.* Teachers and parents are provided with guidelines on the food they can provide for school parties and snack times. In addition to warning against providing foods containing nuts, school wellness advocates advise offering more healthy food choices, such as fruits and vegetables, instead of traditional party favorites of cupcakes and chips.
- *Recess.* School leaders advise teachers to minimize or alleviate using recess as a time for remediation or homework completion. Taking recess away should not be used as a form of discipline.
- *Physical activity as punishment.* Forcing students to do push-ups, sit-ups, or jumping jacks as punishment is discouraged. It is believed that young people will become conditioned to associate physical activity with punishment, which could have long-term effects.
- *Physical activity woven into curriculum.* Teachers are encouraged to provide students with opportunities to move in their rooms during transitions, breaks, etc. Students are provided with adult-supervised opportunities to walk around the school during transitions. These walks are incorporated into the schedule on days that state assessment tests are administered.
- *Health education and nutrition incorporated into the curriculum.* Schools contract with licensed nutritionists/dieticians to provide regular classroom lessons on a variety of related issues.
- *Hydration.* Students are permitted to keep water bottles at their desks.
- *Evening trainings for parents.* Healthy menu planning is conducted by nutritionists as part of evening programs for parents. Babysitting and dinner is provided for participants. Participants also receive various tools to assist their families in remaining healthy. At the last training, each participant receives a pedometer.
- *Before- and afterschool activity programs for children.* Children who are identified as at risk for weight-related health concerns, as well as others who would like to attend, are provided with opportunities to participate in ongoing before- and afterschool programming with school staff. The sessions are supervised by a certified nutritionist and physical education teacher. Programming includes lessons on healthy eating and exercising, fun activities, exercise programs, coping strategies, and emotional/behavioral support as needed.

WAYS TO IMPLEMENT A WELLNESS POLICY IN YOUR CLASSROOM

- When reviewing or summarizing material, have students involved in some type of physical activity. This could be tossing a ball around and having the student who catches it ask or answer a question. This gets the students involved simultaneously in the lesson and in a physical activity.
- Before testing or any lengthy academic activity, encourage the students to do some form of physical activity. When you see your students getting sleepy or slumping in their chairs, get them out of their seats to get moving. This could be walking around the gym, doing jumping jacks in the classroom, jogging in place, doing dances, doing yoga and/or stretching, etc.
- If you are using a classroom reward system, incorporate some type of physical activity into the reward. This could be a dancing activity, extra recess time, time in the gym to play games, etc.
- Encourage students to move during class time. Have students make letters out of their bodies to indicate an answer or spell a word or have them demonstrate or act out a skill (translations in math). Encourage the students to take a break and get moving. For example you could hold up a Uno card. Each color means the students have to do a different activity (e.g., blue means swim in place, yellow is twisting, green is jumping jacks, and red is jogging in place).
- When asking a question that every student in the class has to answer, have the students move to show their answer; for example, "If you agree with me, stand up. If you disagree, bend down."
- When teaching students how to use a computer program or graphic organizer, use part of the wellness policy as your example. For example, teach the students how to use Microsoft PowerPoint by doing a presentation on the effects of smoking. Teach students how to use Microsoft Excel by having them figure out the cost of smoking. Teach students how to use a graphic organizer by including different food groups. The students are learning how to use the program or the graphic organizer, and they are being taught about health and wellness.
- To encourage students to walk quietly down the hallway, have them put an imaginary piece of food in their mouths. Instruct them to choose something healthy.
- Encourage your students to move around the classroom throughout the day. For younger students, have them play a game of "follow the teacher." The students will follow the teacher around the room as they turn in papers, collect papers, etc. You can have them do this to music or sing as they do it.

Strategy 4

Incorporate a research-based prevention and intervention curriculum into the core curriculum. Researchers have advocated that universal school-based prevention and intervention programming is the most effective strategy to prevent emotional and behavioral disorders and related risk factors such as substance abuse, school dropout, violence, incarceration, and academic failure (Kam et al., 2007). Specific strategies must be implemented throughout the K–12 curriculum and should incorporate internal and external protective factors to promote stability and continuity in their ongoing mental, social, and emotional development (Kam et al.). By investing in long-term primary and secondary prevention and intervention programming at all grade levels in all buildings, schools have the potential to reduce the need for more costly programming at the tertiary level (Doll & Cummings, 2008).

PRIMARY, SECONDARY, AND TERTIARY LEVELS OF PREVENTION

A three-tiered model of prevention, popular in many fields, involves primary, secondary, and tertiary levels of prevention. Below is an example as it relates to student behavior.

Primary prevention. Schoolwide discipline at the primary prevention level emphasizes teaching, prompting, and reinforcing appropriate behavior proactively and universally to all children in the school (Sugai & Horner, 2006).

Secondary prevention. Students may be given additional support at the secondary prevention level if they are considered at risk for problem behaviors (Sugai & Horner, 2006).

Tertiary prevention. A few students come to school from the beginning with serious behavior problems that are already well established. These children are in need of tertiary-level prevention interventions, which are preventive in the sense of preventing the problem from getting worse (Tobin & Sugai, 2005).

A plethora of prevention programs is available to school districts that desire to promote social and emotional competence and reduce risk factors (Farmer, Quinn, Hussey, & Holahan, 2001). It is important for those involved in selecting curriculum to review the research and choose programs that meet strict standards of program effectiveness.

PATHS CURRICULUM

The PATHS (Promoting Alternative Thinking Strategies) curriculum has been selected as a Blueprints for Violence Prevention model program. It is a "comprehensive program for promoting emotional and social competencies and reducing aggression and behavior problems in elementary school-aged children while simultaneously enhancing the educational process." This curriculum is facilitated by educators and counselors in a multiyear, universal prevention model. The research on the PATHS curriculum has been found to improve protective factors and reduce behavioral risk factors. Areas in which improvement has been observed include self-control, understanding and recognition of emotions, increased ability to tolerate frustration, use of more effective conflict resolution strategies, and improved thinking and planning skills. Students also showed a decrease in depressive and anxiety symptoms, conduct problems, and symptoms of sadness.

Additional information on research-based prevention models can be found at the Center for the Study and Prevention of Violence Web site (www.colorado.edu/cspv/research/current.html).

Source: Center for the Study and Prevention of Violence, 2006b.

The box titled "Olweus Bullying Prevention Program" provides an example of an evidence-based model for intervention in bullying.

OLWEUS BULLYING PREVENTION PROGRAM (BPP)

The Olweus Bullying Prevention Program has been recognized as a model program by Blueprints for Violence Prevention as a universal intervention to reduce and prevent the incidents of bully/victim problems. This model, designed for the school setting, is to be implemented primarily by the school staff. The program is designed for students in elementary, middle, and junior high schools. All students participate in the program; however, there are additional interventions for individuals who have been identified as bullies or victims.

The content of the curriculum includes a schoolwide component, which includes an anonymous questionnaire to assess the nature and prevalence of bullying. Additionally, the program includes a school conference day to discuss bullying and planned interventions, the formation of a Bullying Prevention Coordinating Committee, and increased supervision of locations where incidents of bullying tend to occur. Within the classroom, rules are established and enforced, and regular class meetings with students are held. At the individual level, teachers, school counselors, and school-based mental health professionals may assist in implementing interventions and managing situations with individuals identified as bullies and victims.

An important component of this model involves investigating the school social climate. One of the primary goals of the program is to create a school climate that is "characterized by warmth, positive interest, and involvement by adults; firm limits to unacceptable behavior; where non-hostile, nonphysical negative consequences are consistently applied in cases of violations of rules and other unacceptable behaviors; and, where adults act as authorities and positive role models" (Center for the Study and Prevention of Violence, 2006a, "Theoretical Rationale/Conceptual Framework: Basic Principles").

Sources: Olweus, Limber, & Mihalic, 1999; Center for the Study and Prevention of Violence, 2006a. Additional information can be found at www.colorado.edu/cspv/blueprints/modelprograms/BPP.html and www.hazelden.org/web/go/olweus/.

Strategy 5

Provide a continuum of school-based mental health, substance abuse, and smoking prevention, identification, and intervention services. The student assistance program (SAP) is one example of a comprehensive, school-based approach that serves to prevent, identify, screen, intervene, and develop support strategies in the school for students. SAP teams help identify "red-flag" behaviors, such as concerns with attendance and changes in appearance and academic performance, which are often due to underlying concerns related to mental health, substance abuse, or social issues (Commonwealth of Pennsylvania SAP Interagency Committee, 2004). Specially trained school personnel collaborate with agency personnel to meet the goals of the SAP program. Services provided by the SAP program can include the following:

- Mental health and drug and alcohol assessments
- Support groups to address a variety of issues, such as coping with a loss and addressing issues of being a child of substance abusers
- Prevention and intervention groups

- Skill development groups (i.e., anger management, coping skills, social skills, etc.)
- Smoking prevention and cessation programs

Additional services often provided by SAP programs include supportive counseling services following the death of a student or school staff member and staff training to educate school professionals in identifying red flags (behavioral indicators) associated with underlying mental health and substance abuse issues. Many SAP teams also provide additional supportive programs that foster the development of internal and external protective factors.

One school in which I served as a mental health liaison has a STAR program in which they identify students with risk factors and organize a variety of Outward Bound activities with supportive and caring adults throughout the school year. Through activities such as rock climbing, spelunking, canoeing, rope course work, and tower climbing, these teachers, school counselors, administrators, and agency liaisons have helped many middle school children over the last 10 years build trusting relationship with peers and adults; develop alternative strategies to deal with anger, stress and frustration; learn to rely on their internal strengths; and improve their decision-making skills as they have gained confidence in their ability to overcome difficult obstacles.

Additional resources on incorporating programs such as the SAP and their related services can be found in the boxed text.

STUDENT ASSISTANCE PROGRAM RESOURCES

Student Assistance Programs, California Department of Education (www.cde.ca.gov/ls/he/at/sap.asp)

Masonic Model Foundation for Children: "The National Masonic Foundation for Children, established in 1986, is a nonprofit 501(c)(3) charitable organization that seeks to promote programs in schools, particularly the Masonic Model Student Assistance Program, to identify the barriers preventing students from achieving academic success and provide intervention to help the youth of this country lead productive, useful, and healthy lives. More than 36,000 educators have attended Masonic Model training, which has resulted in more than half a million school children being successfully referred to and helped by this program." (www.masonicmodel.org)

National Student Assistance Association (NSAA): "Provides cutting-edge school reform, prevention, and intervention services for youth and families." (www.nsaa.us)

Substance Abuse and Mental Health Services Administration (SAMHSA): "School, family, and community resource kits for prevention." (http://mentalhealth.samhsa.gov/publications/allpubs/SVP-0063/action_pamphlet_1/page2.asp)

Student Assistance Program (SAP) Bulletins: "SAP Bulletins have been designed to support school administrators, teachers, counselors, other school district personnel, as well as nonprofit organizations and agencies who are involved with SAPs." (www.cde.ca.gov/ls/he/at/sapbulletins.asp)

Examples of comprehensive models incorporating school-based mental health services include the Systems of Care and Community Schools models, which will be described in more detail in the next section of this chapter, "What Models and Initiatives Exist for Creating a Developmentally Responsive School Environment?"

Strategy 6

Create a safe, secure, and environmentally friendly school that is conducive to learning. In addition to providing the safeguards already in place in districts to protect the health and welfare of children , it is also important to incorporate strategies that not only improve the quality of the school environment but also encourage positive emotions and learning (Veltkamp & Lawson, 2008). The following strategies address the physical environment.

Air Quality and Temperature. To discourage the growth of mold and bacteria, the humidity in a classroom should be maintained within the 40 to 70 percent range, with temperatures ranging from 68 to 74 degrees (Hunley, 2008; Schneider, 2002). Academic performance has been found to be optimal when temperatures are between 68 and 70 degrees (Harner, 1974; Hunley; Wyon, Anderson & Lundqvist, 1991). Smells of chocolate, baby powder, lemon, and lavender are among a variety of scents that have been found to contribute to positive emotional responses, increased time on task, and increased context-dependent memory (Hunley; G. Martin, 1996).

Lighting. Classrooms that are illuminated by natural light have been found to have a positive impact on learning and test scores (Hunley, 2008; Schneider, 2002). A mixture of daylight and other forms of lighting with dimmer switches may provide flexibility for instructional purposes or to adjust to the needs of the class, whether to reduce stress, elevate mood, build morale, or increase performance (Hunley; Tanner & Morris, 2002). During winter when the days are shorter, students may benefit by being exposed to natural light by going outdoors (Hunley).

Acoustics. Many students are distracted by environmental noise. It is important for schools to consider how to minimize distracting and unpleasant sounds. The use of carpets, fabrics, walls, screens, and furniture can assist in buffering noises (Gee, 2006; Hunley, 2008).

Aesthetics. The colors and textures of materials within a classroom have also been found to affect engagement and learning. Reds, yellows, oranges, and deep browns typically have been found to evoke energy in students. Cool colors contribute to feelings of restfulness. Walls painted in pastel colors are more conducive to the learning experience when compared to white classrooms (Hunley, 2008; Schneider, 2002). The manner in which seats are arranged and how teachers utilize the classroom space have also been found to affect emotional reactions and behaviors (Gee, 2006; Hunley).

Strategy 7

Create caring, engaging, and high-quality learning experiences. In creating caring, engaging, and high-quality learning experiences, school systems need to look at the dynamics in the individual class setting, as well as the overall environment of the school setting. Research on healthy school environments has shown that "premium learning communities" must attend to ensuring safety, creating caring connections, maintaining high expectations, and teaching social and emotional skills (Osher & Fleischman, 2005; Osher et al., 2007). Programs that have been found to assist young people in becoming engaged with their schools, communities, and societies include mentoring, child advocacy, and civic engagement. These are discussed below.

Mentoring and Advocacy Programs. Mentoring programs have been found to play a positive role in increasing school engagement, levels of academic self-concept, and academic achievement (Redd, Brooks, & McGarvey, 2002). Bridgeland and colleagues (2006) advised that all schools should consider developing an adult advocacy program, particularly in larger districts subjected to high rates of dropout. In 2003, the National Middle School Association Research Committee reported a similar idea, stating,

> The concept of advocacy [for children and youth] is fundamental to the school's culture, embedded in its every aspect. Advocacy is not a singular event or a regularly scheduled time; it is an attitude of caring that translates into action when adults are responsive to the needs of each and every young adolescent in their charge. (pp. 16–17)

To help personalize the educational experience, the National Association of Secondary School Principals suggested that every high school student have a "personal adult advocate" or mentor (Alliance for Excellent Education, 2004). Such an advocate would be valuable in intervening early with academic and personal concerns, thus providing opportunities to minimize and mitigate the factors contributing to disengagement among at-risk students (Bridgeland et al., 2006).

Mentoring programs are more successful when their goal is to establish a trusting relationship and to help children develop socially, as opposed to addressing a specific behavioral goal (e.g., to stop drinking) (DuBois, Holloway, Valentine, & Cooper, 2002; Garringer, 2003; Herrera, Sipe, & McClanahan, 2000). Second, parental involvement is an important component in successful mentoring programs to ameliorate the perceived threats to child–parent relationship (Barron-McKeavney, Woody, & D'Souza, 2002; A. Johnson, 1998). Additionally, the length of time a mentor can commit can significantly influence the children's outcome. Mentors should strive to commit for at least a year and to meeting the student at least one hour each week (Herrera et al.; Tierney & Grossman, 2000). Many mentor programs have been initiated across the country; one example of an evidence-based Blueprints mentoring program, Big Brother/Big Sister of America (BBBSA), is presented in the boxed text.

BIG BROTHER/BIG SISTER OF AMERICA (BBBSA)

The Blueprints for Violence Prevention has named BBBSA one of its model programs. Volunteers, called "Bigs," interact regularly with assigned youths, the "Littles," in one-to-one relationships. The agency uses a case management approach from the initial contact to the conclusion of the relationship. Outside of the traditional BBBSA program involving a community volunteer, school-based models (SBMs) have grown steadily over the past 10 years (Herrera, Grossman, Kauh, Feldman, & McMaken, 2007). Since the publication of the report *Making a Difference in Schools: The Big Brothers Big Sisters School-Based Mentoring Impact Study* (Herrera et al., 2007), BBBSA has made significant strides to strengthen the school-based mentoring model and practices. One exciting program currently being implemented in schools involves high school Bigs to serve as mentors for Littles within the school district.

More information in establishing a program within schools can be found through the Big Brother/Big Sister of America's Web site (www.bbbs.org).

Mentoring impact studies can be found at the Public/Private Ventures Web site (www.ppv.org/ppv/publications/).

More specific information regarding the BBBSA and the Blueprints for Violence Prevention program can be found at The Center for the Study and Prevention of Violence Web site (www.colorado.edu/cspv/blueprints/modelprograms/BBBS.html).

There are also many informal opportunities within the school setting to provide mentoring relationships to children and youth. Teachers, coaches, principals, teacher assistants, and other school personnel have informally formed mentoring relationships with their students, guiding them and providing them with emotional, social, and academic support as needed.

> *There have been amazing teachers in the district where I work that have created systems of mentoring opportunities. The middle school art teacher, a gregarious and kind woman, meets at least once a week with a small group of students after school to provide them with opportunities to express themselves through a variety of mediums. These students are not necessarily the "gifted artists," but are individuals who have indicated either an interest in art or who appear to be "lost" and not quite sure where they fit in. It has been an invaluable opportunity for her to provide students who could easily fall into the cracks with a safe and creative means to cope with the concerns in their lives and a place to go after school. These students also appear to gain a sense of accomplishment and pride when they create a beautiful clay pot or other form of art reflective of their creativity, effort, and commitment.*

Civic Engagement. Encouraging young people to participate actively in civic activities can promote a sense of purpose, engagement, and connection to their school. Teens who are involved in community work and other types of civic activities have been found to have positive measures in a variety of categories, including school attendance, academic motivation, grade point average, and self-esteem (Balsano, 2005). Young people who have participated in civic engagement activities were also found to develop into adults with a strong work ethic and were more likely to vote and to continue volunteering their services into adulthood (Marin & Brown, 2008; Zaff & Michelsen, 2002).

Community Foundations Leading Change (CFLeads, www.cfleads.org) encourages meaningful involvement by youth in civic life. Through its initiative, Youth Civic Engagement, young people come to understand more fully their link to the broader society and, thus, develop an increased sense of ownership and responsibility. Because one of the pressing concerns our schools face is disengagement by students, schools may benefit by introducing strategies that will foster feelings of membership and connectedness with the larger school environment and community (National Task Force on Community Leadership, 2008). The boxed text describes an example of Youth Civic Engagement in action.

HAMPTON, VIRGINIA: A MODEL OF YOUTH CIVIC ENGAGEMENT

Hampton, Virginia, population 141,000, has led the way in creating a culture and the mechanisms for promoting meaningful roles for young people in the civic life of the community. Young people, working in partnership with adults, influence policy, decision making, and resource allocation in public and private settings throughout the community. Here are a few examples.

To ensure that youth have an ongoing voice in its planning process, the city's planning department employs two high school students as youth planners. Their jobs are to identify what young people want and need in priority areas that have been selected by young people—currently

(continued)

(Continued)

employment, transportation, youth space, and community interaction. The mayor's office, the police department, the school system, public works, and other city agencies also routinely engage young people in designing policies and planning projects. The young people who form the city's Youth Commission are authorized to allocate city funds to neighborhood organizations for youth programs.

In the community, young people and adults work together in several Community Wide Groups to address a particular issue or concern, like the environment, substance abuse or cultural diversity. Neighborhood Groups are made up of young people and adults who have come together to work on projects that will have a positive impact on their particular neighborhood. School Groups consist of student leadership groups in Hampton's middle and high schools who work with each school's administration to help improve the overall learning environment of the school.

Youth Ambassadors—hired by the downtown business district—greet, inform, and entertain visitors and workers, helping the community see young people in a positive light while learning important job skills.

These and other pioneering approaches to young people and adults working together for community betterment are promoted and facilitated by Hampton-based Alternatives Inc. (www.altinc.org) through project implementation, training, technical assistance, consultation, and advocacy.

Source: Used with permission from Community Foundations Leading Change (CFLeads), 2005.

It is important to recognize that the Youth Civic Engagement developmental strategy is still in the formative stages (Benson, Scales, Hamilton, & Sesma, 2006b). Until comprehensive programs are further researched, schools must consider the intrinsic value of providing students with opportunities to be actively engaged in the school environment in a variety of capacities.

Within the school setting, an important strategy to help students feel connected to their school's environment and community is to encourage them to participate in student government, community service, charity drives, or school-based service organizations. Such activities do not need to be complicated (Yazzie-Mintz, 2007).

As part of the educational plan for students identified with emotional disabilities, one of my schools incorporates community service activities into their emotional support services. Several times a year, students go to soup kitchens to serve lunch, clean area parks, help at the food bank, and assist the district during the holiday in their food and clothes drives. Frequently, the students describe these activities as meaningful and eye-opening.

Additional information on civic engagement can be found at the CFLead's Web site. www.cfleads.org.

Strategy 8

Examine the factors that contribute to school dropout rates in your district and develop strategies to keep students engaged. High dropout rates often reflect what our schools are failing to do to keep students engaged. It can be useful to survey students in the school. The environmental qualities that students describe are missing often overlap with the various factors that have been found to undermine the development of a healthy school environment. Since students who have dropped out of school frequently demonstrate warning signs early in their educational careers, it is important to develop an "early warning system" to assist in identifying children at risk for dropping out. Since one of the most significant signs is excessive absenteeism, contacting parents and getting them engaged early is imperative. The development of truancy elimination plans (TEP) is effective in reducing the risk of disengagement in young people. Within TEP meetings, school personnel need to make an effort to understand the factors that contribute to the students' refusal or inability to come to school. Strategies and interventions should be examined at that time to alleviate any barriers influencing their attendance (Bridgeland et al., 2006). The boxed text outlines 10 strategies from the Colorado Foundation for Families and Children to promote school attendance and students' connection to school.

TEN STRATEGIES TO IMPROVE ATTENDANCE

Several key factors compose a comprehensive strategy to promote student attendance and students' connection to school. They include ensuring a safe school climate, encouraging and supporting parental involvement, providing a continuum of supports and services to both students and their families as appropriate, collaborating with the community (including both public and private entities working with youth and families), school-level administrative support, and ongoing program evaluation to verify that your strategies are reducing truancy within your student population. Following are 10 specific suggestions to make this comprehensive strategy possible within your school:

1. Make students and parents/guardians feel welcome. Make a point to say "hello to every parent/guardian or student you see in the halls and outside—make it your business to know his or her name.

2. Create an environment that enables students to feel successful in something—no matter how small it may seem. Award academic and attendance "letters," as you do for athletics.

3. When a student is absent, immediately talk to the parents/guardians—not to their answering machine. Make a personal phone call in the evening or call parents/guardians at work during the day.

4. When a student is absent, immediately talk with the student about why he or she was gone—let the student know you are aware . . . and that you care that he or she is at school.

5. Forge a relationship with local businesses where youth may congregate when truant—encourage them to keep students in school during school hours. Create a poster that states, "We support youth in school and will not serve anyone under 16 during school hours."

6. Forge a relationship with local law enforcement—make them your allies in showing the community, families, and students that school is the place to be. Empower community police officers to return youth to school.

7. Don't provide the temptation for youth to be truant. Close your campuses during breaks and lunch.

(continued)

(Continued)

8. Empower and expect classroom teachers to take action when they think a student may be truant. Ask teachers to make calls to absent youth or families in the afternoon or evenings.

9. Reward and recognize good attendance—not just perfect attendance. Post large signs giving the daily attendance for the day. Reward individuals, classes, and the school for increased attendance.

10. Make your school a place where students feel safe and respected. Adopt a character education program that is planned and implemented by students.

Source: Used with permission from the Colorado Foundation for Families and Children, as cited by the Pennsylvania Truancy Task Force (n.d.).

Strategy 9

Strive toward collaborating and building high-quality preschool and early intervention services. Research has indicated that high-quality early childhood education has tremendous impact on students' outcomes (Begley, 2000; Ritchie, Maxwell, & Clifford, 2007). Research has shown that the best early intervention programs are holistic, nurturing, hands-on, stimulating, and exploratory and integrate interactive learning across the curriculum (Stegelin, 2004). Early childhood services are especially important for children with disabilities, those placed at risk due to family and situational factors, and those in low socioeconomic communities (Stegelin).

Part of a developmentally healthy and responsive school environment is providing students with the supports necessary to ensure that they are reading at grade level and remaining on track for graduation (Bridgeland et al., 2006). Early exposure to books and reading materials is essential to prepare young people for literacy. Additional supports are needed to assist low-achieving students and those with learning disabilities to stay engaged in learning by providing them with differential instruction and research-based interventions as early as possible. The Response to Intervention (RTI) program holds significant promise in ensuring that the "waiting to fail" practices of the past are no longer impeding students' opportunities to receive interventions when they are needed (Fairbanks, Sugai, Guardino, & Lathrop, 2007).

Strategy 10

Provide training to all school personnel on the philosophies underlying a developmentally healthy school environment and what they can do to meet the needs of the whole child. It is important for all staff members who are engaged with children in some capacity during the school day to receive training on the philosophies underlying the school design as it addresses the whole child. Bus drivers, cafeteria workers, teacher assistants, and custodians are just a few examples of the individuals who have regular contact with—and often significant influence on—the young people in our schools but typically receive little additional training on the developmental needs of children. As welcoming and friendly school and positive child–adult relationships take on greater significance for school achievement, school personnel have a greater opportunity to have a positive influence on a child's life.

I have been fortunate to work in such a district that recognizes the value that support staff play in children's lives. An elementary principal in one building frequently finds opportunities to brag about the initiative the cafeteria workers made several years ago to take a few minutes out of their very busy morning schedule to greet students with a friendly face and a big hello when they walk into the building. The principal doesn't need to brag because most people who enter the building notice the energy and enthusiasm that pours through the hallways.

Staff development and training are essential in the development of a healthy school environment. One important step to consider is developing a common language among the various disciplines (Doll & Cummings, 2008). Terminology used by the school nurse and dietician, for example, may be quite different from that used by teachers (Doll & Cummings). One team has developed a vocabulary shared with those in field of special education by creating a list of frequently used terms and acronyms with definitions and descriptions. Through this collaborative effort, teams have gained significant insight into how the various disciplines are interrelated and how to accelerate their services to meet the needs of developing children and adolescents.

WHAT MODELS AND INITIATIVES EXIST FOR CREATING A DEVELOPMENTALLY RESPONSIVE SCHOOL ENVIRONMENT?

Although components of risk, resiliency, and intervention programs have been introduced and utilized in our public schools for several years, the appeal for schoolwide implementation has reached new vigor, as the most needy of schools are being sanctioned for failing to meet legislative demands. Educational leaders have argued that school reform cannot occur until schoolwide mental health prevention and intervention models are intertwined as major components of the school's curriculum and directly tied into the central mission of the entire district (Adelman & Taylor, 2006b; Doll & Cummings, 2008). Kam and colleagues (2007) indicated that schools must consider a long-term developmental model that is science based and considers children's eco-behavioral relationship with the school. To create a prevention and early-intervention treatment continuum efficiently and effectively that offers a full range of care to our most troubled youth, collaboration between mental health systems and educational institutions is essential. School systems cannot succeed without a major infusion of collaborative mental health and social services (Vanderbleek, 2004). The following sections describe models that use systemic approaches and show promise in creating developmentally healthy and responsive school environments.

Community Schools

Numerous barriers continue to prevent young people from accessing mental health services. As a result, a national trend has emerged toward a community school movement, where various sectors of the community, such as mental health, medical, social services, and education, join with others in a partnership to address the needs of children (Melaville, Blank, & Berg, 2006). Under this model, schools are perceived as the logical site to provide therapeutic support, since 16 percent of young people in school receive mental health services and 75 percent of that group receives them in the school setting (Burns et al., 1995; Mennuti & Christner, 2009). There are many advantages to incorporating a community-schools approach when implementing prevention and intervention programs targeting students who are believed to be at risk or in need of intensive therapeutic services. One of the advantages of providing the services in the school system is that the students are more likely to receive needed services. Statistics from community mental health centers have indicated no-show rates of 50 percent or greater (Atkins, Graczyk, Frazier, & Abdul-Adil, 2003). An additional advantage of providing services in the educational environment is that multiple opportunities arise to examine the child's functioning in various situations. This clinical information in important in the examination of presenting problems, and it also allows the clinician to observe the effectiveness of the treatment based on the student's functioning across settings (Atkins et al.).

Since families and children are often reluctant to seek mental health services because of perceived social stigma, accessing services within the school system, where the child goes regularly, may be more acceptable than accessing them in a setting dedicated to mental health (Catron & Weiss, 1994; Corrigan, Watson, & Miller, 2006). In addition, other barriers, such as transportation, costs, and availability of family members who work various shifts, are minimized when the services are provided during the school day in an easily accessible area (Corrigan et al.). Although schools may be an ideal place to provide mental health services, delivering prevention programming and effective mental health programs within the curriculum and during the school day, both consumed by the academic performance requirements of NCLB, remains a daunting task. To meet the mental health needs of young people, it is imperative for collaboration to occur among school districts, policy makers, community agencies, and families.

Systems of Care Model

Comprehensive Community Mental Health Services for Children and Their Families, initiated by the Substance Abuse and Mental Health Services Administration (SAMHSA), is another model that effectively organizes, coordinates, and delivers mental health services to children, adolescents, and their families. The "systems of care" model emphasizes a team approach that incorporates family-driven and youth-guided practice, multiagency collaboration, and culturally competent care (SAMHSA Office of Applied Studies, 2007). The program has been found to be moderately effective, as the data indicated a decrease in the number of referrals from child welfare and educational systems in 2001 (ExpectMore.gov, 2008; SAMHSA Office of Applied Studies).

Coordinated School Health Model

In an effort to meet the complex health, emotional, behavioral, and environmental needs of young people, initiatives such as the Coordinated School Health Program (CSHP) have been proposed. CSHP is designed to improve young people's access to medical and psychological services through partnerships among families, schools, and communities (National Center for Health Education, 2005). This model includes eight interactive components:

1. Health education
2. Physical education
3. Health services
4. Nutrition services
5. Counseling and psychological services
6. Health school environment
7. Health programs for staff
8. Family community involvement

It also involves implementing a K–12 curriculum in which a specially trained teacher addresses health issues at age-appropriate times. Subjects taught include the skills necessary to reduce the risks of

- tobacco, alcohol, and drug use;
- dietary patterns that contribute to disease;
- sedentary lifestyle;
- sexual behaviors that result in STDs, HIV infection, and unintended pregnancy; and
- behaviors that may result in unintentional and intentional injuries.

Services are also made available to students to help them access or receive primary health care services, receive emergency care and avail themselves of educational and counseling services. Additionally, CSHP promotes the value of a school environment that is sanitary and physically and aesthetically pleasing and that provides a positive psychosocial climate. More information on CSHP can be found at the Centers for Disease Control and Prevention Web site (www.cdc.gov/HealthyYouth/CSHP/).

Quality School Health (QSH) Model

QSH is a program of Physical and Health Education Canada (PHE Canada). The QSH model has three major components:

1. *School curriculum*: Focus is on a quality physical and health education curriculum that aids teachers in reinforcing the knowledge, skills, and behaviors that allow students to improve their health and well-being.

2. *School environment*: Attention is on forming a healthy school environment in which the social and physical surroundings preserve and enhance the health and well-being of both students and staff.

3. *Community support and school services*: Services provide support and intervention to at-risk students and regulate aspects of the prevention curriculum (PHE Canada, 2009).

To assist in evaluating progress in implementing a comprehensive schoolwide program, schools are provided with a comprehensive checklist that assesses whether they possess the 12 key characteristics of a healthy school community:

1. Health-minded school administration
2. Holistic view of health
3. Safe and healthy learning environment
4. Community participation and collaboration
5. Meaningful student involvement
6. Coordinated plan or framework
7. Health policies
8. Quality health instruction
9. Access to current, quality health resources
10. Inclusive school health programs and services
11. Spirit of lifelong learning
12. Regular evaluations (PHE, 2009)

More details on the 12 key characteristics can be found at the PHE Canada Web site (www.cahperd .ca/eng/health/qsh_checklist.cfm).

Trauma-Sensitive School Model

Trauma Sensitive School is a model designed to accommodate students who have experienced trauma. The model incorporates six areas:

1. Infrastructure and culture

2. Professional development

3. Linkage with mental health professional

4. Academic instruction for traumatized children

5. Nonacademic strategies

6. School policies, procedures, and protocols (Cole et al., 2005)

Each area relates to the goal of academic success by strengthening relationships between safe adults and the child survivors of trauma. A major theme through all six areas is the importance of building strong healthy relationships. Because trauma creates systemic dysregulation, the goal of treatment is for children to self-regulate.

Positive Behavioral Support

Positive behavioral support (PBS) has been incorporated into educational policy reforms such as the NCLB and IDEIA. Positive behavioral support is not a specific model but rather a process that incorporates a variety of strategies, interventions, and practices designed to eliminate challenging behaviors and replace them with positive, pro-social skills (Doll & Cummings, 2008). Schoolwide PBS has been presented in the literature as an early intervention approach that systematically creates a school climate that is highly conducive to learning, reduces discipline referrals, and improves student academic outcomes (Doll & Cummings). Schoolwide PBS holds a lot of promise in our schools across the country. In reviewing the literature, one finds that the definitions of PBS vary considerably along a continuum from a very structured approach to a general perspective that integrates a broad range of strategies (Doll & Cummings; Horner, Sugai, Todd, & Lewis-Palmer, 2005).

Social and Emotional Learning

Successful implementation of social and emotional learning (SEL) curriculums have been found to improve school related attitudes, behavior, and performance (Osher et al., 2007; Zins, Weissberg, Wang, & Walberg, 2004). In analyses conducted by Zins and colleagues, the following behaviors were found to improve through the use of SEL interventions:

- Students' understanding of the consequences of their actions
- More displays of pro-social behaviors
- Fewer absences
- Higher degrees of classroom participation
- Reductions in aggression and disruptions
- Increased efforts to achieve

- Fewer incidents of conduct problems
- Improved effectiveness in coping with middle school stressors
- Fewer suspensions
- Increased engagement
- Improved transition into middle schools

Incorporating cognitive-behavioral and behavioral instructional methods with SEL models have also been found to be effective in reducing school dropout, attendance, conduct problems, and substance use (Osher et al., 2007; Wilson, Gottfredson, & Najaka, 2001). Additionally, attitudes have been found to improve in students in that they felt more connected to the school, had a more favorable and positive perception of school, and showed an increase in motivation and aspirations (Elias, 2004; Osher et al.).

Blended Model

In recent years, researchers and school personnel have recommended blending the positive behavioral support model with a social and emotional learning model. One such proposition was described by Osher and colleagues as they concurred with previous research that in order for schools to be successful, they must attend to the following four conditions of learning: (a) ensuring safety, (b) creating caring connections, (c) maintaining high expectations, and (d) learning social and emotional skills (Osher et al., 2007; Osher & Fleischman, 2005). These four conditions are described as being interconnected and form the foundation necessary for academic success. By merging PBS and SEL models, schools are in a better position to create school environments that facilitate learning and development in all important domains. The underlying assumption is that a successful PBS program will create a more orderly and safe environment, which, in turn, will provide the support necessary to implement effective SEL programming (Osher et al.). Combining SEL and PBS models holds significant promise in creating a more successful whole-school prevention approach when compared to implementing singular intervention practices (Osher et al.; Osher & Fleischman). Combining the strengths of various models into a comprehensive schoolwide model intuitively "makes sense"; however, it is important to recognize that the results of programs that are in place are inconclusive or too new for their effectiveness to be assessed accurately. Further investigation is warranted (Swearer, Espelage, Love, & Kingsbury, 2008).

CLOSING

This chapter has provided the reader with an overview of the characteristics of a healthy school environment with specific attention on variables that impact students' opportunities to learn. The school's physical environment, school dynamics, teacher–student interactions, health issues, and early literacy all have an impact on student dropout rates, attendance, school violence, substance abuse, and mental health. Therefore, a systematic, integrated approach is necessary to meet the wide range of needs of the children in our communities. The resilience research tells us that protective factors related to social and emotional learning have merit in reducing risk factors and in improving student academic outcomes. Although schools have made significant efforts to reduce violence, improve test scores, and improve graduation rates, the overall system is fragmented and does not efficiently or effectively meet the needs of many of the most needy students. The roles of school personnel and the means to collaborate in developmentally healthy school environments will be discussed further in Chapter 4.

SUMMARY OF KEY POINTS

One of the most important findings from resiliency research is that the environment can be improved to promote the developmental needs of children (Benson et al., 2006a).

- Emerging research has supported the relationship between academic success and physical health and nutrition.
- The physical environment, the school climate, the formation of positive healthy relationships, and school size are among the variables linked with developmentally healthy school environments.
- Research on at-risk youth has found disengagement in school to be a significant precursor to school failure.
- Developmentally healthy schools strive to provide positive mentors and role models.
- True school reform cannot occur until schoolwide mental health prevention and intervention models are intertwined as a major component of the school's curriculum (Adelman & Taylor, 2006b; Doll & Cummings, 2008).

KEY TERMS AND PHRASES

- Whole child initiative
- Resilience
- Developmental assets
- School wellness
- Behavioral engagement
- Comprehensive health

- Safe and secure schools
- Healthy school environment
- Mentoring
- Civic engagement
- Community schools
- Social and emotional learning

3

What Laws Promote Collaboration for the Whole-Child Initiative?

We . . . need to do more to respond to the non-academic needs of students, which make such a difference for how well children learn in school. . . . [That] means support for community programs that address children's social, emotional, and physical needs.

—Senator Edward Kennedy (D-MA, 2007)

CHAPTER TOPICS

- Is the Whole-Child Initiative New?
- What Laws Support Professional Collaboration to Educate the Whole Child?
  - The No Child Left Behind Act of 2001
  - The Safe and Drug-Free Schools Act and the Gun-Free Schools Act
  - U.S. Department of Health and Human Services Interagency Initiatives
  - The Individuals with Disabilities Education Improvement Act of 2004
  - The Carl D. Perkins Career and Technical Education Act of 2006
  - The Workforce Investment Act of 2006 and Rehabilitation Act Amendments of 1998

INTRODUCTION

Everyone concerned with children today—parents, teachers, administrators, counselors, health professionals—is concerned about the need to broaden educational objectives beyond core academics to address the more complex needs of vulnerable children. Susan Neuman (2009), former Assistant Secretary for Elementary and Secondary Education at the U.S. Department of Education during the development of the No Child Left Behind Act of 2001 (NCLB), explained that too many children are growing up in circumstances that make them highly vulnerable. Poverty affects the child completely, and children who come to school from dramatically unequal circumstances often leave school with similarly unequal skills and abilities. Recent education and human service laws and government initiatives include new language that requires schools to find a way to connect students with the supportive services they need during K–12 schooling. These laws challenge professionals to join forces, share expertise, and seek to overcome the barriers to learning that leave too many children behind. However, let's get real. Most veteran professionals know that you cannot legislate change in behavior, or attitudes, or willingness to collaborate in new and different ways. Nor do references to ""resources" in federal or state laws necessarily become a reality for local schools or community agencies. Where great collaboration occurs, despite obstacles, is in communities in which people say, "Okay, we are committed to begin from where we are, and we will find a way to share resources in creative ways."

This chapter provides a short history of the role of schools and school professionals in creating developmentally healthy environments and an overview of the major laws that promote developmentally healthy school environments.

IS THE WHOLE-CHILD INITIATIVE NEW?

The question "What are schools for?" has been debated for centuries: Should schools focus curriculum on academic education, on careers and employment, or upon broader developmental domains? Should schools be portals for providing social services? How these questions are answered reveal our society's beliefs about schools' responsibility for children's development, how school performance will be measured, and how resources will be distributed for academic and nonacademic activities. However, it is important to know that there is a long history in the United States of providing noneducational services to children within a school setting as a shared responsibility between schools and communities.

Since compulsory and tax-supported education was initiated by Horace Mann in 1837, the first Secretary of Education, many educators have challenged the notion of standardized, one-size-fits-all public education. Several early models for educating the whole child emerged in the late 1800s and early 1900s. Early in the 1900s, health services were provided primarily by public health doctors and dentists who volunteered their services. As health and social services became embedded in the schools, the services became more school centered and less family oriented, focusing primarily on improving school attendance and academic performance.

While the "normal" schools, or government common schools, opened the doors of public education to more Americans and immigrants, they were designed to standardize curriculum and regulate teacher training. Many groups within the nation, including Native Americans, members of certain religions, and others who mistrusted the paternalism of the government, wanted the right to choose alternatives to the government-controlled system. The search for alternatives and the tensions about the role of schools vehave been evolving ever since (White & Kochhar-Bryant, 2005). The following are key milestones in that evolution:

1. In the late 19th and mid-20th centuries, progressive schools or free schools that opposed formalized authoritarian procedures and structures were developed either within traditional schools or as alternative schools (Lange & Sletten, 2002; Pulliam & Van Patten, 1999).

2. Leading educational philosopher John Dewey (1899/2006) claimed that the school is the agent of social change and must become an embryonic community, which would include study of the occupations as well as art, history, and science.

3. In the early 1950s, alternative schools ("street schools") for minority and low-income students emerged for students given labels such as "severe learning and behavior problems." To address the needs of those who had been cast off by society and parents, schools in the early 1950s strove to develop a sense of belonging.

4. As a result of the Sputnik launch in the late 1950s and the subsequent rise in public interest to raise academic standards, particularly in mathematics and science, the focus on nontraditional and holistic models diminished.

5. In the 1960s, the civil rights movement and desegregation efforts spurred dissatisfaction with the public schools, and a variety of alternative, nontraditional programs were created in communities to meet the needs of minority children and address social problems (e.g., free schools, open schools, schools without walls, schools within schools, magnet schools) (Raywid, 1998).

6. From the 1970s to the present, significant numbers of students have been dropping out or being pushed out for a variety of reasons: they cannot compete academically, are non-English speakers are bored or uninterested in the courses, or are unable to progress in the traditional learning environments of the schools (Barton, 2005; Bridgeland et al., 2006; Skiba & Knesting, 2002). As a result, many school systems across the nation are experimenting with alternative, whole-child approaches as part of their educational continuum of services.

A growing body of research and years of anecdotal evidence show that students who have been labeled failures, troublemakers, or dropouts in traditional schools can thrive in smaller, more individualized settings (Boss, 1998). This short history of the search for alternatives has advanced the idea that a singular, inflexible system of education that alienates or excludes major segments of the population will not be acceptable (Raywid, 1993). Nontraditional programs have responded to groups of students who have not been served successfully or have not progressed in the ""regular" school programs. In short, not all students learn best in the same educational setting.

WHAT LAWS SUPPORT PROFESSIONAL COLLABORATION TO EDUCATE THE WHOLE CHILD?

As mentioned earlier, you cannot legislate change in behavior, or attitudes, or willingness to collaborate in new and different ways. The existence of a law or policy does not ensure implementation of that policy at the local level. While many laws contain new elements promoting collaboration and whole-child approaches, competing elements make it difficult to implement the laws at the local level. The solutions lie in how local people can use the authority, spirit, and intent of the laws and interpret them in ways that support their collaborative efforts to overcome substantial obstacles. It can be done, and it is being done. This chapter summarizes the aspects or elements of the laws that provide a framework for collaboration that support whole-child approaches.

Over the past few decades, professional collaboration and interagency coordination strategies have become central policy tools or instruments embedded in education laws. The IDEA amendments of 1997 and its reauthorization in 2004 (IDEIA), No Child Left Behind Act of 2001, and Rehabilitation Act amendments expanded cross-agency planning and cooperative arrangements at the federal, state, and local levels. Furthermore, the Gun-Free School Act of 1994 and the Safe and Drug-Free Schools Act of 1994 included provisions that link schools and a variety of community agencies to attend to the need for safe and healthy environments for learning. In addition, two civil rights laws—the Americans with Disabilities Act of 1990 (ADA) and Section 504 of the Rehabilitation Act of 1973 (and 1998 amendments) protect individuals against discrimination on the basis of disability in education and employment settings. These will be discussed in the following sections.

The No Child Left Behind Act of 2001

The No Child Left Behind Act of 2001 (NCLB; Pub.L. 107–110, 115 Stat. 1425, enacted January 8, 2002) is the most sweeping reform of the Elementary and Secondary Education Act (ESEA) since the latter was enacted in 1965. It redefines the federal role in K–12 education and aims to help close the achievement gap between disadvantaged and minority students and their peers. The Commission on the Whole Child (2007) contends that "current educational practice and policy focus overwhelmingly on academic achievement. This achievement, however, is but one element of student learning and development and only a part of any complete system of educational accountability" (p. 3). NCLB has placed a high priority on student academic performance—which has received the most attention since its passage—but it also incorporates provisions that address the broader, nonacademic aspects of development.

The NCLB is the principal federal law that affects education from kindergarten through high school. The four intents, or "pillars," of the Act are (1) accountability for results, (2) emphasis on doing what works based on scientific research, (3) expanded parental options, and (4) expanded local control and flexibility. The law requires states to test children annually in reading and math from third to eighth grades and to analyze and report the results publicly by race, English proficiency, income, and disability (NCLB, Title I, Subpart 1, Sec. 1111, (3) (C), State Plans. From NCLB, Part A: Improving basic programs operated by local educational agencies. Sec. 1111, State Plans. 20 USC 6311). Schools have until 2014 for all students to reach the levels of proficiency on standardized tests that are established by the states (NCLB, Pub.L. 107–110, 115, 115 STAT. 1447, 2001).

NCLB includes a section that grants funds to (a) improve educational services for students in local and state institutions for neglected or delinquent children and youth so that they have the opportunity to meet the same academic content standards that all children in the state are expected to meet; (b) provide services to help children and youth make a successful transition from institutional settings to further schooling or employment; (c) assist youth in locating alternative programs through which they can continue their education if they are not returning from school after leaving a correctional facility; and (d) prevent at-risk youth from dropping out of school (NCLB, 2001, § 1401[a][1–3]). For example, schools are using these funds to support supplemental instruction in core subject areas, such as reading and mathematics, as well as tutoring, counseling, and youth transition services.

NCLB: Parental Involvement

Section 1118 was written into NCLB to ensure that each school within a local education agency develops a parent involvement policy and plan and coordinates with parents in their design, implementation, and evaluation. Under the section, "Shared Responsibilities for High Student Academic Achievement," the school must jointly develop with parents a school-parent compact that outlines how parents will share the responsibility for improved student academic achievement and the means by which the school and parents will build and develop a partnership. Each school compact is required to

describe . . . the ways in which each parent will be responsible for supporting their children's learning, such as monitoring attendance, homework completion, and television watching; volunteering in their child's classroom; and participating, as appropriate, in decisions ingrelating to the education of their children and positive use of extracurricular time. (NCLB, 2001, 115 STAT. 1503 § 1118[d][1], www.ed.gov/policy/elsec/leg/esea02/index.html)

Service Coordination for Children

Recognizing that schools cannot work alone to achieve positive outcomes for all children, NCLB incorporates service coordination and school-community collaboration as a primary policy instrument for creating change (NCLB, Pub.L. 107–110, 115, 1115 STAT. 1535 and 115 STAT. 1440). Many provisions within the Act require new levels of formal coordination between schools and community agencies in order to share responsibility for improving education to help students achieve new academic standards. Each local educational agency (LEA) must have a plan that describes how it will coordinate and integrate services with other educational initiatives or programs at the local educational agency or individual school level (e.g., Head Start, Reading First, preschool programs, transition from preschool to elementary, programs for English language learners, children with disabilities, migratory and homeless children, immigrant children, neglected or delinquent youth, Native American children) (NCLB, 2001, § 1112[b][1][E]). It is expected that such coordination will increase effectiveness of the programs in addressing a broader range of developmental needs, eliminate duplication of services, and reduce fragmentation of the instructional program (U.S. Department of Education, 2004).

How are some schools responding to this challenge? In many schools seeking to improve the performance and overall development of all students, especially those with disabilities, teachers and counselors are being trained as in-school service coordinators with caseloads of students for whom they are responsible. These coordinators become the main contacts for the students, help arrange support services when needed, obtain assessments, and maintain records of the service needs and progress of each student. Examples of service coordination activities, which support broad change efforts or restructuring, include those that

- restructure preschool programs to incorporate health and social services to improve general readiness for elementary school.
- restructure schools, classrooms, teaching, and curriculum to improve basic academic and vocational outcomes for students in K–12 and incorporate social service and family supports.

- restructure secondary schools to link more effectively with two- and four-year colleges and provide outreach to adults in need of retraining and continuing education (Volpe, Batra, Bomio, & Costin, 1999; Wills & Luecking, 2004).

Schoolwide Reform Strategies for Adequate Yearly Progress (AYP)

NCLB promotes schoolwide reforms to improve results for all children in the school but particularly the needs of low-achieving children and those at risk of not meeting state academic achievement standards. Such reforms may include the following:

- Counseling
- College and career awareness
- Career guidance
- Personal finance education
- Applied learning and team-teaching strategies
- Integration of vocational and technical education programs
- Violence prevention programs
- Nutrition programs
- Head Start and reading readiness programs (NCLB, 2001, § 1114[b][1][B])

NCLB funds may also be used for targeted assistance to schools for comprehensive services. *Targeted assistance* means providing resources to help specific groups of students who are at risk for not meeting state academic achievement standards or for dropping out or who are identified as having the greatest need for special assistance (NCLB, 2001, § 1115). Targeted assistance may include health, nutrition, and social services; provision of basic medical equipment (e.g., eyeglasses and hearing aids;) service coordination; and professional development of teachers, parents, and related services personnel. To implement a targeted assistance plan, the school is required to "conduct a comprehensive needs assessment and to establish a formal collaborative partnership with local service providers" (NCLB, 2001, § 1115, 115 STAT. 1478).

Under NCLB, schools are expected to make "adequate yearly progress (AYP) toward meeting state student academic achievement goals" (Subpart 1, Sec 1111, 115 STAT. 1446). In passing NCLB, Congress recognized that some schools experience chronic underachievement and the performance of students on standardized tests in those schools was unacceptable. The AYP status of a school is determined using student assessment data, but the data must be broken out by subgroups of students (general education, students in special education, English language learners, low-income students, and specific ethnic groups (Subpart 1, Sec 1111, 115 STAT. 1446–1447). One hundred percent of students in general education, and in each subgroup (with a 1 percent exception for students with disabilities), must reach the state-defined ""proficient" levels in reading and math assessments by 2013–2014 (NCLB, Pub.L. 107–110, 115, 115 STAT. 1447, 2001; U.S. Department of Education, 2004). A lack of progress (10 percent improvement is required each year) by any of these subgroups can cause an entire school to be designated as "needing improvement" under the federal definition. Districts and schools that fail to make AYP toward that goal face a series of escalating consequences. If a school fails to achieve AYP, then a system of corrective actions comes into play to help the school improve.

What has been learned from the states about how schoolwide reform has addressed school environment and barriers to learning for students? According to several reports of the Center for Education Policy, in most underperforming schools that are restructuring for improvement, students are receiving more tutoring and instructional coaching, and special initiatives are targeting underserved subgroups of students (Scott, 2008).

NCLB: The Safe and Drug-Free Schools Act and the Gun-Free Schools Act

The No Child Left Behind Act amended and reauthorized two important components that affect students' environment for learning: (1) the Safe and Drug-Free Schools and Communities Act (SDFS) as Part A of Title IV, "21st Century Schools: Safe and Drug-Free Schools and Communities," effective July 1, 2002 (Sec 4001, 115 STAT. 1734); and (2) the Gun-Free Schools Act (GFSA) of 1994 (also as Part A of Title IV, Sec 4001115 STAT. 1762).

Safe and Drug-Free Schools Act (SDFS)

Holistic education means ensuring a safe and secure environment, preventing violence and traumatic incidents, and maintaining discipline. The Safe and Drug-Free Schools and Communities Act supports programs "that prevent violence in and around schools; that prevent the illegal use of alcohol, tobacco, and drugs; and that involve parents and communities." (NCLB, 2001, § 4002, 115 STAT. 1734). SDFS also provides grants to state and local educational agencies and Indian tribes to increase student access to quality mental health care services by developing innovative programs that link school systems with local mental health systems.

Local education agencies that receive SDFS funds are required to have a plan for keeping their schools safe and drug-free that includes appropriate and effective discipline policies, security procedures, prevention activities, a student code of conduct, and a crisis management plan for responding to violent or traumatic incidents on school grounds.

WHAT ACTIVITIES ARE REQUIRED OF PROGRAMS FUNDED UNDER SDFS?

- Enhancing, improving, and developing collaborative efforts between school-based service systems and mental health service systems to provide, enhance, or improve prevention, diagnosis, and treatment services to students.
- Enhancing the availability of crisis intervention services, providing appropriate referrals for students potentially in need of mental health services, and providing ongoing mental health services
- Providing training for the school personnel and mental health professionals who will participate in the program
- Providing technical assistance and consultation to school systems and mental health agencies and to families participating in the program
- Providing linguistically appropriate and culturally competent services
- Evaluating the effectiveness of the program in increasing student access to quality mental health services and making recommendations to the Secretary of Education about sustainability of the program (NCLB, 2001, § 4002, 115 STAT. 1738)

States may provide grants to LEAs to establish programs for school drug and violence prevention, but schools must have plans for keeping schools safe and drug free. These include

- school discipline policies that prohibit disorderly conduct; the illegal possession of weapons; and the illegal use, possession, distribution, and sale of tobacco, alcohol, and other drugs by students;
- security procedures at school and while students are on the way to and from school;
- prevention activities that are designed to create and maintain safe, disciplined, and drug-free environments;
- a crisis management plan for responding to violent or traumatic incidents on school grounds; and
- a code of conduct policy for all students that clearly states the responsibilities of students, teachers, and administrators. (NCLB, 2001, §4§ 4114[d][7][A–E])

NCLB: Gun-Free Schools Act

A safe and secure environment for learning means preventing the possession of firearms in schools. As part of the Improving America's Schools Act of 1994, and incorporated into NCLB in 2001, states that received federal funds under the Gun-Free Schools Act (GFSA) are required to establish laws regarding firearms in schools. A policy must be in effect that requires that any student who brings a firearm to a school be referred to the criminal justice or juvenile justice system (NCLB, 2001, Title IV, Subpart 3, Sec 4141, 115 STAT. 1762). GFSAs mandates the expulsion from the general education setting, for "a period of not less than one year, of students who bring a firearm to school" (NCLB, 2001, Title IV, Subpart 3, Sec 4141, 115 STAT. 1762). Alternative educational services may be provided, according to the GFSA, but schools may terminate all educational services to a student who violates this act. The GFSA also requires that police be notified when a student violates the Act and that any action taken by criminal justice or juvenile agencies will be in addition to discipline imposed by a school. State legislatures can enact even more stringent mandates. For example, New Jersey expanded the scope of GFSA to include students convicted of using a firearm in the commission of a crime anywhere in the state (U.S. Department of Education, 2001).

Interim Alternative Placements

NCLB and IDEIA allow greater discretion for local school personnel to remove students, including students with disabilities, who violate codes of conduct. Several NCLB provisions are important for the provision of alternative education to students who are removed from general education settings. Grants support safe learning environments that promote academic achievement for all students by improving the quality of interim alternative educational settings and by providing increased behavioral supports and interventions in schools. Activities may include expanding the scope of behavioral interventions; training for administrators, teachers, behavioral specialists, and other school staff in behavioral intervention planning, classroom and student management techniques, and prevention of behavior problems; and stronger linkages between school-based and community-based resources (e.g., mental health and other service providers).

In conjunction with NCLB, IDEIA also promotes the improvement of interim alternative settings in the following ways:

- Improving training of personnel in behavioral interventions
- Attracting and retaining a high-quality, diverse staff
- Providing for referral to counseling services
- Allowing students to use instructional technology that provides individualized instruction
- Ensuring that services are fully consistent with the goals of the individual student's IEP
- Promoting effective case management and collaboration among parents, teachers, physicians, related services personnel, principals, administrators, and other school staff
- Promoting interagency coordination and coordinated service delivery (e.g., among schools, juvenile courts, community mental health providers, and primary care providers)
- Providing for behavioral specialists to help students transitioning from interim alternative educational settings into their regular classrooms (IDEA, 2004, Sec 665, SEC. 665, 118 STAT. 2786–2787], 20 USC 1465. Interim Alternative Educational Settings, Behavioral Supports, and Systemic School Interventions)

Source: IDEA, § 1465[b][1–2]http://idea.ed.gov/download/statute.html

Together, these laws increase school personnel's emphasis on policies and practices oriented toward safety, security, management of student behavior, and consequences for rule breaking.

U.S. Department of Health and Human Services Interagency Initiatives

Safe Schools/Healthy Students Initiative Grants

The Department of Education describes the background of the Safe Schools/Healthy Students Initiative grants this way:

Since 1999, the U.S. Departments of Education, Health and Human Services, and Justice have collaborated on the Safe Schools/Healthy Students (SS/HS) Initiative. The SS/HS Initiative . . . provides students, schools, and communities with federal funding to implement an enhanced, coordinated, comprehensive plan of activities, programs, and services that focus on promoting healthy childhood development and preventing violence and alcohol and other drug abuse (U.S. Department of Education, 2008b, ¶ 1).

A local educational agency, in partnership with the local public mental health authority, local law enforcement agency, and local juvenile justice entity, may submit a joint application for federal funds

to support a variety of activities, curriculums, programs, and services. The SS/HS Initiative draws on the best practices of education, justice, social services, and mental health systems to provide integrated and comprehensive resources for prevention programs and prosocial services for youth (U.S. Department of Education, 2008b, ¶ 1–2).

For example, LEAs that won SS/HS grants in 2007 proposed integrated, comprehensive, community-wide, and community-specific plans to address the problems of school violence and alcohol and other drug abuse. These plans focused on five elements:

Element 1: Safe school environments and violence prevention activities

Element 2: Alcohol and other drug prevention activities

Element 3: Student behavioral, social, and emotional supports

Element 4: Mental health services

Element 5: Early childhood social and emotional learning programs (U.S. Department of Education, 2008b)

The comprehensive plans are intended to provide students, schools, and families with a network of services that help students do the following:

- Develop the skills and emotional resilience necessary to promote positive mental health
- Engage in prosocial behavior and prevent violent behavior and drug use
- Create schools and communities that are a safe, disciplined, and drug-free environment
- Engage parents, community organizations, and social services agencies to help develop an infrastructure that will institutionalize and sustain successful components after federal funding has ended (U.S. Department of Education, 2008b, ¶ 3)

SS/HS grant applicants are eligible for four consecutive years of funding. The maximum request for each year, based on student enrollment, is $2,250,000 for an LEA with at least 35,000 students (U.S. Department of Education, 2008b).

Comprehensive Community Mental Health Services

The Comprehensive Community Mental Health Services Program for Children and their Families (1992) is another model that more effectively organizes, coordinates, and delivers mental health services to children, adolescents, and their families. The Center for Mental Health Services (CMHS), part of the Substance Abuse and Mental Health Services Administration (SAMHSA), administers six-year federal grants "to implement, enhance, and evaluate local systems of care" (SAMHSA/CMHS, 2004, ¶ 4). The systems of care model emphasizes a team approach that incorporates family-driven and youth-guided practice, multiagency collaboration, and culturally competent care (School Health Policies and Prgrams, 2007, and U.S. Office of Management and Budget, 2009). A system of care is an organizational philosophy and framework that involves collaboration across agencies, families, and youth for the purpose of improving access and expanding the array of coordinated community-based, culturally and linguistically competent services and supports for children and youth with serious emotional disturbances and their families.

Healthy States Initiative and Child Nutrition

In response to the rising rates of childhood obesity in the nation, Congress and the federal government created the Healthy States Initiative. As part of the Child Nutrition and Women, Infants and Children (WIC) Reauthorization Act of 2004, schools participating in the school lunch program are required to develop and implement wellness policies for students and staff. The design of wellness programs was based on two key contributors to the growing rates of overweight children: (1) poor nutrition habits and (2) increasingly sedentary lifestyles (Council of State Governments, 2007). This legislation expands the availability of nutritious meals and snacks to more children in school, in outside-school programs, and in child care, and it improves the quality of food in schools through the following provisions:

- *National School Lunch and School Breakfast Programs.* Simplifies the application process for free school meals; provides migrant, homeless, and runaway children with automatic eligibility for free school meals; requires school districts to adopt local school wellness policies that address healthy eating and physical activity; and expands fresh fruit and vegetable pilot programs (Public Law 108–265, Title I, Sec 1, 118 STAT. 730)
- *Summer Food Service Program (SFSP).* Expands child eligibility for summer food services and provides funds for selected states to implement innovative solutions to rural transportation barriers for three years (Public Law 108–265, Sec 116, 118 STAT. 748)
- *Child and Adult Care Food Program (CACFP).* Extends eligibility for snacks and meals for children in homeless and domestic violence shelters up to the age of 18, allows for-profit child care centers that serve significant numbers of low-income children to feed children using CACFP, and extends the duration of area eligibility from three to five years (Public Law 108–265, Sec 119, 118 STAT. 753)

The Individuals with Disabilities Education Improvement Act of 2004

School collaboration and interagency coordination strategies represent promising interventions that engage both schools and the community in a shared responsibility to support the achievement of all students, including those with disabilities. Figure 3.1 depicts the continuum of shared responsibility among professionals and agencies.

The Education for All Handicapped Children Act has been in effect since 1975 to provide free and appropriate education to students with disabilities who need specialized educational services. In its current authorization, the Individuals with Disabilities Education Improvement Act (IDEIA) of 2004 holds schools responsible for ensuring that students with disabilities receive the range of appropriate educational and related services they need to achieve their fullest potential. Lawmakers recognize that planning for education and support services cannot be accomplished in isolation; rather, schools must reach beyond the school boundaries into the community. As a result, IDEIA requires schools to establish linkages with community and postsecondary agencies and share the responsibility for education and transition supports. States are required to establish statewide, coordinated service systems for students with disabilities, ages 3–21, who need services from the school and other community-based human service agencies (IDEA, 2004, Part A, Sec 602, 118 STAT. 2651).

Under IDEIA 2004, Congress sent a clear signal about its commitment to collaborative and coordinated services, particularly in the early years, and included many new provisions specifically designed to expand cooperative arrangements at the federal, state, and local levels.

Figure 3.1 Continuum of Shared Responsibility for the Whole Child

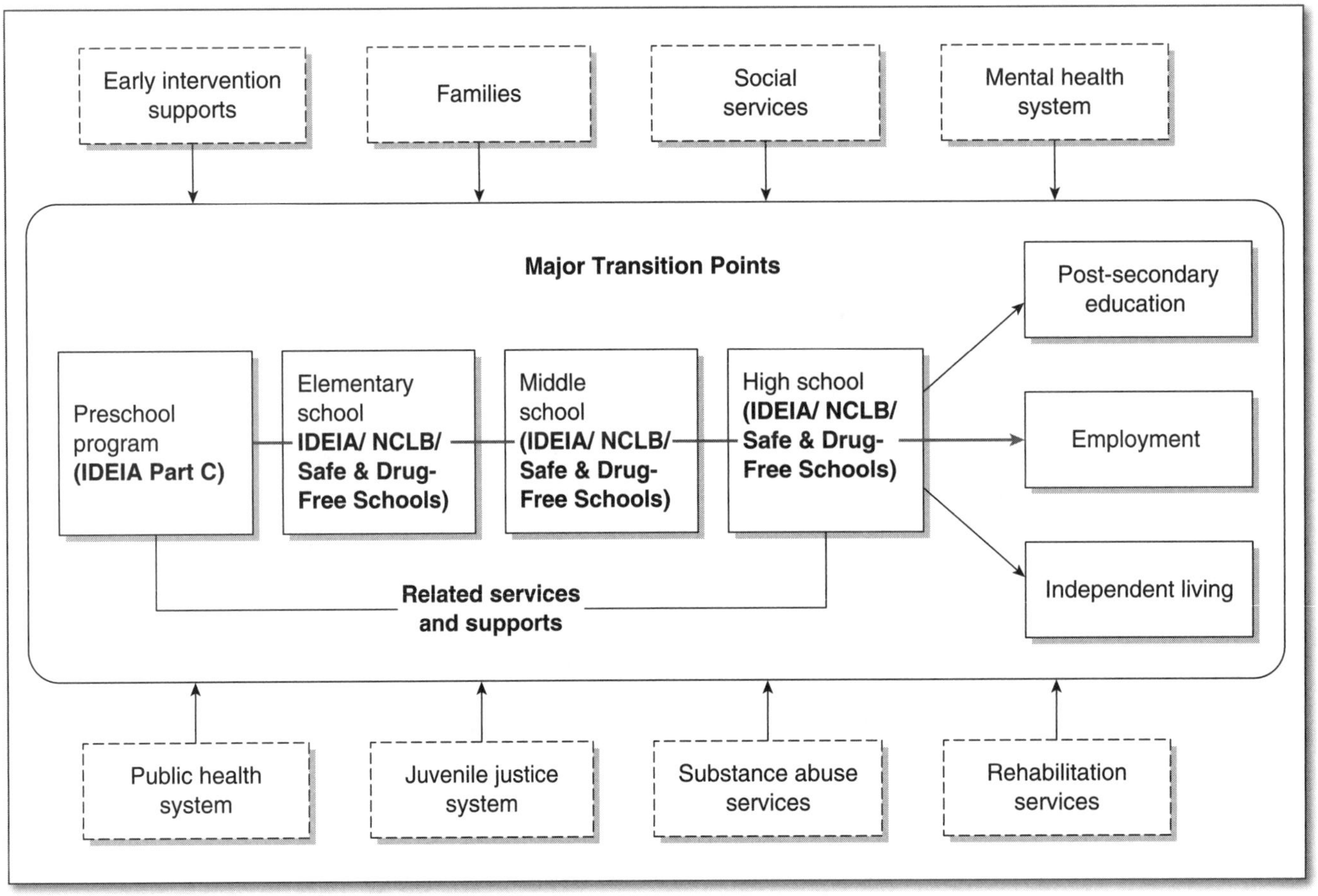

IDEIA PROVISIONS FOR COLLABORATION AND COORDINATION OF SERVICES

- State and local interagency agreements
- Flexibility to allow local educational iesagencies the flexible use of 15 percent of the total federal allotment to develop and implement coordinated early intervening services for students in grades K–12 (focusing on K–1) who need extra academic and behavioral support to succeed in the general education environment
- Requirements for coordination between Part C (early intervention services) and Part B (K–12 special education services) to ensure a smooth transition of services
- Resources to promote systematic school interventions, behavioral supports, and services in interim alternative education settings
- Resources to support stronger links between schools and school-based community mental health services and to improve interim alternative education settings by promoting interagency coordination of service delivery

Source: IDEA, 2004, § 1465.

While local flexibility is permitted in choosing how to design a coordinated service system, all initiatives should be "designed to improve results for children and families, including children with disabilities and their families." (IDEA 2004, Sec 618, 118 STAT. 2742; IDEA, 2004, § 1419[f][4]).

Collaboration and the Individualized Education Program (IEP)

Each child with a disability must have an individualized education program, or IEP. The IEP is developed through a coordinated process among professionals and programs within the school and often between schools and community service agencies as children transition from one grade to the next. The IEP tteam, a collaborative group that addresses the needs of the whole child, includes the following individuals:

- The student and his or her parents
- At least one regular education teacher of such child (if the child is, or may be, participating in the regular education environment)
- At least one special education teacher
- A representative of the local educational agency that is providing services to the child
- An individual who can interpret the instructional implications of evaluation results
- Individuals invited by the parents who have knowledge or special expertise regarding the child, including related services personnel (IDEA 2004, Sec 612, 118 STAT. 2677)

The child's general education teacher is also a member of the IEP team and should participate in the development of the IEP, including the determination of appropriate positive behavioral interventions and strategies, supplementary aids and services, program modifications, and support for school personnel. Finally, the child with a disability should be included on the IEP team and be prepared to participate in the meeting to the extent possible, including directing the meeting if the student is capable (IDEA 2004, Sec 614, Page 118 STAT. 2709). The effectiveness of the contract depends on how well the partners in that contract collaborate to assess students' needs, determine appropriate educational and related services to meet the needs, and deliver services.

Coordination of Related and Supplementary Services

Related and support services refers to a range of interventions that can help students progress in the educational setting and achieve their IEP goals. Connecting the students with these services requires close collaboration among professionals within the school and often with community agencies. The term *related services* is defined as

transportation, and such developmental, corrective, and other supportive *services* (including speech-language pathology and audiology services, interpreting services, psychological services, physical and occupational therapy, recreation, including therapeutic recreation, social work services, school nurse services designed to enable a child with a disability to receive a free appropriate public education as described in the individualized education program of the child, counseling services, including rehabilitation counseling, orientation and mobility services, and medical services, except that such medical services shall be for diagnostic and evaluation purposes only) as may be required to assist a child with a disability to benefit from special education, and includes the early identification and assessment of disabling conditions in children. (IDEA, 2004, Sec 602, 118 STAT. 2657)

The term *supplementary aids and services* means aids, services, and other supports provided in the general or special education class to enable children with disabilities to be educated with nondisabled children to the maximum extent appropriate (IDEA, 2004, Sec 602, 118 STAT. 2658). Examples include modifications to the curriculum or classroom, extended time to complete tasks, assistive technology, or an aide or note taker.

The Carl D. Perkins Career and Technical Education Act of 2006

The Carl D. Perkins Career and Technical Education Improvement Act of 2006 (Perkins Act, Public Law 109–270) (formerly the Vocational and Technical Education Act of 1998) is referred to as the Perkins Act. The purpose of the law is to develop more fully the academic, career, and technical skills of secondary and postsecondary students who elect to enroll in career and technical education (CTE) programs. In the history of the law (Perkins Act, Sec 2, 120 STAT. 684), the 1990 and 1998 Amendments required states to ensure equal access to career technical education for all youth, including those with special learning needs, in recruitment, enrollment, and placement activities in the full range of career technical education programs in the public schools (Perkins Act, 2006, Sec 203, 120 STAT. 720; Sec 122, 120 STAT, 740] [2]). Perkins requires local career technical education programs to coordinate with general and special education and related services to support students in the programs, provide information about career preparation courses, and recruit students into vocational programs and transition services (Association for Career and Technical Education [ACTE], 2005). Youth with disabilities receiving services under IDEIA or Section 504 must be provided the support services to ensure that they have the same opportunity as all other youth to enter career/vocational education. Examples of such supports include curricular accommodations, adaptive equipment, classroom modifications, supportive personnel, and instructional aids.

Career technical education includes several programs that require coordination between schools and outside agencies. One such program is cooperative education, which combines classroom-based and community-based instruction (including required academic courses and related career technical education instruction) in a job context, delivered under cooperative arrangements between a school and employers (Perkins Act, Sec 124, 120 STAT. 726). A tech-prep program combines two years of secondary education with a minimum of two years of post-secondary education. A sequential course of study integrates academic and career technical instruction in a career field using work-based or worksite learning (Perkins Act, 2006, § 203[c], 120 STAT. 738).

The Workforce Investment Act of 2006 and the Rehabilitation Act Amendments of 1998

Preparing youth for responsible adulthood and employment is a central goal of holistic education. The youth provisions of the Workforce Investment Act of 2006 (WIA) can be viewed as a comprehensive whole-person approach to transition to employment and independence. Educators who teach adolescents must necessarily work in cross-agency relationships to assist youth to prepare for and make successful transitions to post-secondary education and employment. WIA, now incorporating the Rehabilitation Act, creates a comprehensive job-training system with local one-stop centers that provide youth with employment and training services at central locations. Services include outreach and intake, initial assessment of skill levels, job search and placement assistance, career counseling, assessment of skills necessary for jobs, service coordination, and short-term job readiness services (National Center on Secondary Education and Transition [NCSET], 2002; Sussman, 2000).

The one-stop centers are very consistent with the holistic philosophy of educators who promote comprehensive whole-child approaches. Because the focus is on inclusion, WIA promotes a philosophy of service delivery that is consistent with the Americans with Disabilities Act (ADA). WIA requires that services be provided in the most integrated setting possible for persons with and without disabilities and that they be universally accessible to all. For youth with disabilities, WIA includes individualized services and access to integrated education opportunities similar to those stipulated under IDEIA. Both Acts include specific provisions for preparing for the transition from school to employment (NCSET, 2002).

Rehabilitation Act Amendments of 1998

The Rehabilitation Act of 1973 was integrated with WIA in 1998. Primary principles at the core of the Rehabilitation Act are nondiscrimination, improved access to rehabilitative services through coordination, and a focus on improving the quality of life for the whole person. Several provisions apply to secondary and post-secondary schools. Section 504 of the Rehabilitation Act of 1973 requires that

> no otherwise qualified individual with a disability in the United States . . . shall, solely by reason of her or his disability, be excluded from the participation in, be denied the benefits of, or be subjected to discrimination under any program or activity receiving Federal financial assistance. (Rehabilitation Act, 1973, § 504[a])

In 1991, the U.S. Department of Education released a landmark memo that affirmed that the appropriate place for most students with ADHD was in the regular classroom, with appropriate modifications. The Student Support Team became the logical vehicle for carrying out the requirements of Section 504 for students struggling in the general education setting.

Several provisions of the Rehabilitation Act address coordination with high schools in order to improve transition services for students who will be eligible for vocational rehabilitation (VR) services after leaving school. Recognizing that some youth with disabilities leaving school will require assistance, state VR agencies are encouraged to participate in the cost of transition services for any student determined eligible to receive VR services. The state educational agency must create a plan that transfers responsibility for transitioning students from the school to the vocational rehabilitation agency. This provision links the IEP and the Individual Written Rehabilitation Plan (IWRP) under the Rehabilitation Act to accomplish rehabilitation goals before high school graduation.

SUMMARY OF KEY POINTS

- Policy leaders are concerned about the need to broaden educational objectives beyond core academics and to address the more complex needs of vulnerable children.
- As a society, we are still defining the schools' common responsibility in relation to that of parents.

- Educators and policy makers advocate models that integrate supportive services into educational settings through collaboration and system coordination as a way to increase a child's chances of progressing along the educational path.
- There are many paths to learning, and the holistic educator values them all; what is appropriate for some children in some situations, in some historical and social contexts, may not be best for others. The art of holistic education lies in its responsiveness to the diverse learning styles and needs of evolving human beings.
- Over the past few decades, professional collaboration and interagency coordination strategies have become central policy tools embedded in education laws. The IDEA Amendments of 1997 and 2004, the No Child Left Behind Act of 2001, and the Rehabilitation Act Amendments expanded cross-agency planning and cooperative arrangements at the federal, state, and local levels.
- The Gun-Free School Act and the Safe and Drug-Free Schools Act have included provisions that link schools and a variety of community agencies to ensure safe and healthy environments for learning.

KEY TERMS AND PHRASES

- General systems theory
- Ecological theory
- Paths to learning
- Alternative school models
- Individuals with Disabilities Education Improvement Act of 2004
- No Child Left Behind Act of 2001
- Workforce Investment Act of 1998
- Rehabilitation Act of 1973
- Section 504 of the Rehabilitation Act of 1973
- Gun-Free Schools Act of 1994
- Safe and Drug-Free Schools and Communities Act of 1994 Americans with Disabilities Act of 1990

- Carl D. Perkins Act
- Adequate yearly progress
- Safe Schools/Healthy Students Initiative
- Comprehensive Community Mental Health Services
- Systems of care model
- Healthy States Initiative
- Individualized EEducation Program (IEP)
- 504 plan
- Supplementary and related services
- One-stop center

4

How Do Schools Create Developmentally Responsive Environments?

A Shared Responsibility

Angela Heishman

While each professional may be interested in the whole elephant, our professional training may prepare us to understand only tails or ears or trunks. To be effective, those who understand tails must talk to those who comprehend trunks, and those who comprehend trunks must converse with those who understand ears. Together we must look and listen, and, in the process, see and grasp more. It is through collaborative dialogue among professionals, patients, and families that a picture of the whole evolves and directions for the most effective treatment are created.

—Seaburn, Lorenz, Gunn, Gawinski, & Maukson, 2003, p. 3.

CHAPTER TOPIC

What Are the Typical Roles of School Personnel, and How Can They Be Expanded to Address the Needs of Students?

INTRODUCTION

In my work as a school psychologist, student assistance program coordinator, and counselor, I have routinely discussed how resiliency, good health, physical wellness, social and emotional learning, and safe and secure environments impact students' academic successful and outcomes. Most people in education agree that relationships exist among these factors and believe that in a perfect world, these needs will be addressed. The dividing lines among the fields of thoughts begin to emerge, however, when people purport the need for comprehensive, schoolwide reform that is designed to address the needs of the whole child. School personnel seem to struggle in determining what their roles are and whether they conflict or overlap with the responsibilities of families. They also describe their concerns about fulfilling the responsibilities of physicians, psychologists, crisis workers, substance abuse counselors, social workers, charities, and so forth when discussing the initiatives that strive to address the social, emotional, mental, and physical health of young people. In listening to their concerns and reflecting on the experiences of school personnel over the last 15 years, I have heard a waxing and waning of various philosophies of school professionals in regard to their specific responsibilities and roles in addressing children's needs. Within this section, the typical roles of various school personnel are reviewed and discussed to explain how these positions positively lend themselves to promoting the needs of the whole child.

WHAT ARE THE TYPICAL ROLES OF SCHOOL PERSONNEL, AND HOW CAN THEY BE EXPANDED TO ADDRESS THE NEEDS OF STUDENTS?

Administrator

VOICE OF A SUPERINTENDENT

I view both the principal role and the role of the superintendent as being in transition. Both roles have always included a high level of managerial skills and relationships to subordinates, and that continues as necessary; however, I recognize a greater need for each leader to possess a wider leadership skill set, including collaborative processes, instructional leadership, shared decision making, caretaker of school culture, tireless lead learner, master communicator, cheerleader/ follower, motivator, questioner, and supreme advocate.

I think responsibilities are growing for everyone, including teachers, because needs have changed. We find ourselves in a world demanding continual improvement. Information is decentralized and available. Brain research has led to a greater understanding of the science of how children learn. Educational research has combined with brain study and electronic data analysis to produce definitive instructional practices to improve learning.

While society calls for every student to attain proficiency, students have probably never been so unequal in developmental skills when starting school and background knowledge for new learning. Poverty, language barriers, and apathy continue to be roadblocks for many students in finding school success.

I think the school as an organization has a complex set of needs. While once a place of extreme structure, we find ourselves in need of autonomy/flexibility to make grouping and regrouping opportunities for children who have varying social and educational needs. Teachers no longer desire or need to have "John Wayne" leadership—a more collaborative team approach is necessary to concentrate on individual learning needs. Decisions at the team level will likely have a greater impact on student success.

—Bill Chane, Pennsylvania Superintendent

VOICE OF AN ELEMENTARY PRINCIPAL

In the past, the traditional role was to follow the Central Office's directions and to call with problems for anything. The role has changed dramatically! Now the Principal is the Site-Based Manager. I am responsible for maintenance, curriculum, budget, etc. It is my belief that I am also responsible for the mental, emotional, and physical health of my students, faculty, and staff. If my cup is empty, I cannot do this well. Therefore, it is important for me to keep myself "healthy." I also believe in touching base, on a one-to-one basis, with each teacher at least three times weekly. I do a "check-in" to see how they are doing. This check-in helps me to understand the background of issues that may come up.

Students have changed because our society is changing. I'm concerned about my students' "character" (who you are when no one is looking). Some of my students don't take responsibility for their role in a "bad situation." For example, one student told another student to type in "hot girls" while working on the computer. The student did. Neither one took responsibility. The student who said to do it actually meant to say "don't do it." The student who typed it in was not to blame because another student told him to do it. Perhaps students have always had difficulty taking the blame, but I wonder if there is a change in people's character. Based on my 20 some years as an educator, I believe that one of the most important contributions I have made is implementing character education into my building's curriculum. I want to make sure that we are preparing them to be "good people" in addition to being academically strong.

In regards to children's behaviors and emotions, I also have noticed that students are getting labels earlier. For example, we have a child in kindergarten labeled "bipolar." Maybe putting labels on kids makes them feel less responsible for their actions. "It isn't my fault. My neurotransmitters caused me to act this way." I certainly see parents using this excuse to explain unruly behavior. It has really been difficult to discipline students when students and their parents aren't allowing them to take full ownership of their actions, regardless if they have been identified with a disability.

*There are certain people that are meant to be elementary principals. They are the kind of people that can be distracted several times a day and still not lose focus. They are the kind of people that you can tell are "passionate" about their job. However, we are all still different. The right elementary principal is the person who is right for the entity. Each entity changes in relationship to its leadership. In a nutshell, either you fit in or you don't. If you don't, I think it is important to try to find a way to fit in while also being true to yourself. I believe that this is where I was supposed to be for the past nine years. I feel honored to be here and to touch the lives that I do. I am both servant **and** leader.*

—Elizabeth, Elementary School Principal

Traditional Role

School administrators, including principals, assistant principals, and superintendents, have and generally continue to be the people ultimately responsible to oversee the school's functioning, which includes ensuring compliance with the laws, rules, and education codes guiding day-to-day practices. Traditionally, schools ran in a top-down manner, in which there was little compromise regarding who made the final decisions. Students and teachers generally viewed principals as the disciplinarians, and the general tactic was to avoid them at all costs.

Emerging Perspectives

An important role currently being fulfilled by principals and superintendents is that of curriculum leader. Glatthorn and Jailall (2008) wrote, "NCLB has ratcheted up the role of the principal as curriculum leader in a standards-based environment" (p. x). As part of this responsibility, administrators have found themselves in a position of quickly becoming proficient in curriculum design and understanding content in a variety of disciplines. It has become a central role in their leadership to develop curriculum and ensure that it aligns with the standards and methods of assessment. Questions have been presented regarding principals' preparedness to play such a substantial role in curriculum leadership and development (Glatthorn & Jailall). Not only may their knowledge base in the content of all subjects be incomplete, but also their training on collaborative leadership may be insufficient. Based on the changing expectations of school districts, school leaders need to increase their understanding of the theoretical underpinnings of collaborative leadership in order to lead successful schoolwide reform efforts.

Although building principals, directors of pupil services, directors of special education, assistant superintendents, and superintendents continue to fulfill the duties of supervising all elements of the school system, opportunities have emerged in recent years for administrators to develop relationships with school personnel that allow collaborative leadership to occur. In other words, a school counselor with expertise in population-based mental health models may have the opportunity to work within a committee and can make recommendations regarding the implementation of such programs. School nurses, nutritionists, and physical education teachers may be able to collaborate with various other committee members to facilitate changes in how schools incorporate physical activity into the school day, address unhealthy eating patterns, and teach students to pause before making a poor decision that could be detrimental to their health (e.g., smoking). Administrators will likely continue to make the "big decisions," but through collaborative leadership, the entire committee and the school as a whole feels a sense of ownership.

The principal's role has expanded from being the disciplinarian; in fact, many principals at the secondary level are typically not directly involved in handling disciplinarian concerns. These concerns are frequently handled by assistant principals or the dean of students. In elementary schools, however, the principal's disciplinary role is dependent on whether additional administrative positions exist. Smaller schools, for example, may continue to have school principals as the only administrators in the building. In general, administrators' roles in the schools have become varied. Although recent research has focused primarily on administrator's role in curriculum development, other researchers have examined the other duties they fulfill (Glatthorn & Jailall, 2008). Trail (2000), for example, indicated that the principal's roles have expanded significantly from the "traditional model." A few of the emerging roles in this age of school reform include the following:

- *The principal as psychologist.* This is the idea that principals are more likely than in the past to reach out to children and their families. They are more likely to listen to teachers and their students and to use feedback to create effective change.
- *The principal as teacher.* As described earlier, principals are emerging as curriculum experts, and many are knowledgeable in strategies to address academic and behavioral difficulties. If they do not know, they are often willing to defer to someone who can point them in the right direction.

- *The principal as facilities manager.* Chapter 2 of this book presented information on the role that the environment has on learning. Administrators are ultimately responsible for the manner in which students, staff, custodians, and others take care of the building. Many principals have described incidents in which it was up to them to clean the vomit in the hallway or to deal with a clogged toilet. School leaders also influence whether the school's climate is warm and welcoming or closed and off-limits to the family and communities.
- *The principal as police officer.* This role includes not only enforcing the rules but also establishing high expectations for behaviors and promoting a safe and secure environment where any form of bullying, harassment, or intimidation is not tolerated.
- *The principal as diplomat and public relations director.* School leaders must often fulfill the duty of negotiating among stakeholders. This may involve managing a conflict between a teacher and a parent or disputes among teachers, such as those that may occur in determining inclusion or pullout services for special education students. In expanding services to meet the developmental needs of the whole child, diplomatic skills are important so as to portray to the critics the value that such programming efforts will have for improving students' outcomes (Trail, 2000).

New Directions

As described throughout this book, there is growing evidence to support the notion that students' achievement and outcomes are closely intertwined with their own internal resiliency, physical health and wellness, social and emotional strengths, and cognitive abilities. Additionally, the physical environment and social climate of the school interplay with these various dynamics. Based on these findings, principals, superintendents, and other school leaders will need to serve as the catalyst in schoolwide reform efforts to expand services already in place and to incorporate additional programming that addresses the needs of the whole child. Listed below are a variety of recommendations for school administrators to consider in facilitating the collaborative process.

Recommendations for Facilitating Collaboration in the School Setting

- *Provide inservice training* for all school personnel on the principles and related research underlying the need for developmental practices that address the needs of the whole child.
- *Allocate funding* to assist the school district in expanding services and resources. It is important to note that through collaborative and resource-oriented teams, schools may be able to utilize services and programs already in place in a more efficient manner. For example, instead of using several different social and emotional learning curriculums in various elementary and middle school buildings, it may be more effective to invest in one schoolwide research-based developmental model that builds on skills and uses a common language across grade levels.
- *Provide time* for school personnel, teams, and committees to work. This may include providing release time during the school day and offering some form of compensation for work completed outside of the scheduled workday.
- *Include information* regarding schoolwide initiatives to support the whole child as a regular agenda item at administrative team meetings, school board meetings, buildings'

faculty and staff meetings, Parent Teacher Organization (PTO) meetings, and other times when parents and other community members may be present. Cultivating positive public relationships will be invaluable in forming community, business, agency, and school partnerships.

- *Serve as a positive role model.* School personnel, including district office personnel, should teach and model good health practices. This can include eating healthy, not smoking, exercising, and demonstrating healthy conflict resolution skills and coping strategies.

- *Engage school personnel in the decision making process.* By encouraging staff involvement in the decision-making process, they may feel more empowered to influence changes in the school environment and in their interactions with students.

- *Facilitate the process of using assessments* to evaluate schools' current and ongoing activities that address the developmental needs of children. This information would be valuable for building capacity as well as for finding gaps. Valuable resources to assist in assessing, planning, and developing services in the school setting can be found at Developing Safe and Civil Schools (DSACS), in particular a coordinated approach to Social-Emotional and Character Development (SECD; www.teachSECD.com). Figure 4.1 outlines six steps that have been developed by Dr. Elias and his colleagues at DSACS to assist teams in their efforts to coordinate SECD into the school setting.

Figure 4.1   Six Starting Points for Putting the Pieces Together

1. Assess Your Schoolhouse

   Look at the SECD skills and values being taught across various programs in your school and organize them into scope and sequence charts. Examine where objectives overlap. Look for gaps, discontinuities, or inconsistencies and plan to resolve them, beginning either by grade level, schoolwide, or sequentially.

2. Assess Your School's Climate

   Reports generated from assessments collected on the school's climate, students' perspectives, and parents' perspectives can be shared with school leaders, staff members, and student leaders, and priorities can be set for addressing school needs. The data are presented by gender and ethnicity, as well as by grade level, within school and by staff position so that differential perceptions of the school climate can be uncovered.

3. Unify Problem-Solving Strategies

   Students are taught many different steps to take for problem solving, decision making, self-awareness and self-management strategies, conflict resolution, etc., both across subject areas within grade levels and then across grade levels. This leads to uncertainty among students as to how to solve real-life problems, especially when they are under stress. Bring these various steps and processes into alignment so that students are learning a common method within grade levels and that continuity or coordination occurs across grade levels.

4. Articulate Shared Values, Themes, and Essential Life Habits

   Examine the values, themes, and essential life habits that are being presented within grade levels and then across grade levels. Examine the context and way in which these value/themes/life habits are being presented. Bring them into alignment so that students are learning a common set of themes/values/life habits within grade levels and that continuity or coordination occurs across grade levels.

5. Shift Services Toward Event-Triggered Support and Anticipatory Guidance

   Examine the procedures in place to provide students with support when they are in difficulty. To what extent are they anticipatory (i.e., triggered by children experiencing difficult life circumstances) versus reactive to negative student behaviors. Event-triggered services reduce negative incidents in school, allow more energy and attention to be directly toward learning, and improve climate and morale.

6. Improve Faculty Readiness to Teach SECD

   Try to show how teaching SECD, or using SECD approaches, aligns with responsibilities and expectations that faculty already have. Show how core content standards emphasize problem solving, decision making, and critical thinking—all part of SECD—across content areas. Having an SECD planning group or committee of some kind provides a chance for faculty to support one another as their skills develop. It provides a forum for sharing approaches, getting help in overcoming obstacles, and being recognized for accomplishments.

Source: Excerpted and adapted with permission from Developing Safe and Civil Schools (DSACS): A Coordinated Approach to Social-Emotional and Character Development (www.teachSECD.com), a project of the Rutgers Social and Emotional Learning Lab and the Center for Applied Psychology, Rutgers University.

Teacher

VOICE OF A TEACHER

The role of a teacher has changed a great deal. In 1983 I taught my first class at the University of Iowa, and had you asked me then what teaching was all about, I would have said it's 100 percent about curriculum and the kids be damned. At that time, I also was not sold on being a teacher. By 1995 I recall telling a student teacher that it's not about the curriculum at all, that it's always about working with kids, and the curriculum be damned. Now in 2009 I think that it's the kids in the room who determine the curriculum. They're the bosses, and what they need changes like every few weeks, but it's our job to keep up with them. Right now, more than ever, a teacher has to be child centered.

Here's another way of looking at the progression. In the '80s, I was all about teaching Classics, and knowing about the Classics, and the kids just better get the book I was teaching. In the '90s, I felt that not all classics were the same, but there were certain ones the kids should know. Now I believe that any book the kids find boring should be tossed. It's all about the kids. And you can't teach them without engaging them.

We just read The Curious Incident of the Dog in the Night-Time. *There were no quizzes. They read 20 minutes in class sustained silent reading (SSR) every day and then did like 10 pages at home. Everyone, and I mean everyone, read the entire book. Then we did an assignment using a multiple-intelligence response to the book. It was great; it was fresh; everyone enjoyed it. That's real teaching. Oh, and don't go thinking I know what I'm doing because I don't. But so far, this is how it's been.*

—Bob Hankes, High School Teacher

Traditional Role

Teachers were generally expected to be experts in their content area. The phrase "sage on the stage" reflects the philosophy that teachers would "pour" out their knowledge to the students in their classrooms and the students would sit and soak it in. When specific children were found to have difficulty learning, it was frequently attributed to an issue "within" them; factors related to environmental conditions, learning style differences, or other extraneous variables were minimized or not considered. Teachers typically would design their own form of evaluations to measure the students' understanding of the content. Data were collected in the areas of reading and math during group-administered achievement tests every few years. The local education authority determined how this information would be used and whether changes in the curriculum or grouping of students needed to be made. There was little training in managing classroom behaviors or in addressing the needs of the abused, depressed, or angry child. Students with learning disabilities were not frequently in the regular education classrooms, as they were either pulled out for instruction or were placed in a class with lower expectations. Teachers also tended to be isolated from their colleagues, with minimal opportunities built into the day to consult with others.

Emerging Perspective

I don't recall having any training in what to do with the difficult student or how to differentiate my instruction to meet the needs of a child with learning difficulties. In fact, when I look back, homogenous grouping was the trend, and it really wasn't that much of an issue. If students learned, they learned. If they didn't, they were retained. It seems that we now need to become pseudo-psychologists as we attempt to figure out our students' emotional and behavioral issues, while also designing our instruction using techniques that incorporates various learning styles and is research based. This is while I am also to be preparing my students for the state assessments. In all of this, I wonder what I am to do when I know that a child is truly going through some pretty bad stuff at home. I know from my own experiences that it is hard to concentrate in school when you are overwhelmed with "life." I wish there was more I could do, but that isn't my role.

In talking with teachers about the changes that have taken place since the 1990s, with the emphasis now being placed on accountability in addition to the implementation of prevention and intervention models, I hear that the role of the regular education teacher has changed significantly. A variety of variables have influenced teachers' styles of teaching and the methods that they use to provide instruction in their content areas.

Heterogeneous Grouping, Inclusion, and Least Restrictive Environment. After significant evidence was presented about the negative effects of segregating special education students from their nondisabled peers and the ill effects that homogeneous grouping can have in lowering achievement and expectations, the composition of students in the regular education classroom changed. Instead of assigning students to specific sections based on their ability level, students were placed in classrooms more randomly (Crockett & Kauffman, 1999). In more recent years, the changes have become even more dramatic, as schools have been criticized for pulling students out of the regular education classroom for instruction that could be differentiated or modified. Lawsuits have been filed across the nation in response to the belief that students identified with disabilities are not truly being placed in the least restrictive environment (Pennsylvania Training and Technical Assistance Network [PATTAN], 2009).

One of the significant changes that has occurred in recent years and continues to leave staff bewildered is in technology and the role it plays in the day-to-day functioning of the teacher. Educators are not only able to communicate quickly via e-mail to their colleagues, supervisors, and parents about students and curriculum concerns, but they also have access to a wide variety of resources on the Internet. Within a few minutes, teachers can expand their knowledge base in their content area, strategize on alternative means to teach or evaluate a specific skill, or gain additional information regarding specific behaviors that appear to be impeding students' academic performance. Through collaboration through new technologies, teachers are better able to examine the "big picture" and understand how their students present across settings. This information is invaluable in determining whether a pattern of red-flag behaviors warrants additional assessments or if concerns are class specific.

New Directions

With the advancements in neurobiological research and ability to examine brain functioning, educators are gaining an incredible amount of insight to guide them in tailoring their instruction to meet the specific learning needs of struggling children. This research has also supported the belief that stress, emotional well-being, nutrition, physical activity, and overall health influence students' memory, learning, attention, and academics. In recognizing the relationship that exists among these factors, educators may be more inclined to incorporate strategies and modules that address holistic health and mental health prevention.

With the growing consensus that teacher quality significantly influences school achievement, their involvement in formulating schoolwide policies is central (Berry et al., 2005; Darling-Hammond & Youngs, 2002). Teachers play an especially important role in the implementation of strategies and practices that promote the needs of the whole child. Listed below are a variety of recommendations that teachers and other school personnel can incorporate in their practices to enhance the educational experiences of children.

Recommendations for Meeting the Needs of the Whole Child in the Classroom

- *Demonstrate a positive belief about all children.* This implies more than just saying, "I have a positive belief about children." It involves maintaining positive high expectations for their academic progress as well as their social-behavioral development, encouraging them to be the best that they can be, and providing them opportunities to be successful beyond performance on tests. This includes utilizing the resources reported in Chapter 2 for building resilient children.
- *Participate in training* that examines the role that holistic health plays in student achievement. Integrate holistic health strategies into your lessons as often as possible.
- *Become aware of the needs and skills necessary to work with culturally linguistically diverse individuals.* Review the research on "culturally relevant pedagogy" to ensure that instruction is designed and delivered in a manner that best meets students' needs (Center for Research on Education, Diversity & Excellence [CREDE], 2002). (See Chapter 7 for an extended discussion of this topic.)
- *Advocate for healthy physical environments*, which include safe playgrounds, comfortable classrooms, sanitary and clean conditions, and secure settings. Volunteer to be a member of your school's wellness committee to help in identifying and implementing the changes necessary to create a safe school environment.
- *Integrate opportunities to discuss health topics*, such as good nutrition and physical activity, into your curriculum. A variety of resources for teachers and students that can be used in the classroom can be found at BAM! Body and Mind, a resource of

the Centers for Disease Control and Prevention (www.bam.gov). BAM! offers resources to help students learn about diseases, food and nutrition, physical activity, safety while outside, life (i.e. managing stress, bullying, peer pressure, anger, and more), and taking care of the body (i.e. hand washing and oral hygiene).

- *Provide opportunities when appropriate to practice pro-social skills* learned in prevention and intervention curriculums, such as conflict resolution, refusal, active listening, anger management, and decision making. Consult and collaborate with your school's counselors, who have expertise in these areas.
- *Ensure that professional staff teaching health and nutrition are knowledgeable* about current findings in the pertinent fields. Contact local medical providers and establish a collaborative relationship with them when gaps are found in staff members' training. For example, invite a guest speaker, such as a dietician, to talk to students about healthy eating and the dangers of obesity.
- *Collaborate with school personnel to promote a positive behavioral support system* to help reduce negative behaviors and alleviate the need for more punitive discipline.
- *Encourage opportunities for physical fitness* and refrain from withdrawing recess as punishment. Examine alternative forms of discipline, such as those established by positive behavior support approaches.
- *Actively seek out and incorporate programs that provide students with mentors* and other positive relationships with adults. This may include adding extracurricular activities that meet a variety of students' strengths and interests (e.g., intramural sports, art, theater, chess, robotics, etc.). Contact Big Brother and Big Sister to initiate the school-based mentoring program if it is not already in place (www.bbbs.org).
- *Serve as a role model of healthy lifestyles*, modeling self-restraint and healthy coping strategies. Eat an apple instead of chips or drink a bottle of water instead of soda when students are watching.
- *Be cognizant of red-flag behaviors* and refer to appropriate school-based resources as needed. If unsure about a student's behaviors, contact the building principal, school counselor, school psychologist, or other professional with experience in assessing for risks. Recognize the importance of maintaining appropriate professional boundaries and practicing within the boundaries of certification and training. Remember not to work beyond your level of training and expertise.
- *Utilize a variety of teaching strategies* to engage students actively in instruction.
- *Encourage students to participate in civic organizations in the community.* Assist students by reaching out to business leaders, community agencies, and politicians to build these connections.
- *Reach out to parents* and strive to form positive school–family partnerships. Routinely connect with parents and provide them with positive reports about their children's behaviors when possible. Invite parents to participate in classroom and school activities (e.g., conduct an art show of student work, present student writings to the class, put on classroom plays, demonstrate science projects, etc.).
- *Collaborate with staff in the school when possible.* This can include sharing "what works" with more difficult behaviors and consulting as necessary when help is needed. Realize that teachers, administrators, school nurses, counselors, and other school personnel are part of the same team.
- *Play an active role in monitoring the school's success in meeting the needs of the whole child.* Additional materials to help in this endeavor can be found at Quality School Health Web site (www.cahperd.ca/eng/health/about_qsh.cfm) and the Social-Emotional and Character Development Web site (www.teachSECD.com).

Special Education Teacher

> ### VOICE OF A SPECIAL EDUCATION TEACHER
>
> *When I started teaching in 1977, I was more of a traditional teacher. Most of my time was actually spent on planning and teaching. I would say it was 90 percent planning and teaching and 10 percent paperwork. I had time to develop my craft, as they say, and learn from my mistakes. IEPs were just starting, and actually I liked them in that they kept me focused on what students really needed. However they are so tedious now—it has just gotten out of hand! They seem more like a legal contract and less of a teaching tool/guide.*
>
> *Even back in 1977, I wore many hats as I do now, so I don't think that has changed that much. What is different is that I would call myself a case manager now. And as far as the percentage goes, I hate to admit it, but I really think most of my energies go to paperwork. So I see it as 50 percent for planning and teaching and 50 percent paperwork combined with the other thousand things that happen each week. It hit me a few years ago as to how little time I spend planning good, creative lessons. Luckily I have a reservoir of ideas to pull from. If I were a new teacher, I would really struggle with being a good teacher. It still eats at me that I cannot always be the quality teacher I want to be because there just is not enough time. I have always worked with multiple aides, but now I find I give my aides way more responsibility than ever. I find that I could almost use a full-time secretary. Because of that, I think that the more stringent guidelines are good for my aides. I can see in time that aides may need to have almost a teaching certificate. I give my aides more teaching duties as well as other organizational duties. I am, or used to be, a perfectionist so I did everything myself. Now I have learned that in order to survive, I have to delegate more.*
>
> *As a result of these changes, things are not the way I would like them to be done. I have to let it go and I do. Otherwise I would go crazy. Another difference is that I find that I not only parent my students, I am also parenting their parents. The population just seems to need more direction. I also find that I spend more time at school. For the past 5 years I spent very long days—10 to 12 hours on many days. And again, the last thing I do is lesson plans . . . other stuff comes first. Another difference is in professional development. Teacher inservices for special education used to be about being a better teacher (learning new strategies, etc.). Now they are about doing your paperwork better. And it's been this way I would say since IDEA '97. I would say that IDEA reauthorization in 1997 seemed to change things a lot in our field. I am not sure if that is just my imagination or not. I could probably go on, but lunch is over.*
>
> —Kathy, High School Life Skills Teacher

Traditional Role

Until more recent years brought an emphasis on inclusion, special educators have typically worked with students with disabilities in separate classrooms from their regular education peers. Individuals with more severe disabilities may have spent their entire day in a classroom with one or two special education teachers located in a section of the building isolated from the mainstream, or they may have been housed in a building designed for children with special needs. Often, teachers designed their instruction to meet the particular learning needs of the students, while acknowledging that the material might be several grade levels below that of their same-age peers. Less was at stake regarding the ability of the staff in preparing students with disabilities to perform at an achievement level comparable to their peers. Additionally, minimal attention was directed toward helping these individuals transition into adulthood, and there was even less focus on their opportunities to pursue post-secondary training and educational options.

Emerging Perspective

One of the changes that has occurred in recent years relates to the "highly qualified teachers" mandate in the No Child Left Behind Act of 2001, which requires special education teachers to specialize in additional content areas instead of being certified only in special education, particularly for secondary-level professionals (Wasburn-Moses, 2005). In addition to this requirement, pressure has been placed on school districts to minimize the gap between regular education and special education students' performance on high-stakes test. Holding special education students responsible to meet the same standards established for regular education students has placed exorbitant pressure on special education teachers, as their students continue to be an identified group failing to make adequate yearly progress. These factors have led many trained special education teachers to wonder if it is worth teaching in this field when they could teach in regular education, where there seems to be inherently less paperwork, less pressure to meet reevaluation and IEP deadlines, and more time to actually teach (Pugach & Warger, 2001; Wasburn-Moses). Schools may well continue to lose trained special education teachers, and filling these positions may continue to be difficult.

New Directions

With the implementation of RTI, special educators can play an invaluable role in providing consultation services to other school professionals in designing interventions to address very specific skill deficits. Special educators understand the importance of implementing interventions with fidelity; how to document data; and how to assess progress, a central requirement in measuring IEP goals. Special education teachers also have been steadily moving into the regular education classroom with initiatives for more inclusive practices. Co-teaching or team teaching provides regular education and special education teachers opportunities to collaborate on an ongoing basis about strategies that may benefit students with more significant learning difficulties. These experiences are beneficial in assisting implementation teams with understanding the needs of the "neurodiverse learner" when expanding services to meet the needs of the entire population of students.

Special education teachers also understand the importance of examining students' learning style preferences and of developing strategies to keep them actively engaged in instruction. Teachers working with students with ADHD, for example, have learned that strategically placing students in certain areas of the room during instruction, using cues to keep students focused, using multisensory teaching techniques, breaking instruction into chunks, and providing breaks when indicated have helped identified children to learn. Actively forming collaborative relationships with special education teachers will allow all teachers to access a wealth of resources when determining how to expand services to address the needs of all students.

Recommendations for Meeting the Needs of Children With Disabilities

- In addition to the recommendations provided previously for regular education teachers, special education teachers need to offer their experience to help others understand and address the daily challenges of disabled students. By sharing their insight regarding the vulnerability that students with disabilities face, for example, they may help school leaders and implementation teams become more willing to explore additional remedies to minimize the risks of bullying behaviors.

- Special education teachers need to collaborate with school staff, coaches, athletic directors, parents, and administrators to advocate for extracurricular activities that allow more opportunities for all children. This includes identifying activities that will not exclude individuals with physical, developmental, or cognitive disabilities. Such activities can include intramural sports, art groups, theater, and music classes.

- It is recommended that special education teachers become knowledgeable in the role that holistic health, nutrition, and physical health has on the learning, memory, and overall performance of students. Examining these variables within their caseload may help them become more adept at noticing external factors that may be contributing to a particular student having a bad day. When conducting functional behavioral assessments, for example, knowing that the child did not have breakfast, was sick, or didn't have an opportunity to go to recess may help to explain patterns of disruptive behaviors.

VOICE OF A DRUG AND ALCOHOL LIAISON

I think my role has changed a little in that I work with more kids and involve parents more. Groups are a big difference since we have been able to facilitate without a school staff member. I think it's great we can do ongoing support groups for kids who lack ongoing support. Unfortunately, I see teachers and school counselors being more overworked, and Student Assistance can suffer due to this. I worry that not enough time is given to support our at-risk students. Some schools have tried to hire crisis intervention counselors, and I have seen their roles change into a support for school counselors and working less with at-risk youth.

From what I've seen, schools are more accepting of outside supports if the administration is. If there is a clear support by the administrators in districts, it seems to follow that teachers are more supportive. Student Assistance perceptions seem to follow that same suit. I think it has to do with a lack of knowledge about the mission of Student Assistance services, which can lead to a lack of general support. Overall, the majority of school personnel and families appear to be more accepting of school-based services. I find, however, that there are some teachers who seem to resent the time students devote to substance abuse prevention and intervention services because they lack information about the short-term and long-term impact it has on student's success.

—Jenn, Drug and Alcohol Liaison to Student Assistance Teams

Counselor

VOICE OF A SCHOOL COUNSELOR

I believe a "guidance counselor" was traditionally viewed as someone who sat in his/her office all day and waited for students to come down. Most counselors were teachers who decided they wanted a change, and most of the issues would have been academic in nature (e.g., What career choice is best for me?). I believe the role of the counselor is now more proactive and global. We look at the entire system and make suggestions for maximizing student learning. Accountability is huge also—how can we show that students are changing as a result of our interventions? We do more looking and listening for student needs and then creating programs to meet those needs. For example, we have been seeing a lot of students individually over the past few years with concerns about not being treated properly by their friends or a boyfriend/girlfriend—hence, our "Safe Dates" curriculum in seventh grade. We have moved "Second Step" lessons to Grade 6 because we are seeing more students with lack of empathy and anger control issues in younger grades. It's all about looking at the needs and trying to find the intervention that will reach the most students and make good use of our limited time. We have added more support groups and some topic specific workshops to further meet student needs. We also spend the majority of our individual counseling time on personal/social issues rather than on academic issues—I think because students have learned about confidentiality and know that we are here to help them.

—Anne, Middle School Counselor

Traditional Role

School counselors typically fulfill a number of responsibilities as they help meld the fields of education and mental health. Their responsibilities generally include providing academic counseling and helping students plan for the future; teaching a variety of psychosocial skills, such as stress management, study skills, coping strategies, and anger management; collaborating with teachers in developing strategies to address behaviors that may be impeding student learning, such as hyperactivity, poor inhibition, disorganization, and lack of motivation; providing supportive counseling and crisis services to address concerns such as grief/loss, depression, bullying, pregnancy, and peer pressure; providing transition services when students are preparing to move between grades and buildings; and providing consultation and support to students, parents, and school staff (ASCA, 2004; Kochhar-Bryant, 2008).

Emerging Perspective

Some issues have arisen related to role ambiguity in school counseling (Lambie & Williamson, 2004). Concerns have been mounting regarding the amount of time school counselors are pulled away to participate in noncounseling, clerical tasks (Burnham & Jackson, 2000; Lambie & Williamson). For example, many school counselors have been assigned to the scheduling, organizing, distributing, and administering of state assessment tests. These tasks generally take large chunks of time out of their scheduled time to meet with students. They are also asked to "fill in" when administrators are out of the building and cover classrooms if a teacher is sick. Because school counselors have continuously been asked to provide a wide range of services that goes beyond the traditional role of a modern-day career counselor, the ASCA (2003) recommended a change from the term *guidance counselor* to that of *school counselor* or *professional school counselor* (Lambie & Williamson). These terms appear to reflect more accurately the skill sets and responsibilities of today's school counselor.

From a historical context, *guidance counselor* was used at the onset of the profession because of its implication that these professionals would prepare young people for transition into the workforce (Lambie & Williamson, 2004). The word *guidance* was slowly replaced with terms referencing counseling as the field began to emphasize the person rather than the problem (Cobia & Henderson, 2003; Lambie & Williamson). More recently, the role of the school counselor has continued to emerge, and this role is continuously expanding as these professionals provide support services to special education students; consult with other school professionals, families, and community agencies; and are required to perform additional responsibilities, such as bus duty, lunch duty, teaching guidance lessons, organizing team meetings, conducting classroom observations, designing behavior plans, and fulfilling a variety of clerical duties. It is important to consider that although the role of the school counselor has expanded, no duties have been removed (Lambie & Williamson). Although the role of the school counselor may vary, it is apparent that this role is critical in expanding school services to address the needs of the whole child.

New Directions

School counselors are finding themselves in the position of having to work with children with serious mental health issues when they may be the only mental health professional available to meet these students' needs. Based on their wide range of experiences in bridging the gaps between education and counseling, school counselors can provide valuable insight into the development and design of population-based prevention and intervention programs. Additionally, they can serve as an excellent resource in assisting with collaborative efforts to scale up services already in place, while also providing insight into the role that social and emotional health and other holistic aspects of health play in learning. Listed below is a variety of recommendations as to how school counselors can aid in expanding services to address the needs of the whole child.

Recommendations for Expanding Services to Address the Needs of the Whole Child

- *Collaborate with school personnel to promote a positive behavioral support system* to help reduce negative behaviors and alleviate the need for more punitive discipline and out-of-district placements for special education students. It is important to work with administrative staff experienced with schoolwide reform to assist in the training and implementation of PBS. Likewise, it is important to work with other school personnel to receive their feedback regarding their specific concerns regarding students' behaviors.
- *Facilitate and oversee the incorporation of resiliency-based activities* into the K–12 grades. This includes collaborating with other school personnel on incorporating mentoring and civic engagement programs. This may include adding extracurricular activities or inschool activities that engage a variety of students' strengths, abilities, and interests (e.g., intramural sports, art, theater, chess, robotics, bowling team, dancing, music, etc.).
- *Serve as a role model for healthy lifestyles.* For example, model self-restraint and the coping strategies taught in the classroom when addressing problematic or stressful situations that occur during the school day.
- *Assist teachers, paraprofessionals, principals, bus drivers, custodians, and other staff with recognizing red-flag behaviors.* Educate them about how to refer these students to appropriate school-based resources as needed. Provide checklists and other resources to assist school personnel in recognizing risk factors. Emphasize for staff the importance of working within their level of expertise. Be available for consultation or refer staff to other experts in the field of mental health to address questions they may have.
- *Reach out to parents* and strive to form positive school–family partnerships. Routinely connect with parents and provide them with positive reports about their children's behaviors when possible.

- *Play an active role in monitoring the school's success* in meeting the needs of the whole child. Become an active member of the team and communicate the need for research-based interventions that are developmentally appropriate for specific age groups.
- *Participate in inservice trainings or other forms of professional development* that examines the relationship between emotional and social health and learning. Also, work collaboratively with the school nurse, physical education teacher, nutritionists, school physician, and others involved in school wellness activities to educate others about the relationship that health issues have on learning and behaviors. The school counselor could help develop strategies with these individuals to find healthy strategies to cope with stress, to eat healthy, and to manage emotions.
- *Form an ongoing, collaborative relationship with district office staff and other school leaders to assess the schools' success in meeting its objectives.* Share information you observe in the schools and provide feedback gathered from school staff prior to such meetings.

School Psychologist

VOICE OF A SCHOOL PSYCHOLOGIST

I remember in one my first graduate classes in preparing to become a school psychologist, gatekeeper was the term used to describe our role in the school setting. Although the "evaluation team" made the ultimate decision about special education identification, school psychologists were the ones holding the keys to get into the world of individualized educational planning. It now seems that school psychologists are frequently caught between the realms of regular and special education. We strive to meet the needs of all students in our schools, but due to student and school psychologist ratios, our attention is usually directed toward the most problematic students. I like putting the pieces of the puzzle together to figure out why a student is having difficulty learning and brainstorming strategies that may help improve a student's behavior in the classroom. I don't like being a testing machine and would like the opportunity to play a more preventive role. I am excited about the move toward RtI and hope that we will continue to be recognized for the variety of services we can provide to address the needs of all students.

Traditional Role

School psychologists have typically been considered "gatekeepers," while teachers and parents have had minimal input into determining educational placement, primarily due to the emphasis placed on standardized instruments. A number of additional practices, once considered typical and traditional practices of the school psychologist, are no longer considered ideal. During a National Association of School Psychologists conference, the High Plains Educational Cooperative summarized the following practices as central to the "old role" of a school psychologist: make student comparisons using nationally normed tests; heavily weigh the IQ/achievement ratio when determining eligibility for special education placement; use the majority of time for administering and scoring standardized tests; test a high percentage of individuals for multidisciplinary evaluations; view the problem as "within" the child without considering environment, instruction, or curriculum; focus on the source of the problem rather than developing strategies; identify one's level of expertise in giving psychoeducational evaluations; and spend the majority of time serving special education students (High Plains Educational Cooperative, 2005).

Emerging Perspective

In recent years, particularly with the attention directed toward RTI, the perceptions of the duties that should be fulfilled by the school psychologist have changed drastically. Although the significant discrepancy model between ability and achievement is still used to determine eligibility for special education services, the move toward an RTI model has contributed to using additional forms of data to assess for learning disabilities. Instead of relying only on the results of individually administered standardized tests, the team is able to examine children's results on benchmark assessments and curriculum-based measures and results generated from students' responses to research-based interventions. These data provide a more accurate picture of young people's specific learning needs.

School psychologists are also being used more frequently to provide consultation services to a variety of school personnel, including regular education teachers, instructional support teams, student assistance teams, school wellness committee members, and intervention specialists. They are being recognized as individuals with many skill sets that can be invaluable in meeting the needs of all children, not just those identified or in the process of being identified for special education. School psychologists are becoming more involved in assisting school professionals with developing strategies and interventions to help students learn and with managing classroom behaviors. Additionally, their training and experiences provide them with a level of expertise to assist teams in the development and implementation of population-based mental health prevention- and intervention-based services (Doll & Cummings, 2008). Also, psychological services are increasingly recognized as an important service school psychologists can provide. School psychologists recognized as having a wealth of training and experience that could be further capitalized on when attempting to bridge the gaps among services.

New Directions

With advances in technology and an increased understanding of neuroscience and learning, school psychologists are likely to be called upon more often to explain and help staff design and implement an RTI model. In other words, instead of haphazardly administrating strategies that the teachers hope will work, teams can use assessments to examine closely students' specific levels of need and design strategies that are tailored to address areas of weakness. Instead of automatically providing instruction in phonics instruction to a child with reading difficulties, for example, school psychologists can help teams link assessments to interventions to find the right intervention. School psychologists possess a number of skills that will prove to be valuable in creating systemwide change in improving students' academic outcomes, and they also have a substantial knowledge base and expertise in other domains that will help in expanding services designed to meet the needs of the whole child. School psychologists' training in collaboration and consultation can also offer tremendous assistance to school districts in the development, implementation, and evaluation of comprehensive service delivery models (Canter, 2006). Listed are recommendations of activities school psychologists can consider when systematically expanding their role to meet the developmental needs of all children.

Recommendations for Facilitating a Safe and Supportive School Environment

- *Provide inservice and other modes of training* to explain the research supporting a whole child initiative.
- *Engage in more extensive prevention activities.* This may involve becoming more involved in curriculum meetings, participating in the development of positive behavioral interventions and supports, overseeing mentoring activities, and becoming more involved in consulting and training staff on nonacademic and academic variables that may be impeding classroom engagement (Canter, 2006).
- *Assist in conducting assessments* to identify what is currently in place, examine gaps in services, and understand the concerns of stakeholders invested in the school system.
- *Play an active role in schoolwide reform teams.* Possible services include overseeing district-level implementation and ongoing evaluation and engaging in ongoing consultation with administrators, school staff, and families.
- *Assist in reviewing, selecting, and implementing* comprehensive, research-based prevention and intervention programs as a core component of the school's curriculum.
- *Play an active role in advocating* for comprehensive, school-based counseling and medical services to meet the needs of the many underserved young people requiring mental health care. Collaborating with other mental health providers in the school (e.g., social workers, school counselors, etc.), school nurses, teachers, and administrators will help ensure success in implementing these services. Recommendations reviewed previously will assist in this process.

Social Worker/Home–School Visitor

VOICE OF A HOME–SCHOOL VISITOR

My graduate training did not even come close to preparing me for my duties as a home–school visitor/school social worker. I believe I went through a fantastic graduate program and I am licensed. My training did not sufficiently prepare me for the vast number of duties I am expected to fulfill. I realize that there are some challenges I face that no amount of education could have prepared me to handle. Most of my training has focused on meeting the basic needs of children. I pretty much prescribe to the idea that students cannot learn until their basic survival needs are met. I was not prepared in how to manage a child who is wrestling with his mother while she is attempting to shove him out the door to get him to school. I understand that I work in a school system, but my perspective is quite different from that of the majority of personnel in the district. It is frustrating for me to hear complaints by teachers regarding students not getting their homework completed when I know they have horrendous home lives. Many of these students have little opportunity in the evening to do schoolwork, as they are busy watching their younger siblings, making dinner, and handling various crises caused by one or both of their parents. There are more kids with hard lives that are beyond what educators can fathom. My hope for the future is to see more people buying in to the idea that we need to bring the services to the child. Perhaps then I will be better able to appreciate educational demands.

Traditional Role

The roles of the social worker and home–school visitor can vary substantially from one school district to another. The traditional role of many social workers generally meant a hands-off approach when it came to addressing specific academic issues. The training for social workers varies, but typically they view children's needs from an ecological or systems perspective that entails looking at issues occurring in the home and within the dynamics of the family (Canter, 2006). Additionally, schools often hold them responsible to assess whether needy students are being well fed, need warm clothing for the winter, or need assistance in scheduling a doctor's appointment. Sometimes they assume the responsibility of ensuring that students are attending school and, if they aren't, may drive to the home to investigate and even pick up students with excessive absences. When a young child has frequent incidents of lice, the school social worker and nurse may work collaboratively to discuss and provide guidance to families on how to treat lice infestations appropriately. Some schools have utilized their social workers as a chauffeur service when a child misses the bus. Some districts use their social workers strictly for the students in special education services, and they may provide supportive counseling and instruction in effective coping strategies.

Emerging Perspective

Many of the roles that could be described as "traditional" continue to meet the current job description of the school social worker. Social workers are typically skilled in forming collaborative relationships, which has led to recognizing them as essential to involve in the collaborative process of developing schoolwide programming that addresses the social and emotional needs of children (Canter, 2006). Due to the attention now placed on mental health and environmental factors, social workers' roles have also been expanding to include assisting with assessing the role these variables have on young people's ability to learn. With their training in promoting people's strengths and skills in collaboration, it is believed that social workers are natural leaders in the scaling-up process and in the refinement of schoolwide programming (Canter).

New Directions

School social workers will be a valuable resource in advocating for programs that are designed to address the developmental needs of the whole child. They possess important skills to help bridge the gap between social sciences and academics. Listed below are recommendations on how school social workers' and home–school visitors' roles can be expanded.

Recommendations for Social Workers in a Developmentally Responsive School

- *Reallocate time to assist districts in developing more extensive prevention activities.* This may involve being more physically available to classrooms; engaging in more curriculum meetings with teachers, administrators, and related service personnel; participating in the development of positive behavioral interventions and supports; overseeing mentoring activities; and becoming more involved in consulting and training staff on nonacademic variables that may be impeding classroom engagement (Canter, 2006).
- *Play an active role on schoolwide reform teams.* Services may include overseeing district-level implementation and ongoing evaluation and engaging in ongoing consultation with administrators, school staff, and families.
- *Explore the recommendations previously described under school counselor and school psychologist,* due to the nature of the social worker position.
- *Examine the effectiveness of collaboration teams* and assist teams that may be at an "impasse" or struggling to work together effectively.

School Nurse

VOICE OF A SCHOOL NURSE

Before returning to graduate school to become a certified school nurse, I worked in an emergency room. I thought the demands were intense in that position, but when I came to the school setting, I had no idea of what busy meant. As the only nurse in this building, I am isolated from other adults most of the day, except on those occasions when a child is quickly escorted to my office by a building administrator to assess if he or she is "doing drugs." I am often in the position of providing emergency medical care that probably should have been implemented hours before the student even entered the school building. I wish I had a dime for every time I heard a child or parent report that they decided just to wait to see the school nurse. I have to administer medications to a long line of students during lunch time and also to students in the morning who refuse to take them with their parents at home. I spend an incredible amount of time directing students back to class, as my office is often seen as a refuge from the demands of the classroom. I have several students a day feign sickness in order to go home. I also have to serve those students who are legitimately sick and whose parents I have not been able to contact. There are many more responsibilities that I need to fulfill that range from catheterizing children in wheelchairs, administering insulin, and providing general supportive services to young people just wanting a caring adult to listen to them. Although it sounds like I am complaining, I have to say that I love my job and I love the kids. I have those students who really appreciate me and who light up my day. I have seen tremendous growth in some of these students, and I am proud to see them maturing toward adulthood. I work with a wonderful staff that I know do the best they can to meet the needs of the "whole child," but we could always do more.

Traditional Role

School nurses meet the medical and overall health needs of students in the school setting. They administer routine hearing and vision screening and check height and weight. School nurses serve as consultants to parents who are unsure if they need to pursue additional medical attention for their child and offer guidance to teachers regarding whether a student's symptoms or behaviors should raise alarm. First-aid care is often a primary part of their position, as they take care of skinned knees, sprained ankles, jammed fingers, and other accidents that may occur in gym class or on the playground. They also have been in the awkward position of being one of the first people to know that a teenage girl is pregnant and must consult carefully with administrators regarding communicating this issue with parents. Issues of confidentiality remain and continue to be an issue of contention when determining whether the nurse fulfills the obligation toward her school or toward her license.

Emerging Perspective

School nurses' responsibilities go beyond addressing the physical health needs of children. They are often one of the first individuals to identify red-flag behaviors indicative of depression, an eating disorder, or drug addiction. School nurses are also one of the first individuals involved when students attempt suicide or when they are cutting "to relieve their internal pain." The job continues to be intense, and it has become recognized that school nurses need more help. School districts have been raising their expectations of the nursing support staff. Although nurses continue to complete mandated health screening (annual height, weight, vision, and hearing), immunization compliance, and care for stomachaches and scrapes/bruises, such tasks take a backseat to more critical responsibilities. These may include medication administration; management of chronic illness; participation in team/committee meetings (e.g., SAP); data collection and reporting; and coordination of care and communication with students, school personnel, parents, and the students' medical providers. Students with chronic illness and multiple disabilities are now in the classroom. Teachers and aides provide basic care, and nursing personnel administer medications, give tube feedings, and perform procedures such as urinary catheterizations. The school nurse initiates Individual Healthcare Plans (IHPs), service contracts, and emergency medical plans for the management of diabetes mellitus, seizures, asthma, severe allergies, and other medical conditions to ensure safe and optimum student functioning at school.

New Directions

Due to the significance their role has in identifying mental health and substance abuse risk factors, school nurses are often considered a core member in many prevention and intervention teams, such as Student Assistance Programs. They are also valued as important members of schoolwide reform committees, as they attempt to incorporate districtwide strategies to reduce childhood obesity and health risks. School nurses can provide invaluable input on how to improve school lunch programs, increase physical activity, and explain the role that holistic health has on student outcomes. For school nurses to be used efficiently on these teams, it is important for schools to provide them with time fulfill their duties. Listed below are recommendations on the role that school nurses can have in expanding services to students.

Recommendations for Meeting the Mission of Holistic Health

- *Participate as a core member of healthy school committees.* In this role, school nurses can assist the team in evaluating the school's policies and practices in managing disease control (e.g., hand washing; maintaining sanitary conditions, especially in food preparation areas); taking care of students' health needs via physical activity, nutritional choices, and safety and security at recess and in physical education class; incorporating health instruction into the classroom that covers topics such as sexually transmitted diseases, HIV infection, tuberculosis, and hepatitis; developing programs and interventions that reduce the risk of tobacco, drug, and alcohol use in young people; and promoting research-based prevention/intervention models that increase resiliency and reduce the risk for problematic behaviors and mental health issues.
- *Advocate for comprehensive school-based health services.* School nurses are in a strong position to fulfill this role, as they possess the background knowledge and experiences to train school personnel on the influence that preventive health has on increasing school attendance, improving academic engagement, and improving the overall quality of life of students who may not have regular access to a health care professional. This training can serve as a stepping-stone in helping the school community buy into school-based services. Offering educational sessions to families about preventive health and other timely issues would also be a valuable step in building home–school collaboration to meet the health needs of children.

- *Facilitate collaboration between medical clinics and the school environment.* School nurses are a natural link between these settings, as they are versed in the languages of both, which can help bridge the "semantic gaps" that can occur when developing multidisciplinary teams.
- *Play an important role in guiding students to make healthy decisions.* With their influence, school nurses may encourage students to develop youth planning committees that will address similar needs, but delivered through the voices of young people. The school nurse, school counselor, social worker, physical education teacher, and trained nutritionist are among the individuals who can mentor this youth group through the various stages of its development.
- *School nurses can provide a variety of additional services* to create a healthy and positive learning environment for children. Since there are limited nursing personnel in the school setting, however, nurses may take a relatively pragmatic approach in designing policies and practices that address the needs of students.

CLOSING: TOWARD A CULTURE OF COLLABORATION

As we attempt to transform our school environments to address the needs of the whole child, one thing remains clear: we must involve virtually everyone in this collaboration—teachers, school counselors, school nurses, administrators, teachers' assistants, school psychologists, nutritionists, service workers, custodial and maintenance staff, resource officers, administrative assistants, and related service personnel. Schools must also involve families, community leaders, mental health/substance abuse agencies, physicians, police officers, and others who serve to protect and support young people and their schools. Collaboration may seem to be a goal toward which everyone should move naturally; however, it takes considerable effort, organization, patience, and a general willingness to examine other perspectives. It takes mental flexibility to change an opinion when the evidence presents itself.

This chapter presented readers with an opportunity to explore the roles of various positions within the school setting. Most school professionals and support staff can find roles that overlap with those of other positions within the school setting. In recognizing that programs and responsibilities overlap, and that gaps in services exist, one realizes that the formation of a strong culture of collaboration is essential to identify these areas and to develop a comprehensive program that addresses the needs of the whole child. Since many professionals at times become overwhelmed when considering the needs of the developing child and their implications for one's professional life, it is important to remember that school professionals need to work as a team. The days of working in isolation have passed. Through collaboration, each member of the school community is playing an important role in putting the pieces of the puzzle together to meet the needs of the whole child.

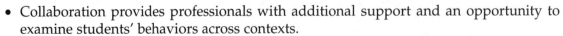

SUMMARY OF KEY POINTS

- Collaboration provides professionals with additional support and an opportunity to examine students' behaviors across contexts.
- Administrators have emerged as requiring collaboration skills and requiring the fulfillment of a variety of roles.

- Active involvement in the collaborative process by school leaders is an important component of protecting the integrity and overall functioning of programs.
- With the growing consensus that teacher quality significantly influences school achievement, the involvement of teachers in schoolwide policy development is essential.
- The school counselor's role has expanded from being a professional who guides career decisions to one who demonstrates flexibility while fulfilling a wide variety of capacities, including providing therapeutic and educational supports to needy students.
- The expertise and knowledge base possessed by school social workers and nurses are invaluable in the development and continuation of schoolwide programs that address the needs of the whole child.
- School psychologists no longer serve as the "gatekeeper" of special education. Rather, they offer a variety of skills and services to meet the needs of the entire school population, including providing consultation services to personnel.

KEY TERMS AND PHRASES

- Collaborative leadership
- Least restrictive environment
- Inclusion
- Gatekeeper
- Response to Intervention
- Homogeneous grouping
- Heterogeneous grouping

5

How Do Professionals Collaborate to Educate the Whole Child?

Collaboration is like dancing with an octopus. The work of building and sustaining school/community collaborations is a dance with multifaceted partners.

—C. Levine, 1998, ¶ 1

CHAPTER TOPICS

- Why Is There a Growing Interest in Collaboration to Address the Developmental Needs of the Whole Child?
- How Does Collaboration Lead to Schoolwide Change?
- The Many Uses of Collaboration: The Four Action-Dimensions
- Is Collaboration a Developmental Process?
- Collaboration in the Early Years
- Collaboration in the Middle Years
- Collaboration in the High School Years
- Ten Principles for Successful Collaboration and Coordination

INTRODUCTION

Collaboration and coordination among teachers, administrators, parents, and community agency personnel are arguably the most important factors in the success or failure of educational programs for students with special barriers to learning—and indeed for all children. Since the education system has a mandate to educate the whole child, collaboration among professionals is the pivot upon which that mission turns. The skills and abilities of professionals to form professional partnerships have become so important that just about every set of new standards for the professional qualifications of teachers, administrators, and related school personnel now addresses collaboration and system coordination.

Every aspect of educational development to improve teaching, support and student learning, involves the ability of people to effectively work together for positive change. Many educational reforms, initiatives, innovations and good ideas have failed primarily because of human problems with implementing them or sustaining them. Conversely, many initiatives owe their success to human creativity, perseverance and the power of the basic human drive for continuous learning. However, an important paradox for collaboration among human beings is this—human nature and human interaction harbor both the promise of, and the threat to, creative problem solving. With skilled leadership that harnesses the creativity and basic motivation of people to apply new knowledge in solving problems, collaboration can result in powerful and positive long-term change.

The journey of each child from family to preschool and through schooling and into responsible adulthood involves changes in the self-concept, motivation, and development of the individual, and it is a fragile passage for each child or adolescent seeking to make difficult life choices (Benson, 2007; German, Martin, Marshall, & Sale, 2000; Michaels, 1994). This passage is even more delicate for children with complex learning needs. For professionals seeking to help students on their journey, the process requires creative and durable linkages among educators, parents, and human service personnel.

This chapter discusses the challenges that professionals face in responding to the wide range of developmental needs of children and youth in schools. It explores why school collaboration and system coordination have been so difficult to accomplish within the field of education. We define *collaboration*; discuss the essential relationships and skills for effective communication, collaboration, and coordination to take place; and describe the characteristics of effective collaborative teams. A foundational belief for these efforts is that developmentally healthy school environments depend upon the positive and constructive relationships among teachers and counselors, which requires preparation for collaboration and mutual understanding of roles.

WHY IS THERE A GROWING INTEREST IN COLLABORATION TO ADDRESS THE DEVELOPMENTAL NEEDS OF THE WHOLE CHILD?

Why are collaboration and coordination watchwords in education today? Why have researchers and policy makers over the past few decades put out a clarion call to improve collaboration among professionals, between schools and community agencies, and between professionals and parents? There are several answers to this question. First, over the past 20 years, major transformations have occurred in educational, social, political, and economic arenas that continue to impact the education and development of children and youth. Second, more children with complex educational support needs are now served in the general education setting. Third, antidiscrimination laws have improved access to early childhood education programs, community schools, and post-secondary education and employment. As a nation, a greater investment is being made to assist all children to progress academically and prepare for independent adulthood. To achieve these goals, a host of nonacademic barriers to learning must be recognized and overcome.

Four Reasons for the Growing Interest in Collaboration

Reason 1: Growing Complexity of the Educational System

Collaboration and system coordination are vital characteristics of an effective education and human service system. The education and human service system has become increasingly complex and, thus, more difficult for the individual family to navigate when their child needs specialized services. Such children and youth often need a variety of support services from different agencies to help the family cope as a unit, as well as to help the student participate and progress in education and social settings and function as independently as possible. However, "cracks" or "gaps" often appear in the service system when students need specialized educational or support services from the school or from external community agencies. These insufficiencies present several perplexing challenges for education and human service personnel:

- The frustrations and anxieties that arise when a single individual in need must acquire specialized services and supports from several separate and uncoordinated sources
- The risk that the youth or family will be unable to find help because of the gap in services (e.g., absence of speech and hearing services near the school, elimination of a school-based mental health counselor position due to budget cuts, or inadequate transportation to service agencies in a rural or remote area)
- The differences among families in their capacity to access and effectively use services within the system

A system gap means incomplete or weak links between schools and community service agencies. There may be no single access or entry point to help students and families identify the services they need and understand eligibility processes. The boxed text presents an example of collaboration to address the diverse needs of students.

A DIVERSITY INITIATIVE

From Rocky Beginning to Positive Change

The following case example illustrates how collaboration for change in a single school may begin as an untidy process but lead to long-lasting and positive schoolwide changes. An interdependence emerged among people working together for a common purpose—the well-being of youth. The culture and organization of the school were permanently changed. This experience with systemic change also established new patterns of relationships, which were very different from the traditional isolation and independent work that had been characteristic of teachers, school support staff, and parents.

(continued)

(Continued)

The Brookville High School ninth-grade teachers shared a common challenge. They were about to receive a group of 12 students with emotional, behavioral, and learning disabilities who had been transferred from a separate special education center into the community school. The special education center was being closed as part of a countywide budget reduction, and the 12 students were to be part of a new inclusion initiative. The students were to be integrated into general education classes with the support of a collaborating special education teacher. Due to circumstances beyond the control of the high schools, the program was implemented on very short notice; the special education lead teacher/coordinator was brand new, and none of the teachers had planning time to prepare for their new charges.

In August, before the fall semester began, a few of the teachers met briefly with the principal to discuss their roles, how they would collaborate to develop IEPs, and how they would deliver a more integrated curriculum model with curriculum accommodations. For the first time, this year they were combining English and history into a blocked class and math and science into another block for all students. While the teachers were excited and very supportive of the inclusion initiative, they did not feel ready to receive the 12 new students and had to spend a great deal of extra time before the semester reviewing the students' backgrounds to become familiar with their instructional and behavioral needs.

Several problems arose during the fall semester. Some of the general education teachers had not been involved in the August meetings and, therefore, were not aware of the students' disabilities and needs. Other school staff, such as the physical education staff, cafeteria staff, the new nurse, the new guidance counselor, and the music teachers, were unaware that these students were to be transferred in under the new inclusion initiative. Several of the students requested extra help with the long-term classroom projects, help with organizational skills, and extensions of time for taking quizzes and tests and turning in assignments. Numerous adjustment difficulties and behavioral incidents arose with a few of the students, which resulted in a variety of consequences, such as in-school suspensions. In three cases, the use of in-school suspensions resulted in student midyear course failures. When under in-school suspension, students were not permitted to complete their work and turn in homework and, as a result, lost all points for projects and homework. Teachers did not know how to put behavioral strategies to work in their classrooms to prevent escalation of incidents leading to disciplinary action. In addition, three of the students had probation officers who were not known to the teachers but who were required to visit the students in their school. None of the 12 students were adjusting well to their new school. Several parents of other students joined forces to complain to the principal about what was wrong with the "inclusion experiment."

In mid-December, the teachers met again to review the outcome of the inclusion initiative. They determined that many things were seriously wrong with the initiative and a major intervention was needed—quickly! Linda Forrester, the special education coordinator, had done some homework and had researched the special education center from which the students had been transferred. She learned that they had been taught in classes with ratios of one teacher to six to eight students. The students also had regular group counseling and the support of a mental health therapist, who frequently intervened before small problems became big ones.

Linda believed that a great deal needed to be done to improve collaboration among the teachers. First, in collaboration with Principal Harris, she arranged for a series of meetings and discussions with all of the teachers involved with the students, including key support staff, to discuss the students and their needs. An external specialist/consultant experienced with educating youth with emotional and learning disabilities was brought in to consult on strategies for positive behavioral supports, classroom management, instructional modifications (changes in the instruction or curriculum materials), and classroom accommodations (changes in the physical classroom or seating).

Second, a series of follow-up training sessions were arranged with Linda and the consultant to prepare general education teachers to increase their skills in working with students with special needs. In addition, ongoing technical assistance and staff coaching by the consultant were arranged with in-school observations over the balance of the year and continuing follow-up in the subsequent year. This training series included "critical analysis" sessions in which teachers learned to model, observe, and analyze their own teaching techniques and coach each other. Consultation and training were built into a two-year personnel development plan for the school.

Third, the special educators and teachers established a process for interacting and communicating with parents on a regular basis to intercede early when student issues emerged. Parents typically were the first to anticipate student problems or crises, and open communication between parents and teachers could alert everyone involved and defuse problems early. Parents were invited to communicate openly with the special or general education teachers or guidance counselor. They were encouraged to call to alert staff when situations arose that could affect student behavior in school; for example, if the student (a) was having trouble adjusting to a new medication, (b) needed extra help to organize assignments, (c) was stressed out about a large project coming due, or (d) had just been placed on house arrest by a probation officer for violating curfew. Teachers would be on alert and be ready to provide extra support.

Fourth, an emergency response policy was defined and implemented for students whose behavior was challenging and disruptive in class. This policy included a process of teacher staffing for students who were having difficulty adjusting and who needed a team consultation for problem solving and creating solutions. The caseload of one of the school counselor was reduced so that he could establish an ongoing support group for students throughout the year. Linda, the special education coordinator, located an online "academy" program for the resource library that teachers could use to research useful and tested strategies for their classrooms to improve accommodations for students with emotional and behavioral disabilities or any student with challenging behaviors.

Fifth, a process was created by which information on students with special needs identified for transfer into the school would be forwarded well in advance. In addition, transition visits to the school were arranged for the students and their families to promote the students' adjustment. A teacher-mentor was assigned to each incoming student to provide continuity of support.

Finally, the special education coordinator, a general education lead teacher, and Principal Harris held a series of meetings with the general school staff to orient them to the goals of an inclusive community, the needs of the new students, and the channels of communication available if students needed additional support or intervention. As an alternative to the traditional label of inclusion program, *the staff adopted the term* diversity initiative *to emphasize the goal of building a community that emphasizes quality educational experiences and responds to the diverse needs of* all *children and youth. The Brookville High School diversity teachers established a learning community to advance their own ongoing professional development and, in turn, improve their work with students with special needs. They established a system for evaluating the diversity initiative and making adjustments along the way. They also arranged learning seminars with other high schools to share their challenges and successes with the initiative.*

This story about Brookville High School illustrates that collaboration for change typically does not develop in a tidy, step-by-step, linear fashion. Instead, it was messy, complex, and unpredictable. However, the initial challenges and instability provided ample motivation for the principal and teachers to find solutions to some serious problems. This challenge led to creative thinking, close collaboration, and unity among personnel who had not worked together previously and new leadership among staff. It also resulted in relationships, practices, and policies that were unprecedented for the school.

Reason 2: New Philosophies in Education and Human Services

Collaboration with families has become more important as a result of new philosophical views on risk and resilience, student and family engagement, and an emphasis on empowering consumers and families to make decisions about services and assume more control over educational planning (self-determination). For example, there is a growing interest in developing strategies to empower students and families to participate in decisions that affect their long-term graduation goals. Empowering parents also means equipping them with the tools—knowledge and skills—to help their children and to collaborate effectively with professionals. Student self-determination and individual planning to achieve educational goals have become central to collaboration and coordination initiatives for students. Furthermore, teachers, administrators, parents, and students are explicitly prepared to collaborate and coordinate services in ways that support student self-determination.

Reason 3: Collaboration's Improvement of Conditions for Learning

The traditional structure of schools promotes isolation and impedes collaboration. Teachers work in isolation, administrators try to accomplish tasks alone, and the responsibility of implementing new ideas falls to individuals. Overcoming these barriers is worthwhile, however. Collaboration has gained attention because people achieve more, make better decisions, and accomplish important tasks more effectively when they work together. Collaborative teams have many advantages over individuals working in isolation. Teams tend to be better at solving problems, have a higher level of commitment, and include more people who can help implement an idea or plan. Moreover, teams are able to generate energy and interest in new projects. Both research and practice demonstrate the advantages that teams bring to accomplishing goals. Collaborative groups or teams may work on decision making, curricular reform, development of new programs, or restructuring. But effective teams do not develop by accident. Teams take time, skills, and knowledge to be successful (North Central Regional Educational Laboratory [NCREL], 2004).

Reason 4: Effectiveness of a Shared Responsibility

Schools and school-linked agencies are finding that as they improve their work together, outcomes for students improve as well. A shared responsibility and shared approaches to addressing student educational and developmental needs—helping the whole child—bring to bear the combined thinking, planning, and resources of many professionals, both in the schools and in a variety of agencies, upon the needs and problems of a child and family (Conzemius & O'Neill, 2001). Furthermore, the economic value of sharing resources across agencies to close persistent gaps in services for children and families is gaining recognition. Although schools experience widespread difficulties establishing cooperative agreements and sustaining interagency relationships that support holistic education, there is emerging evidence of their effectiveness (Fowler, Donegan, Lueke, Hadden, & Phillips, 2000; Kochhar-Bryant, 2008; Kohler, 2002).

The Role of Professional Collaboration in Creating Healthy School Environments

Developmentally healthy school environments depend upon positive and constructive relationships among school professionals. These professionals work in partnership to help their students achieve their potential and build upon their strengths, abilities, and talents to shape personal visions for their future. Professional collaboration is essential for developing and sustaining school environments that address the needs of the whole child. Education of the whole child (holistic education) is concerned with the breadth of the curriculum, but it is also about teaching methods that facilitate a balanced learning process that encompasses the whole human being. Furthermore, it is about preparation of students for responsible living in a democratic society. But underlying these aims are deeper challenges: What motivates students? What keeps them engaged? What kinds of relationships with peers and adults connect them to the learning community? The case illustration presents the story of Montel, a bright and talented child, who is at risk of failing in school.

LET'S SEE IT IN ACTION

What's Up With Montel?

Montel, a 15-year-old with suspected but not yet identified ADHD and emotional disabilities lives with his maternal grandparents, who have been caring for him since he was 7. He tested in the superior range of intelligence at the age of 7. His special talent is music, as he taught himself how to play an electronic keyboard when he was 10, and he spends a great deal of time creating "beats" for contemporary songs and mixing music on a synthesizer. Through preschool and elementary years, Montel had difficulty sitting for long periods. On occasion, teachers would accommodate by allowing him to stand in the rear of the class as long as he was quiet and even permit him to complete tests standing up.

While Montel is very bright, articulate, and athletic, he has been getting into more trouble with his family, in school, and in the community. Teachers report that his grades have plummeted and that he sleeps in class, is truant more often, and is becoming a disciplinary problem at school. They view him as capable but defiant and unwilling to work, and they take the position that in ninth grade, all students are expected to take responsibility for their learning. His grandparents report that he has become secretive at home, refusing to tell them where he is after school, staying out long past curfew, arguing about everything, and becoming destructive at home. He has been banished from the local supermarket for petty theft. He has been returned home by the police for smoking marijuana under a bridge in the neighborhood. Montel has a lot of strengths but cannot tap them to succeed in school and in other areas of life. From Montel's point of view, he is bored by school and only wants to get home to his music and video games.

What questions should be asked about Montel? How should professionals intervene? To ask much broader questions: What role and responsibility do the school and school professionals have to look beyond Montel's academic progress? What responsibility do they have to examine the multiple challenges a student like Montel may face that prevent him or her from being successful academically, socially, and eventually in a career? What is their responsibility to explore the underlying factors that are impeding academic progress, in essence looking at the whole child to find a way to reach and teach? How might Montel's special talents serve as a bridge to his reengagement in his education?

HOW DOES COLLABORATION LEAD TO SCHOOLWIDE CHANGE?

Collaboration in Systems: An Untidy Process

Collaboration is about change—in people, practices, or organizations. More broadly, it is about *systemic change,* or changing a system (Chrispeels et al., 1999; Dettmer et al., 2005; Pounder, 1999). The term *system* has emerged over the past 60 years from the biological and physical sciences. Almost three decades ago, Kauffman (1980), borrowing from von Bertalanffy's (1968/1976) seminal work on general system theory, defined a system as a collection of parts that interact to function purposefully as a whole. For example, a pile of airplane parts is not a system, but a functioning jet is. A system, therefore, is an interdependent group of things that work together to achieve a common purpose. The following set of general system principles can be applied to collaborative work for educating the whole child.

The Individual Is Viewed as a Whole Person (Holistically)

In general system theory, people are viewed as whole individuals who are greater than the sum of their parts. The individual is a dynamic, whole system that is in continuous interchange with his or her environment—the individuals with whom they interact, the physical surroundings, and the culture. System thinkers seek to understand individuals and their needs in the context of their relationships with their environment or surroundings. For example, when a student requires multiple services and supports within an education setting, he or she needs them addressed—not in isolation—but through a collaborative, coordinated process.

Interdisciplinary Communication Is Essential

Working together, specialists from diverse fields can better attend to the holistic needs of the student and help the service system develop responses that are integrated rather than fragmented.

Bronfenbrenner (1979) built on the ideas of general systems theory and proposed in his ecological theory that a child's development occurs within the system of relationships that forms his or her social environment. Bronfenbrenner's theory defines complex "layers" of environment, each having an effect on a child's development (Bronfenbrenner, 1979, 1986). He claimed that in order to create a change in an individual child (the system), all the parts of that system must be attended to—physical, cognitive, social-emotional, health, peer and family relationships, and home and school environment. Bronfenbrenner (1986) later referred to a "social context system," which involves interaction among people who influence a student at multiple levels of a student's social organization—family, peers, school, and wider community. Applications of this model include interdisciplinary teaming (Hart, Zafft, & Zimbrich, 2001) and the student support team, now prevalent in schools across the United States.

Nothing Is Irrelevant

Human systems involve interdependent groups of people who work together for a common goal. Relationships among people and the contexts in which they live and work become interrelated aspects of change. We all live in systems and with systems: a nation, a family, a school, a community, or a person can be viewed as a whole system. Acting within a whole-system, or ecological, perspective means that if we want to create a change in a system, we have to examine all the parts of that system—personnel, relationships, roles, resources, leadership, organization, and others—and how they are related to each other in context (Bronfenbrenner, 1979). Nothing is irrelevant.

Systems are "open" when they are free to interact with their larger environment. They are not isolated or cut off from that environment or any component of the setting. Because of their constant state of interaction with their environment, such systems do not grow, develop, or change in a linear fashion. In the opening chapter case illustration teacher collaboration did not develop in a linear fashion or in a tidy, step-by-step manner. Instead, it was messy, complex, at times unstable, and usually unpredictable.

Collaboration Changes How We Think

Understanding systemic change and our individual relationship to it as a professional requires a change in our worldview—a paradigm shift. Such a shift requires a change in the way we think about our professional role and practices, our relationships, and the environments in which we work. As the case illustration at the beginning of the chapter showed, the teachers changed their traditional assumptions about how to work together in order to help the new students with disabilities for whom they shared responsibility.

Group or organizational change processes mirror the process of individual change. As mentioned earlier, the paradoxical nature of humans can both facilitate and threaten collaborative relationships. When individuals are challenged to change their thinking or behavior, they typically react with resistance or fear (Abrams, 2008; Cooperrider, 2000; Costa & Kallick, 2000). Often they require a powerful psychological stimulus, either internal or external, to motivate the change. The initial stimulus for change is frequently situational, such as a life crisis. Internal motivation may include guilt, dissatisfaction with one's life, or a desire for self-improvement. Examples of external motivation include spouses' or parents' demands for change, fear of the judgments of colleagues, a counselor's encouragement to change, or a court order to cease a behavior. In the Brookville illustration, the teachers' "crash course" in systemic change followed a path similar to that shown in Figure 5.1.

Figure 5.1   Systemic Change Process for Collaboration for the Whole Child

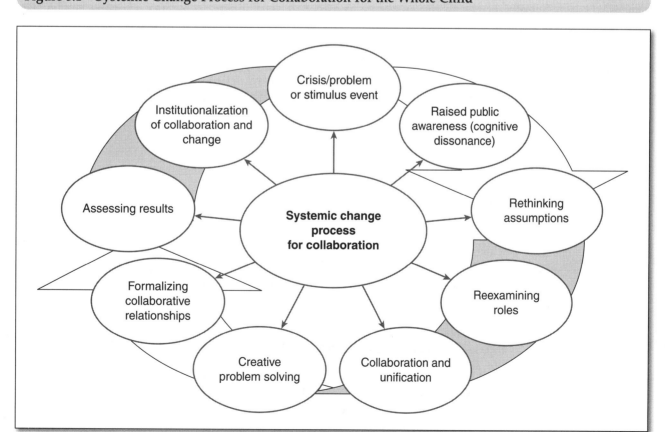

The teachers were highly motivated by the strong stimulus (crisis or problem) provided by the hastily introduced inclusion initiative, which was in turn triggered by the county budget crisis. These conditions, which challenged their base of knowledge and created great discomfort, also led to a re-examination of their assumptions and beliefs about collaboration, teaching, and learning. As they searched for new structures for collaboration to solve the problems of including students with disabilities in the general education classroom and the school system as a whole, they also had to reexamine their professional roles. First, they created informal analysis and problem-solving teams. Then they formalized the collaboration by establishing long-term learning and support teams and by assessing results through evaluation teams. The creation of long-term teams institutionalized the collaboration, or helped increase the likelihood that the collaboration would be sustained over time. The school was forever changed, as were the teachers.

Collaboration Means Constructing Solutions Together

One might argue, in hindsight, that the early "errors," "failures," "barriers," or "challenges" for the school could have been prevented. However, in the framework of system theory, they could not. When introduced to a new and complex set of stimuli, or changes in the environment (i.e., the sudden mandate to implement the inclusion initiative), the system was not yet ready for the change required. The problem-solving process and actions could *not* have been forecast or anticipated. Instead, they had to be constructed together by a group of creative people sharing a common experience. Therefore, the initial stimulus presented by the inclusion challenge can be viewed as powerful condition for the development of deep and sustainable change.

Several forces in the system can affect the change process and, ultimately, the success of the school's response: (a) the clarity and strength of the mission or task required, (b) leadership to guide the initiative, (c) the needs of the students, and (d) the budget resources to support the initiative. If these change forces are aligned well to support the process, a stronger collaborative unit in the school will be created. However, if one of the interacting forces or conditions is weak (e.g., the plan is well conceived and the students are ready, but resources or leadership is inadequate), then the initiative may be seriously undermined.

Change Is a Process, Not an Event

While crisis is not a necessary condition for effective collaboration and sustainable change, untidy and unpredictable processes are typical. For these reasons, systemic change can at once be thrilling, fascinating, and extremely challenging. Leading such change is not for the lighthearted. As Hall and Hord (2001) observed, change is a process, not an event. It is rare that human systems transform both rapidly and effectively; they need time for adjustment, reflection, problem solving, and evaluation. Without these, new processes or reforms are likely to erode and decay over time.

How Strategic Collaboration Achieves Change Goals

Research on organizational change has demonstrated that attempts to change educational systems to improve teaching, learning, and support for the whole child involve new collaboration among people and their roles and involve ongoing inquiry and reflection (Cooperrider et al., 2000; Cushman, 1998; Ettling, 2002; Fullan, 1999; Hall & Hord, 2001; Hargreaves, Earl, Moore, & Manning, 2001; Hinde, 2003; Osguthorpe & Patterson, 1998). Thus, change requires people to

- learn new information and reflect on what they have learned in the past (discovery).
- think and work together differently and in new combinations (synthesis).
- clarify expected results or define what needs to be changed or improved.
- create new practices and processes (development of practices).
- decide who takes responsibility for the process and how to resolve problems when the collaboration is "broken."
- participate in continuous self-development and learning in connection with the wider professional community (building professional community).

Strategic collaboration involves a purposeful effort to change how people work together, how they perform their roles, and how the environment supports their goals. For example, never has collaboration been more important than in the design of educational environments to address the needs of the whole child. The effectiveness of collaboration depends on how well the desired results are envisioned and defined, how carefully the goals are developed, and how precisely the collaborative activities are aimed at the actual problem or need being addressed.

For example, suppose a physician is presented with a complex set of symptoms in a few new patients. Suspecting that this may be a new or previously unidentified illness, she decides to collaborate with physicians from two other specialty areas to diagnose the problem and develop appropriate treatment plans. The effectiveness of that collaboration (defined by results) depends upon the clear goals defined for the collaboration. Evaluators could examine only the *processes* of collaboration (e.g., the roles of the other physicians, how they worked together, how often they met, how they established the treatment plan, or how decisions were made). Or they could evaluate the *results* of the collaboration (e.g., accurate diagnosis of the problem, appropriate treatment plan, new combination of medications prescribed, and, ultimately, improvements in the patients' conditions within a reasonable period). The patients improve, the doctors have identified a new illness, and the collaboration is deemed essential to the overall effort.

Obviously, in the example above, the target results of the collaboration are quite clear—heal the patient. With collaboration in education and human services, the target results or outcomes are seldom as clear and are typically highly complex. But the old adage still applies: if you don't know where you're going, you'll probably end up somewhere else. Adding to this complexity is the challenge of determining appropriate results from collaboration along the developmental continuum of the child.

A Caring Community of Learners: Creating a Protective Shield

Caring communities are defined as places where teachers and students care about and support each other, actively participate in and contribute to activities and decisions, feel a sense of belonging and identification, and have a shared sense of purpose and common values (Blank & Berg, 2006; SAMHSA Office of Applied Studies, 2007). The caring community concept differs sharply from the "factory-model" school, which emphasizes competition among students and hierarchical authority and still exerts a strong influence on our educational system. Schools organized as caring communities foster a shared sense of responsibility for teaching and learning. In comparison with traditional schools, they are characterized by student self-direction and a strong motivation to learn, experimentation, reduced absenteeism, greater social competence, respect for individual differences, and higher educational expectations and academic performance of students (Clark & Astuto, 1994; Lewis, Watson, & Schaps, 1999).

A central goal of these schools is to create a positive school climate by carefully attending to interactions and relationships between teachers and children and among children. Along with families, all members of the school community contribute to the care and education of young children. Caring community schools recognize that emotional competence is learned through interactions with peers and adults (Villa & Thousand, 1999). School personnel emphasize the crucial role they play as models of attitudes and behaviors. Children are also helped to reflect on their own feelings and are required to increase their awareness of others' feelings.

THE MANY USES OF COLLABORATION: THE FOUR ACTION-DIMENSIONS

Collaboration places complex demands on professionals and can be thought of as having four overlapping action-dimensions. These dimensions reflect the purposes and applications of collaboration to problem solving and change. In other words, collaboration is used in different ways as an instrument, tool, medium, or lever to create change in knowledge or understanding, relationships among people, practices, or problem-solving approaches. The four dimensions include discovery, synthesis of ideas, development of practice, and building professional community (Kochhar-Bryant, 2008):

1. *Collaboration as discovery* refers to the use of collaborative relationships to construct new knowledge about how to educate the whole child, through action research or team investigation, or to transfer knowledge between and among professionals. Examples include the use of classroom- or school-based action research teams, study groups, committees and task forces, teaching internships, and teacher exchanges. In the Brookville School illustration, the teachers developed an inquiry team to explore strategies that other schools use to include students with emotional and learning disabilities in the secondary curriculum.

2. *Collaboration as synthesis of ideas* refers to the use of collaboration to connect the thinking and knowledge of people in different disciplines, units, or groups within a school or organization in order to guide decisions and actions, redefine or solve problems, or develop new policies and processes. Examples of collaboration as synthesis include teams involved in the development of RTI plans, student support teams, Individualized Education Plans, and interdisciplinary problem-solving groups. In the Brookville illustration, teachers established a response team that combined the thinking of the general education and special education teachers, counselors, and related services personnel to solve immediate student problems and create new policies.

3. *Collaboration as the development of practice* refers to the application of collaborative practices to analyze, develop, or make more effective educational and support

practices and role relationships. Examples include collaborative or team teaching, teacher networks, personnel development programs, partnerships with institutions of higher education, interschool planning teams, mentoring or coaching relationships, parent and family resource centers, and local school improvement teams. In Brookville High School, a professional development program was established and embedded within a long-term technical assistance initiative to support the teachers for the balance of the school year and the next year.

4. *Collaboration as building professional community* refers to the creative use of collaboration to connect school personnel with the larger external professional community to create broad, sustainable change within the school. It means bringing the professional community into the school to facilitate change. This dimension may also involve the creative use of collaboration for the purpose of linking the first three dimensions: new knowledge creation, development of practice, and collaborative decision making. Examples include linking with professional associations, connecting teachers with national or regional resource centers, connecting with Web-based professional communities, and forming partnerships with universities to enhance the school's capacity to improve learning for all children (Kochhar-Bryant, 2008).

A collaborative initiative typically involves a blend of two or more of these dimensions.

IS COLLABORATION A DEVELOPMENTAL PROCESS?

The process of achieving collaborative relationships that can result in deep change in the educational environment is developmental whether the goal is individual, group, or institutional change. Such relationships occur in stages.

Degrees and Stages of Collaboration

The degree of collaboration among professionals will depend on a variety of factors, including the strategic goals of the partners, the administrative and organizational support and culture, the kinds of stresses or threats to the process, and the complexity of the learning that is desired or required to accomplish the task. Figure 5.2 depicts the five degrees of collaboration.

The degrees of intensity of collaboration range from the less complex communication and networking to the most complex and less common state of total integration of roles, groups, units, or organizations. The difference in degree reflects the complexity of the kind of interaction required and the kind of learning that needs to occur. At one end of the continuum, teachers may simply request and provide information. But at the highest level of learning, thinking and interaction within the group are characterized by the exchange of ideas and integration of perspectives, attitudes, and opinions (Cohen, 2004; Friend & Cook, 2009). The concept of degrees of collaboration is interpreted below in the context of professional collaboration between general and special educators.

Figure 5.2   The Five Degrees of Collaboration

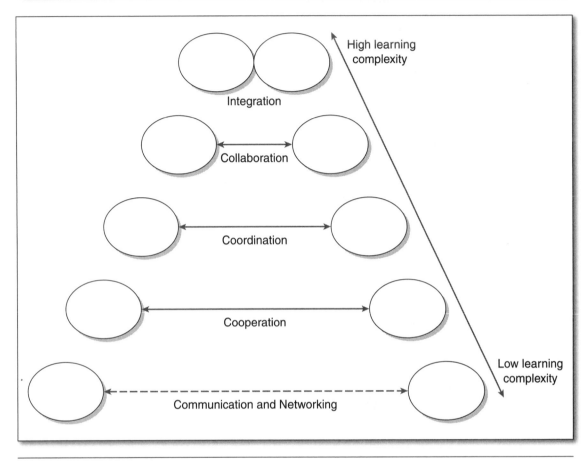

Source: Adapted from the work of Dettmer, Dyck, & Thurston, 2005; Friend & Cook, 2009; and Himmelman, 1996.

A series of stages proposed by Stump and Hagie (2003) mirrors the five degrees of collaboration introduced in Figure 5.2. They include

1. sharing information,

2. discussing adaptations and modifications,

3. providing supports in the classroom,

4. sharing instruction in the classroom, and

5. co-instruction.

Each stage represents an increasingly closer collaborative relationship between professionals.

Let's apply these stages of change in the case of student "Anita's" needs before she is referred to special education.

1. *Sharing information* about the strengths, needs, and talents of Anita. Anita has been identified as having reading difficulties, has been found eligible for services under RTI, and is experiencing emotional stress. She has special talents in drawing, which she expresses in art class.

2. *Discussing adaptations and modifications.* These are the types of interventions most appropriate to support Anita's participation in the classroom, including integration of art interests and talent into reading skill building.

3. *Providing supports* in the classroom. These might include monitoring Anita's reading progress and engagement in learning or preteaching or reteaching.

4. *Sharing instruction* in the classroom. Examples would be alternating roles of lead and support teacher and experimenting with collaborative activities between the art teacher and academic subject teachers.

5. *Co-instruction.* An example would be team teaching.

Understanding the developmental nature of collaboration can aid teams in setting reasonable goals for their work together and can lead to sustainable collaborative programs (Stump & Hagie, 2003).

Collaboration in Communities of Practice

An important concept that underlies collaborative practice is that of shared learning. In educational organizations, knowledge involves shared learning that is the basis for change and growth among professionals within the education community. This process of shared learning has been termed community of practice (CoP). Theories of professional communities underlie collaborative or collegial learning on the basis of a shared curiosity and a desire to expand skills and knowledge both individually and collectively (Kofman & Senge, 1993; Pugach & Johnson, 1999; Wald & Castleberry, 2000; Wenger, 1998; Wenger & Snyder, 2000). Communities of practice are aligned with the collaborative action-dimension introduced earlier—building professional community—or using collaboration to connect school personnel with the larger external professional community.

Etienne Wenger's pivotal work "Communities of Practice: Learning as a Social System" (1998) builds on previous work of developmental psychologists and social learning theorists. A *community of practice* is a group of people who share a concern or a passion for something they do and who interact regularly to learn how to do it better (Wenger; Wenger et al., 2002). Communities of practice are formed by people who engage in a process of collective learning in shared activity, such as a group of teachers and counselors working on similar problems with student learning, a gathering of first-time district administrators helping each other cope with new legal requirements on school discipline, or a small group of students with learning disabilities in community college who support each other as they seek to negotiate needed accommodations in their classes.

A community of practice is not just a club, a group of friends, a chat room, or a group of people who share similar interests. Rather, according to Wenger (1998), a CoP has an identity that is defined by a shared domain or area of interest. Membership implies a commitment to the domain and, therefore, a shared competence that distinguishes members from other people. In pursuing their interest in their domain, members engage in joint activities and discussions, help each other, and share information. They build relationships that enable them to learn from each other. A group of teachers having the same job title is not a community practice, unless they interact and learn together to achieve a common purpose.

Members of a community of practice are practitioners. They develop a shared repertoire of resources: experiences, stories, tools, ways of addressing recurring problems—in short a shared practice. This takes time and sustained interaction. . . . In the course of all these conversations, they have developed a set of stories and cases that have become a shared repertoire for their practice. (Wenger et al., 2002)

Communities develop their practice through a variety of activities. A few examples are provided in Table 5.1.

Table 5.1   Examples of Activities Based on Communities of Practice

Problem solving	"Can we work on designing an accommodation for my students who have attentional difficulties and brainstorm some ideas? I'm stuck."
Requests for information	"Where can I find the text of the law related to school safety and student discipline?"
Seeking experience	"Has anyone dealt with a student in this situation before?"
Reusing assets	"I have a proposal for a collaborative program between the music teacher, math teacher, and counselor, which I wrote for the principal last year. I can send it to you, and you can easily tweak it to resubmit it."
Coordination and synergy	"Can we pool some of our budget funds to purchase and share the assessment instruments we need?"
Discussing developments	"What do you think of the new online professional development academy? Is it helping you with new strategies for working with students?"
Documentation projects	"We've talked about this problem of student engagement, and some of us are creating some effective strategies. Let's write down our strategies and describe what's working."
Visits	"Can we come and see your new student court program? We would like to establish one in our school."
Mapping knowledge and identifying gaps	"Who has expertise with behavioral assessment? What are we missing? What other groups should we connect with to learn more?"

Source: Adapted from Etienne Wenger, *Learning for a Small Planet: A Research Agenda*, 2006.

For Wenger, indicators for the formation of a community of practice include the following:

- Sustained mutual relationships, whether harmonious or filled with conflict
- Shared ways of engaging in doing things together
- A rapid flow of information and propagation of innovation
- Quick set-up of a problem to be discussed
- Substantial overlap in participants' descriptions of who belongs
- Knowing what others know and can do and how they can contribute to an enterprise
- Ability to assess the appropriateness of actions and products
- Shared stories, inside jokes, jargon, and shortcuts to communication
- Shared symbols of membership reflecting a certain perspective on the world

Communities of practice are becoming vital instruments for knowledge acquisition and the exploration of new ideas. So important have CoPs become in education that the

U.S. Office of Special Education Programs (OSEP) established a National Communities of Practice Technical Assistance Network to help state educational agencies establish CoPs to develop new insights into problems and solutions (see the Idea Partnership, www.ideapartnership.org).

COLLABORATION IN THE EARLY YEARS

Several comprehensive models for supporting children in the elementary years emphasize professional collaboration and a shared responsibility among parents, schools, and community. These models reflect research on effective practices, including developmentally appropriate practice, child-centered planning, instructional teaming, inclusive curriculum, and a collaborative environment. A few examples are highlighted below.

Collaboration for Early Intervention and Preschool for Children With Disabilities

IDEIA 2004 includes two programs for young children and their families that depend upon professional collaboration and interagency coordination: (1) the Early Intervention Programs for Infants and Toddlers with Disabilities, Part C, which covers services to children from birth through age 2; and (2) the Preschool Program of Part B, which covers services to children from ages 3 to 5. The purpose of the Part C program is to (a) enhance the development of infants and toddlers with disabilities and minimize their potential for developmental delay, (b) enhance the capacity of families to meet the special needs of their infants and toddlers with disabilities, (c) provide financial assistance to increase the capacity of state and local agencies to create statewide, comprehensive interagency systems of services for children 0 to 3 with disabilities or developmental delays. Together these programs represent an important effort to expand the scope of services available to the nation's youngest children with disabilities and their families.

Several collaborative practices have been found to be particularly effective for families. Families said that it was especially helpful when the service coordinator was also the primary therapist, when service coordinators had frequent contact with families, and when coordinators were deliberately matched with families based on needs and personalities. Families also identified flexibility in scheduling and service location and ease of communication with the coordinator as helpful. Many families appreciated home visits and viewed them as enhancing collaboration; that is, they met on their "own turf" where the parents were more relaxed and the setting was more comfortable and natural for the children. If home visits were unavailable, then transportation to the centers was helpful. Administrative policies and practices that contribute to collaboration include allowing employees to work on flexible schedules and enabling service coordinators to work on weekends or evenings (Research and Training Center on Service Coordination, 2001).

Collaboration Strategies at the Elementary Level

In comparison to preschool, elementary school is a more structured and challenging academic environment for all children, particularly for those with learning barriers and disabilities. Children with disabilities in the general education classroom are held to the same expectations for performance as their peers. Serving all learners in the general elementary classroom demands educational planning and instructional teaming. For example, addressing the teaching and learning needs of an elementary student with learning disabilities and a mental health disorder may require the combined expertise of the general education teacher, special education teacher, psychologist, and school counselor.

Instructional teaming often relies on collaboration with other staff members, such as paraprofessionals, teaching assistants, and volunteers. Another important, and often "unsung," member of the instructional team is the school librarian or technology resource room specialist. Library services and technology services are now expected to be integrated into instruction and student learning, and these roles are therefore crucial to collaborative teaming.

New Roles for Families at the Elementary Level

Parents serve a variety of new collaboration and coordination roles as their child enters elementary school—as teachers, decision makers, partners, service coordinators, and advocates. They are teacher-collaborators when they reinforce at home the skills acquired in preschool, school partners when they communicate needs to school personnel, and decision makers when they participate in the educational planning or evaluation process. They must communicate and collaborate closely with their child's teacher to understand the academic requirements in the elementary school, the requirements for homework assignments and projects, and the new responsibilities students have for delivering home–school messages and communications. In the elementary school, many parents are committed to participate in the life of the school to be closely engaged in and supportive of their children's learning.

Parents are service coordinators, decision makers, and advocates when they participate in the IEP process and help to ensure that their child with special needs receives needed support services. They take the initiative to understand the laws that guarantee their access to and coordinate the supports and service they need. They are informed about the difference between early intervention services (Part C of IDEIA) and early childhood services (Part B of IDEIA). Parents provide a vital bridge between preschool programs and elementary school, visiting the new program with their child, helping the child to become familiar with the new setting, and discussing concerns and fears connected with the upcoming change. They can also help bridge the gap by arranging visits with former preschool friends and teachers, as well as with new classmates (Pinkerton, 2004). Family members play a pivotal role in providing information about the child's abilities, strengths and weaknesses, and interests and talents. Parental insights complement information obtained from preschool sources and provide a broader picture of the child's capabilities and needs (National Center for Early Development and Learning, 2005; Pinkerton; Wandry & Pleet, 2003). The boxed text provides an example of the important role of coordination and support for children with multiple developmental needs.

THE INDIVIDUALIZED INTERAGENCY PLAN

Well Worth the Effort!

The following case example describes a new coordination model that is focused on a child's strengths and a family-centered philosophy. It has resulted in great progress in the life of a child with multiple needs.

My name is Carolyn, and I live in Minnesota with my husband, Bob, and our seven children. Bob and I have been married for 23 years. In 1990 we became foster parents for Clay County. As a stay-at-home mom for most of those years, we became blessed with four biological children, one adopted daughter, and two permanent foster children. In 1994, our then foster child, Sara, was showing signs of developmental delays, and so began our journey into the world of special services.

When we adopted Sara at the age of six, she had two diagnoses: attention deficit/hyperactivity disorder (ADHD) and fetal alcohol syndrome (FAS). Since then, Sara has also been diagnosed with reactive attachment disorder (RAD) and bipolar disorder. At first we worked with a special education team to develop an IEP that included occupational therapy, adaptive physical education, special education, a support paraprofessional in the classroom, and a pediatrician to coordinate Sara's medications. This process worked well.

As Sara moved into the K–12 education system, the need for home, community, and educational supports increased. I became involved with our local Interagency Early Intervention Committee (IEIC) at this time. This committee addresses the needs of children ages birth to seven. Our two permanent foster children also have FAS and other complications from premature birth. They required intensive services from birth onward and were placed on an Individual Family Service Plan (IFSP). One of the first things I heard about at the committee meetings was the Individualized Interagency Intervention Plan (IIIP). Because the IIIP was modeled after the IFSP and was to be phased in by age groups, the Interagency EI Committee was the first to discuss this document and its implementation. The Committee was asked to form a IIIP training team with a parent component to help implement the IIIP process in the local county and school district. The more I learned more about the IIIP, I knew this was exactly what Sara needed.

By the time Sara was in third grade, the complications resulting from her psychiatric and learning disabilities were overwhelming our family. The county stepped in to provide case management services and psychiatric medication monitoring services for children with mental health diagnoses. The next year we added developmental services through the county, a behavioral specialist, and in-home support. As Sara's mom, it became my full-time job to coordinate communication among agencies, educate staff regarding Sara's mental health issues, and coordinate five different individual care plans under different service agencies. During every meeting or phone call, I was bombarded with comments regarding Sara's manipulative behaviors, her raging and manic episodes that interfered with her day and with staff's ability to teach her, and her ability to "work the system," accepting no accountability for her behaviors. Sara's strengths were never discussed.

Weekly meetings at school became routine, along with many phone calls in between. When Sara began showing signs of another manic episode, it was my job to notify all the professionals with whom we were working, gather input needed for a medication change, and monitor Sara for 24 hours a day to ensure her safety. My husband and I were the only ones who had a complete, comprehensive understanding of Sara's needs. Just getting through the week was exhausting, leaving us with very little time or energy to focus on the needs of our other children.

Our county had implemented the Wraparound Process, a coordinated team effort to address the needs of high-maintenance children. While the team helped with general communication, I continued to coordinate the majority of Sara's services and supports. Our school district was slowly moving forward with the IIIP process, but it would be another year before this new system would be available for Sara's age group.

I approached Sara's special education staff and requested that they consider the IIIP for Sara. It was decided that it was in Sara's best interest to coordinate her care and start addressing her needs using a comprehensive, strengths-based process. So, Bob and I and 15 professionals sat down to write an IIIP for Sara, completing the process in less than two hours. After years of hearing what Sara couldn't do, we finally had a document that not only addressed her needs and concerns but also acknowledged her many strengths! Sara learned very quickly through manipulatives because she was a tactile and kinesthetic learner. She was also very interested in music and art, particularly sculpture. She also excelled in gymnastics. We remain forever grateful for the effort of the team that day.

Sara's progress during that first year on her IIIP was remarkable. We used Sara's strengths to provide her with more accountability for her learning. Her teachers agreed to use her interest in art and sculpture to design class

(continued)

(Continued)

projects. She was also permitted to join the gymnastics team. Most importantly, we were able to develop a behavior plan that encompassed all areas of Sara's life and was consistently implemented in school and home environments. One of Sara's greatest achievements this past year was participating in the regular education classroom for up to three hours a day without behavioral supports. Coordinating Sara's care through the IIIP has meant far fewer meetings (reduced to two or three times a year), fewer phone calls, and the development of a cooperative working relationship among staff whose focus is on ensuring that Sara reaches her full potential in all environments. Most importantly, I can now be a Mom again to Sara and our other children.

Source: Minnesota System of Interagency Coordination, 2003, by permission.

As you reflect on the case of Sara, consider the following questions:

- Who had the most complete understanding of Sara's needs?
- Who were the primary case managers?
- How did the focus on strengths make a difference for Sara?

The case example shows that the coordination process was shifted to create a shared responsibility within the system for children with disabilities and their families. The new IIIP service model simplified the way in which services were provided. It built a unified, coordinated service system that served Sara's multiple needs and reduced the crushing burden on the family to coordinate services from multiple agencies. The most important shift was philosophical—moving toward a strengths-based, family- and person-centered approach to services. This meant that for Sara, there was a deliberate shift in focus from her disabilities (problem focused) to a focus on her strengths, assets, and abilities. This represents a move away from traditional service delivery approaches to a more family-centered model of care. While traditional approaches focus on deficits (what's wrong with the child so we can "fix" it), the new focus asks, "What is working well, and what strengths and capacities can be drawn upon to help Sara manage her own difficulties?" As a result, the IIIP reflected the full range of Sara's assets and strengths.

Strategies for Effective Transition From Elementary to Middle School

Transition from elementary school typically occurs either in the fifth or sixth grade, as students move on to middle school for their sixth, seventh, and eighth years. Once again, the child must adjust to a new environment, a new set of expectations, and, often, a new set of peers. For most children, their elementary experiences have prepared them to manage the adjustment within a few days or weeks, and they quickly grow comfortable with the new demands. However, many children—both with and without disabilities—may not be adequately prepared in advance for these changes in the educational setting.

During these years, parents, teachers, administrators, and support personnel play a crucial role in helping students develop a positive self-image and the skills they need to deal with the changes in their learning environment and the new demands and pressures they face. Their ability to communicate and collaborate as a team to address the individual needs of youth in the middle school can make the essential difference for child during the transition and for the remainder of their school years. The following collaborative activities represent a synthesis of those used in elementary and middle schools across the United States to support students with learning needs and disabilities:

- In the sixth-grade teachers (or fifth-grade if the first middle school year is sixth grade) fills out a transition plan, which includes information on reading and math levels; writing ability; IEPs as appropriate; students' strengths, interests, and special talents; counseling needs; home support; learning styles; behavior problems; and organizational problems. These forms are used to guide placement.
- The middle school counselor meets with students in each rising elementary class to give a presentation about middle school, homework, organization, scheduling, typical school day, teachers, school activities, clubs, and athletics.
- Middle school "ambassadors," including students with special needs, are sent to the elementary schools to speak to the fifth-grade students.
- Short videos are used to introduce students to the schools; these can even be produced by middle school students as special projects under the guidance of teachers.
- Middle school students are paired with rising elementary students for a day at the middle school. The "shadows" attend classes and take notes on what they experience. Then they share the information with their home elementary classmates.
- Parent question-and-answer nights are held. These include the principal or assistant principal, a member of one of the middle school teacher teams, and a counselor in the school that the children will be attending.
- Tours of the middle school are arranged for students and parents with reviews of discipline rules and regulations.
- An assembly or roundtable mixer is held in the gym at which rising elementary students can mix with middle school students.
- Rising elementary students write down the top questions that they would like answered about middle school. Middle school students then write back or videotape their responses.
- The last two or three classroom guidance sessions for rising elementary students are devoted to answering questions and easing fears about transition.
- A list is developed of rising elementary students who are identified as possibly needing extra support in the adjustment to middle school. Extra support to these students is provided through a special small "early bird" group that meets a week before the start of the school year (the invitation, however, should go out to all students). During this time, students get their lockers and schedules; practice opening their lockers; and review daily procedures such as getting lunch tickets, checking out library books, and other tasks. This group could continue occasionally during the first few months of school to monitor how students are adjusting and if they need continued support.

The transition to middle school is an important pathway toward ultimate graduation that must be successfully navigated. The National Middle School Association (NMSA, 2002) has called upon schools at both levels to adopt early transition plans to help youth to achieve a sense of belonging in their new school. Educators are being asked to collaborate and coordinate to create transition plans, implement teaching teams, and work more closely with school counselors. Teachers and counselors at the elementary and middle level are beginning to work together to share information about students with special needs before they make the passage to the next level. And parents are not just encouraged to find out about the program at the next level but are being actively helped by professionals in the process. This new attitude shifts the old practice of inducing parents to take the initiative to find out about middle school to one in which communication, information sharing, and direct assistance occur.

A Case Example: Saving Paul

The case example that follows illustrates how communication and collaboration between teachers and parents in the middle years can make a great difference in the life of a young adolescent transitioning from elementary to middle school.

Paul:	When I started at Chadwick Middle School, I was afraid, but I didn't want anyone to know. There was so much pressure. Things were easy at my other school because I only had one teacher and one classroom and I always kept my books and papers in one desk. Now I have a locker, a combination to remember, and a bunch of classes to get to with so little time. I have to keep all my subjects organized, my papers and stuff organized, get different homeworks in to different teachers, prepare for lots of different tests on different days, and there's so many big projects. I have trouble with organization and remembering things, and no one gave me help with this. I started falling behind slowly day by day and feeling worse and worse about myself. After a while, I just gave up.
Paul's mother:	Paul was always a very active child and had trouble with attention. Conversations were difficult with him because his mind was always flitting away like a butterfly. During elementary years, this high activity level and lack of attention created difficulty, but he was very bright and could always compensate. We didn't have him diagnosed because he seemed to find a way to keep up. He was never identified as needing special education because he could perform average or better. Each year, though, his teachers reported problems with minor disruptions in class, disorganized behavior, and trouble paying attention. Because I had continuous communication with his elementary teachers, I could stay on top of the problems and provide supports at home. When Paul was 10, he was diagnosed with attention deficit/hyperactivity disorder.

Once Paul hit seventh grade, though, everything changed. He had to develop organizational skills for homework assignments, subjects, schedule of classes, teachers, and long-term projects and papers. Organization was his Achilles' heel. He began to change, became distant, hang out with friends who I was very concerned about. I thought at first this was Paul just being a preteen, but by the end of the year, his grades has plummeted, and by the end of eighth grade, he was nearly failing every subject. More frequently he was refusing to go to school, and we had to start using structured behavioral strategies.

During the seventh grade, no teachers had attempted to communicate with me about his situation, and no one provided any extra help to Paul to organize himself. When I went to back-to-school night, I expressed my concerns, and one teacher said, "In middle school we expect them to manage independently. This isn't elementary, and they have to take more responsibility for themselves." I asked, "What if they have difficulty with this and need extra help? What if they fall too far behind?" The teacher responded, "Well, if they're in the general education class, we treat everyone alike. No special treatment." Paul did pass eighth grade by a small margin, and I feared for the following year when he shifted to ninth grade.

High School Counselor:

Paul's mother made an appointment to talk to me just before the end of his eighth-grade year. She was very concerned about her son's experience in seventh and eighth grades and worried about his near failure and what that meant for the coming year. Unfortunately, I have a caseload of 300 students, so it's hard for me to spend much time with each child. But I was interested in this case and appreciated the mother's concern and involvement. I pulled his file and found that, yes indeed, Paul had nearly failed all of his classes. Yet, what was amazing was that he had taken the state assessment tests in eighth grade and had scored "advanced proficient" on all of them. Moreover, he had early psychological tests that showed that he was a very bright kid. How could he be failing his grades yet scoring "advanced proficient"? Something was terribly wrong.

I spoke with some of his teachers in middle school, and they reported that Paul was known to sleep in class, routinely failed to turn in homework, and often showed disruptive and attention-seeking behavior in class. I asked if any of the teachers had let his parents know about this behavior or had provided any extra support for Paul, and they all said no. They believed Paul could do the work, could pass the tests, but was just unmotivated. They did not believe he needed special education. They were reluctant to report on his behavior because they wanted to "give him every chance to make the changes on his own." Furthermore, the special education screening team refused to evaluate Paul for services because of his high state standardized test scores and teacher reports. And so, in my opinion—and his mother's—we had failed him in the middle school. This student clearly needed help and was at particular risk of academic failure in ninth grade. His marginal adjustment in middle school and growing sense of isolation had left him even more vulnerable to the pressures and demands of high school.

I met with Paul and talked with him about his feeling of being overwhelmed with the work and promised to get him some help with organization and time management during the year. We set up a time to visit the high school and meet with a few of the teachers and classrooms. I discussed what he could expect in terms of schedule and workload and other expectations. I also stayed in close touch with his mother for the balance of the year to give suggestions about how she might provide extra support at home and prepare him for the transition at the end of summer. During ninth grade, we held a teachers' roundtable with Paul and his mother and the high school counselor to discuss progress at midyear and share what supports were being used in his classes. By the middle of the year, Paul's grades had improved from failing to Bs and Cs and his attitude toward school was improving. The frequency of disruptive and attention-seeking behavior began to decline.

Questions for Discussion

- How did middle school teachers characterize middle school expectations for Paul? How were these expectations different from those in elementary school?
- How does Paul characterize the new demands placed on him?
- Why was Paul not screened for special education services in the elementary years, even though he was diagnosed with ADHD?
- How did the school counselor intervene and provide support to Paul and his mother?

What can we learn about this case? First, Paul's experience of change in his educational environment placed great stress on his coping skills. He was predisposed to being at risk of poor adjustment to the new demands of middle school. He had not received professional help during his elementary years because he was bright and able to compensate for his learning challenges. Paul also had no one with whom to share his feelings and fears.

Second, Paul's parents had little communication from the middle school teachers about Paul's behavior, so they missed many opportunities to intervene at home. While the teachers may have been well meaning in "hoping" and giving Paul a chance to "change on his own," they inadvertently contributed to his deterioration. Opportunities were lost to intervene early, to provide supports in school, and to help Paul turn around his sense of failure and defeat.

A serious and gathering situation was diffused, however, due to the persistence of Paul's mother, the support of an astute and caring school counselor, and the willingness of ninth-grade teachers to coordinate and provide support. Close collaboration around Paul's needs was achieved. Without such a response on the part of the school, Paul may well have deteriorated further in ninth grade and have become a dropout statistic. Paul's case mirrors that of a growing number of middle school students who may or may not be diagnosed as having disabilities yet are at significant risk for alienation, academic failure, and dropout.

COLLABORATION IN THE MIDDLE YEARS

Collaboration and Coordination in Middle School

While there is consensus that the elementary school is a "'nurturing,' 'child centered,' and 'self-contained,' descriptions of middle school learning environments are inconsistent" (NMSA, 1999). As the NMSA (1999) has observed,

Middle schools may implement enabling practices, such as interdisciplinary teaching, thematic units, flexible scheduling, and flexible grouping to address student needs. On the other hand, many middle schools mirror traditional high school departmentalization, 50 minute classes, and ability groupings. Some middle schools are organized to create a gradual transition from self-contained to departmental configuration. For example, the fifth grade is self-contained, the sixth grade has 2 person teams, the seventh has 2–3 person teams with larger blocks of time, and the eighth grade has 4 or more teachers each specializing in a subject area. With such a great variety of middle school configurations, any discussion of transition therefore examines the substance of the setting young adolescents are entering before addressing the appropriate grade of transition.

Despite variations across the United States, the middle school concept today is based on the following components:

- *Educators committed to young adolescents:* Teachers and professionals are trained to understand and teach young adolescents, including those with special needs, and have a passion to deal with the unique characteristics of the middle school student.
- *Interdisciplinary teams:* A team of teachers work together, with other support professionals, to help educate the same group of youngsters. Interdisciplinary teams plan their own schedule and build a sense of community with their core of students.
- *An adult for every student:* Each student is given the opportunity to connect with at least one adult. This occurs within the context of a teacher mentor/advisory program.
- *Exploratory curriculum:* The curriculum is structured so that all students, including those with disabilities, have the opportunity to explore their various abilities, including those that may have been hidden to this point.
- *Integrative curriculum:* Connections are made among content areas, and students are able to identify these connections.

Because middle school students want to and need to be involved in their own learning, teachers in effective middle schools make every attempt to involve all students actively in the educational process (NMSA, 2002).

Classroom Strategies Compatible With Adolescent Brain Development

As research has indicated, there is a disconnect between standards-based educational environments and the nonstandard, individual, variable social and cognitive development, learning preferences, social development, and rapid physical changes that occur during early adolescence (A. Jackson & Davis, 2000; Haugaard, 2000; Urdan & Klein, 1999; U.S. Department of Education, 2000). Neuropsychologists agree memory and attention are affected during adolescent development, when the prefrontal cortex of the brain undergoes changes. They also agree that the way to hold attention in young adolescents is to engage the senses and emotions and to combine this with problem-based learning (Casey et al., 2000; Immordino-Yang & Damasio, 2007; L. Wilson & Horch, 2004). After students are introduced to a problem in a unit, teachers encourage them to ask questions that interest them. Using essential questions to frame the unit, incorporating the senses and emotions to focus the learning, and then facilitating students as they find multiple ways to solve problems can focus adolescent learning while building complex neuron connections within the brain (Wilson & Horch). Classroom activities that are compatible with attention and memory in adolescents include the following:

- Problem-based activities that engage students in working together to examine real-life issues and solve problems using all their senses
- Activities that require students to take responsibility for directing their own work and for team participation
- Playing music to link memory to specific learning tasks to facilitate young adolescents' sensorimotor connections
- Having students write reflectively to reinforce and consolidate learning

- Using physical challenges as a context for solving problems and building collaboration (e.g., low ropes courses)
- Involving students in real-life apprenticeships in which they shadow workers in various jobs or learn skills in short internships that either connect to an area of study or help them understand one of the problems they have posed
- Peer collaboration or cooperative learning to promote group problem solving

In addition, more middle schools are establishing subschools and adopting a small-team-based model of student management and support. The team-based model establishes home groups and rooms and provides a supervised catch-up or makeup room with flexible timetables (L. Wilson & Horch, 2004).

Development and Traditional School Settings

There is compelling evidence that many students believe that traditional school settings contribute to their struggles in school. Interviews with students reveal that they perceive their former teachers as having little interest in them. Many feel isolated, gravitate toward other students like themselves, and end up hanging out and missing too many days in the classroom. Students place high value on relationships with teachers, administrators, and counselors and on their ability to learn at their own pace with their own focus. They also place high value on individualized attention, caring, and support (Lehr et al., 2004).

These desires are expressions of adolescents' developmental needs as they search for their own identity, yet the school environment, particularly in the middle years, typically limits opportunities to exercise decision making. Many schools respond to students with highly controlling management and discipline practices, which can actually increase problem behaviors and decrease motivation (Stuhlman, Hamre, & Pianta, 2002). Educators' perceptions of students' capacity for decision making and autonomy tend to mirror those at the elementary level and clearly do not match students' self-perceptions. Students believe that they should be allowed to make decisions in middle and high school (Alspaugh, 1998; Mullins & Irvin, 2000; Phelan, Davidson, & Yu, 1998; Phelan, Yu, & Davidson, 1994).

Several studies have concluded that factors associated with the middle school setting may have a deleterious effect the successful transition and adjustment of students, both those with and without disabilities (Alspaugh, 1998; Mulhall, 2007). Young adolescents mature at vastly different rates and are at different stages between Grades 4 and 10. Transitioning students from classrooms designed for children to those designed for young adolescents cannot be done effectively by treating all students as though they develop physically, emotionally, socially, and cognitively at the same rates (Hough, 2003).

Much more research is needed to understand more clearly students' experiences as they move from elementary into middle and high school and how programs and professional collaboration might be better structured to respond to the developmental needs and capacities of young adolescents. Recent reforms in middle schools are showing great promise for addressing barriers to successful transition and lessening the often overwhelming challenges facing students, particularly those with special needs, at this vulnerable stage in development. School professionals, who are generally knowledgeable about student developmental differences, may not be aware of how professional collaboration can mediate the impact of these differences on student progress.

Lippmann and colleagues (2008) provided a developmental perspective on what competencies young people need to be ready for college, the workplace, and the transition to adulthood. Drawing connections with youth development research that has identified the assets that youth need to make a successful transition to adulthood, they organize competencies into five domains of youth development: physical, psychological, social, cognitive, and spiritual (see boxed text). Lippman and colleagues report also focuses on strategies that have proven helpful for groups that face greater challenges in meeting the readiness criteria for college, the workplace, and the transition to adulthood. These include low-income and minority students, Latinos and English language learners, students with disabilities, disconnected youth, youth aging out of foster care, and sexual minority youth.

YOUTH DEVELOPMENT COMPETENCIES

To succeed as adults, youth must acquire adequate attitudes, behaviors, and skills in five areas:

1. *Health*: Good current health status and evidence of knowledge, attitudes, and behaviors that will assure future well-being; for example, exercise, good nutrition, and understanding the consequences of risky behaviors

2. *Personal/social skills*: Intrapersonal skills (i.e., the ability to understand emotions and practice self-discipline) and interpersonal skills (e.g., working with others; developing and sustaining friendships through cooperation, empathy, and negotiation; and developing judgment skills and coping systems)

3. *Knowledge, reasoning, and creativity*: A broad base of knowledge and an ability to appreciate and demonstrate creative expression; good oral, written, and problem-solving skills; and an ability to learn and an interest in lifelong learning and achieving

4. *Vocational awareness*: A broad understanding of life options and the steps to take in making choices; also, adequate preparation for work and family life and an understanding of the value and purpose of family, work, and leisure

5. *Citizenship*: Understanding national; community; and racial, ethnic, or cultural group history and values; also, having a desire to be ethical and to be involved in efforts that contribute to the broader good

Youth development competencies are

- *social competencies*, such as work and family life skills, problem-solving skills, and communication skills.
- *moral competencies*, such as personal values and ethics and a sense of responsibility and citizenship (including participation in civic life and community service).
- *emotional competencies*, such as a sense of personal identity, self-confidence, autonomy, and the ability to resist negative peer pressure.
- *physical competencies*, such as physical conditioning and endurance and an appreciation for and strategies to achieve lifelong physical health and fitness.
- *cognitive competencies*, such as knowledge, reasoning ability, creativity, and a lifelong commitment to learning and achievement.

Source: Lippman, L., Atienza, A., Rivers, A., & Keith, J. (2008). *Developmental perspective on college & workplace readiness.* Washington, DC: Child Trends.

Collaboration Strategies for the Developmentally Responsive Middle School

Effective middle schools provide a strong academic program that is developmentally responsive to the unique needs of young adolescents. In the developmentally responsive middle school, welcome activities may include orientation to the school for students and families, meetings between parents of students at both levels, assignment of a peer mentor and adult advisor, orientation to the year's curriculum, and orientation to new expectations for student behavior and responsibility and available supports. During the year, supportive structures and activities for special needs students "wrap around" these youth during the school day. Such structures and activities include mentors or peer partners for support during the first visitation days and throughout the year, help with lockers and schedules, ongoing advising to choose extracurricular activities, drop-in problem-solving sessions for dealing with peer problems or homework assistance, peer mediation, and parent support groups.

According to the NMSA's *This We Believe: Developmentally Responsive Middle Level Schools* (1995), an adult advocate is a key feature of a developmentally responsive middle school. Middle school students often need assistance in resolving both educational and personal issues they face during these transitional years. NMSA's report, based on decades of research on what works, describes 12 characteristics of an effective, student supportive school:

1. Educators committed to young adolescents

2. A shared vision

3. High expectations for all

4. An adult advocate for every student

5. Family and community partnerships

6. A positive school climate

7. Curriculum that is challenging, integrative, and exploratory

8. Varied teaching and learning approaches

9. Assessment and evaluation that promote learning

10. Flexible organizational structure

11. Programs and policies that foster health, wellness, safety

12. Comprehensive guidance and support services

These 12 characteristics provide a framework for what middle schools should and can be, according to NMSA (Hough, 2003; NMSA, 1995; Swaim, 2003). Specific strategies that middle schools use to address the developmental needs of their youth are discussed below.

Focus on Students' Strengths and Positive Development

Often parents and teachers of adolescents focus on the problems and needs and fail to ask: What is right with this teen? What is working in their lives? What are their special talents and interests? The answers to these questions—which should be asked of the youth—can often serve as essential levers for motivating adolescents during the delicate passage through the middle years. The developmentally appropriate curriculum for middle school students builds upon their strengths and experiences and continues to be personalized and responsive to each individual's development and learning patterns. This is achieved with small classes and low student/teacher ratios. Students also benefit from multiage groupings in which they learn from their peers and at their own pace. Strength-based student assessment directs professionals to identify and build upon the existing strengths and skills that the child and family present (Epstein, Rudolph, & Epstein, 2000; Friedman, Leone, & Friedman, 1999).

Use Interdisciplinary Teaming to Deliver Developmentally Appropriate Curriculum and Instruction

Research demonstrates that schools engaged in interdisciplinary teaming have a more positive school climate, have more frequent contact with parents, have higher job satisfaction among teachers, and report higher student achievement scores than nonteaming schools (Aubusson, Steele, Dinham, & Brady, 2007; Flowers, Mertens, & Mulhall, 1999). Several factors related to curriculum and instruction are important for helping young adolescents who are special needs learners adjust to the new demands placed on them. These factors include the way in which curriculum is organized, how instruction is delivered, and the way decisions are made about course selection, and all depend on effective collaboration among teachers, parents, and students.

Several strategies have been associated with student achievement in middle schools, for all students. When teachers are engaged in teams with fewer students (90 or less), they can participate more frequently in team activities, particularly curriculum coordination and coordination of student assignments. Common planning time is needed between teachers and with counselors so they can meet frequently when students have learning difficulties (Commission on the Whole Child, 2007). To assess the effectiveness of their strategies, teachers should document the teaching and learning approaches used within their classes and document student results. Administrators are pivotal in helping teachers appreciate the value of their teaming in creating a positive climate, particularly for special needs learners, and for improving their relationships with students, parents, and other professionals (Flowers et al., 1999).

Use Teaming to Develop and Deliver Exploratory Curriculum

Developmentally responsive middle schools provide an inviting, challenging, and exploratory curriculum that connects subject areas. An exploratory curriculum balances attention to academic basics with students' need to explore a wide variety of interests and experiences. Exploratory classes in areas of art, music, drama, technology, foreign languages, and others offer students opportunities to explore their interests (NMSA, 2002).

Developmentally appropriate curriculum is delivered by interdisciplinary teams that consist of two or more teachers from different subject areas and the group of students they commonly instruct. Team teachers plan, coordinate, and evaluate curriculum and instruction across academic areas. Teams cultivate meaningful and regular communication with families. Teams often share the same schedule and the same area of the building. For teachers, teams provide a collaborative and supportive work group. For students of all abilities, this structure offers stable relationships with teachers and peers (A. Jackson & Davis, 2000). Of principals in middle-level schools, 79 percent report that they had teams in 2000, up from 57 percent in 1992 (NMSA, 2002; Valentine, Clark, Hackman, & Petzko, 2002). The team of teachers makes possible small communities of learners, which enhance personal relationships among students and teachers.

Practices such as these are recommended in middle schools for young adolescents, particularly those with disabilities, because they connect the content of the curriculum and the teaching strategies with the personal experiences of students. The ability of such connections to motivate students demonstrates in practice what brain research hypothesizes.

These strategies reflect the four action-dimensions of collaboration introduced earlier—collaboration as discovery, as synthesis of ideas, as development of practice, and as building professional community. The research of Kilgore, Griffin, Sindelar, and Webb (2001, 2002) suggests that inclusion of students with various learning needs is most likely to be accepted and supported by faculty and staff when schools alter traditional cultures, transform themselves into learning communities, and develop the capacity for continual professional growth (see also Senge, 1994; Wenger, McDermott, & Snyder, 2002).

COLLABORATION IN THE HIGH SCHOOL YEARS

High schools have many opportunities to serve youth better by expanding to include training in the competencies necessary for the development of the whole young person. If the scope of expectations for readiness continues to be limited to specific competencies that serve only college or the workplace, many youth will continue to struggle to make a successful transition to adulthood, and their full potential may not be realized (Lippmann et al., 2008).

Strategies for Serving Low-Income and Minority Students

Schools serving high percentages of low-income and minority students that use the career academies approach have been found to be effective in preparing students for successful school-to-work transitions without compromising academic goals and college preparation (Kemple, 2004). Three features distinguish these schools: (1) a school-within-a-school structure in which a team of teachers is linked with a group of students to create a small and personalized learning environment; (2) an integrated academic and vocational curriculum linked to the academy's occupational focus; and (3) the use of business partnerships in which employers assist in designing the academy program, provide workplace experiences, and offer summer or even permanent employment to some students. Additionally, mentoring programs are frequently cited as successful school-based interventions that can result in increased academic motivation, better school attendance, and reduced problem behavior (Dance, 2001; D. Martin, Martin, Gibson, & Wilkins, 2007; Whiting, 2006).

Students With Disabilities: Graduation and Diploma Options

For students with disabilities, graduating from high school is the key first step toward positive future outcomes. While high school graduation is an important milestone on the path to adulthood, the type of courses that students take during high school is also critical to later success. Additional coursework may be needed for students with disabilities so that they can develop skills and abilities that nondisabled students may already have. These critical skills and abilities include basic study skills; social skills, including interactions with teachers, authority figures, and peers; emotional and self-esteem skills; goal setting; the ability to understand strengths and weaknesses; self-help skills and habits that are needed in work and school settings, such as attendance and time management; and a knowledge of their rights as a people who have disabilities (Wehmeyer, 2007).

In addition to obtaining a high school diploma, there are several other pathways to success for students with learning disabilities. Transition planning services—particularly those that enable students to provide input into the decision-making process—are essential to the success of students with emotional and learning disabilities (Baer & Kochhar-Bryant, 2008). Students who take the lead in planning for their transition to college or work show greater responsibility for their lives beyond high school (P. Levine & Wagner, 2005). Participation in career-technical education is another pathway to successful transition to adulthood for students with special learning needs. Data from the National Longitudinal Transition Study show that students who took courses in an occupational area were more likely than those who only participated in academic work to get competitive employment after graduation and were also more likely to have jobs with higher earnings (Levine & Wagner).

The National Center on Education Outcomes (D. Johnson, Thurlow, & Stout, 2007) examined graduation requirements and diploma options for youth with disabilities and recommended the following:

- Clarify the assumptions underlying state graduation requirements and diploma options.
- Ensure that students with disabilities have an opportunity to learn the materials they will be tested on in state and local assessments.
- Make high school graduation decisions based on multiple indicators of students' learning and skills.
- Clarify the implications of developing and granting alternative diploma options for students with disabilities.

Through all of these studies, one theme resounds: Programs must be implemented to help high school youth with special learning needs to build relationships and build on their strengths so that they can succeed in school, work, and the world around them. A common strategy recommended is building relationships between youth and adults, such as teachers, mentors, tutors, or guidance counselors, who can help youth make a successful transition to post-secondary education and employment.

Collaboration for the Student Support Team

The success of the broad approach used by student assistance programs (SAPs, part of the federal Drug-Free Schools initiative) has demonstrated the value of collaboration within schools and between schools and school-linked agencies for at-risk youth. Within the SAP, the Student Support Team (SST) is a collaborative problem-solving process that is a hallmark of schools in most states. SSTs illustrate several functions of collaboration for the purposes of addressing the needs of the whole child. Their purpose is to find paths around roadblocks to academic and social success for any student referred for services. SSTs are the responsibility of both regular and special education professionals. Furthermore, most Section 504 requirements for IEPs can be met through SST documentation, as can requirements under NCLB and IDEIA for better teacher support and parent involvement. The SST process is designed around a problem-solving model that is used districtwide to help develop effective interventions to address and improve student learning and behavior at school. The SST also serves as the single portal of entry to determine the need for evaluation to assess eligibility for Section 504 accommodation plans or special education services.

WHAT IS A 504 PLAN?

The *504* in "504 plan" refers to Section 504 of the Rehabilitation Act and the Americans with Disabilities Act, which both protect people with disabilities from being excluded from participating in programs or activities that receive funding from the federal government. Such programs include elementary, secondary, or post-secondary schooling. The term *disability* means a "physical or mental impairment that substantially limits one or more major life activities" (ADA, 1990, § 12102[1][A]). A disability can include physical impairments; illnesses; injuries; communicable diseases; chronic conditions such as asthma, allergies, and diabetes; and learning disabilities. A 504 plan is a written plan that specifies the accommodations and modifications that are necessary for a student with a disability to perform at the level equal to his classmates. Examples of such accommodations include a wheelchair ramp, a tape recorder for taking notes, a double set of textbooks, blood sugar monitoring, an allergy-free environment or lunch menu, and in-home instruction.

Source: Mauro, n.d.

Membership in School Support Teams (SSTs) varies among schools, but teams typically consist of three to seven members. These may be an administrator, a counselor, a regular education teacher, a special education teacher, a school social worker, a parent, a media specialist, and a school psychologist or other specialist (e.g., English language learner specialist, reading specialist, or speech pathologist). When a classroom teacher or parent has a concern about a student's academic achievement, behavior, health, or social competence, either may seek the assistance of the Student Support Team.

The SST process helps teachers to develop interventions to assist the student. Specific areas of concern are identified; information is gathered through observation, interview, review of school records, and informal assessment. The SST develops new strategies to help address the concerns, and classroom teachers implement these strategies over a period of several weeks. The SST then reconvenes to assess the student's progress. For example, a teacher may implement a behavior contract for a child who has difficulty maintaining appropriate classroom behavior and completing classroom assignments. If the intervention is not successful, however, the SST may refer the student to the school's 504 Committee or the Special Education Team. Parents who have concerns about their child's academic achievement, behavior, health, or social competence should be encouraged to discuss their concerns with the classroom teachers first. Teachers and parents working together often establish informal strategies that successfully address concerns.

Use "Backward" Planning to Help High School Students Achieve Their Goals

The common characteristic of collaboration at the secondary level, along with a focus on academic progress, is an additional focus on achieving specific quality postschool outcomes (Turnbull, Turnbull, Wehmeyer, & Park, 2003). Therefore, planning at this level must "begin with the end in mind" and should use a process known as "backward planning" (Wiggins & McTighe, 2005). Backward planning uses future goals to identify future student performance needs. This process is therefore proactive and pragmatic. The focus is on developing the most direct route to postschool quality-of-life outcomes by using students' strengths and support systems (rather than developmental milestones) (Baer & Kochhar-Bryant, 2008).

Backward planning is important because it is based on the expectation that students can achieve their desired postschool outcomes through early planning and a team commitment to immediate action. Teachers, counselors, and transition coordinators develop a sense of urgency with regard to taking concrete action steps to help students prepare to achieve their post-secondary goals.

IEPs: Not Just for Students With Disabilities Anymore

Students without IEPs, but who need educational supports, benefit from personalized learning plans that address their specific area(s) of need. Nineteen states currently require what can be termed *individual learning plans* for identified students (Education Commission for the States, 2007). These policies include Arkansas's requirement that personal education plans be implemented for students identified as at risk for academic failure and New Mexico's requirement that identified eighth graders be retained or provided with a graduation plan. Additionally, Kentucky has introduced a Web-based program that will help students map out their academic careers and give them an idea of what vocational career path they'd like to explore—all while teaching them how to write a resume and apply for financial aid. Table 5.2 presents the 19 states and their requirements for individual learning plans.

Table 5.2   States Requiring Individual Learning Plans

Alabama	Yes, local boards are required to submit a plan for the provision of educational services to at-risk students. Local boards are required to budget at least $100 per at-risk student to be expended on tutorial assistance programs, including afterschool, Saturday school, summer school, or any combination of these programs.
Arkansas	Yes, students failing to demonstrate a proficient level of achievement are required to participate in individual academic improvement plans. Districts are required to implement personal education plans for students identified as at risk for academic failure.
Connecticut	Yes, local and regional boards of education are required to "identify a course of study for those students who have not successfully completed the assessment criteria to assist such students to reach a satisfactory level of competency prior to graduation."
Delaware	Yes, ninth graders who score at Level 1 or Level 2 on Delaware Student Testing Program reading or mathematics assessments must have an individual improvement plan. At a minimum, improvement plans must identify a specific course of study and the academic improvement activities that the student will undertake to help the student progress toward meeting the standards. (Appears in practice in ninth grade, although policy no longer includes ninth grade.)

(continued)

Table 5.2 (Continued)

Florida	Yes, students not meeting district or state requirements for proficiency in reading, mathematics, or science must be provided with an individualized progress monitoring plan to target instruction and identify ways to improve academic achievement.
Georgia	Yes, each high school is required to have at least one student support team and must establish policies providing for the following: • The identification of learning problems • Assessment, if necessary • An educational plan • Implementation • Follow-up and support • Continuous monitoring and evaluation
Indiana	Yes, parents of students who do not receive a passing score on the Indiana Statewide Testing for Educational Progress, (ISTEP) and/or ISTEP, must be notified, and a parent/teacher conference set up to discuss the student's scores and a proposed remediation plan.
Kentucky	Yes, extended day instructional programs (which must be offered to identified students) must include (1) a method to assess the priority educational needs of each individual student and to determine the academic expectations to be exhibited by the student at the end of the program; (2) an appropriate educational program designed for the individual student that assists the student in mastering the academic expectations within the timelines specified by the program; (3) an ongoing method of informal and formal assessment to document the student's progress toward mastery of the academic expectations; (4) a schedule of services, which shall be of the duration and regularity necessary to allow mastery of the academic expectations within a reasonable and projected timeline.
Louisiana	No. (Although students must be provided with 50 hours of instruction in the subject in which they failed to achieve proficiency on the Graduate Exit Exam.)
Michigan	Yes, each student failing to meet expectations for each standard on the Michigan Merit Examination must be provided with an individual report that will allow the student's parents and teachers to assess and remedy problems before the student moves to the next grade.
Minnesota	Yes, districts are required to develop a remediation plan for identified students.
Mississippi	Yes, intensive interventions specifically designed for individual students must be provided for students who have failed two grades or have been suspended or expelled for more than 20 days in the current school year.
New Mexico	Yes, students in the eighth grade failing to make adequate yearly progress are to be retained or provided with a graduation plan to meet their needs for entry into the workforce or a post-secondary educational institution.
North Carolina	Yes, students identified as being at high risk of failing or who fail competency tests must be provided with plans designed to meet their specific needs. Additionally, students who do not meet district promotion standards (which must include statewide accountability standards) must be provided with personalized education plans.

Oklahoma	Yes, required alternative education programs must be designed to serve secondary school students in Grades 6–12 who are most at risk of not completing high school. Programs must include the development of a plan leading to graduation for each student in the program that will allow the student to participate in graduation exercises for the school district after meeting the requirements of the school district as specified in the individual graduation plan for that student.
Texas	Yes, a personal graduation plan must be administered for each student who (1) doesn't perform satisfactorily on a Texas Assessment of Knowledge and Skills exit exam or (2) isn't likely to receive a high school diploma before the fifth school year following the student's enrollment in ninth grade, as determined by the district.
Virginia	Yes, each school division is required to record for each eligible student attending a state-funded remedial program (1) the state or local criteria used to determine eligibility, (2) the expected remediation goal for the student in terms of a target score on a locally designed or selected test that measures the Standards of Learning (SOL) content being remediated, and (3) whether the student did or did not meet the expected remediation goal.
Washington	Yes, individual student learning plans must be implemented for each student in Grades 8–12 who was unsuccessful in a Washington Assessment of Student Learning content area the previous year.
West Virginia	No. (Although school counselors are required to work with individual students in providing developmental, preventive, and remedial guidance and counseling programs to meet academic needs, including programs to identify and address the problem of potential school dropouts.)
Wisconsin	Yes, school boards are required to identify at-risk students enrolled in the district and annually develop a plan describing how the board will meet their needs.

Individualized learning plans are reported to increase student engagement with the curriculum material and improve students' ability to deal independently with problems as they arise. The teacher can shift his or her role to that of individual coach and progress monitor rather than deliverer of information and troubleshooter (see boxed text).

A TEACHER'S REFLECTION ON INDIVIDUAL LEARNING PLANS

The hardest change for me has been getting used to a new classroom dynamic where my control of the situation has to rely far more heavily on students being responsible for their own behavior and trusting that they will be. Previously a class that was working well had a quiet hum, and movement in the classroom felt organized and purposeful. However, this was not always the case with Year 8 French classes. Now, as I experiment with different ways of implementing project-based individual learning plans, it feels like chaos. It is much noisier, and at first glance, movement around the classroom seems social rather than learning centered. But when I really look and listen, I see individuals working on their project and getting up and consulting other students about things.

(continued)

(Continued)

I see a knot of students perched on a couple of tables discussing the TV show they are doing as a project, one of them making notes. Later I see them all copying the notes into their workbooks so they can meet the organizational requirements of the task. I see four or five students at the interactive whiteboard doing an interactive language quiz. One student is doing the quiz; the others are loudly calling out instructions to this student. Another student across the room has looked up from her work and is watching this intently. I also see the student who is always messing around doing just that with her buddy, so this is where I target a question about whether they need to see me about anything. They briefly discuss this; then one of them puts their names on the board for an appointment, and they return to their seats.

Previously students put up their hands for assistance or called me when they needed help. I moved around the room to the students. Now, they write their names on the board, and I tend to stay in one spot with the laptop and my record book, where I have all their details, etc. They come to me, have a brief tutorial to address a situation, and go back to their tables. A big group usually sends a delegate or two to ask language or procedural questions, then the delegate returns to the table and teaches the others.

I sit at the side of the room rather than at the front. I can scan the room and see what's happening without intruding upon the situation. Removing myself from the prime position—at the front, controlling the information and the whiteboard—has had positive benefits, such as students seeing the actual project requirements as the controlling force in their work. For example, I am hearing more often now "It says I have to . . ." rather than "You said I have to . . ." Depersonalizing the control mechanism of the situation means that I am in a better personal position to sit beside someone and help them. I am a resource (and a pretty good one)!

Recommendations for the High School Years

Professionals collaborate to make high school more challenging and meaningful to students in the following ways.

- *Personalize learning.* Enable students, teachers, and parents to develop a learning plan and graduation pathway that ensures each child graduates while meeting high standards.
- *Make it relevant.* Show students the real-world applications of their education through different lessons outside the school building. For example, they might learn about music in a music store or by doing an internship with a local musician or band. Teach the importance of chemistry and photosynthesis by spending one day a week at a working farm. Just because it's learning doesn't mean it can't be fun!
- *Provide mentors and meaningful relationships.* Research consistently demonstrates that kids do better in school and remain engaged if they have a good relationship with at least one adult in the building. These relationships include academics but go beyond if necessary to offer students assistance and insight into situations outside the classroom.
- *Give teachers flexibility.* Teachers need flexibility to work differently and freedom to design exciting and innovative lessons. They also need options to expand their own education. Empower and invigorate teachers with opportunities for new approaches and ideas so that they can ensure high academic achievement for all of their students (Lippman et al., 2008).

The case example describes one high school, Swain County High School, that used a variety of collaborative strategies to meet its students' needs, leverage their strengths, and enable them to succeed in school and beyond.

SCHOOL REFORM IS A CONTINUOUS PROCESS

One School's Journey From School Failure to Student Success

Swain High illuminates a central fact of school reform: it is a continuous process that requires persistent pursuit of excellence guided by a core set of values. When the Southern Governors' Association (SGA) teams visited Swain in May 2004, Principal Janet Clapsaddle, teachers, and counselors talked proudly of the school's journey dating back to the mid-1980s. Administrators and faculty began the journey with an honest, data-driven evaluation of their own school. They found a high dropout rate, a low college entrance rate, academic courses taught in isolation, undemanding vocational classes, and the "middle 50 percent of students" feeling neglected and not even considering post-secondary education. Over more than a decade, Swain has been guided by what it calls its "key practices." These touchstones include higher expectations of students, more rigorous career-technical studies, upgrading of academic studies, integration of studies, active engagement of students, and guidance and advising that involves not just the counselor but all the faculty.

The following list itemizes several of the best practices, as well as state and district policies, that the SGA teams identified as a result of their visit to Swain County High School:

- *Data-driven decision making is a central feature of school operations.*
- *State and district policies on assessment allow school administrators to benchmark their progress against other schools and to implement a system that provides schools with test data in a timely manner.*
- *School benefits from state supplemental funding of "low-wealth" schools and from federal funding to offset lack of local tax base as a result of national park in county.*
- *State policy also provides for suspending of drivers' licenses for failure to pass coursework.*
- *A positive, nonaggressive school climate focuses on academic achievement.*
- *High-quality teachers are recruited through a system of interviews in March, with contracts offered in April.*
- *Teachers are paid for six hours of credit per year toward advanced degrees.*
- *Teacher-leaders meet during the summer for two days to examine results from state tests and other assignments, to identify trends and patterns in need of improvement, and to identify low-performing students in need of special services.*
- *Team leaders meet with teachers and develop strategies for academic departments and teachers.*
- *The school emphasizes a collaborative "team" approach to teaching across disciplines, often combining academic and applied learning in a 90-minute class presided over by two teachers (e.g., combining geometry with drafting, technology with math).*
- *Literacy instruction flows across the curriculum. Ninth grade students get a double dose of English and grammar. English, science, and business teachers work together to teach students how to do research papers.*
- *The school district provides flexibility to school administrators so they can experiment and find better ways to do their work.*
- *School leaders have developed a strong relationship with the local community college and nearby university that results in more than half of Swain's seniors completing courses for which they earn post-secondary credit.*
- *All students are expected to complete either a college preparatory or career/technical program of study that prepares them for post-secondary study.*
- *The school has increased its graduation requirements from 20 Carnegie units in 1990 to 28 in 2004, with students earning a possible 32 units.*
- *The school has developed an outstanding guidance and advisement system in which each student and his or her parent works with a school representative to develop a plan of high school study leading to further learning. Each teacher also works as a mentor to approximately 15 students throughout all four years of high school.*

Source: Developmental Perspective on College & Workplace Readiness. "School Reform is a Continuous Process: One School's Journey From School Failure to Student Success." *New traditions: Options for rural high school excellence.* Southern Governors' Association. (2004), p. 14.

Coordinated Planning for Transition to Post-Secondary Settings

The Individuals with Disabilities Education Improvement Act provides a framework for a systematic, cumulative, and long-range transition-planning and decision-making process, which is becoming a model not just for students with disabilities but for all students in some schools. IDEA Amendments redefined *transition services* as a

coordinated set of activities aimed at a specific student outcome (e.g., employment enrollment in college); activities which promote the movement of a student from school to post-school activities which may include post-secondary education, career technical training, integrated employment (including supported employment), continuing and adult education, adult services, independent living, or community participation" (§ 1401[34][A]).

This coordinated set of activities must (a) be based on the individual student's strengths, preferences, and interests and (b) include needed activities in the areas of instruction, community experiences, the development of employment and other postschool adult living objectives, and, if appropriate, daily living skills and functional vocational evaluation.

The word *coordinated* is the only reference—and an oblique one—to a systematic approach to transition. The term was first defined in the regulations for the IDEA of 1990 to mean both "(1) the linkage between each of the component activities that comprise transition services, and (2) the interrelationship between the various agencies that are involved in the provision of transition services to a student" (Assistance to States for the Education of Children with Disabilities Program and Preschool Grants for Children with Disabilities: Final Regulations, 1992). Thus, the various support and transition activities must complement and be coordinated with each other, and the different agencies responsible for providing the services must do the same, making sure that the services they provide to the student meet, in a coordinated, nonduplicating fashion, his or her transition needs. Because the transition process relies on the involvement of many individuals and many service providers, this coordination of effort is essential. Transition viewed as a systematic, individualized process that incorporates a coordinated set of activities

- is a continuous process through transition from middle school and through high school.
- incorporates a coordination strategy that provides continuity of planning and links each student with a transition coordinator, counselor, or ombudsman.
- considers students' anticipated post-secondary goals.
- is a long-range planning and decision-making framework for students and families that addresses a variety of domains of education and life preparation.
- addresses curriculum options, including participation in the general education curriculum, career-technical, community-based learning, nonacademic learning activities, and standardized assessments.
- incorporates related and supportive services (opportunities) identified by students, parents, and professionals.
- incorporates the coordination of appropriate community-based and adult service agencies, vocational rehabilitation, health and mental health agencies, post-secondary institutions, and employment development services.

Transition planning is foundational for the IEP-planning process. Long-term transition planning provides an overarching framework that guides the development of the

IEP and provides continuity throughout the process regarding the immediate and long-term future of the student (Kochhar-Bryant & Bassett, 2003). It is a blueprint for direction setting and for constructing a plan that is aimed at high school diploma and exit goals most appropriate for the individual. The transition plan is vital to accessing and progressing in the secondary education curriculum because it defines specific needs and services in regard to the secondary curriculum and associated assessments, services, and supports. While IDEIA 2004 initiates transition once again at age 16, many states are choosing to continue their practices (begun under IDEA 1997) to initiate planning when the student turns 14.

TEN PRINCIPLES FOR SUCCESSFUL COLLABORATION AND COORDINATION

Successful collaboration begins with the adoption of a common set of principles that can serve as an anchor and guide for building a collaborative culture in schools. Based on evidence from theory and research, the following 10 principles have been defined. They can be applied in the development and evaluation of both intraschool and interagency collaboration and coordination practices.

Principle 1. Collaboration and system coordination are long-term developmental processes that impact students' ability to achieve their maximum level of potential. Some students require short-term support in education and community settings and during periods of transition from one setting to another. Others require extended support services or intermittent intensive support services. Effective collaboration for educational planning and support is flexible and designed to assist the student to develop as fully as possible in all areas of functioning—academic, social-emotional, language, and physical. School and school-linked agency personnel also work together to strengthen the service system. For example, efforts to improve K–12 education for students depend on engaging related services within the school, such as speech and audiology, counseling, psychological services, social work services, and medical diagnostic services.

Principle 2. Collaboration and system coordination initiatives are interventions to achieve change in relationships, processes, services, institutions, or systems. Expected results must be clearly defined for these interventions, and outcomes must be evaluated and communicated to all professionals and consumers affected. Federal and state education laws now require collaboration within schools, as well as interagency agreements between schools and community service agencies, to provide needed services for students as required by their IEPs. In most communities, however, collaboration and interagency linkages are still largely informal and voluntary collaborations. Although collaboration may be mandated, its results cannot be, because collaboration and coordination depend upon local processes and the will and abilities of people to work cooperatively (Hagebak, 1992; Slater, 2004). The intended student outcomes must be clearly specified and interagency resources focused to achieve those outcomes.

Principle 3. Planning for collaboration and system coordination initiatives is vital to their strength and sustainability. While many collaborative initiatives spring up in response to crises or sudden changes (as illustrated in the Brookville example), an organized planning process should be established as soon as possible to provide a "rudder" for navigating the change process.

Planning also involves assessing the readiness of people or groups for collaboration or coordination by asking several guiding questions. What is the goal or mission for our collaboration? What are the expected results and how will they be measured? What do the participants (or participating school units or agencies) bring to the relationship in terms of resources, missions, and philosophies? What is the extent of their knowledge, skills, and attitudes about collaboration and about the population of students being served? What combination of people could help to address the goals of collaboration and coordination? Planning that is focused by such guiding questions joins people strategically and leads to sustainable change.

Principle 4. Collaboration must engage all the people who will be affected by the change process. The success of any collaboration or coordination effort will depend on the ability of the planning team to create a supportive community environment and involve all stakeholders in decision making.

Principle 5. Collaboration initiatives can start small and can emerge from any part of a system. As discussed earlier, human systems involve complex relationships and interdependent groups of people who work together for common aims. Change in human systems does not develop in a tidy, linear, step-by-step fashion; rather, it is often messy, unstable, and unpredictable. A collaboration for change that emerges in one part of the system can trigger a larger change process across the whole system.

Principle 6. Student- and family-centered collaboration and coordination promote the self-determination and engagement of the student and family. Effective collaboration promotes the student's and family's ability to make decisions (i.e., self-determination) in planning for education and support services. Collaboration and system coordination activities strengthen or reinforce self-help and informal support networks, which may include the student's parents, siblings, and extended family.

Principle 7. The effectiveness and sustainability of collaboration and system coordination are based on the level of commitment people have to the process. This principle may seem like a platitude, but if a school or organization attempts systemic change without clear commitment from the people being affected, the change is not likely to last. Collaboration among people of different professional roles, disciplines, beliefs, and attitudes is a complex undertaking even under the best of circumstances. Systemic change is not likely to occur if the leader, the principal, or the administrator alone is committed. Nor can it be successful if only some of the people have a clear picture of what needs to be accomplished.

Principle 8. The effectiveness and sustainability of collaboration and system coordination depend on how professionally prepared people are to participate. Along with commitment, professional preparation is vital to the effectiveness of collaboration. The ability to collaborate effectively with others is not innate but rather involves a complex repertoire of skills that must be modeled and learned. That repertoire includes knowledge of the underlying foundational ideas and principles related to collaboration, skills to participate effectively and facilitate collaboration, and the dispositions (beliefs, attitudes, and ethics) that are essential to effective practice in collaboration and coordination.

Principle 9. The environment for collaboration influences its potential. Many aspects of the local environment can either support or undermine the effectiveness of collaboration or system coordination. A supportive environment for collaboration or system coordination is one in which there is dedicated leadership for the initiative and a focus on the outcomes and benefits of the collaboration for students and families. In addition, there are adequate resources, sufficient technical assistance and support, formal agreements where needed, and a quality review and evaluation process.

Principle 10. Early defeat in an attempt to collaborate does not necessarily mean long-term failure; such initiatives often lie dormant and rise again when conditions change. In any system, a collaborative initiative, once begun, is hard to suppress. Once a collaborative relationship is brought to life and a small core of "champions" or leaders has emerged who are invested in it, it will find a way to express itself. The boxed text, based on a true story, illustrates principle 10.

COLLABORATION FOR HIGH SCHOOL TRANSITION

A Window Opens Somewhere...

Representatives of three agencies met with excitement to talk about cooperation among the Ames Public School District; the Community Services Agency (CSA), which was the mental health and substance abuse services system; and the One-Stop Career Center. The representative of the Community Service Agency initiated and hosted the meeting. The goal was to draft the very first cooperative agreement among the three agencies to improve access to and coordination of services for youth with disabilities exiting the school system who needed adult services and One-Stop services. The initiative would be led by the CSA with the school district and rehabilitation agency as equal partners. After several meetings, a cooperative agreement was crafted and the "pioneer" team was feeling very pleased with its work. The agreement was presented to the director of the CSA, who praised the initiative but did not approve the agreement. It was "dead on arrival."

The team was extremely discouraged and asked for an explanation for the decision. The CSA director explained that it was not considered within the scope of the CSA to be the lead agency in initiating and managing such an agreement with the school system and it would require additional resources that the CSA did not have. The team believed the decision was very short-sighted but was forced to disband. However, after one year, the team member from the Ames School District dusted off the agreement and carried it forward, creating a public school-initiated agreement with the One-Stop and CSA. The CSA signed on this time, since the school system would take the lead and manage it.

This story began over 25 years ago. The interagency agreement has been sustained and strengthened and is now a nationally known interagency collaborative that expanded statewide and has served as a model for other states. While the original pioneer of the interagency agreement at the CSA may feel wistful that she will never be recognized for her initial leadership, she learned that when a door closes on an initiative in one part of the system, often a window opens up somewhere else.

SUMMARY OF KEY POINTS

- The concepts of collaboration and coordination are not simply pleasing abstractions—they represent effective practices that affect student outcomes.
- *Collaboration* is generally defined as a process of participation through which people, groups, and organizations form relationships and work together to achieve a set of agreed-upon results.
- Strategic collaboration involves a purposeful effort to change how people work together, how they perform their roles, and how the environment supports their goals.

- Expectations for collaborative practices are a centerpiece of the No Child Left Behind Act of 2001, the Safe and Drug Free Schools Act, the Individuals With Disabilities Education Improvement Act of 2004, and related education and disability laws.
- A positive youth development framework views youth with the glass half full—seeing what can go right with youth rather than what can go wrong. It is more productive to understand what kinds of attitudes and behaviors might promote thriving and optimal development than to focus on deterring antisocial development.
- Collaboration and coordination among teachers, administrators, parents, and community agency personnel are arguably the most important factors in the success or failure of educational programs aimed at meeting the needs of the whole child.
- The Brookville High School case study illustrates that collaboration for change typically does not develop in a tidy, step-by-step linear fashion. Instead, it was messy, complex, and unpredictable.
- The success of the broad approach used by student assistance programs (SAPs, which are part of the federal Drug-Free Schools initiative) has demonstrated the value of collaboration within schools and between schools and school-linked agencies.
- Collaboration is a developmental process; each stage in the process represents an increasingly closer collaborative relationship among professionals and includes sharing information, discussing adaptations and modifications, providing supports in the classroom, sharing instruction, and co-instruction.
- Many states are introducing individualized learning plans for all students, not just those with disabilities.

KEY TERMS AND PHRASES

- Collaboration
- Consultation
- Developmental continuum
- System coordination
- General system theory
- Student support team model
- Strategic collaboration

- Developmental aspects of collaboration
- Communities of practice
- Collaboration for transition
- Positive behavioral intervention
- Coordinated planning
- Action-dimensions of collaboration

6

What Is the Role of Community Agencies?

What we know about the individuals, no matter how rich the details, will never give us the ability to predict how they will behave as a system. Once individuals link together they become something different. . . . Relationships change us, reveal us, evoke more from us. Only when we join with others do our gifts become visible, even to ourselves.

—Wheatley & Kellner-Rogers, 1999, p. 67

CHAPTER TOPICS

- How do Coordinated Services Support Developmentally Responsive School Environments?
- Which Community Agencies Should Be Engaged With Schools?
- How Do Schools and Community Agencies Work Together?
- How Do Schools and Community Agencies Coordinate for Youth Placed at Risk?
- How Is an Interagency Agreement Developed?
- What Is the Role of the Local Interagency Planning Council?

INTRODUCTION

It has long been recognized that schools alone cannot provide all the services that children with disabilities and their families need. As discussed in Chapter 1, the idea of shared responsibility for a community's children has recently become a watchword for educators and human service personnel. The notion of shared responsibility implies working across agency boundaries to create a well-coordinated service system to meet the holistic needs of students. Coordination means connecting people within systems and requires extraordinary commitment to accomplish.

This chapter explores the role of community agencies and presents strategies for coordinating services between schools and community agencies to support the development of the whole child. The chapter also discusses practical issues associated with building a local coordinated system, including interagency agreements and preparation of service coordinators. Finally, the chapter explores new directions in the use of interagency agreements for school improvement.

Over the past few decades, the benefits of interagency service coordination in systems such as health care, mental health, rehabilitation, and adult disability services have caught the attention of educators and education policy makers. Because of the growing population of children who are placed at risk in schools and communities, interest is growing in linking the educational system and the community-based human service system to provide comprehensive and seamless structure of services and supports for children and their families (Dunst & Bruder, 2002; Kendziora, Bruns, Osher, Pacchiona, & Mejia, 2001; National Center on Outcomes Research, 2001; Research and Training Center on Service Coordination, 2001; U.S. Department of Education, 2003; U.S. GAO, 2004; Whelley, Hart, & Zafft, 2002). Such an approach requires that schools reach out beyond their boundaries and seek shared responsibility with the many agencies that provide services for students.

HOW DO COORDINATED SERVICES SUPPORT DEVELOPMENTALLY RESPONSIVE SCHOOL ENVIRONMENTS?

A systematic approach to interagency service coordination means developing strategies to address the complex needs of children and youth in an organized and coordinated manner to support healthy development and academic success. A *coordinated interagency service system* is defined as a systematic, comprehensive, and coordinated system of support services in primary or secondary education that allows students placed at risk and students with disabilities to receive services in the most integrated settings possible and in a manner that promotes individual choice and decision making (Kochhar-Bryant, 2008). *Interagency service coordination* may also be defined as a strategy for mobilizing and organizing all of the appropriate resources to link the student and family with needed services to achieve individual goals and successful long-term outcomes.

What Is a Coordinated System?

Recently, educators and human service leaders have come to recognize that successful collaboration requires much more than collaboration among professionals within the school environment. Rather, it involves a wider collaboration among schools, local and state human service agencies, and a wide range of community public and private agencies that are concerned with children and youth. The term *system coordination* builds on earlier terms that emerged in the fields of health, mental health, mental retardation, and rehabilitation in the 1960s—*case management* and *interagency coordination*. More than two decades ago, Bachrach (1986) defined *case management* within the mental health discipline as

the integration of services on the patient level. . . . Someone in the system is taking charge and seeing to it that all the little bits and pieces of the fragmented service system begin to come together in some coherent way for the chronically mentally ill individual. It embodies the concepts of continuity and comprehensiveness in a personalized manner. (p. 174)

In education and human services, a *systematic approach* means developing goals, activities, and approaches in an organized and coordinated manner to address the complex developmental and support needs of children and youth. The student who is placed at risk by life circumstances is viewed as having complex and interconnected needs that require coordinated responses from multiple service agencies (e.g., the school, mental health, family services, public health services, social services, juvenile services, and/or legal services). The underlying principle of system coordination is that the individual remains at the center and must be **self-determined,** or exercises as much personal decision making in planning for graduation and adult life as is possible.

A Framework for Defining System Coordination

The term *coordinated services* refers to the delivery of services across systems to address the holistic (whole-person) needs of students. Students in need of special education services are typically also in need of mental health services, social services, or other human services. When families seek services from two or more agencies with different eligibility requirements, a mechanism for connecting these families with the agencies is essential. School–community partnerships can facilitate coordinated services by serving as liaisons between families and service providing agencies (Bonner-Tompkins, 2000).

Interagency partnerships and agreements are relationships that involve the school and at least one other agency that coordinate for a common purpose. To meet the variety of educational and support needs of students, schools must coordinate with a broad range of service agencies and professionals to create connected and supportive systems within the school and between school and community. This means that each part of the system is dedicated to ensuring that each child, from early intervention through transition from high school, is connected with the services he or she needs along the way. Each professional or agency in a system is dedicated to contributing to the well-being and development of children with disabilities and their families as they respond to their changing needs and the changing educational environment. The definition of system coordination reflects four assumptions:

1. Interagency relationships are formalized in *written cooperative agreements* in which the role of the agencies and professionals are made clear.

2. Interagency relationships are *dynamic and responsive to changes* in the needs of children and families and in the service environment.

3. Interagency relationships are *continuous* throughout the course of the child's educational journey from early childhood through to high school graduation.

4. The system relationships should result in *goals and strategies* that systematically address the problems and priority needs of persons being served by the system.

A synthesis of the literature (Kochhar-Bryant, 2002) on planning for educational services for students placed at risk and those with disabilities shows that a coordinated system has several important elements.

- *A formal, long-range interagency plan for a system of education and support services* for students in integrated settings, from early intervention through post-secondary transition.
- *Special supports for the critical passages,* or transitions, between educational settings, such as from early intervention to preschool, elementary to middle school, and high school to post-secondary education.
- A *statewide system of personnel development* to prepare teachers and support personnel to work within a coordinated interagency system of services, which includes preservice preparation and continuing (inservice) preparation of educators and the training of parents.
- *Innovative cooperative partnerships* among public schools, related service agencies, area colleges and universities, private service providers, and parents to achieve common goals for including students who are placed at risk and students with disabilities into mainstream education.
- *Ongoing evaluation* of system coordination efforts and student outcomes (Benz, Lindstom & Yovanoff, 2002; National Center on Outcomes Research, 2001; U.S. GAO, 2003).

Service system coordination is a cornerstone in the educational success of students and families. A coordinated interagency service system is both an ideal and a strategy. The general goal of service coordination is to ensure that students with complex, multiple needs receive education and support services in a manner that is timely, appropriate, accessible, comprehensive, and flexible.

How Do Coordinated Services Address the Whole Child?

In today's education policy environment, there is little question that the primary emphasis in schools is on the cognitive domain as measured by student performance on standardized tests (Blank & Berg, 2006). With the recent focus on academic achievement, attention to other developmental domains that make up the whole child has been diminished. In 2006, the Association for Supervision and Curriculum Development (ASCD) commissioned *All Together Now: Sharing Responsibility for the Whole Child* (Blank & Berg) as a resource document for the Commission on the Whole Child. Blank and Berg urged the Commission to identify and adopt a unifying framework that would respond to research on the conditions that promote the development of the whole child. Organizations that focus on youth development and education have begun to build frameworks that incorporate these factors. These frameworks are remarkably similar in their focus and are guided by an abundance of authoritative research on the development of the whole child. For example, the National Research Council and the Institute of Medicine identified eight features of positive developmental settings:

1. Physical and physiological safety
2. Appropriate structure
3. Supportive relationships
4. Opportunities to belong
5. Positive social norms
6. Support for efficacy and mattering
7. Opportunities for skill building
8. Integration of family, school, and community efforts (Blank, Melaville, & Shah, 2003)

The Learning First Alliance (2001) cites physical and psychological safety, a challenging and engaging curriculum, a sense of belonging and connection to others, and reassurance by others of capability and worth as key factors to development. The central theme of this action plan is that every school must make the creation of a safe and supportive learning community one of its highest priorities. Each of the four components of this phrase—safe, supportive, learning, community—is crucial (see Figure 6.1).

Figure 6.1   Core Elements and Outcomes of Safe and Supportive Learning Communities

A supportive learning community includes the following:

1. A challenging and engaging curriculum for all students

2. Respectful, supportive relationships among and between students, school staff, and parents

3. Frequent opportunities for student participation, collaboration, service, and self-direction

4. A physical plant that promotes safety and community

5. Systematic approaches to supporting safety and positive behavior, including

   o schoolwide approaches to climate, safety, and discipline;

   o orderly and focused classrooms; and

   o a continuum of supports for the few students who need them.

6. Involvement of family, students, school staff, and the surrounding community

7. Standards and measures to support continuous improvement based on data

The essential question that Blank and Berg (2006) and other leaders of the whole-child movement are asking is this: Who is responsible for creating the conditions for learning? Schools? Families? Communities? The Commission on the Whole Child answered the question this way:

> Schools, families, and communities must work together to get the results that we all want for our nation's children. By bringing together the assets and resources of communities and families at schools to help support students, while ensuring that the school sees the community as an important partner and resource, we can truly develop and nurture the whole child. (Blank & Berg, 2006, p. 11)

Centers for Disease Control and Prevention: Eight Components of a Coordinated School Health Program

As mentioned in Chapter 2, because a healthy school is a vital part of a healthy community, a commitment to successful collaboration is required from school administrators, staff, students, parents, and the community. Effective coordinated school health programs are based on the eight-component model developed by the Centers for Disease Control and Prevention (CDC; 2008) to encourage lifelong healthful behaviors that contribute to productive citizens. Schools by themselves cannot, and should not, be expected to solve the nation's most serious health and social problems. Families, health care workers, the media, religious organizations, community organizations that serve youth, and young people themselves also must be systematically involved. However, schools can provide a central facility in which many agencies might work together to maintain the well-being of young people (CDC). Following are descriptions of the eight interactive components.

1. *Health education:* A planned, sequential, K–12 curriculum addresses the physical, mental, emotional, and social dimensions of health. The curriculum is designed to motivate and assist students to maintain and improve their health, prevent disease, and reduce health-related risk behaviors. It allows students to develop and demonstrate increasingly sophisticated health-related knowledge, attitudes, skills, and practices. The comprehensive health education curriculum includes a variety of topics such as personal health, family health, community health, consumer health, environmental health, sexuality education, mental and emotional health, injury prevention and safety, nutrition, prevention and control of disease, and substance use and abuse. Qualified, trained teachers provide health education.

2. *Physical education:* A planned, sequential K–12 curriculum provides cognitive content and learning experiences in a variety of activity areas such as basic movement skills; physical fitness; rhythms and dance; games; team, dual, and individual sports; tumbling and gymnastics; and aquatics. Quality physical education should promote, through a variety of planned physical activities, each student's optimum physical, mental, emotional, and social development, and it should promote activities and sports that all students enjoy and can pursue throughout their lives. Qualified, trained teachers teach physical activity.

3. *Health services:* Services are provided to appraise, protect, and promote students' health. These services are designed to ensure access or referral to primary health care services or both; foster appropriate use of primary health care services; prevent and control communicable disease and other health problems; provide emergency care for illness or injury; promote and provide optimum sanitary conditions for a safe school facility and school environment; and provide educational and counseling opportunities for promoting and maintaining individual, family, and community health. Qualified professionals such as physicians, nurses, dentists, health educators, and other allied health personnel provide these services.

4. *Nutrition services:* Access to a variety of nutritious and appealing meals accommodates the health and nutrition needs of all students. School nutrition programs reflect the U.S. Dietary Guidelines for Americans (DHHS, 2005) and other criteria to achieve nutritional integrity. The school nutrition services offer students a learning laboratory for classroom nutrition and health education and serve as a resource for linkages with nutrition-related community services. Qualified child nutrition professionals provide these services.

5. *Counseling and psychological services:* Services are provided to improve students' mental, emotional, and social health. These services include individual and group assessments, interventions, and referrals. Organizational assessment and consultation skills of counselors and psychologists contribute not only to the health of students but also to the health of the school environment. Professionals such as certified school counselors, psychologists, and social workers provide these services.

6. *Healthy school environment:* The physical and aesthetic surroundings and the psychosocial climate and culture of the school are conducive to student health. Factors that comprise the physical environment include the school building and the area surrounding it; any biological or chemical agents that are detrimental to health; and physical conditions such as temperature, noise, and lighting. The psychological environment includes the physical, emotional, and social conditions that affect the well-being of students and staff.

7. *Health promotion for staff:* Opportunities are provided for school staff to improve their health status through activities such as health assessments, health education, and health-related fitness activities. These opportunities encourage school staff to pursue a healthy lifestyle that contributes to their improved health status, improved morale, and a greater personal commitment to the school's overall coordinated health program. This personal commitment often translates into greater commitment to the health of students and creates positive role models. Health promotion activities have improved productivity, decreased absenteeism, and reduced health insurance costs.

8. *Family/community involvement:* An integrated school, parent, and community approach enhances the health and well-being of students. School health advisory councils, coalitions, and broadly based constituencies for school health can build support for school health program efforts. Schools actively solicit parent involvement and engage community resources and services to respond more effectively to the health-related needs of students (CDC, 2008).

WHICH COMMUNITY AGENCIES SHOULD BE ENGAGED WITH SCHOOLS?

Schools across the nation are establishing relationships with community service agencies in an effort to address the wide range of developmental needs of students and their families. Schools can serve as a hub for the delivery of services that complement and support education. Implementation of school-linked services, however, is a complex endeavor requiring the development of collaborative partnerships connecting schools, service agencies, families, and the community. To support coordinated service efforts and improve outcomes for students and families, schools must make many important changes as part of a comprehensive school restructuring effort.

What School-Linked Services Might Community Agencies Provide?

As mentioned in Chapter 3, schools traditionally have provided some health and social services such as vision and hearing screenings, immunizations, and school lunches. However, recent initiatives to link schools and community agencies are aimed at broadening these programs by establishing partnerships with a broader range of service agencies. Examples of these services include the following:

- Mental health services
- Counseling
- Substance-abuse programs
- Teen pregnancy programs
- Dropout prevention
- Health care

- Dental care
- Child abuse programs
- Gang diversion programs
- Conflict resolution programs
- Literacy training
- Job training
- Tutoring and remedial education
- Mentoring
- After- and before-school care
- Parenting education
- Programs for homeless youth

Integrated services are school linked when these services are available at a school or a nearby site in close partnership with a school. The school itself serves as the link between the service delivery system and families. In a school-linked approach to integrating services for children, (a) services are provided to children and their families through a collaboration among schools, health care providers, and social services agencies; (b) the schools are among the central participants in planning and governing the collaborative effort; and (c) the services are provided at, or are coordinated by, personnel located at the school or a site near the school. Most often, the school-linked approach requires agencies that typically provide health and social services off the school site to move some of their staff and/or services to the school.

A school's decision to provide school-linked services, however, will be successful only if it is part of a larger restructuring effort (Volpe et al., 1999). Over 15 years ago, Jehl and Kirst (1992) commented:

> Just as there cannot be effective school restructuring without school-linked services, there cannot be effective school-linked services without school restructuring. The earlier practice—"adding on" social or health services without changing the way the school interacts with families and community agencies—will not work. (pp. 98–99)

When a school restructures to make services available to its students and families, it makes basic changes in the way it operates. The school takes steps to reach out to the community and becomes a hub for providing services so that each service provider is not trying to work alone. Examples of such operational changes that promote coordinated services include the following:

- The school building is used by community agencies to provide easier access for clients and may remain open when school is not in session.
- The services provided by community agencies become an integral part of the educational opportunities that the school offers students and families, and educators and service providers work together in teams rather than in isolation.
- Administrators are active within the community and become catalysts for partnership development.
- Teachers are familiar with available services in the school and community and are comfortable recommending them to students and families.
- Professional development time is used to help teachers learn about community services, the referral process, and practical applications for families (e.g., teachers can learn about literacy programs available for parents and how they can work with parents to improve learning opportunities for children).

In a "full-service" school, there is a sense that everyone is works together to address the needs of the whole child.

HOW DO SCHOOLS AND COMMUNITY AGENCIES WORK TOGETHER?

What Does a Service Coordinator Do?

Service coordinators provide the link between the academic and developmental needs of students and families and appropriate services in the school and community. Service coordinators facilitate the efficient and effective use of resources. They provide a single contact, or single point of entry, into the broader service system within and outside the school for students and their families. A service coordinator (often referred to as a *case manager*) facilitates a service plan or the IEP (if the student is receiving special education) by linking the student and his or her family with the needed services within and outside the school. The coordinator identifies the role of each provider and coordinates all needed services. The student and family can expect the coordinator to provide the following services:

- Meet with the student and family on a regular basis and include the student and family in all aspects of planning services to meet needs.
- Ensure that service providers identified in the student's plan are of high quality and are the best match for the student and family.
- Work with service providers to ensure that the student and family can access the services and help resolve problems with service providers.
- Assist in obtaining and maintaining all services that the student is entitled to under the law.

Service coordinators also assess the needs of the child and family; broker the needed services; and act as liaisons between district staff, classroom teachers, other school staff, and parents. They facilitate school-based team meetings, IEP team meetings, and other collaborative meetings and maintain records and facilitate smooth transitions between school levels. They determine eligibility for services, provide monitoring and tracking of services, and advocate for families and for greater service availability.

The coordinator's role is dynamic—that of advocate, mentor, and coordinator of a spectrum of services. As a student's needs change, the service coordinator notes these changes and adjusts the mix of services as necessary. For example, a coordinator at the elementary level may recommend tutoring for a child with learning difficulties in the general education classroom, but in middle school, the student may be referred for counseling and family support.

Effective service coordinators are well trained and know the community, individuals, and families whom they serve. They are competent, sensitive, and committed to representing the interests and preferences of the individual and/or family. They provide reliable information, help students and families explore options, and coach students and families and guide them to make informed decisions about services and supports. Finally, they assist in the coordination of service providers in a manner that strengthens the informal resources (family, friends, neighbors, place of worship) and ensures the participation of students in defining personal goals for the future (T. Jackson, 2003).

What Are the Eight Essential Functions of Service Coordination?

This section defines the essential elements or functions of service system coordination in the educational continuum. A synthesis of over three decades of literature (1970–2005) by this author resulted in a set of eight categories by which system coordination activities can be categorized. These categories represent eight basic functions that are performed by schools and school-linked agencies to provide services to students and families (Kochhar-Bryant, 2008). They include the following:

1. Information and referral

2. Identification and preparation

3. Needs assessment

4. Individual program planning

5. Service coordination and linking

6. Service monitoring and follow-along

7. Individual and interagency advocacy

8. Evaluation and follow-up

These functions operate at both the individual and system levels. They are discussed separately in the following sections.

Function 1: Information and Referral. Information and referral activities vary widely among schools and service agencies and are defined either (a) narrowly, as information giving to the public and the referral of youth and families to agency services for which they are eligible, or (b) broadly, with extensive outreach activities, aggressive parent and community education, and interagency case-finding activities to identify different groups of individuals needing services. Information and referral activities include the following:

- Outreach to eligible in-school students or those in alternative educational placements who are not currently benefiting from related and supportive services
- Distribution of information to students and families about community resources and how to access them
- Development of a single point of entry or contact for services
- Decreasing the amount of time between initial contact and entry into services or programs.

Improved outreach and identification of eligible target groups of students increases the likelihood that needed services reach the students who need them.

Function 2: Identification and Preparation. Identification and preparation involve procedures for matching individual service requests with appropriate supportive agencies. Identification and preparation activities may include the following:

- Creating a reliable system database on students identified and served
- Developing criteria for early evaluation and diagnosis of the disability or learning need
- Making services accessible in terms of physical access, hours of operation, transportation, and cost
- Obtaining and documenting informed consent
- Involving families in early planning

Function 3: Needs Assessment. Needs assessment is a process by which diagnostic evaluation and general information is collected, analyzed, and interpreted among the service coordinator, student, family, teachers, and other relevant personnel. A needs assessment should focus on both the individual's current level of functioning as well as his or her highest level of functioning before seeking services. A needs assessment should also address the whole person, including academic, social-emotional, career-technical, and independent living domains (Tindle, Leconte, Buchanan, & Taymans, 2005). Based on an assessment of individual needs, the service coordinator can establish priorities for services to the student.

Comprehensive assessment of the whole child addresses strengths and developmental needs in relevant functional domains, including physical development, independent functioning, social, family/natural support, behavioral, academic and vocational, employment, health, and psychological. It also involves periodic renewal of assessments, communicating and interpreting assessment information, adapting assessment tools for students with learning disabilities, and making recommendations for interventions on individual education and transition plans. Needs assessment is an ongoing process that extends throughout the course of the student's school program. Broader system-level needs assessment involves activities such as data analysis and surveys of systemwide needs of populations for services.

Function 4: Individual Program Planning. An essential function of service coordination from early childhood through high school transition is the development of a comprehensive service plan. Individualized student development plans, or IEPs, are service agreements or contracts among the student, family, school, and service providers that document their responsibilities and commitments. They are based on information obtained from the individual assessments described under Function 3. Planning activities

- engage the interdisciplinary team and families in education planning.
- consider all of the functional domains, including family supports.
- address the continuity of needed supplemental and support services as the student moves from one educational level to the next.
- involve regular review of the plan.
- ensure active participation and decision making of students and their families in the process.

Program planning also occurs at the broader system level, where it typically results in the development of an interagency cooperative agreement.

Function 5: Service Coordination and Linking. At the individual level, service linking means identifying appropriate service agencies and individuals to deliver the services identified in an individualized education plan. For example, for families of children and youth with disabilities, service linking may mean providing a central point of contact to link the student and family with a variety of services such as speech and hearing, school counseling, and assistive devices or equipment. For individuals with chronic health needs, it may mean providing information about and linkage to public health services, nursing services, and providers of in-home health-related and adaptive equipment. For secondary youth preparing for post-secondary placement, it may mean linking the student with post-secondary education personnel, employment services, or vocational rehabilitation services. For individual students, linking activities may include establishing a service coordinator or point of contact for each individual or family; identifying and contacting needed services within the agency's service area or outside it, if needed; and linking students and families to needed services during key transitions from early childhood through exit from high school.

At the broader system level, linking means coordinating and sharing resources among agencies on behalf of children and youth. Shared resources include the financial, human and intellectual, and material resources of cooperating agencies that could be dedicated to the system coordination activities defined in a cooperative agreement. Interagency linking activities can prevent duplication of services among many agencies and make the service system more efficient.

Function 6: Service Monitoring and Follow-Along. At the individual level, the purpose of service monitoring is to (a) ensure that students receive the services that are described in their individual support plans and (b) evaluate the student's progress in achieving the goals and objectives in the plan. Monitoring also involves documenting services actually received, documenting gaps in services for students and efforts to locate services outside the community, documenting barriers in services for the student, and maintaining continuity in service coordination through key transition points. Monitoring requires that the service coordinator and IFSP or IEP team maintain ongoing contact with students receiving services and the agency(ies) providing them.

Service monitoring at the broader system level means

- observing the delivery of services of cooperating agencies and contract service providers to ensure that services are delivered according to the intended schedule.
- ensuring that services reach the students they were intended to serve.
- ensuring that services are delivered in a manner that complies with established local, state, and national laws and are delivered with an acceptable level of quality.
- documenting progress and performance of cooperating agencies and contract service providers.
- collecting data on referrals to agencies and services needed by individuals or families.
- collecting information from students and families about how they perceive the quality, appropriateness, and accessibility of services.

The monitoring function can offer valuable information about the quality and effectiveness of service coordination in the service delivery system.

Follow-along activities are an important part of the monitoring function. The service coordinator provides mentoring and emotional support, fosters relationships of trust with the student, and maintains close contact and communication with the family. Follow-along activities may include the following:

- Making home visits to families
- Visiting youth in their school or their work-based programs
- Providing informal and supportive counseling with students or families
- Addressing family support needs
- Providing behavioral (or other) crisis intervention

The follow-along function includes the personal support component of service coordination. It can be instrumental in preventing student dropout from needed services or programs and even preventing dropout from school.

Function 7: Individual and Interagency Advocacy. Advocacy is a very broad term that has different meanings to different groups of people, but it is a particularly important function of service coordination. At the **individual level,** advocacy means actively seeking services on behalf of a student or assisting the student to advocate on his or her own behalf (self-advocacy). Advocacy activities at the individual level include recommending specific services to student support teams or IEP teams, sharing information with a family about services to solicit their consent to approve a student's participation, or educating general educators about how supportive and assistive services can help a student with special needs progress in general education.

System-level advocacy means advocating in ways similar to those described above but doing so on behalf of a whole group of students. Examples of advocacy activities include the following:

- Developing a shared interagency understanding of the needs of groups of students with disabilities or special learning needs
- Addressing multicultural and language minority issues with service agencies to negotiate the development of special supports or accommodations
- Communicating service barriers and service gaps to decision makers
- Communicating and protecting human rights and due process procedures for groups of students
- Promoting an emphasis on self-determination and informed decision making for students and their families
- Helping local agencies meet new legal requirements
- Increasing support services for groups of students as they transition between grades or programs

As local agencies respond to new requirements for system coordination, advocacy can help build a shared capacity to meet the multiple needs of students and their families.

Function 8: Evaluation and Follow-up. Evaluation and follow-up are essential to effective service coordination. Although evaluation may be a *final step* in assessing the value and quality of services for children, it is the *first step* in their improvement. Evaluation is a process by which (a) information about educational programs and services is collected to measure the results or effects of services and programs on students and families and the educational environment, (b) determine if the interagency partnership is achieving the goals that it set for itself, and (c) make decisions about the future of the interagency agreement. Because evaluation is closely linked to the decision-making process, it is more powerful if the information it generates becomes part of the decision-making process (Rossi, Lipsey, & Freeman, 2003), particularly for school improvement or restructuring.

Follow-up activities are used to track the path or disposition of students once they have exited the program or service agency (e.g., from preschool to enter elementary or from high school to enter college or employment). Follow-up activities are designed to answer questions such as these:

- What happens to students once they have left the school and the services in which they have been participating?
- Do the students return to community agencies for additional services, and are they more likely to access services again in the future?

- Do students experience long-term benefits or impacts as a result of receiving services (e.g., enrollment in post-secondary education and/or improved independent living, physical health, mobility, social situation, financial situation, family relations, employment, and general functioning)?

Follow-up methods used in school include student or family surveys or interviews to determine perceptions about quality, accessibility, and appropriateness of services; outreach to students who did not complete high school to determine what additional services are needed; and evaluation of post-secondary transition plans for students and their families. Follow-up information also informs school personnel about whether or not the benefits or progress made by students who receive school-based or school-linked services is sustained over time.

While the eight functions discussed above may be known by different labels in different communities, they describe the basic tasks performed system coordinators in schools and school-linked agencies.

HOW DO SCHOOLS AND COMMUNITY AGENCIES COORDINATE FOR YOUTH PLACED AT RISK?

How Do Coordinated Services Support Children and Youth in Alternative Programs?

Failure to educate youth placed at risk is usually a failure of coordination of needed services, both within and outside the school. The majority of students attending an alternative education program require support services, not only from their school but also through other providers, such as social services, court services and mental health. Raywid (1998) observed,

An alternative [program] must have broad aims, making its concern the full development of each youngster—character and intellect, personal and social development, as well as academic achievement. It is concerned with the person, not just with the person's academic achievements. (p. 12)

The type of collaboration most widely reported by districts with alternative schools and programs for at-risk students was with the juvenile justice system (84 percent) (Kleiner, Porch, & Farris, 2002). Over 75 percent of districts collaborated with community mental health agencies, while 70 percent collaborated with police or sheriff's departments. Sixty-nine percent collaborated with child protective services. Only 23 percent of districts reported collaboration with parks and recreation departments.

Since the reasons for placement in an alternative program vary widely, from chronic behavior problems to a specific incident of disruptive behavior, substance abuse, and mental health problems, the a full-service approach to service delivery is a necessity. The conditions that place students at risk are typically so complex that schools alone cannot intervene in the multiple problems that interfere with student success (Vaughn, Bos, & Schumm, 2003). A team of professionals can offer more knowledge and experiences to respond to the varied needs of the student. Each team member, including the student, is held accountable for the success of the collaboration;

the student, therefore, is an integral member of the team. Through participation in the interdisciplinary team process, students are encouraged to practice the skills of self-determination.

A member of the student support team usually facilitates the coordination of non-school professionals to form a multidisciplinary team of persons to work together to provide a holistic approach to service delivery. The interdisciplinary team provides a safety net against individual errors in judgment. The coordination of services also ensures that there is no cessation of services for the student through transitions from one setting to another. In many local districts or counties, a central student tracking system shared by many agencies (e.g., the school, mental health agencies, family services agencies, juvenile courts, probation and parole officers, substance abuse system, and others) ensures that student information is centrally maintained. Meanwhile, the student is the core member of the team, exercising personal decision making in life planning as a central part of the process.

System Coordination and Young Offenders

Educational services for young offenders in correctional facilities have been notoriously weak across the United States. Similarly, coordination during the transition from correctional facilities to employment, post-secondary education, and the community has been fragmented, inefficient, and disconnected (National Center on Education, Disability and Juvenile Justice [EDJJ], n.d.).

Coordinated systems of support are now being developed in most states to increase the likelihood of successful youth transition and reentry into the community (EDJJ, n.d.). Effective transition practices for youth released from correctional facilities involve close coordination among correctional education personnel, the public schools, and community-based agencies such as mental health and social services agencies. Transition coordination can increase the likelihood that incarcerated youth will reenroll in their home school, complete high school, and become gainfully employed in their communities (Stephens & Arnette, 2000).

Several promising practices are being implemented in many states to overcome the obstacles identified above. Cooperative contractual agreements among local agencies that provide transition services to juveniles are being established to maintain a seamless continuum of care. Such linkages result in increased postrelease options for youth leaving corrections. A consistent transition-planning process, curricula to support transition planning, databases to track and monitor student progress, and a planned sequence of services after release are the key ingredients of successful transition. Individualized wraparound services that focus on the strengths of the individual and his or her family are also being established. Finally, there is evidence that juveniles who receive prerelease training in social skills, career exploration, and vocational education are more likely to succeed after release from juvenile correctional facilities (National Center on Education, Disability and Juvenile Justice, n.d.; Stephens & Arnette, 2000).

Successful transition between correctional facilities and schools requires integrated and coordinated prerelease strategies developed and implemented collaboratively by all agencies involved in providing facility-based and aftercare services to youth and their families (Stephens & Arnette, 2000). Coordinated aftercare and follow-up can make the difference for youth and prevent their return to detention.

HOW IS AN INTERAGENCY AGREEMENT DEVELOPED?

Interagency agreements are formed among schools and community agencies to provide support services that are needed to address students' complex developmental needs in a coordinated manner. Such agreements define the activities, responsibilities, and resource contributions of each agency. The focus of the agreements is to (a) reduce the barriers that exist when a student and family need services and supports from several separate and uncoordinated sources and (b) achieve progress and a successful transition to adult life. In this chapter, the terms *interagency agreement* and *multiagency agreement* will be used interchangeably.

Interagency coordination for services that support educational goals is strongly encouraged under NCLB and IDEIA 2004, but specific formal relationships are not yet mandatory. The voluntary nature of these interagency linkages affects how they can and should be managed. As Hagebak counseled in 1992,

> Cooperation doesn't really work very well when it's mandated, because it depends so heavily on the attitudes of the people involved. You can't really buy a ready-made cooperative human service system, although having some flexible funds to use in supporting the special mechanisms you develop can certainly help the process along. You've got to get close if cooperation is going to work.... You have to work at it and keep it central to your purposes.... Cooperation is a contact sport and unless you build contact among administrators and managers, school and business staff and their boards, your effort will fail. (pp. 73–74)

Involuntary or "discretionary" associations and relationships among people take on great importance and must be carefully nurtured if the interagency relationship is to endure.

The following sections describe 10 strategic-planning steps for the development of interagency agreements to promote coordination of schools and community services for transition.

Ten Steps to Develop and Implement Interagency Agreements

The process of developing and implementing interagency agreements can be divided into the following 10 steps:

1. Engage the community.

2. Conduct preplanning assessment.

3. Assess interagency coordination needs.

4. Identify opportunities for matched resources.

5. Establish a joint vision and shared mission.

6. Design cooperative agreements.

7. Define the management structure and the role of interagency teams (councils).

8. Develop an "adoption" plan: personnel development for student transition.

9. Develop team problem-solving strategies.

10. Evaluate for service improvement.

These steps, offered as a framework for developing local interagency agreements and action plans, are based on the practices of collaborating agencies around the nation. They provide a menu of options for the development of agreements. The 10 steps

- can be initiated by a single school or agency or jointly by several.
- are relevant for service systems with very underdeveloped school-linked services and interagency relationships.
- are useful for strengthening transition systems with more advanced interagency relationships.
- can form the basis for the design of evaluation of interagency partnerships.

These steps, which provide a "path" of activities and strategies for those who are beginning the process of developing new interagency agreements, are suited to the local system and community.

Step 1. Engage the Community: The Spectrum of Key Stakeholders

The process of interagency collaboration begins by conducting activities that engage key stakeholders, or personnel within the cooperating agencies, in discussing transition services, legal requirements for cooperation, and intentions to improve the transition service delivery system. The quality and effectiveness of interagency agreements among service agencies relies on the commitment of a spectrum of people within those agencies to cooperate, including those listed in the boxed test.

SPECTRUM OF PROFESSIONALS WHO PARTICIPATE IN INTERAGENCY AGREEMENTS

- Parents and students
- General and special educators and administrators
- Career and vocational/technical educators
- Related and support services personnel
- Rehabilitation personnel
- Adult and community-based services personnel
- Public and private health services personnel
- Post-secondary agency personnel
- Employers, employment services, and private nonprofit agency personnel

- Business/industry personnel and school-business liaisons
- School board members and key community decision makers
- Probation and parole workers
- Police
- Advocacy agency workers and leaders
- Recreation and leisure services providers
- College and university personnel
- Local and state politicians concerned with the needs of children and youth
- Civic and religious group leaders
- Job-training program personnel
- Social services personnel

There are several strategies for identifying interagency stakeholders who could be enlisted to initiate or improve interagency collaboration.

Enlist Students, Parents, and Parent Leaders as Advisors and Planners. Parent leaders are often the best champions for new initiatives—if they support the effort. Parent and student organizations can also serve as essential links between educational agencies and the community (Rosman, McCarthy, & Woolverton, 2001; Wandry & Pleet, 2003). Parent groups may include school alumni, parent association leaders, school board members who are parents of students with disabilities, PTA leaders, parents who are business leaders, parent volunteers, and advocates. The strongest champions for interagency collaboration can emerge from any sector of the community, once the value of the initiative is communicated.

Forge Partnerships With the Business Community. The business community is a key partner in developing secondary school initiatives to link education and work environments. Table 6.1 provides examples of such business involvement.

Table 6.1   How Can Business Support Interagency Collaboration for Secondary Support?

Goals	*Examples of Partnership Activities*
1. Support schools' efforts to integrate academic, career-oriented youth leadership, and community-based learning activities.	Business employees can • serve as tutors, mentors, career advisors. • offer summer jobs, special courses, and after-school activities. • create work-based programs for secondary youth to gain work experience. • develop entrepreneurial clubs, sponsor activities in subject areas such as science fairs. • help teachers and students link with community and social service agencies.
2. Strengthen teachers' knowledge of business and industry environments.	Help teachers develop new instructional strategies to integrate academic and community-based learning; provide opportunities for teachers to learn more about the applications of an academic subject within an industry; provide teacher internships in business and industry; sponsor workshops; train volunteer teams; and help schools appeal for community support.
3. Develop effective strategic planning models and tools.	Help schools generate, manage, and use needs assessment information for strategic planning; assist interagency teams to create effective organizations for coordination; institute an evaluation process.

Businesses recognize that effective school-community programs help orient youth to work settings and expectations and the value of career planning and, ultimately, produce a more prepared workforce.

Plan for Interagency Collaboration. Schools and districts use a variety of strategies for informing and engaging community agencies to provide needed services for children and youth. However, effective interagency agreements begin with community information activities that can help secure agency participation in the mission. Through the process of informing a wide spectrum of agencies about the interagency partnership, interagency planners can begin to identify participants in the planning process. The first questions for an interagency team might be these:

- Who among the stakeholders can best help define goals and make decisions?
- What combination of people could help address students' service and coordination needs?

The strategic planning meeting brings people together in combinations that are likely to bring about new relationships and needed change. An interagency agreement depends on effective relationships among the representatives in the cooperating agencies who are most likely to be working together. Several questions may be helpful in deciding whom to invite to strategic meetings:

- Which agencies or service specialists are needed immediately to provide services for children and youth?
- What agencies or individuals are the best champions for the cause of developing an interagency agreement?
- Who are the "weakest links" (i.e., Who will need the most encouragement to get involved)?
- Which agencies most need to understand each other's roles and begin working together first?
- How can I get my state, regional, and local interagency personnel working together?

Meetings that are carefully crafted to join people strategically typically produce very creative results and accelerate the development of interagency agreements. Table 6.2 provides strategies for informing community agency personnel, students, and families about new initiatives for interagency service coordination.

Table 6.2   Thirteen Strategies for Engaging the Community

1. Engage parent, student, and consumer organizations.	Inform parent, student, and consumer organizations, such as the PTA, and parent advocacy groups about the plans for an interagency agreement. Distribute information and solicit input to the plans and roles of these groups in the development of the collaboration.
2. Engage educational leaders and school principals.	Inform educational leaders and school principals who have primary responsibility for a new student support initiative that will affect instruction or student services. Principals and other administrators should be among the first to be informed of the effort, and they should be helped to see how the initiative will aid them in achieving their educational goals and objectives for students.
3. Engage personnel in community agencies.	Inform staff and directors of relevant community and adult services agencies, because their support is vital to a service coordination initiative. Each cooperating (or potential) partner needs to know about the intent to collaborate and the process for forming or revising the interagency agreement.

(continued)

Table 6.2 (Continued)

4. Develop mission and goals statements.	Develop mission and goals statements to help each potential cooperating agency understand the relationship between the student support initiative and its own individual agency mission, goals, and objectives. Each must understand how the new collaboration will help it to achieve its individual agency goals, improve its outcomes for children and youth, improve its services and resources, and/or evaluate its efforts. The mutual benefits to all cooperating agencies must be defined early in the process.
5. Inform and engage relevant teacher unions and educational associations.	Inform relevant teacher unions and educational associations about new initiatives that involve teaching staff and help them understand the potential benefits of the collaboration for the students and professionals. It might also be helpful to have input from the county or district educational association.
6. Include the initiative in local education reform seminars.	Include, in local education reform and accountability seminars, information about the student support initiative.
7. Conduct brainstorming meetings.	Conduct special seminars or brainstorming meetings with heads of agency personnel to discuss the interagency agreement.
8. Develop informational brochures and materials.	Develop informational brochures and materials that explain the mission and benefits of interagency collaboration. Include information packets in the local budget documents that are distributed to educational and community agency planning boards. Develop interagency brochures to inform the community of the key partners in the initiative and to promote the interagency partnership as a distinct entity.
9. Conduct seminars with business.	Include information about the initiative in local business–education seminars or in chamber of commerce, one-stop center, workforce investment council, or school-to-work meetings.
10. Use local media newspapers.	Feature articles about the support initiative in local newsletters and newspapers.
11. Meet with community leaders.	Conduct meetings with community leaders and solicit their assistance in championing the initiative.
12. Links with local universities.	Link with local colleges or universities to develop meetings or seminars related to interagency coordination.
13. Utilize annual reports.	Include descriptions of interagency initiatives, accomplishments, and impacts in school improvement plans and report cards and in the annual reports of cooperating agencies

Step 2. Conduct Preplanning Assessment: How Prepared Are Interagency Partners for Collaboration?

Assessment of the readiness, or preparedness, of community agencies for interagency coordination can benefit agencies developing new interagency partnerships, as well as those seeking to improve existing relationships. Preplanning assessment at the interagency level helps measure how ready the agencies are to enter a partnership. It is important for interagency planners to know what each cooperating agency brings to the relationship in terms of resources, service mission, and service philosophy. It is also important to know something about the structure of the agencies that are collaborating, their investment in the interagency partnership, and the extent of their knowledge about the population of students to be served. Understanding what each agency can contribute in a collaborative relationship will help interagency transition planners understand how they can function as an effective team.

Assess Environmental Supports for Interagency Agreements for Transition. Many aspects of the local environment can support the development and effectiveness of interagency agreements for transition. The important questions related to the local environment are these:

- Are the key agencies in the community of the interagency coordination plan?
- Are the necessary resources available to implement the interagency plan?

In the planning process, if environmental supports are found to be weak, then interagency planners should focus efforts on student needs assessment and resource development.

Step 3. Assess Interagency Coordination Needs

The third step in the development of interagency agreements involves assessing the needs of each agency in the support service network. Such needs may include resources and mutual understanding of resource limitations; staffing, policy, and procedural changes; and service delivery area considerations. The first set of goals and activities that is defined among coordinating agencies will provide only a blueprint or map for defining early relationships. As the agencies' activities expand or diminish, cooperative agreements must be revisited and modified. Ongoing needs assessments can help the system remain sensitive to changes. It is important that interagency planners show a clear relationship among the developmental support needs of students, the mission and goals of the interagency agreement, and the contributions of each cooperating agency.

What Should Be Assessed? Each agency that joins an interagency partnership for service coordination may have different reasons for cooperating and a different understanding of its role and responsibilities in providing transition services. How, then, can the planning personnel help agencies determine a common mission to create a systematic and coordinated service program? What strategies are needed to form an effective working relationship that can achieve results? The first question has to do with *what* the collaborative relationship should focus on (principles, goals, and objectives), and the second with *how* (the processes).

In thinking about what needs should be addressed by an interagency partnership and how it should do so, two propositions may be helpful:

Proposition No. 1: The primary focus for an interagency agreement for service coordination should be on helping agencies understand the nature of support services that address the developmental needs of the whole child and the legal authority for coordination across agencies. Such a focus helps build the necessary commitment to work together to help children, youth, and families prepare for and succeed throughout their school years and beyond.

Proposition No. 2: The interagency partnership should focus on how it can improve the coordination and linkage of services to children, youth, and families so they can achieve developmental and educational goals.

Assessment activities at the system level involve the following:

- Defining the range of local services available to identify a foundation for a service coordination initiative
- Identifying service gaps and service needs that are not now being met within the system
- Determining the level of readiness, in terms of structure, attitudes, and knowledge, of cooperating agencies to establish formal interagency agreements
- Determining the expertise and resources that each organization brings to the partnership
- Assessing the needs of the cooperating partners to address a common goal

A thorough needs assessment can provide important information for determining how prepared each agency is to perform the eight core service coordination functions.

Step 4. Identify Opportunities for Matched Resources

Once the interagency planning team has completed a needs assessment, the next logical questions are these:

- How does the team find the resources to start action?
- What should be asked from partner organizations? Should financial resources be requested, or should a different kind of investment be expected?

Often new resources continue to be identified long after the cooperative relationship begins. They may emerge as a result of a needs assessment or an evaluation of interagency activities.

The question of resource sharing should be raised early in the interagency planning process. Visits to other districts that have cooperative agreements can be helpful for identifying resource-sharing arrangements.

Step 5. Establish a Joint Vision and Shared Mission

Once needs have been assessed and potential resources identified, the action phase of the collaboration process can begin—that of establishing the shared vision (what does the organization or partnership want to become?) and mission (reasons for the partnership's existence). This step involves discussing a joint vision and mission for student support service improvement and hammering out broad goals and strategies for achieving them. The goal of this step is to provide a foundation for the cooperative relationship and a signed, formal interagency agreement that embodies the principles of shared responsibility and community participation in development of comprehensive coordinated services. As the interagency planning team discusses the common vision and mission, it is important to view the agreement as more than a linkage; rather, it is a shared change strategy for improving developmental outcomes for the whole child.

A local change strategy is designed to improve the availability of and access to student support services. It may also be used to solve specific coordination problems among agencies that are identified in the local interagency needs assessment. A statewide systems change strategy is designed to help all local education agencies build the capacity to develop student support services and agreements.

What Are the Components of the Interagency Mission Statement? The mission statement should describe the service issues or barriers that need to be addressed by the cooperating agencies. It can be stated in terms of "opportunities for change." Each community defines its interagency mission differently, so no two mission statements will look alike. However, a few fundamental elements should be included in mission statements.

The statement should describe the broad purpose of the interagency agreement and the areas of joint responsibility. It generally describes what each cooperating partner will contribute toward the goal of student developmental service delivery and improvement, and it may describe what the partnership is not designed to do. A mission statement generally includes several of the following four parts:

1. *Statement of context or history:* This is usually a brief introductory paragraph that broadly describes the interagency partnership: how it was initiated; how it addresses current student needs; how it improves on current developmental practices; and how the partnership may differ from, or expand on, what has been in place before.

2. *Statement of the authority for the interagency agreement:* This introductory section of the mission statement refers to the legal basis for the agreement and may list the local, state, and federal laws, statutes, regulations, or policies that give authority to this agreement.

3. *General statement of purpose of the agreement and expected outcomes:* This includes a broad statement of what the partnership expects to accomplish, including what results it hopes to see for children and youth.

4. *Broad goal and outline of roles and responsibilities:* This describes what the agreement provides and the roles and responsibilities of each cooperating partner.

The mission statement is a broad description of the "vision" of the interagency partnership; it is not a specific set of goals and objectives. Mission statements generally serve as a preamble to a cooperative agreement that defines specific goals, objectives, and actions for the partnership. The next step discusses how to develop the cooperative agreement and annual action plan.

Step 6. Design Cooperative Agreements That Support the Development of the Whole Child

Once the mission statement is completed, the next step is to negotiate among collaborating agencies the specific agreements for action to achieve the mission. The cooperative agreement incorporates the mission statement and provides more detail about the commitments of the agencies involved. How does the team develop such a cooperative agreement to meet specific annual goals? How can goal statements be crafted in such a way that the team can measure the results of the interagency coordination activities? How does the team develop a timetable for action? This section discusses the development of a cooperative agreement and goals for coordinating and improving services.

What Should the Cooperative Agreement Accomplish? The cooperative agreement is essential to the development of effective interagency coordination. The agreement defines the structure, processes, and local authority for action among the collaborating agencies. It also defines what can be expected from each agency—its activities, responsibilities, and contributions to the transition service delivery system. Cooperative agreements should accomplish four things:

1. *Identify resources to support the interagency relationship.* Cooperative agreements outline the particular contribution each cooperating agency will make; agreements may include staff, funds, equipment, consultation time, vehicles, space, and other resources. Plans to transfer, redistribute, or match these resources are also defined.

2. *Identify goals, objectives, and activities of each cooperating agency.* Cooperative agreements should also describe the role and authority of the members of the interagency planning team.

3. *Identify expected results of the interagency partnership.* Cooperative agreements define the expected results for students and families involved in transition services and for the cooperating agencies. Methods to evaluate results should be described, along with the roles of cooperating agencies, students, and families in the evaluation process. Agreements should also describe clearly the interagency planning team's authority for evaluating and monitoring the coordination activities (more details on evaluation are provided under "Step 10. Evaluate for Improvement").

4. *Establish timetables for the activities.* Cooperative agreements include the date the interagency relationship takes effect, the schedule for accomplishing objectives, and the dates for reviewing and modifying the agreement.

Although cooperative agreements look different in each service system, there is a basic blueprint for crafting an agreement to accomplish a set of goals within a specific period.

Develop Goals and Objectives for the Agreement. Two definitions are useful in developing goals and objectives for an interagency relationship.

1. An *interagency goal* is a broad statement about what two or more cooperating agencies intend to achieve.

2. An *interagency objective* is a specific statement of intent to carry out an activity to reach a goal. It is stated in explicit, measurable, and time-limited terms. The objectives also form the basis for developing the intended outcomes of the interagency relationship (Fowler et al., 2000; Mager, 1984; Zemke, 1999).

The following compares objectives written in measurable and nonmeasurable terms.

Measurable Terms

- By September 15, 2010, Mankato County Public Schools will identify and enroll 20 high school juniors and 30 high school seniors in the Work Readiness and Training Partnership at Northeast National Bank and Trust.

- By January 30, 2011, Stanton County Elementary school will identify all children who have reading difficulties and will assign a literacy coordinator to work with teachers to develop individualized plans for each student.

Nonmeasurable Terms

- The Mankato County Public Schools, in partnership with Northeast National Bank and Trust, will work to help Mankato County High School graduates enter the field of banking and commerce.
- Stanton County Health Department will seek to assess children's reading issues using literacy coordinators.

The first two objectives are preferable because they are specific and measurable. The first objective, for example, is time limited (students will be enrolled by September 15) and measurable and quantifiable (20 juniors and 30 seniors), and the goal is clear (students will be enrolled in the Work Readiness and Training Partnership at Northeast National Bank and Trust). The third and fourth statements, written in nonmeasurable terms, are broad goals that need more specific, measurable objectives. The language "help . . . graduates enter the field of banking" is vague and gives little information about the specific actions the partnership intends to take to accomplish this goal. Exactly how will it "help . . . graduates enter" banking jobs? What does "enter the field of banking" mean? Does it mean taking nonskilled jobs as filing clerks? Or does it mean entering bank management-training programs? And how will the goal be measured?

If the interagency team defines its goals and objectives early in the development of the relationship, it is much easier later to evaluate what has been accomplished. It is also easier to determine whether students are benefitting from the coordinated transition services and if the quality of and access to services is being improved. The boxed text provides an example blueprint for a cooperative agreement that begins with the mission statement. This blueprint reflects elements of many actual agreements used in the field today (Kochhar & Erickson, 1993; Kochhar-Bryant, 2008).

BLUEPRINT FOR A COOPERATIVE AGREEMENT FOR SERVICE COORDINATION

Mission Statement

The mission statement describes the broad purpose of the interagency relationship and the areas of joint responsibility. The statement generally describes the transition service needs the collaborating agencies will address and what each will do.

Parties

The cooperating partners (e.g., adult and community service organizations; state, local, or federal government agencies; businesses; educational agencies; health agencies; organized labor; employment services; and others) are identified by their full names.

(continued)

(Continued)

Terms

Stipulates the length of time the agreement will remain in effect before it is reviewed. Usually, agreements are reviewed annually by the cooperating agencies.

Purpose

Describes the broad purpose of the agreements and broad areas of joint responsibility.

Commitments, Objectives, and Actions

Describes the specific commitments and actions to which the cooperating agencies agree. Examples include the following:

- Resources that have been pledged for interagency service coordination by each cooperating agency
- An annual calendar describing activities required by the agreement and schedule for annual review and modification
- Ongoing interagency training and sharing of information, including interagency service coordinators, teachers, support personnel, counselors, administrators, instructors, supervisors, and others as appropriate
- Annual goals and objectives for each cooperating agency
- Joint review and evaluation (quarterly, biannually, or annually) of the service coordination efforts and goals
- Data sharing among cooperating agencies, which might include resources shared among agencies, service assessments of student needs, service dropout rates, services provided to families, projections of individuals entering transition activities or programs, and other relevant information that helps cooperating agencies address the needs of joint clients
- Meetings, as appropriate, to determine which individuals or families are eligible for interagency services
- Interagency coordination evaluation meetings to determine how effective the partnership is for students and families and to solve problems related to collaboration

Partnership Evaluation

Defines the criteria by which the interagency coordination activities will be evaluated, including the expected benefits and outcomes for the students and the community.

Assurances for Participants

Describes how collaborating agencies will comply with local, state, and federal laws to ensure nondiscrimination in the provision of services on the basis of race, religion, national origin, sex, and disability.

Confidentiality

Describes how collaborating agencies will ensure confidentiality of individual records and information. Also describes procedures for getting written consents (if needed) from individuals served and parents/guardians, providing access to individual records, and sharing information about individuals served. May include mediation and procedures for settling conflicts over confidentiality or the services of the agencies.

Administrative Responsibility

Identifies the interagency coordinator(s) and persons with responsibility and final authority within the collaborating agencies.

Terminating the Partnership

Describes the procedures for ending the relationship among agencies and other related organizations. For example, an agency desiring to quit the partnership may have to give at least 60 days' notice to other agencies of its intent to terminate.

Authorizing Signatures

The responsible persons within each agency sign and date the cooperative agreement.

Attachment to the Cooperative Agreement

Joint tools or forms, such as referral forms, an interagency coordination activities calendar, release and confidentiality forms, and evaluation forms, may be attached to the agreement.

Comprehensive agreements are not "token" agreements but are "living," active, working documents that guide and direct a system of well-coordinated activities.

Incorporate Milestone Schedules Into the Agreement. The cooperative agreement should include (1) dates that the agreement takes effect, (2) dates by which the collaborating agencies will accomplish annual objectives, and (3) dates for review and modification of the agreement. A well-defined schedule of activities, as in the example in Table 6.3, helps collaborating agencies ensure that milestones are met.

Table 6.3   Example Timetable for Implementing a Cooperative Agreement

Time (Flexible)	Activities
Six months to one year before developing the interagency agreement	Contact potential collaborating agencies and explore mutual needs, understanding, and capacity to participate in an interagency partnership for support services. Conduct student and agency needs assessments.
One to three months before formal interagency commitment	Obtain informal agreements from committed agencies. Based on identified needs, determine human, financial, and material resources that each agency is willing to commit for service coordination. Set a date to develop the cooperative agreement. Several weeks before the initiation of the formal interagency partnership, begin a media/public relations campaign to help initiate the interagency coordination initiative.

(continued)

Table 6.3 (Continued)

Time (Flexible)	Activities
Immediate period after the agreement takes effect	Formalize the interagency partnership in a cooperative agreement document. The cooperative agreement should include all applicable components listed previously (goals, objectives, resources, activities, and expected results). Designate an interagency liaison or coordinator.
Summer or early fall of the current school year	Initiate the service coordination activities.
Fall and winter of the current school year	Throughout the fall, winter, and spring, monitor the service coordination activities. Conduct periodic meetings with collaborating agencies. Through observations and verbal and written communication, assess the ongoing effectiveness of the service coordination activities. Make adjustments in the activities as needed. Compile and share data collected from the informal monitoring. Set a date to initiate the evaluation process.
During the final month of the school year	Initiate formal measures to determine whether the interagency objectives have been met. Interview participants and disseminate surveys developed to assess students, families, and cooperating agencies' perceptions of effectiveness of the coordination activities.
At the close of the school year	Analyze outcomes and determine whether the objectives of the cooperative agreement have been met. Celebrate the success of the interagency partnership by conducting appreciation activities for cooperating agencies and personnel. Conduct a year-end meeting with the collaborating agencies to review and modify the agreement if needed.

Step 7. Define the Management Structure and Role of Interagency Teams

Interagency collaboration often begins with a few activities shared between agencies, but as the relationship begins to grow, interagency coordinators may need to change the way they manage the coordination activities, communicate the mission of the interagency relationship, and measure the benefits for or effects on students and families.

How Do Interagency Teams Make Management Decisions? In many communities throughout the United States, interagency linkages for student service coordination are still largely informal and voluntary collaborations, and administrators are reluctant to impose regulations and procedures on these often fragile relationships (Crane, Gramlich, & Peterson, 2004). Instead, many choose approaches that encourage new collaboration through technical assistance, training, and sharing of models. How the interagency linkage is managed will depend on the number of agencies involved and whether the school has the lead role and is the "center" for coordination of the partnership.

There are often few guidelines for developing interagency linkages, particularly in rural communities. Linkages tend to be loosely managed with a great deal of local flexibility and discretion over the types of relationships formed among service agencies. Local educational agencies have been the primary initiators for coordinating and managing activities of interagency partnerships. However, strong state and local encouragement and support, through personnel training and technical assistance, can be powerful in assisting schools as lead agencies and in stimulating effective service coordination (Baer, Simmons, & Flexer, 1997; Crane et al., 2004; Kochhar-Bryant, 2008).

Since NCLB and IDEIA require school systems to develop interagency partnerships, the center for the primary coordination of services typically lies with the school. However, coordination may be shared among agencies through an interagency council. There is no one way to manage or coordinate services among multiple agencies, but there are a couple of important considerations. Research on interagency coordination has demonstrated that coordination is more effective when the lead agency, typically the school, understands the staffing constraints of the collaborating agencies and is sensitive to the economic circumstances that may be affecting each agency (Baer et al., 1997).

Step 8. Develop an "Adoption" Plan: Personnel Development for Student Transition

When people sense they are entering an era of change and that traditional ways of doing things are being abandoned, some may resist or feel negative about the future. The interagency planner and leadership need special knowledge to champion systemic change. How can interagency coordinators foster a sense of investment or ownership in an interagency partnership? How should agency personnel be oriented to the changes that the new collaboration may bring? What kinds of training will be needed? How can the agencies celebrate their successes and honor those who have made important contributions to the effort?

How Will Interagency Personnel "Adopt" New Roles and Ways of Working? Systemic change usually means that people will be traveling on new and unfamiliar paths in their work. These paths will require different methods, relationships, procedures, norms, values, and attitudes from all who are involved in the process. No new student support initiative will be successfully "adopted," or fully accepted and implemented by agency personnel, unless the representatives are adequately trained in their field, understand the purposes of the collaboration initiative, and are prepared for systemic change. New training and development activities are needed to help key personnel adopt, sustain, and evaluate the effectiveness of new practices. Change cannot occur without the efforts of change agents who have new knowledge and can guide the needed changes.

Step 9. Develop Team Problem-Solving Strategies

Educators and human service professionals take pride in their professional status and independence. Such independence can sometimes create barriers to interagency cooperation. This section presents some of the common problems that present when building interagency relationships to support student transition and describes strategies to overcome them.

What Are Common Barriers to Interagency Relationships? Barriers to service coordination can be clustered into three categories: organizational, attitudinal, and knowledge.

1. *Organizational barriers:* Barriers related to the differences in the way interagency relationships are structured and managed and how the agencies define their missions, how they operate and develop policies, and how they provide services. Personnel may fear that funds will not be available for the cooperative arrangement or that there will be competition for resources.

2. *Attitudinal barriers:* Barriers related to the beliefs, motivations, and attitudes that different agencies have about students and families and their roles in the student support service system and community participation in general. Personnel may fear control and scrutiny by other agencies, that their jobs may be threatened, or that quality of services might be compromised.

3. *Knowledge barriers:* Barriers related to the differences in the knowledge and skills of various agency personnel. Personnel may lack awareness and understanding of other organizations, be unable to imagine possibilities for cooperation, or lack strategic planning skills.

The cornerstones of a cooperative interagency relationship are the personal relationships of the individuals involved. The most powerful of these relationships occurs among those closest to the students and families. Often both the successes and difficulties with the cooperative process can be traced to problems in professional and personal relationships. Interagency coordination initiatives can be much more effective if agency personnel are alert to these barriers to cooperation. In addition, diverse agency structures can make interagency service coordination a challenge.

Step 10. Evaluate for Service Improvement

The final step in the development of an interagency agreement is evaluation—the measurement of effectiveness. Local interagency teams can be a powerful force within the community for systemic change and improvement of developmental support services to youth. As a collaborative interagency team, they see the system as a whole and can make strategic decisions about what resources are needed to improve services and what services best match the assessed needs of youth in the community. Evaluation is an important tool in this process. It involves acting upon evaluation data collected from multiple sources and agencies to improve the educational support service system. Such improvement requires a constructive process for the following:

- Analyzing and communicating the information in a manner that is understandable and usable by different stakeholder groups (e.g., service coordinators, students/families, administrators)
- Systematically using the information to make changes and improvements in the service system to ensure that services match the assessed needs for children, youth, and families.

Armed with valuable evaluation information, interagency councils can promote actions through school boards and other governmental entities in areas such as policy and funding. The case study in the boxed text illustrates the power of community schooling and interagency coordination to affect positive changes for students, families, schools, and communities.

THE CHICAGO PUBLIC SCHOOLS (CPS) COMMUNITY SCHOOLS INITIATIVE: STUDENT AND SCHOOL OUTCOMES

The Chicago Public Schools reported in the summer of 2007 that it was beginning its fifth full year of implementation of the CPS Community Schools Initiative (CSI), which was now beginning to demonstrate the power of community schooling to effect positive changes for students, families, schools, and communities. The CSI has brought about improvements in student achievement and grades and reduction of disciplinary problems.

The CSI represents the largest community schools initiatives in the United States, with 110 community schools operating during the 2006–2007 school year and 40 more planned to open in 2007–2008. These public schools have become centers of their communities, with campuses open mornings, afternoons, evenings, weekends, and into the summer. Students attend traditional classes, but in addition, parents can receive job training, families can access medical and dental care on-site, and children can participate in music and art lessons.

The community schools model requires that

- schools partner with one or more community organizations that have demonstrated that they provide educational and related activities that improve the academic performance and development of CPS students.
- out-of-school-time programs offered through the partnership support the school's academic program.
- each school employs a full-time resource/site coordinator who oversees programs, identifies and engages additional resource providers, and coordinates with the partner organization(s) and advisors.
- each school have an advisory group that includes the school principal, teachers, parents, representatives from the partnering organization, and other community stakeholders.

According to CPS, students who participated in CSI programs demonstrated a small but significant improvement in grades and performance on standardized tests. Students showed a rise in Out of School Time (OST) attendance, which correlated with greater improvement in student grades and reading, math, and science scores on Illinois Standards Achievement Test (ISAT). CPS also reported that among program participants who began the academic year with reading or math grades of C or below, 43 percent and 42 percent, respectively, improved at least one half grade by the third quarter. CSI participants also improved their performance in other important school domains, including quality of homework, class participation, and class behavior. Furthermore, schools participating in the CSI have consistently demonstrated reductions in the number of serious disciplinary incidents compared to other schools with similar demographics.

Source: Chicago Public Schools, 2007.

WHAT IS THE ROLE OF THE LOCAL INTERAGENCY PLANNING COUNCIL?

An interagency planning council is one mechanism to increase the availability, access, and quality of services. Such a council achieves this by developing and improving policies, procedures, systems, and funding. The local planning council may have different names in different communities, including "community interagency support team," "interagency planning council," "interagency planning team," or "local advisory group." The planning council may be purely advisory, or it may have decision-making authority. As a decision-making body, the council may determine the direction and operation of the interagency partnership, its goals and objectives, its management and staff, the use and distribution of resources, and target populations. The goals of an interagency planning council typically include the following:

- Coordination of services to ensure nonduplication and cost-effectiveness
- Sharing responsibility for helping students and families link with community services
- Providing a quality, local service delivery system to support transition
- Anticipating current and future needs for services and developing plans to build capacity to meet those needs
- Improving student outcomes in adult living, learning, and employment roles
- Developing a registry of community service agency representatives who can attend student service planning meetings and act as resources in the process
- Developing formal interagency agreements in which information about eligibility can be shared, needs assessed, gaps in services identified, and service capacity strengthened

Developing the Local Advisory Council Team

The local advisory council should include a relatively small group of concerned, knowledgeable, and committed individuals. The local council should include a balance in representation among school and community agencies, including individuals with disabilities, special education professionals, parent representatives, and individuals from a variety of backgrounds. A council chair should be designated to serve as the lead interagency coordinator or liaison. A long-range plan of two to five years should be developed to sustain the program. The council should define short- and long-range goals within an established timetable, assess the developmental support needs of youth in the system, and define expected outcomes or impacts. It is important that the council have the authority to determine the direction of the interagency partnership and review its accomplishments on a regular basis.

SUMMARY OF KEY POINTS

A coordinated interagency service system provides a systematic, comprehensive, and coordinated system of education and support services for children and youth who are placed at risk. This network of support is provided in their communities in the most integrated settings possible and in a manner that promotes individual choice and decision making.

- School and community leaders are applying the concept of community to creating new partnerships and structures for the benefit of children, youth, and families.
- There is no one model for successful system coordination; best practices need to be tailored carefully to the particular circumstances of the schools and communities and the students and families they serve.

- Educators and related services professionals are challenged to look beyond traditional service boundaries and to consider relationships across their disciplines, across the educational continuum, and across agency boundaries.

KEY TERMS AND PHRASES

- Shared responsibility
- Interagency service coordination
- Coordinated interagency service system
- Coordinated school health program
- Integrated services
- Cooperative agreement
- Service coordinator
- Single point of entry
- Eight functions of service coordination

7

How Does Cultural and Linguistic Diversity Affect Professional Collaboration?

The future calls each of us to become partners in the dance of diversity, a dance in which everyone shares the lead.

—Howard, 1993, p. 41

CHAPTER TOPICS

- Who Are Culturally and Linguistically Diverse Students and Families?
- What Is Cultural Diversity?
- How Does Cultural and Linguistic Diversity Enrich School Environments?
- How Does Cultural and Linguistic Diversity Affect Professional Collaboration?
- What Strategies Are Effective for Working With CLD Students and Parents?

INTRODUCTION

Previous chapters have discussed the challenges and promise of collaboration and system coordination for improving outcomes for students and families. This chapter introduces another factor in human interaction that makes collaboration and coordination even more complex, yet deepens our understanding of the concept and its importance. That factor is cultural and linguistic diversity (CLD). Every individual is rooted in a culture—a family, community, and ethnicity. All of us are constrained by our cultural lenses through which we see the world and the behavior of others. If educators are to help students to develop socially and emotionally and make meaning of their worlds, they must step outside their own cultural boundaries to view the world from multiple perspectives. The greater our ability to appreciate perspectives that are rooted in different cultures, the more likely we are to (a) help students develop healthy relationships with their peers and (b) help personnel develop deeper collaborative relationships with their colleagues.

This chapter explores the question of how cultural and linguistic diversity shapes developmental healthy school environments and professional collaboration and how educators can improve collaboration and coordination of services for culturally and linguistically diverse students and families. The chapter introduces principles for professional collaboration to address the needs of the culturally and linguistically diverse whole student, discusses barriers to communication and collaboration associated with diversity, and lays out strategies for overcoming them.

WHO ARE CULTURALLY AND LINGUISTICALLY DIVERSE STUDENTS AND FAMILIES?

How Is the Nation's Population Changing?

Racial and ethnic diversity has grown dramatically in the United States in the last three decades. This increased diversity appeared first among children and later in the older population and projected to increase even more in the decades to come. Here are some important facts:

- In 2007, 57 percent of children were White, non-Hispanic; 21 percent were Hispanic; 15 percent were Black; 4 percent were Asian; and 4 percent were of other races. (Federal Interagency Forum on Child and Family Statistics., 2009)
- The percentage of children who are Hispanic has increased faster than that of any other racial or ethnic group, growing from 9 percent of the child population in 1980 to 21 percent in 2007. (Federal Interagency Forum on Child and Family Statistics., 2009)
- By 2020, nearly one in four children in the United States will be of Hispanic origin, and by 2030, more than 40 percent of all students in the K–12 population will have cultural and/or linguistic backgrounds that are not European-American (Li & Associates, 2004).
- In 2007, 18 percent of children were native-born with at least one foreign-born parent, and 4 percent were foreign-born with at least one foreign-born parent. (Federal Interagency Forum on Child and Family Statistics., 2009)
- The percentage of children living in the United States with at least one foreign-born parent rose from 15 percent in 1994 to 22 percent in 2007 (Federal Interagency Forum on Child and Family Statistics, 2009).

- California has the highest population of English language learners (ELLs) in the United States with 33 percent; Texas is second with 12 percent (California Department of Education, 2005).

In 2006, 20 percent of school-age children spoke a language other than English at home, and 5 percent of school-age children had difficulty speaking English (U.S. Department of Education, 2009).

- Students speak 400 languages across the nation, although students whose native language is Spanish represent 76.9 percent of students learning English in America (Zehler, Fleischman, Hopstock, Pendzick, & Stephenson, 2003).
- Of U.S. teachers, 45 percent have at least one student with limited English proficiency (LEP) in their classrooms (National Clearinghouse on English Language Acquisition, 2005).
- The percentage of school-age children who spoke a language other than English at home varied by region, from a low of 11 percent in the Midwest to a high of 34 percent in the West (Federal Interagency Forum on Child and Family Statistics, 2009).
- An estimated 9 percent of ELL students in U.S. schools have disabilities (Li, R. & Associates, 2004).

In the context of these population changes, there is a severe shortage of culturally and linguistically diverse teachers in the workforce. School personnel have difficulty distinguishing between language acquisition–based learning difficulties and actual learning disabilities (Zehler et al., 2003). Students therefore have difficulty obtaining services from both special education and ESL (English as a second language) departments when they have both challenges.

Are CLD Students and Families Alike?

CLD families are not a homogeneous group. To collaborate effectively with CLD students and families, it is important to consider the spectrum of linguistic diversity that this population represents, examine the concept of culture, and recognize the importance of acknowledging and respecting native cultures. This understanding is essential to the successful application of the principles presented later in this chapter.

Linguistically diverse students are generally defined as those who speak, or whose families speak, a language other than English (English language learners, ELL). Some are in families that are in or near poverty status, but many are in technical or professional families who earn relatively high incomes. As simple as this concept may appear, non-English speakers as a group have a great range of English language skills. Some students and their parents may not speak English at all. Some parents may not speak English, while their children have acquired English to varying degrees but may not be fully proficient (limited English proficient; LEP). Many parents and students are bilingual. The possible combinations of language proficiency among students and families from the same linguistic background are numerous; therefore, educators should not generalize their experiences with non-English speakers to all ELL students and families.

WHAT IS CULTURAL DIVERSITY?

Appreciating Differences: Linguistic Diversity, Literacy, and Cultural Diversity

Cultural and linguistic diversity affects collaboration and communication among school professionals, students, and families as they work together to create developmentally responsive environments. When considering the nature of students' "diversity," it is important to distinguish among literacy, linguistic diversity, and cultural diversity.

Literacy has traditionally been defined as the ability to read and write. Today the definition has been expanded to include the ability to locate, evaluate, use, and communicate using a wide range of information resources including text, visual, audio, and video sources (Fagan, 2001).

Linguistic abilities can place limitations on how the student becomes literate. For instance, a parent who only speaks Latvian, the official language of Lithuania, will probably only be fully literate in Latvian. Socioeconomic status and level of education also impact literacy. Some immigrants flee their native countries because of limited resources and poor conditions; therefore, their level of literacy in their first language may be far below their spoken language ability in that same language. Conversely, some bilingual or multilingual immigrants have emigrated to work in technical and professional fields in the United States and are literate in several languages.

Cultural diversity is defined as the presence of individuals who are from a variety of cultural backgrounds. More specifically, cultural diversity refers to differences among people based on a shared ideology and valued set of beliefs, norms, customs, and meanings evidenced in a way of life. Diversity includes differences in gender, race, ethnicity, language, nationality, disability, or religion among various groups within a community, organization, or nation. Cultural and linguistic diversity is reflected in several characteristics by which groups differ, including their perceptions, concepts of time, personal space concepts, thinking processes, social groupings and relationships, appearance, posture, symbolism and nonverbal communication (Dahl, 1998). Diverse populations include all groups in the region or nation, including indigenous and immigrant populations.

Regional Differences Are Important

Within an ethnic group, culture may vary widely. Regional differences within the same nation can be significant. For example, imagine two European-American families with French heritage whose past five generations have lived in the United States. The only difference is that one has lived in Vermont their entire lives and the other in Mississippi. Although surely they will have some elements of culture that are similar, they also will differ on any number of beliefs, customs, and linguistic patterns. Similarly, differences are also found within the same ethnic groups who emigrate to the United States from other countries. Individuals who all may be considered Hispanic or Latino may not be at all similar. For example, people from El Salvador are very different from people who have emigrated from Honduras, Mexico, Peru, Argentina, or Bolivia. And all of them differ from families who have emigrated from Spain.

Embedded Cultures

In the United States, there are individuals from multiple cultures, but an overarching American culture exists. This is referred to as the *macroculture*. The *macroculture* is composed of numerous *microcultures,* which are the specific cultural practices of individuals within the population (J. Banks & McGee-Banks, 1992; Guerra & Knox, 2008). So within specific families, there may be various combinations of cultural practices. For example, many Latino or Asian families participate in a traditional American Fourth of July celebration with fireworks and a picnic; others don't acknowledge the holiday and continue with routine activities. Many immigrant children create traditional Valentine's Day cards, yet their parents and grandparents may not acknowledge the holiday. Obviously, a student or child may be more receptive to accepting new cultural values and norms than a parent or grandparent for whom these practices are unfamiliar. Since many cultures embrace an extended family that actively participates in the family structure, within one household there may be a blending of cultures from both the macroculture and the family's microculture (Guerra & Knox; Midobuche, 2001)

Culture, therefore, is a kaleidoscope of infinite combinations and variations of an individual's micro- and macroculture and languages. This provides a challenge for collaboration and coordination of services for culturally and linguistically diverse populations (Soodak & Erwin, 2000), since no two families or individuals are the same, regardless of their ethnic heritage. Each family is a cultural system within a larger culture, as Figure 7.1 shows.

Figure 7.1   Embedded Cultures

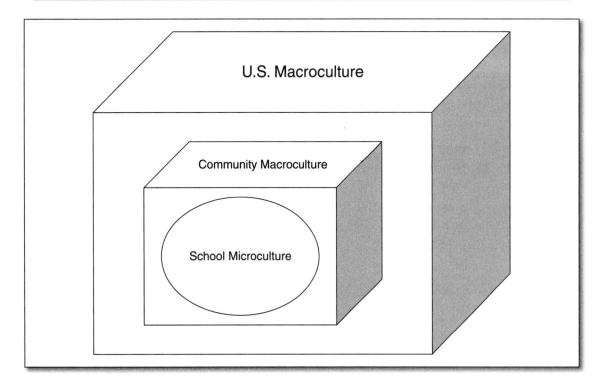

While it is important that educators be very careful not to generalize about people from different regions of the world, it is also important that they understand that some families have come to the United States from countries that are in deep poverty or in conflict. The cultural practices and value sets they bring with them sometimes create conflict as their children adjust to an "American" way of life. The boxed text provides an example of such a conflict.

A CLASH OF CULTURES

Problems for the Hmong in America

Kim-ly Tran is 13 and lives in a large Hmong community in the Midwest. Her parents fled from a mountain village in Vietnam in the 1970s through Laos and then came as refugees to the United States. They only speak Hmong in the home, and her parents do not read.

Kim-ly has many friends in the Hmong community and outside, and so she is aware of the differences between Hmong culture and mainstream American culture. It is common for Hmong girls as young as 14 to enter into marriages to men ranging in age from 17 to 35. A 14-year-old wife may have two children by the age of 16 or 17, and she will usually not be able to complete high school. Thus, her educational opportunities are often limited. Like many Hmong girls, Kim-ly is also burdened by the heavy responsibilities that are heaped upon her at home. Both her parents work in the evening, often leaving her, the oldest girl, to run the household, preventing her from having a social life.

In the eighth grade, Kim-ly began to experience anxiety reactions during school and had to isolate herself from people. Her previously strong grades began to plummet, and she could not pay attention in class or complete homework at home. She agreed to speak to a school counselor, who met with her on a weekly basis in school. The counselor had studied Hmong culture and began weekly group counseling sessions with several Hmong girls who were experiencing problems similar to Kim-ly's. In addition, the school counselor matched the girls with older, successful Hmong high school students, who acted as mentors for the younger girls.

Source: Adapted as a composite of factual information on the Hmong from Lindsay, 2004.

For example, educational systems in some regions of the world are minimal or nonexistent due to sustained conflict. Even if education is available, many children leave school because of lack of security or economic pressures to go to work to help support the family. Consequently, individuals who have left their countries due to war or poverty may not have experience with or exposure to traditional education. This can place the students and parents at a distinct disadvantage when attending schools in the United States as they try to interact with educators and make educational decisions, particularly if the children have special learning needs. However, these families may also be very resilient and possess many other resources that enable them to adapt to requirements of the schools. It is the responsibility of the educator to identify these sources of resilience. The illustrative cases in the boxed text underscore the diversity of students and families and complexity that often challenges them as they respond to the educational needs of their children.

A SHORT STORY

A Parent Asks, "Where Do I Begin?"

Lili Bear, a Native American, was referred for a child study to determine her need for special education services. Her grades had dropped markedly in the past two years in the sixth and seventh grades, following the divorce of her parents, and she was showing serious signs of restlessness and inability to pay attention in class. Her mother had moved off the Cherokee reservation at the time of the divorce three years ago.

The child study team concluded from a variety of assessments that Lili had auditory processing problems, attention deficits, and depression and could benefit from speech and language therapy. The team recommended to Mrs. Bear (in the presence of a Native American advocate) that she (1) have Lili see a counselor or mental health therapist through the county system, (2) seek consultation for ADHD treatment and depression, and

(3) seek family therapy to improve support to Lili at home. The team also suggested that she seek financial help through her insurance for some of the mental health costs.

While Mrs. Bear was appreciative of the all the time, attention, and recommendations of the team, she could not understand how she could possibly locate, arrange, attend, or pay for any of the services recommended. Since her divorce, she had worked two part-time jobs, and she was uncertain what her insurance coverage was, let alone whether it would cover mental health services. She had only completed fifth grade on the reservation and struggled to understand the terms and labels being used to describe her daughter. She left the team meeting feeling overwhelmed.

It is important for educators to realize that wide differences can exist among people who share a common language and culture. Furthermore, while it cannot be assumed that CLD parents and students have minimal experience with the process of education, educators should be sensitive and aware of that possibility. Families such as Lili's can be overwhelmed by educational recommendations from well-meaning team members. Such families may have few resources to follow up on recommendations that require them to navigate a complex service system.

COMING TO AMERICA . . . WITH A LIMITED VIEW OF SCHOOLING

The Story of Domingo—Part 1: History

Domingo, an immigrant from the South American country of Colombia, came to the United States five years ago. Like many immigrants, he left his country of birth to seek a better life here. Employment was a major consideration for him, but so was education for his son.

In the town where Domingo grew up, children only attended school for half a day. Sometimes the teachers would go on strike because they weren't getting paid for weeks, and there would be no school. When classes were held, they were in large rooms that were empty except for desks, a blackboard, and minimal supplies. If children could not pass the annual end-of-year test, they could retake it, but many eventually dropped out. Sometimes students who misbehaved were forced to kneel in the gravel during recess. There were no programs for students with disabilities. In fact, children with moderate to severe disabilities were rarely seen in public. The only contact between parents and teachers was the report card. There were no afterschool activities, conferences, or PTA. People who had more money could send their children to private schools that were better equipped and provided a more consistent and substantial education.

When Domingo immigrated to the United States as a teenager, he brought with him his ideas and attitudes about education: bare rooms, minimal supplies, no help in learning, little interaction with teachers, and the belief that quality education is only for the privileged.

In reference to the case illustration about Domingo from Columbia, how can teachers structure parent-training sessions so that Domingo or other immigrants can begin to understand the U.S. educational system? The story of Domingo is continued is the boxed text.

LIVING IN AMERICA . . . STRUGGLING TO PARTICIPATE

The Story of Domingo—Part 2: The Present

Domingo now lives in the United States, and his son attends elementary school. The school contacts him and asks him to come to a Local Special Education Screening meeting to discuss some serious learning problems that

(continued)

(Continued)

his son is experiencing in school. It is at this point that Domingo begins to try to integrate what he knows about education with his experiences with the American school. Because Domingo has minimal education and little understanding of the needs of children with learning problems, he promptly agrees to the diagnostic testing that is recommended by the team. He asks no questions because he has no previous experience with these processes. To Domingo, this is obviously better than what might have happened back in Columbia.

It is important to understand that blind agreement is **not collaboration.** Domingo might have been able to provide valuable assistance to his son at home or valuable information that would provide some insight into the challenges that his son is facing. It is the responsibility of educators to uncover this information, engage the assistance of parents, and begin to establish a meaningful collaborative relationship.

HOW DOES CULTURAL AND LINGUISTIC DIVERSITY ENRICH SCHOOL ENVIRONMENTS?

Beyond the Demographic Data: What Does Diversity Mean for Schools?

As mentioned above, humans differ greatly in language and in cultural heritage. For example, even among those who speak English, differences in regional accents and lexicon across the United States often create barriers to communication and relationships. In addition, accents and vocabulary can disclose levels of education, social status, personal biases, and a range of other personal characteristics. These differences, however, also add a richness to our experience, if we are willing to step outside our own cultural confines. However, for those who are immigrants struggling to learn the English language, the challenge of learning in American schools is enormous. Policy makers and educators have identified several challenges associated with the needs of the rapidly growing numbers of ELL or LEP students, both with and without learning disabilities, in schools across the United States.

Challenges for Schools and Appropriate Placement of Students

In the face of NCLB accountability requirements for state testing of students, many school districts are struggling to address the needs of this population in order to achieve AYP goals (Cronin, Kingsbury, McCall, & Bowe, 2005; P. McLeod, 2005; Ruiz-de-Valasco & Fix, 2000). States must now provide data on how ELL students are performing on state assessments, and ELL students must participate in these assessments (U.S. Department of Education, 2008a). The research and education policy community is divided as to whether bilingual education or English immersion is best for non-English speakers (Albus & Thurlow, 2005; Educational Policy Reform Research Institute, 2004).

The needs of CLD students are largely unmet in today's schools, as reflected by two important statistics:

1. A disproportionate percentage of Hispanic, Black, and Native American students drop out or do not obtain a high school diploma (Garcia, 2005; Orfield, Losen, Wald, & Swanson, 2004).

2. A disproportionate percentage of Hispanic, Black, and Native American students are placed in special education classes (Cronin et al., 2005; Kozleski, 2005; Obiakor & Wilder, 2003).

Although special education may meet the needs of students with disabilities, it can be inappropriate for students without disabilities. Improperly placing CLD students in special education can negatively impact their educational outcomes and potential career possibilities (Artiles, 1998; Greene & Kochhar-Bryant, 2009; Obiakor & Wilder, 2003; Salend, Garrick Duhaney, & Montgomery, 2002).

These conditions and the growth in diversity of the student population is driving many changes in curriculum and instruction, student assessment, school organizational structure, administration, and personnel preparation. NCLB and IDEIA require that in order to evaluate properly a child who may not be proficient in English, schools must assess the child's proficiency in English as well as in his or her native language to distinguish language proficiency from disability needs. These goals require close collaboration among teachers, ESL specialists, and special educators.

New Responses Needed From School Personnel

Children for whom English is not their primary language have numerous challenges to learning that require special responses on the part of teachers and administrators so that all students are given every opportunity to succeed in school. These challenges include the following:

- Language differences that require teachers to understand how students learn to speak and read English when their primary language is different
- How a student's immersion in the mainstream language affects academic progress and student assessment
- How student and family cultures affect students' learning and progress and how curriculum and instruction can adapt appropriately
- How CLD students are evaluated and referred for support services or to special education so as to avoid their overrepresentation or underrepresentation in special education
- Implications of cultural and linguistic diversity for accessing community services
- Impacts of attitudes and practices that negatively affect ethnically and linguisitically diverse student groups
- Implications of culture for high school transition planning and preparation for employment and post-secondary education.

These challenges demand that educators appreciate the complex interaction of language, culture, and professional knowledge and attitudes in the education of culturally and linguistically diverse students. However, those advocating or undertaking school reform and improvement are not fully considering the implications of this new reality (B. McLeod, 1996; P. McLeod, 2005; Zehler et al., 2003). So important are cultural factors in preparing educators that the Council for Exceptional Children (2001) developed specific content standards for teachers and administrators that address diversity and the role of families in the educational process. Highly qualified educators, counselors, and administrators must be familiar with the special needs of CLD students, both with and without disabilities.

How Can Parents Play a Powerful Role?

Educators are also expected to appreciate the potentially powerful and valuable role of parental participation in the education of their children. Parents provide essential information to educators that cannot be obtained from any other source. They provide an important window into the unique culture of the family and the broader culture of the ethnic community. Active participation of culturally and linguistically diverse parents in the educational decision-making process improves their children's academic achievement (C. Brown, 2004; Cummins, 2001). Culturally and linguistically diverse parents also feel more empowered when they are invited into meaningful collaboration and decision-making processes with educators. When CLD parents are knowledgeable and empowered, overreferral and underreferral to special education is less likely to occur (Obiakor, Utley, Smith, & Harris-Obiakor, 2002; U.S. Department of Education, 2002, 2009). It is essential, for example, to include parents in prereferral or early intervening processes to ensure that students are receiving every possible support for language acquisition before they are referred to special education. The boxed text provides an example of the role collaboration plays in addressing the needs of culturally and linguistically diverse students.

CREATING A SYSTEM TO IMPROVE THE ACHIEVEMENT OF CULTURALLY AND LINGUISTICALLY DIVERSE STUDENTS

The following teaching case provides an example of the role of collaboration in addressing the needs of culturally and linguistically diverse students.

It is April, and Mr. Clayton just became the new principal of Diaz Elementary School. He was chosen because of his experience and success at his previous school with a demographically similar population. Diaz Elementary School has a very diverse student population. Forty percent of the students receive free and reduced lunches, and 52 percent have culturally and linguistically diverse backgrounds, speaking 15 different languages. Of the minority students at Diaz Elementary School, 23 percent are in special education, well above the county average of 9 percent. Mr. Clayton knows that minority overrepresentation in special education has complex roots, but he also knows that with proper staff training, resources, collaboration, and coordination of services, CLD students can successfully participate in general education classes and misidentification can be reduced. One of the primary challenges that Mr. Clayton faces is trying to develop the systems needed to support the diverse student population at Diaz Elementary School.

Mr. Clayton met individually with general education, special education, and English for Speakers of Other Languages (ESOL) teachers; guidance counselors; and the school social worker. After these conversations, Mr. Clayton realized that all of these units in Diaz were functioning as separate entities, widening the gaps in what already was a very fragmented system. Teachers were duplicating efforts with some students, while other students failed to receive the assistance that they needed to improve their academic success. Collaboration and coordination were needed to produce more effective and efficient results.

A staff meeting was held to discuss the challenges facing staff members, as well as the accomplishments that had already been achieved (What's working?). Teachers expressed concerns about language and cultural differences, lack of resources, lack of planning time, and their need to understand how cultural and language differences affect learning. These conditions were contributing to problems and complicating communication and collaboration with students and parents, particularly in IEP and evaluation meetings. Several accomplishments or strengths from which they could build were identified:

- *A moderate rate of parent and student participation in extracurricular activities, such as potluck dinners and movie nights*
- *Minimal behavior and discipline problems*

- *Teachers' ability to provide needed structure and their commitment to student achievement*
- *A parent population that was eager to participate and had not yet become apathetic to challenges their students faced*

Mr. Clayton knew that in order to create a new system within the school, he would have to provide the staff with new tools to work with diverse populations. He knew that encouraging and cultivating CLD parents as resources and decision makers was a crucial factor in the students' and school's success—one that was missing from Diaz. Mr. Clayton also knew that change would not be easy and that it would require a major shift in thinking among his teachers.

First, a series of interactive information sessions *was designed to assess staff knowledge and needs regarding CLD students, the extent of collaboration with CLD parents, and available resources. Next, a series of* training sessions *was developed to help personnel understand the complexities of teaching and supporting CLD students and communicating with their families. Finally,* committees *were established to provide support to staff members throughout the school year.*

Second, blocks of time *were set aside for collaboration across subject areas and within disciplines. All grade-level teachers met on a regular basis, but so did general education, special education, ESL, and guidance teachers for each grade level. For the collaboration periods to be effective, an* outside consultant *was brought in to train teachers on the issues encountered in teaching CLD students and effective collaboration with CLD parents. In a process of* continuous peer review *(critical friends approach), problems related to collaboration were raised in staff meetings and used as examples for analysis, information sharing, and problem solving by teams. Successful collaboration processes were also highlighted, analyzed, and supported.*

Third, the concept of shared responsibility *was introduced to staff—the notion that they all shared a common "client." This was applied not only to students receiving services but also to the* early intervening services *(prereferral intervention) team, the team that decided whether the student needed special education or if the learning problem was related to second language acquisition. It was decided that no decision regarding at-risk or CLD students or students receiving multiple services would be made unless it was a team decision involving each service provider. This meant that each teacher became familiar with the functions and expertise of each other's disciplines and roles while initiating a teaching approach that facilitated the use of language. This approach was designed to prevent duplication of efforts and to ensure the most efficient use of resources. Most importantly, using a* multidisciplinary team approach *established a unified profile of students based on coordinated information about each student. Such coordination increased the school's ability to implement and evaluate appropriate supports in the classroom before students were prematurely or inappropriately referred for special education.*

Teachers were also introduced to the concept of integrated, meaningful, and structured parental participation. *The staff brainstormed how they could engage all parents —not just CLD parents—as* cultural capital *(valued resources) to enhance the learning environment.*

1. *The first program was an afterschool computer-based writing program that helped parents compare their own childhood experiences to the childhood experiences of their children. This was a very successful activity, and the products were published in a book to raise money for future projects.*

2. *The second project was a series of parent training sessions designed to help parents understand the processes, procedures, and expectations of American schools. One expectation specifically addressed was the responsibility of parents to assist their children with homework and to encourage consistent scheduling of study times at home.*

3. *Finally, a special education assistance team was established to assist CLD parents with the special education process to ensure that they had the skills and expertise to be active participants in education decision making.*

Together, these programs encouraged active participation of CLD parents.

(continued)

(Continued)

A teacher action research team was also established to complete two tasks:

1. *The first task was to conduct diversity self-assessments for team members and then to determine how to assess the needs of immigrant students and parents. The team developed a demographic profile of the parent community and then researched strategies used by other schools and organizations to assess the general needs of CLD populations. Next, they sought out several successful programs that served CLD students and arranged time to observe them and meet with their staff.*

2. *Based on this research, they compiled a portfolio of general needs and characteristics along with an inventory of successful teaching and collaboration strategies. The product was presented to the staff at an interactive inservice session and has continued to evolve. Staff plan to develop a Web site to share effective teaching and collaboration strategies.*

Finally, it was decided that Diaz students and families needed a resource center. School and community agency goals were coordinated to ensure access to the community services necessary to support the needs of students. A survey was sent to families to obtain information that helped in establishing a compatible school-based resource center for Diaz's population.

Consider these questions as you reflect on the Diaz Elementary case.

- What made Diaz Elementary School staff realize that change was needed?
- How would you describe the "new kind of collaboration" that was needed?
- What strengths were identified that could be built upon?
- What steps did Mr. Clayton take to provide staff with new tools to work with a diverse population?
- What collaborative teams were established to create the needed changes?

The rapid change in the Diaz Elementary School community population signaled to the school that they needed a new kind of response to students and families. The school was unprepared. As the school assessed the nature of the needs of the students and families, individuals within the system were challenged to create new structures and relationships within the school community. *There was no returning to the way things had been in the past; the school had to re-create itself.* The challenge of including diverse populations of students extended well beyond ensuring the presence of translators or providing materials in native languages. Staff at Diaz Elementary learned that a new kind of collaboration was required. This collaboration took them on a new journey in which understanding and respecting differences in life experiences, world views, cultures, mores, and values led to mutual, respectful, collaborative relationships. Ultimately, collaboration led to improved achievement for CLD students of Diaz Elementary.

HOW DOES CULTURAL AND LINGUISTIC DIVERSITY AFFECT PROFESSIONAL COLLABORATION?

Cultural differences can potentially impede collaborative relationships among students, families, and school personnel. The most obvious challenge is language. Other differences include style of interaction, notions of acceptable participation, and attitudes toward disability. These differences can be challenging to overcome, because cultural characteristics are so integrated into our behavior and identities that often it takes considerable effort to acknowledge and change behavior.

Critical to seeing and understanding the children we teach is the courage to face our own biases openly. Recognizing the limits imposed by our embeddedness in our own culture and experience, acknowledging the values and beliefs we cherish, and accepting the influence of emotions on our actions are extraordinary challenges (Balaban, 1995). Sensitivity toward cultural differences provides the foundation on which collaborative relationships can be built.

Cultural Sensitivity: A Powerful Method of Accommodation

One of the first steps teachers can take is to engage in reflective self-analysis to examine their own attitudes toward different ethnic and racial groups and toward gender and social class. Because our own cultural patterns and language are seldom part of our conscious awareness, we often forget that our taken-for-granted beliefs and values are interpretations, which are culturally and historically specific (Bohn & Sleeter, 2000; Waxman, Lee, & MacNeil, 2008).

Cultural sensitivity, or *cultural competence,* is the ability not only to be aware of and understand an ethnic group's unique norms, values, beliefs, and traditions but also to appreciate and respect these differences. Those who embrace a culturally sensitive approach view differences without value judgment (Huffman, 2003; Zionts, Zionts, Harrison, & Bellinger, 2003). Professionals who are culturally sensitive make accommodations to increase such appreciation and respect among different cultural groups.

Three models represent levels of cultural sensitivity that schools can incorporate (Huffman, 2003; Sanchez, Stuckey, & Morris, 1998).

1. *Promote access through translated materials.* In many school districts, educational documents for students and parents are translated into the most common languages used in that district. Nothing is changed in the practices of the school except the languages in which the documents are produced.

2. *Use culturally adapted or transcultural model.* Schools or programs that adopt this model may not only provide translated materials but also incorporate values, norms, and/or traditions of the target population within the materials. The program maintains its original integrity, but it is modified to make it easier for CLD populations to use, access, or participate in.

3. *Use culturally specific models.* These models are designed for a specific cultural population. Changes in school practices are much more dramatic than in a culturally adapted model (Gorman & Balter, 1997).

According to Kalyanpur and Harry (1999), "Awareness of cultural differences provides the scaffolding for building collaborative relationships" (p. 118). Kalyanpur and Harry used the term *cultural reciprocity* to refer to the ways of thinking and behaving that enable members of one cultural, ethnic, or linguistic group to work effectively with members of another. Lynch (1997) used the term *cross-cultural competence,* which is characterized by the following:

- Awareness of one's cultural limitations
- Openness, appreciation, and respect for cultural differences, including subtle differences
- Avoidance of stereotyping

- Ability to apply cultural awareness universally to all situations
- View of intercultural interactions as learning opportunities
- Ability to use cultural resources in interventions
- Empowerment of families and professionals as each learns from the other (Kalyanpur & Harry; Lynch, E. W., 1997; University of Central Florida, 2004).

The boxed text presents a set of guiding questions to assess one's own cultural competence.

ASSESS YOUR CULTURAL COMPETENCE

The following questions can serve as a guide for assessing your own cultural competence.

- To what extent do you know the demographics, characteristics, and resources within the ethnic communities in your service area?

- How well are you able to describe the strengths of ethnic groups in your school, district, or service area?

- Are you familiar with the prevailing beliefs, customs, norms, and values of the major ethnic groups in your service area?

- Do you attend cultural functions or community forums or interact socially with people of different ethnic groups? Do you patronize businesses or pursue recreational or leisure activities within ethnic communities?

- Does your agency work collaboratively with other programs or have linkages with institutions of higher education and/or civil rights or human relations groups that provide accurate information concerning ethnic populations?

- Do staff members use cultural consultants who can help them work more effectively within a diverse cultural context?

- Does your organization subscribe to publications to stay abreast of news and events concerning ethnic populations. Do staff have access to culturally related materials, and does your organization maintain a library with cultural resources?

- Are people of ethnic minority groups on staff in your organization at all levels?

- Does the agency discuss barriers to working across cultures?

- Do personnel use culture-specific assessment instruments for diagnosis, use culture-specific treatment approaches, and use cultural references or historical accomplishments as a source of empowerment for ethnic populations?

Source: Adapted from Chaisson-Cardenas & Moore, 2003.

Sensitivity to Family Beliefs About Children With Behavioral and Learning Challenges

Members of diverse cultures may vary in child-rearing practices, in their views about social-emotional and learning difficulties, and in their responses to the authority of the school (Harry, 2002; Valle & Aponte, 2002). A family's cultural beliefs will impact the nature of their participation with professionals and schools and how they view disabilities.

Family responses to having a child with any type of learning challenge or disability differ greatly among cultures. In some nations, children with learning and physical disabilities are hidden and not presented as part of the family. The type and severity of a child's disability also affect social attitudes toward the disability. Children with mild disabilities are often assimilated into the culture, while those with more severe disabilities are often socially isolated and cared for only within the immediate family. For instance, a learning disability or mild cognitive disability might go unnoticed in a developing nation or in a remote rural community that provides limited education and has low levels of literacy. In that setting, disabilities may only be acknowledged if they are readily apparent, either physically or behaviorally. It may be difficult for parents to comprehend the concept of a learning or cognitive disability in a child who functioned adequately within the context of their home or community. An understanding of cultural factors is fundamental to implementing educational and related services that are culturally sensitive.

Sensitivity to Rates of Language Acquisition

Cultural and linguistic experiences greatly affect the ease with which CLD students can adapt and progress within "mainstream American society." Second language acquisition takes about five to seven years (to reach content proficiency), but students can reach conversational language proficiency well before that (Zehler et al., 2003). Although parents may appear to understand conversations and discussions fully, it is important that professionals are sensitive to language capabilities.

Unfortunately, language differences often appear to be communication disorders, such as language delays or deficiencies (Obiakor & Wilder, 2003). In many instances, these perceived delays or deficiencies trigger referrals to special education. Once a CLD student is referred to special education, it is likely that he or she will be found eligible for services (Zehler et al., 2003). To ensure that students are being fairly assessed, collaboration among speech and language therapists, bilingual specialists, and general and special education teachers is essential in the early intervening services stage to determine whether the student is exhibiting a communication disorder or expected language differences.

Technical language and frequent use of acronyms by school professionals can present obstacles to communication. Educators and special educators are particularly reliant on acronyms with which many individuals outside of the field are unfamiliar with. It may help to develop a list of acronyms and their definitions to distribute to parents in their native language or to use as a reminder when conversing with individuals whose primary language is not English. Many parents are uncomfortable expressing their lack of understanding and may not ask the questions necessary for them to comprehend and actively participate in a conference or conversation with teachers. It is important to be mindful of the technical language that is used to communicate with all parents, but especially culturally and linguistically diverse families. The boxed text continues the story of Domingo begun earlier in the chapter.

LIVING IN AMERICA ... WITH LIMITED ENGLISH LANGUAGE SKILLS
The Story of Domingo—Part 3: A Meeting

The day of the special education eligibility meeting is approaching, and Domingo is contacted to come to the meeting. Test results are discussed, and a translator is present. The Woodcock Johnson III Test of Achievement

(continued)

(Continued)

and Stanford Binet were used, and numerical scores are presented. Domingo dutifully sits through the entire meeting, unable to understand the discussion and overwhelmed and intimidated by the room full of professionals all discussing his child. His son is found eligible for services for learning and emotional disabilities. Domingo is passed a paper to sign, and the meeting is ended.

Domingo needed help from the special education assistance team to prepare him to be an active participant in this decision-making process. NCLB and IDEIA support Domingo's right to be present *and* to participate actively in the meetings and decisions. The presence of a translator **does not mean active participation,** because the translator simply translates discussion without interpreting it for Domingo.

It is apparent that the inclusion of CLD populations into schools requires different strategies and knowledge for school personnel. A flexible and responsive educational system is designed to recognize the challenges students and parents must overcome and provides them with necessary supports and reasonable timetables to achieve it. At a minimum, most school districts provide translators to minimize language barriers during special education-related meetings with families. The availability of translators for other types of meetings varies among school districts, but some schools have engaged parent liaisons who act as translators. At minimum, school districts should have most legal documents translated into the most common languages of the community.

Sensitivity to Different Styles of Interaction

Different cultures have different styles of interaction, and when these styles clash, or are incongruent, they can become barriers to effective collaboration (Harry, 2002). Interaction style refers to the body language, spoken language, voice tone, intensity, attitudes about personal space, and role perceptions that make up human interactions. The concept of interaction styles can be applied directly and indirectly to collaboration and coordination of services. Parents who do not access available services for their children may be perceived as uninvolved or neglectful. However, the problem may actually be limited knowledge and experience with community services, pride, or cultural values that reject state-funded assistance (Geenan, Powers, & Lopez-Vasquez, 2001). In some cultures, teachers are considered dominant, and parents have experienced few opportunities to participate in decisions about their child's education. Culturally and linguistically diverse parents, therefore, may not believe they are entitled to participate in educational decisions and that the school should make such decisions. Different cultural beliefs need to be acknowledged by educators in order to avoid misinterpretation and to facilitate a collaborative relationship.

Sensitivity to Parents' Ability to Participate

Strict adherence to traditional ways of engaging parents can actually have a negative impact on collaborative relationships with CLD parents (López, 2001; Waterman, 2006; Waterman & Harry, 2008). Educators often define *appropriate parent participation* as attending parent–teacher conferences, volunteering in the classroom, and participating in the school PTA, and they may believe these the only legitimate means for parents to participate in their children's education. However, different cultures, lifestyles, and family resources often dictate different levels of participation. Furthermore, many CLD families are at a distinct disadvantage when confronted with complex education laws, eligibility, placement processes, and procedures. Inadequate understanding about these procedures and processes often prevents these families from making informed decisions about their children and from participating in school decisions in a meaningful way.

WHAT STRATEGIES ARE EFFECTIVE FOR WORKING WITH CLD STUDENTS AND PARENTS?

Coordination to Support English Language Learners With Disabilities

Language development should be the shared responsibility of all teachers, not only those in bilingual and ESL classes (Ortiz, 2004). General education teachers provide access to the general curriculum, special education teachers help to modify the curriculum or adapt instruction, and ESL/bilingual teachers support second-language acquisition. ESL/bilingual teachers understand that acquiring a second language is not the same as acquiring a first language, and they understand the impact of culture on a child's behavior in class. With an ELL child with disabilities, general education, special education, and ESL/bilingual teachers must collaborate closely to develop individualized education and supports. P. McLeod (2005) and others have conducted reviews of strategies related to English language learners (see also Callahan, Wilkinson, Muller, & Frisco, 2009; Ortiz, 2004). The following sections draw on her synthesis.

- *Bilingual education* is developmental; that is, it helps the student develop and maintain proficiency in two languages, English and the native language.
- *Transitional bilingual* means providing instruction in the native language while English is used increasingly, until the student enters a regular instructional program. When the student has a disability, the special education teacher consults with bilingual teachers to adapt instruction. Other services can be provided through trained related-services personnel.
- *English as a second language* services are now being provided in general education classrooms rather than pullout settings. Students have access to high-quality instruction designed to help them meet high expectations. Teachers collaborate to employ strategies known to be effective with English learners, such as drawing on their prior knowledge; providing opportunities to review previously learned concepts and teaching them to employ those concepts; organizing themes or strands that connect the curriculum across subject areas; and providing individual guidance, assistance, and support to fill gaps in background knowledge (Callahan et al., 2009; Center for Equity and Excellence in Education, 2002, 2006).

Differentiating Language Acquisition Problems and Learning Disabilities

ELL students with disabilities may need to receive both language support services and special education services. However, ESL educators and parents are concerned about the overrepresentation of culturally and linguistically diverse students (CLD) in special education services. Also, once students are classified as individuals with disabilities, the current school structure often strips them of their ESL support (Callahan et al., 2009). Although IDEIA 2004 attempted to provide comprehensive quality services to students with disabilities, lack of language support or bilingual services for ESL students in special education programs is likely to impact ESL teachers' decision making when referring a student for special education.

The process of distinguishing between students with language acquisition problems and learning disabilities should begin with several questions. What exposure have these students had to the curriculum? What are their cognitive and learning characteristics? What is their academic experience and background (McCardle, Mele-McCarthy, Cutting, Leos, & D'Emilio, 2005; Yates & Ortiz, 1998)? When looking at speech and spelling errors, a question to consider is: Does the child have an auditory or speech problem, or are the difficulties a result of learning two different language systems? Many speech and spelling errors are rooted in differences between an English language learner's home language and English. These kinds of assessments are essential before a student is placed into special education.

In terms of evaluating the language status for non-English speakers and the possible presence of a disability, the following guidelines are offered:

1. *LEP, recent arrival:* Evaluate the student in the native language. Provide native language instruction or ESL instruction. The IEP should include plans for English language acquisition (bilingual instruction and/or ESL). Special education services should not be provided in English only.

2. *LEP, one to three years:* Evaluate the student in the native language and in English. Determine language or languages in which special education and related services will be provided—this information should be included in the IEP (Albus & Thurlow, 2005; Artiles & Ortiz, 2002; Goldenberg, 2008; Klinger, Hoover, & Baca, 2008).

3. *Long-term LEP, over three years:* Evaluate the student in the native language and English but do not discontinue language support services.

The "appropriate placement" does not have to be a self-contained classroom for ELL students. Both bilingual/ESL and special education services can be provided in the general education classroom. Collaboration with bilingual and ESL teachers is essential, especially when general and special educators are not bilingual.

EIGHT PRINCIPLES AND STRATEGIES TO STRENGTHEN PROFESSIONAL COLLABORATION IN HIGHLY DIVERSE SCHOOLS

There is no cookbook for effectively working with diverse populations. People need opportunities to share their experiences and cultural views, whether they are part of a teaching team, interdisciplinary planning team, transition team, interagency coordination team, or other collaborative working group. The following sections present eight principles that undergird effective collaborative relationships and service coordination in diverse settings.

Principle 1

It is the responsibility of all citizens in a democratic, multicultural society to promote a collaborative climate that appreciates individuals from all cultures (Bernhard, Freire, Pacini-Ketchabaw, &

Villanueva, 1998; Swick, Boutte, & Van Scoy, 1995/1999). At its simplest level, multicultural education is a critical forum for reforming schools in ways that support pluralism and equity (Bohn & Sleeter, 2000; Riehl, 2000). Professionals who value a culture of appreciation seek to increase their factual knowledge about diversity while at the same time integrating new information into their worlds, world views, relationships, and interactions. Through this process, they create new personal meaning. Creating new personal meaning means extending our understanding of the world as we have seen it, gaining a new perspective or changing a belief traditionally held, strengthening a personal value, or renewing a commitment to a goal.

The value of appreciating diversity should extend from district to local levels and from administrators to all staff (Swick et al., 1995/1999). Improving students' understanding of cultural diversity should also be a part of a comprehensive multicultural education program. A greater understanding of diverse patterns of behavior and cultures helps educators more realistically perceive the life experiences of diverse groups (Bohn & Sleeter, 2000). This understanding, in turn, helps reduce preconceptions and biases and provides a foundation for more effective collaboration.

Principle 2

Personal biases and prejudices must not influence collaborative relationships with diverse individuals. It is useful for educators to examine their position in society in relation to culture and class privilege (Kumashiro, 2001; Nieto, 2000). For example, it is common in many nations for each race to be afforded a specific place among the other races and within the class structure. Often, exploring these issues illuminates discrepancies, disparities, and injustices among individuals that are contrary to democratic ideals yet nonetheless present in society. Once societal positions are explored, this can be a catalyst to foster meaningful discussion related to biases, preconceived stereotypes, and prejudices that negatively impact collaboration.

Principle 3

The collaborative professional acknowledges that CLD families do value education. Many students and families are confronted with insurmountable obstacles to participating in educational processes: language barriers, negative perceptions, exclusionary practices, employment obligations, cultural differences, and failure to understand educational processes and procedures. These factors contribute to behaviors that could be perceived as contradictory to positive, supportive parental participation (Bernhard et al., 1998; Cummins, 2001; López, 2001; Valencia & Black, 2002). A CLD parent's participation in collaborative interactions should not be judged until every attempt has been made to eliminate or minimize the barriers to such participation.

Principle 4

Actively build collaboration upon cultural and linguistic diversity in the school. Schools and institutions that succeed in empowering students and parents to participate communicate respect for cultural diversity. They act to marshal diversity to the advantage of everyone (Bernhard et al., 1998; Zehr, 2003). The incorporation and respect for diversity can be visualized along an "additive-subtractive" continuum (Cummins, 2001). At the positive end of the continuum are educators who acknowledge the benefits of bilingual and bicultural students and parents. In contrast, at the other end of the continuum sit educators whose goal is the replacement of native cultures with that of the dominant mainstream. As Figure 7.2 depicts, the positive end of the continuum is empowering, and the negative end is demeaning. *This not to say that the dominant American culture is at the negative end but, rather, that the goal of eliminating native culture is disempowering.*

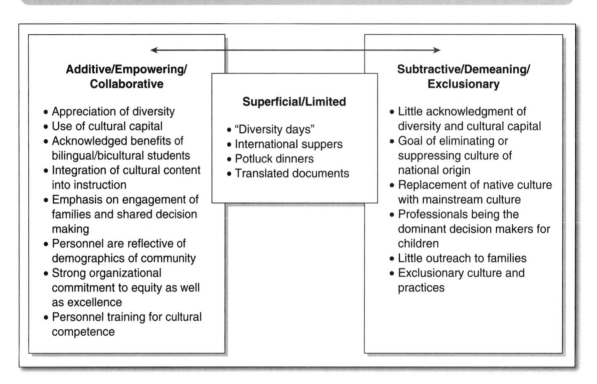

Figure 7.2   Continuum of Respect for Diversity

Additive/Empowering/ Collaborative

- Appreciation of diversity
- Use of cultural capital
- Acknowledged benefits of bilingual/bicultural students
- Integration of cultural content into instruction
- Emphasis on engagement of families and shared decision making
- Personnel are reflective of demographics of community
- Strong organizational commitment to equity as well as excellence
- Personnel training for cultural competence

Superficial/Limited

- "Diversity days"
- International suppers
- Potluck dinners
- Translated documents

Subtractive/Demeaning/ Exclusionary

- Little acknowledgment of diversity and cultural capital
- Goal of eliminating or suppressing culture of national origin
- Replacement of native culture with mainstream culture
- Professionals being the dominant decision makers for children
- Little outreach to families
- Exclusionary culture and practices

Parallel to the additive–subtractive continuum is the collaborative–exclusionary continuum, which applies specifically to working with culturally and linguistically diverse parents. On one end are the educators who unconsciously or consciously want to create an educational system based on equality for all. They actively encourage CLD parents to support the educational progress of their children in the home and school, and they make accommodations to encourage parent participation. At the opposite end of the continuum are educators who perceive themselves solely as "the teacher" and are neutral or negative about parent participation (Cummins, 2001). These educators fail to acknowledge the cultural capital and positive impact that diverse parents can have on their child's education.

Principle 5

Create school-based resource centers to promote collaboration with diverse populations. Many schools are creating school-based community resource centers to expand participation of CLD families. Resources fall into two main categories:

1. *Family-oriented resources:* An example is support groups that provide opportunities for families to discuss issues such as daily demands, triumphs, and obstacles they encounter (Barron-McKeagney et al., 2002; Driscoll, Russell, & Crockett, 2008)

2. *Service-oriented resources:* The resource center becomes a logical hub for facilitating frequent and regular participation and linking with school-based and community services (Riehl, 2000). Service-oriented resources include health care options, child care options, coordination of services through mental health facilities, housing, language instruction, economic resources, and other social resources available thorough public agencies.

Principle 6

Make expectations for participation and collaboration explicit. The *hidden curriculum* means the implicit rules and structures that are part of the unique culture of the organization or school. "Acceptable" parent participation and collaboration is no exception (Bernhard et al., 1998; López, 2001). Several strategies have been shown to be effective in communicating expectations for parent collaboration and engagement with the school. Administrators must be committed to improving relationships with families and provide staff development with focus on cultural sensitivity. Hiring bilingual staff and engaging bilingual volunteers can support these goals. Outreach to the community is strengthened by a welcoming environment in the school. This includes family-friendly, flexible meeting hours that accommodate families' schedules and transportation assistance to help families attend meetings. Essential to improving outcomes for CLD students is helping parents understand what "high standards for all children" means.

Principle 7

Acknowledge alternate forms of parental participation and collaboration. CLD parents frequently participate in their child's education indirectly or outside conventional participation activities (Geenan et al., 2001; López, 2001; Valencia & Black, 2002). For instance, they may use stories with their children to convey the importance of education. Valencia and Black found that *consejos,* or advice-giving narratives, were a common method that Latino families used to convey their commitment to education to their children. Similarly, "funds of knowledge," or teaching by example, is used to communicate values and commitments. It is important to identify, acknowledge, and support these valuable means of participation within a family.

Principle 8

Involve parents in meaningful, structured activities. Culturally and linguistically diverse parents want the best for their children, but they are often constrained by logistics, attitudes, and experience. Educators need to establish creative means to showcase the cultural capital of students and families while involving them in meaningful educational activities (Perez & Pinzon, 1997). Sometimes parents may need to be shown how to participate in homework and other school-related activities (Cummins, 2001).

It is important to differentiate between single events and social activities and meaningful participation designed to empower parents. Potluck dinners and multicultural nights are important social events. International show-and-tell in class can be educational and beneficial to children and families. However, using students or parents from other countries and cultures as "authorities" may appear to be empowering but must be used with caution, because it can be perceived by the students as demeaning and therefore not a meaningful activity. Academic supports for CLD students and administrative resources for parent participation are two examples of activities designed to build long-term capacity to engage parents. Inviting and encouraging parents to serve on committees that support decision making in the school or district is another empowering activity.

SUMMARY OF KEY POINTS

- The number of CLD students in the United States is has risen dramatically in the past decade.
- Educational performance gaps persist for many CLD students, and educators have difficulty differentiating between second-language acquisition challenges and the presence of a disability.
- Both IDEIA 2004 and NCLB have focused on the performance gaps of CLD students and challenged schools to close them.
- Culturally competent teachers and related service personnel appreciate the complex interaction of language, culture, knowledge, and attitudes in the education of culturally and linguistically diverse students.
- Culturally competent personnel recognize diversity as enriching education; they also appreciate the potentially powerful and valuable role of parental involvement in improving student achievement and providing a window into the culture of the family.

KEY TERMS AND PHRASES

- Culture
- Cultural and linguistic diversity
- Literacy
- Acculturation
- Ethnocentrism
- Assimilation
- Accommodation
- Deficit perspective
- Cultural mismatch theory
- Cultural model perspective
- Macroculture and microculture
- Cultural sensitivity
- Cultural competencies

Celebrating Our Work

The Benefits and Positive Impacts of Professional Collaboration

School people and their relationships to one another will make or break reform. How do teachers relate to each other? How do school professionals interact with parents and community? What are principal-teacher relations like? The answers to such questions are central to determining whether schools can improve.

—David T. Gordon, 2002, p. 1

CHAPTER TOPICS

- The Power of Collaboration: Can the Success of Professional Collaboration and Interagency Coordination Be Measured?
- Does Professional Collaboration Improve Results for the Whole Child?
- How Do We Know That Whole-Child Approaches Impact Student Learning?
- Does Collaboration Promote Student and Family Self-Determination?
- Why Is It Important to Celebrate Our Work and Renew Our Commitment?

INTRODUCTION

Collaboration and coordination are essential to change processes aimed at improving student achievement. Our final question, which this chapter will address, is this: *What evidence is there that collaboration and service coordination actually result in the kinds of changes or outcomes we expect—in student achievement and developmental progress, improved practices, and organizational change?* This question about evidence becomes a little more complex when we begin to think about the effects of collaboration at different points along the developmental continuum for students. The chapter discusses the link between professional collaboration and positive results for students, families, and a variety of professionals who work together on their behalf.

Collaboration should occur with clearly defined results, or desired effects, in mind for students, families, and professionals. The driving questions are these: Does collaboration work? What do we mean by "effective" collaboration? What results are expected from collaboration and from interagency service coordination? This chapter explores evidence that both professional collaboration and interagency service coordination promote the academic achievement and progress of the whole child, parent engagement in education, and more effective linkages between schools and community service agencies.

THE POWER OF COLLABORATION: CAN THE SUCCESS OF PROFESSIONAL COLLABORATION AND INTERAGENCY COORDINATION BE MEASURED?

About Maps, Mileage, and Navigation: Making Decisions and Measuring Results

Policy makers, researchers, and practitioners recognize the benefits and positive outcomes of professional collaboration and interagency service coordination to support children and their families as they enter, progress in, and exit the school system. Although current legislation emphasizes the need for a shared responsibility for educating all children, collaboration and service coordination continue to be great challenges for school systems. The challenge remains for three reasons:

1. It is difficult for professionals in different disciplines and agencies to make decisions about what results they expect from the collaboration and service coordination.

2. It is difficult to decide how to measure collaboration and coordination and what measures to use.

3. It is difficult to navigate, or lead, collaborative efforts among different people who have different attitudes about change processes and expected results.

Benefits and *outcomes* refer to the results that school personnel hope to see from the professional collaboration or interagency coordination efforts. Outcome evaluation involves measuring how the collaborative service delivery process leads to the desired change in the student/consumer population and in partner agencies. The expected results or outcomes are like the map that points us in the direction we want to go; the measures are the ways we determine the distance we have come in achieving the results;

and the leadership factor is the ability of professionals to lead, or navigate, through the change processes that necessarily come with collaboration and interagency coordination.

Effective Professional Collaboration: A Shared Responsibility for Results

Systemic change for educating the whole child is not likely to occur if only the principal or administrator has a clear understanding of what needs to be accomplished. To create a shared commitment to collaboration, everyone involved in producing results needs the following:

- A clear rationale for why a change is needed, including expected results
- An explanation of how collaboration will help achieve the desired results
- An understanding of all participants' roles in the process, including how they can expect their roles and work to change
- Incentives or rewards associated with participation in the collaborative initiative (tangible and intangible)

It is important to determine the purpose for the collaboration, outcomes or results desired, the environment in which collaboration will take place, the tasks and responsibilities involved, and the manner in which the initiative's success will be measured. The following mnemonic—POETRE—might help with remembering the essential questions for evaluating a collaborative initiative.

P   What is the *purpose* for the collaboration? (What problems need to be addressed? What questions need to be asked?)

O   What *outcomes* (results) are collaborators expecting?

E   What is the appropriate *environment* in which to accomplish the outcome (people, location, setting, materials)?

T   What is the sequence of *tasks* to be accomplished?

R   Whom should be assigned *responsibility* for the tasks?

E   How do we *evaluate* so we know if we have achieved the results we want?

Focusing on these questions helps collaborative leaders make decisions that can carefully guide the collaborative activity and keep it focused. The example in the boxed text applies the POETRE questions.

KNOW WHAT YOU WANT FROM COLLABORATION

Middle school principal Mr. Sawyer and a few of her teachers decided to bring people together to "talk about" ways the school could improve students' preparation for transition from middle to the high school. The meeting was planned hastily, and invitations were sent out broadly to individuals within and outside the school. When the meeting came together, there were elementary and middle school teachers, a high school counselor, a speech and language therapist, a social worker, as well as district staff and a school improvement specialist.

(continued)

(Continued)

The meeting was unproductive, since it degenerated into a tense complaint session in which school personnel were put on the defensive about what resources were available to make changes, who was responsible, why there were no high school teachers there, and why this had not been brought up during the last school improvement team meeting. It felt to some participants like a monitoring meeting.

After the meeting, Principal Sawyer and school staff stayed to debrief. They had not thought through what they wanted from the meeting. The debriefing yielded the following information about purpose, outcomes desired, environment, tasks, responsibility, and evaluation (POETRE).

P What was the purpose (question being asked)? *How can our school improve transition support services and supports for students moving from middle to high school?*

O What outcomes/results did they expect? *While Principal Sawyer expected to produce a set of brainstormed ideas about strategies that could be pursued further with the high school staff, this expected result was not clearly communicated to participants.*

E What is the appropriate environment to accomplish the outcome (people, location, setting, materials)? *Principal Sawyer realized that perhaps first she should have held a smaller brainstorming session with staff to organize their thinking, examine needs within the middle school, and prepare to present needs and set goals for a larger meeting. Also, realizing that place and setting is important and symbolic, staff suggested finding a more neutral setting or having the next meeting at the high school.*

T What are the next tasks to be accomplished? *Another meeting was set for school personnel to hold an open discussion about transition and adjustment to high school and prepare for a larger meeting in which concrete plans could be developed.*

R Whom should be assigned responsibility for the tasks? *Principal Sawyer took responsibility to invite participants from the middle school and assigned the assistant principal the task of conducting a schoolwide survey of ideas that could be brought to the next meeting.*

E How do we evaluate so we know that we have achieved the results we want? *Principal Sawyer decided to evaluate the activities by providing staff with a summary of the needs survey, the group discussion outlining the suggested ideas and strategies to improve transition, and proposed next steps. All staff were invited to provide feedback, whether individually, in writing, or at a general staff meeting.*

Facilitators of Effective Interagency Service Coordination: Knowledge, Organization, and Attitude

Achieving coordination between schools and community service agencies is one of the most challenging endeavors that schools take on. While many organizational, attitudinal, and knowledge factors serve as barriers, many others can facilitate the development of effective collaboration and coordination. These can serve as measures of success (the "mileage") for collaborative efforts that support the needs of the whole child.

Knowledge facilitators include the following:

- Research on effective models for collaboration and coordination of services
- Adapting models to fit local conditions
- Working in boundary-crossing tasks or roles
- Leadership styles that favor collaboration and coordination

- State standards that communicate the responsibilities of local education agencies for collaboration or system coordination
- Shared definitions and service philosophies among schools and agencies

Organizational facilitators include these:

- Formal interagency agreements with community organizations
- Timelines for action in developing holistic educational services
- Investment of agency resources
- Reward systems for staff to reinforce group-centered approaches and collaboration
- Reasonable caseloads for professionals who support students
- A focus on outcomes and accountability for results among professionals
- A broad range of services offered by organizations
- Geographic proximity among organizations
- Clear lines of communication and clear roles
- Shared evaluation of the effectiveness of the collaborative relationship or the interagency agreement

And here are some examples of *attitudinal facilitators*:

- Perceived need for collaboration
- Prevailing organizational and environmental norms that value collaboration
- Relationships among participants that are based on trust, respect, and mutual understanding
- Flexibility and adaptability
- A process for recognizing and celebrating collective achievements and individual contributions
- A process for sharing information between families and professionals that facilitates access to needed services and supports

Seven Action Steps for Evaluating Interagency Agreements

The following action steps are useful for designing an evaluation of interagency agreements for service coordination.

1. Who will participate? Decide who will participate in design of the evaluation and in defining outcomes to be measured. Ensure that all agencies, units, or organizations that will be impacted by the interagency agreement are represented in the evaluation. Engage a consultant if needed.

2. What will you evaluate? Select the elements of the interagency agreement that need to be evaluated (e.g., informing the community, assessing needs, developing shared resources, shared mission, cooperative agreement, outcomes, or all of these).

Decide also whether to evaluate individual-level outcomes or system-level outcomes. Individual-level outcomes include measures of achievement or progress of children and families in education or transition from one educational level to the next (e.g., successful transition from early intervention to preschool, improved academic performance, improved access to related services, increased involvement of families in their children's education, reduced dropout, and successful transition from high school to post-secondary settings. System-level outcomes include measures of improvements in the service system as a whole, in the way agencies coordinate their services to serve students, and in how well the system is assuring access to services for all students who need them.

3. What questions will you ask? Outcome evaluation addresses several questions: How do we know that the programs and services are helping students and families achieve education goals? How can we improve the interagency partnership to increase access to services included in students' education and support service plans? How do students and families judge the quality and accessibility of the education and support services? How well are the interagency partners accomplishing the goals in their cooperative agreements? To what extent are students and families benefiting from the services?

4. What will be your evaluation design and methods? Evaluation should support decision making and, thus, should be built into the cooperative agreement early in the planning stage. Evaluation measures should be closely aligned with objectives in the cooperative agreement. Interagency coordinators play central roles in the planning and implementing of evaluation and in defining measures of "success." It is important that interagency evaluation is supported at the highest leadership levels and that the partners communicate evaluation results and use them for future planning. Interagency evaluation planning teams include representatives from all collaborating agencies and families.

5. How will you collect and analyze your data? Data collection and analysis should yield useful information about results and benefits for participants. Identify the sources of information needed to answer evaluation questions (e.g., interviews, surveys, site visits and observations, records reviews). Select data analysis procedures, such as quantitative measurements of numbers of participants and measures of student progress, or qualitative measurements, such as analysis of interviews and open-ended questionnaires related to students' judgments of the quality of the services.

6. How will you report evaluation results? Distribute the final report to partners and key stakeholders. How will you use the evaluation information for change and improvement? Ensure that evaluation results are acted upon. Evaluation reinforces and supports program management, accountability, and continuous improvement. Have the evaluation design and methods evaluated by an external consultant.

7. How will evaluated results be used? Equally important as collecting evaluation data from multiple sources is acting upon evaluation data to improve the service system. Evaluation information should be (1) analyzed and communicated in a manner that is understandable and usable by different stakeholder groups (e.g., service coordinators, students, families, administrators) and (2) applied in decisions about service system change and improvement. Evaluations reveal valuable information about the general quality of services, their weaknesses, and any barriers and gaps that may exist, and they inform future decisions about how the interagency agreement needs to change to improve services.

DOES PROFESSIONAL COLLABORATION IMPROVE RESULTS FOR THE WHOLE CHILD?

Professional collaboration has become even more important for schools in recent years: collaboration is essential to improving academic achievement for all students in response to new accountability requirements. Accumulating research is providing evidence of links between student achievement and collaboration: professional to professional, teacher to student, special educator to general educator, teacher to parent, IEP team collaboration, and school to community professional coordination. Effective collaboration and system coordination have been linked to a variety of student, family, and professional outcomes. These include the following:

- Gains in student achievement, motivation, attendance, conduct, and other measures of commitment to learning
- Improved collaboration among teachers and related services personnel and systematic assistance and support to beginning teachers
- An expanded pool of ideas, methods, and materials that benefits all teachers
- Greater engagement of parents in their children's education
- Improved coordination among schools and school-linked agencies to support student services and school improvement planning (Bush, 2007; Bush & Glover, 2002; Dettmer et al., 2005; DuFour, 2003; Friend & Cook, 2009; Glover, 2003; Kendziora et al., 2001; Knight & Boudah, 2003; Sharpe & Hawes, 2003).

Creating a professional collaborative culture may be the most important factor in successful school improvement initiatives to improve student outcomes (Gordon, 2002; Lambert, 2003).

HOW DO WE KNOW THAT WHOLE-CHILD APPROACHES IMPACT STUDENT LEARNING?

Whole-child approaches are grounded in a set of assumptions and challenges for practice that includes the following:

- Healthy kids make better students. What can we do to ensure that all kids arrive at school healthy and ready to learn?
- Students who are scared have trouble concentrating. What can we do to ensure students feel safe and secure, both physically and emotionally, in their schools?
- Academic engagement is critical for success. How can schools and communities engage students in ways that are relevant and tied to the broader community beyond the classroom?
- Students who are supported by caring adults are most likely to excel. What elements of student support, both inside and outside the classroom, are critical to ensuring success? What does support for students mean, and how can we ensure all students have it (Commission on the Whole Child, 2007)?
- Students must be prepared for life outside school. What must we do to provide a challenging, rigorous curriculum that prepares today's students for success in the workplace and higher education (Commission on the Whole Child, 2007)?

The following sections provide a summary of research on whole-child approaches and student learning from the Learning First Alliance (2001), interwoven with more recent research. The summary is organized around core elements of safe and supportive learning communities.

A Supportive Learning Community Promotes Student Achievement and Positive Development

A great deal of research has confirmed a positive relationship between educational environments that address the needs of the whole child and student achievement. The National Longitudinal Study of Adolescent Health (Resnick, Ireland, & Borowski, 2004; Greenberg et al., 2003), a study of 90,000 middle and high school students, found that students who feel "connected" to school—measured by the strength and quality of their relationships with teachers and other students—are more likely to have improved attitudes toward school, learning, and teachers; heightened academic aspirations, motivation, and achievement; and more positive social attitudes, values, and behavior. In addition, when students feel connected to school, they are less likely to use drugs, be violent, commit suicide, or exhibit other at-risk behaviors. Students' sense of school as community is related to a number of improved student outcomes:

- *Research from the Developmental Studies Center:* Increased positive interpersonal attitudes, enjoyment of school, school engagement, and academic motivation; reduced delinquency, drug use, misbehavior, violence, and sexual activity (D. Gottfredson & Bauer, 2007; G. Gottfredson, Gottfredson, Payne, & Gottfredson, 2005)
- *Research on implementation of the Comer School Development:* Improved school climate, reading and math achievement, behavior, and anger control (Cook, Murphy, & Hunt, 2000)
- Increased tendency to abide by the classroom's expressed norms and values (Benson et al., 2006b)
- Reduced drug use, victimization, and delinquency (Anderson, Christenson, & Lehr, 2004; L. Johnston, O'Malley, Bachman, & Schulenberg, 2009)

These effects may be most pronounced for students who are at most risk (L. Johnston et al., 2009). In summary, decades of research provide evidence that young people have basic psychological needs for autonomy, belonging, competence, and physical security (Learning First Alliance, 2001; Berliner, 2009; Blank et al., 2003; Brener, Weist, Adelman, Taylor, & Vernon-Smiley, 2007; Deci & Ryan, 2006, 2008).

A Challenging and Engaging Curriculum Promotes Student Achievement and Positive Development

Student engagement and enthusiasm are critical to student achievement, school attendance, and staying in school. Results related to challenging and engaging curricula that promote student achievement include the following:

- Increased student achievement is found in schools and classrooms with high expectations, a challenging curriculum, and instruction that focuses on the development of both thinking skills and content understanding (Deci & Ryan, 2006; Patton & Trainor, 2003).
- Effective instruction engages students in higher levels of thinking; uses multiple ways of working with students, such as lectures, small groups, and independent projects; and connects schoolwork to real-life contexts (Linnenbrink & Pintrich, 2003).
- Student achievement is best achieved when schools and communities have clear goals to help all students meet high standards and teachers, administrators,

students, and families take collective responsibility for meeting those goals (Deshler, 2005; Deshler, Schumaker, & Woodruff, 2004).

- Failure to support the academic achievement of students is related to students' disengagement from school and increased risk-taking behavior. National longitudinal data show that regardless of ethnic background or social class, youth who have problems with schoolwork are more likely than others to be involved in every health risk studied, including alcohol, sexual intercourse, and weapon-related violence (Blum, Beuhring, & Rinehart, 2000).

Respectful, Supportive Relationships Among Students, Staff, and Parents Promote Student Achievement and Positive Development

Many studies substantiate the importance of belonging and support for students, for staff, and for parents (Adelman & Taylor, 2006a; Education Commission of the States, 2007; Resnick et al., 2004). The following findings demonstrate the importance of respectful and supportive relationships:

- Teacher satisfaction and effectiveness is related to teachers' sense of the school as a community; research on the separate components of teachers' sense of community has verified the importance of teacher collaboration (Aubusson et al., 2007, DuFour, 2004; Noddings, 2005).
- Teachers who experience the school as a community try to provide parallel experiences for their students; when teachers are active participants in professional learning communities with a strong sense of voice and authority, they create a similar learning context for their students (Aubusson et al., 2007).
- Small schools help promote positive administrator and teacher attitudes and collaboration. Among students, small schools contribute to positive interpersonal relations, attitudes, and behavior; a greater sense of belonging; participation in extracurricular activities; enhanced school attendance; and lowered dropout rates. Achievement is highest in schools of 600 to 900 students and was most equally distributed (across socioeconomic groups) in very small schools (Crosnoe, Johnson, & Elder, 2004; Finn, 2002; Watt, 2003).
- The effects of school size on learning are greatest in schools with many low socioeconomic status or minority students. In a comparison of large (over 1,500 students) and small (under 500 students) schools, there was more support and caring in the small schools. Also, while small schools had more limited curricula, they offered more personalized counseling and guidance of students (Crosnoe et al., 2004).
- Reduced class size has positive effects on achievement in the early grades, with effects beginning to appear when class size is reduced to 15 to 20 and increasing with further reductions. The positive effects are greater for disadvantaged and minority students than for others. Smaller class size improves the quality of classroom activity (Achilles, 1997; Bohrnstedt & Stecher, 2002; Fidler, 2001; Finn, 2002; Nye, Hedges, & Konstantopoulos, 2004; Speas, 2003). Changes that are attributed to smaller class sizes that may help explain achievement gains include the following:
  - More positive classroom atmosphere
  - More opportunity for individual attention
  - More flexibility for teachers

- o More space
- o Less noise and fewer distractions
- o More time for each student to speak
- o Friendlier atmosphere with better student-student and student-teacher relations
- o Increased student engagement
- The practice of "looping" (keeping students with the same teacher for more than one year) increases student achievement and results in more positive student attitudes toward school and a more positive approach to classroom management on the part of teachers (Rodriguez & Bernard, 2007).

Frequent Opportunities for Participation, Collaboration, Service, and Self-Direction Promote Student Achievement and Positive Development

Many studies have focused on the positive developmental consequences of structured extracurricular and afterschool programs for youth. Autonomy, self-direction, and influence are important to students, and cooperative learning promotes students' enjoyment of school and interpersonal relations, development of social skills, sense of the classroom as a community, and academic achievement (Berkowitz, 2001; Deci & Ryan, 2006; T. Dodge & Jaccard, 2006; Eisenman, 2001; A. Jackson & Davis, 2000; Stonehill et al., 2009; Wehmeyer, 2007). The following findings demonstrate the importance of student participation, service, and self-directedness (self-determination).

Participating in helpful activities, or being given responsibility to perform a helpful role for extended periods (service learning), can promote students' dispositions toward being helpful to others (L. Fredericks, 2003; Little, 2009; Little, Wimer, & Weiss, 2008; Roehlkepartain & Scales, 2007). Staub (1992) first described this process, in which individuals learn desired behavior by participating in the activity, as "natural socialization." Positive findings of such participation include the following:

- Improved personal and social development
- A sense of social and civic responsibility
- Academic progress
- Greater career exploration and aspirations
- Improved school climate and youth-community relations
- Decreased risk-taking behaviors

Programs are most effective when they involve high levels of student responsibility, autonomy, and choice; reflection activities; and well-prepared teachers (Conzemius & O'Neill, 2001; Deci & Ryan, 2006; Wehmeyer, 2007).

- Students who participate in extracurricular activities have better attendance, lower dropout rates, lower rates of drug use, higher academic achievement, and higher aspirations than nonparticipants, presumably because such participation reflects and enhances student connection with and attachment to the school (Dumais, 2006; Feldman & Matjasko, 2007; Jenkins & Ball, 2000).
- Excessive time spent in leisure activities has a negative effect on math achievement scores, while school-related activities, such as student government, student academic clubs, and sports, have positive effects (Dumais, 2006; Eccles, Barber, Stone, & Hunt, 2003). A youth culture in American society that focuses on leisure is associated with lower achievement test scores.

A Physical Plant That Promotes Safety and Community Impacts Student Achievement and Positive Development

The student's physical environment, including ventilation, day lighting, and indoor environmental contaminants, can have a profound effect on the health of children and on their ability to learn efficiently (Basch, 2009; CDC, 2007).

Systematic Approaches to Supporting Safety and Positive Behavior

Considerable research has been conducted on systemic approaches to supporting safety and positive behavior and examining the educational benefits of safe school interventions (Adelman & Taylor, 2007a; Gastic, 2005; Gottfredson & Bauer, 2007; Guilamo-Ramos, Litardo, & Jaccard, 2005). The following findings address these systematic approaches.

Safety and Positive Behavior. Gottfredson and Bauer (2007) listed the following models or approaches derived from programs that have shown evidence of effectiveness:

- Setting rules, communicating clear expectations for behavior, consistently enforcing rules, and providing rewards for rule compliance and punishments for rule infractions
- Organizing the delivery of instruction in ways that promote maximum learning and that encourage a sense of community
- Improving general management functions, such as coordination, resource allocation, and communication, and establishing and maintaining clear goals for the organization
- Increasing social control through an extended network of caring adults who interact regularly with the students and who share norms and expectations about their students (communal social organizations)

Providing Behavior Management Interventions.

- Providing instruction, training, and coaching in the development of social competency skills for the general population
- Providing instruction, training, and coaching in the development of social competency skills for high-risk populations

Teaching Appropriate Behavior. Comprehensive approaches to school discipline emphasize systematic teaching of appropriate behavior (not just punishing), matching the level of intervention to the level of behavioral challenge posed by each student, and designing integrated systems that deal with a full range of discipline challenges (Sugai, 2007; Sugai & Horner, 2006).

Reducing Antisocial Behavior. Three general types of programs reduced youth antisocial behavior: programs focusing on anger control, those emphasizing administrative techniques (including classroom management, schoolwide norms and rules, school organization, etc.), and those providing social skills training (Derzon, Wilson, & Cunningham, 1999).

Conflict Resolution and Mediation. Programs that emphasize schoolwide conflict resolution, peer mediation, and direct teaching of social skills and self-management strategies have shown positive effects (Bear, 2008; University of Illinois, 2009; Zimmerman, 2002).

Classroom Management. Effective classroom management can improve student learning by increasing time devoted to instruction (as opposed to discipline), decreasing discipline referrals, promoting more active teaching strategies, and improving classroom climate (Freiberg, Connell, & Lorentz, 2001; Sugai, 2007; Sugai, Horner, & Gresham, 2001).

Caring Orientation. Opportunities for student influence and a caring orientation have been identified as important factors in studies of effective "alternative schools" (G. Gottfredson & Gottfredson, 2007; White & Kochhar-Bryant, 2005, 2007).

Discipline Practices. Finally, discipline practices that involve suspension and expulsion have been shown not to have positive effects on students. Expelled or suspended students are more likely to become further alienated and to drop out of school. There is also evidence that suspension and expulsion are disproportionately meted out to minority students (Irvin et al., 2006; Schiraldi & Ziedenberg, 2001; Skiba & Knesting, 2002). The boxed text presents the transformation of a school and the positive outcomes of a whole-child approach.

BROAD ACRES ELEMENTARY SCHOOL TRANSFORMATION
Positive Outcomes From Serving the Whole Child

The school was failing, but the kids had done extraordinary things. This was the paradox at Broad Acres Elementary School in Silver Spring. If test scores are awful but the children have walked through deserts, waded across rivers, and learned new languages, the question becomes not so much "Why are the children failing?" as "What's wrong with this school?"

At Broad Acres eight years ago, test scores were so low that the state threatened to take the place over. Montgomery County Superintendent Jerry Weast and Principal Jody Leleck decided to remake the school. They negotiated with the teachers union to add extra hours to the workweek for extra pay. Teachers would offer no more excuses about poor kids from dysfunctional families; expectations would soar. About a third of the faculty left; Leleck hired 27 veteran teachers that first summer.

At Broad Acres, 88 percent of students qualify for meal subsidies, and three-quarters come from homes where English is not spoken. Two-thirds are Latino, 22 percent are Black, and the rest are Asian. Kids move in and out at a breathtaking rate; only 30 percent of fifth graders have been there since first grade. "Thirty apartments in the complex next door are scheduled for evictions in January," says Principal Michael Bayewitz. "That's several dozen kids we'll lose. One-third of our families have no working phone numbers. The families are in survival mode."

In the spring of 2000, results of state testing showed that students at Broad Acres were performing at very low levels. Scores on Maryland State Performance Assessment Program tests were similar to those of schools being taken over by the state: only 11.8 percent of third graders were proficient in reading, and only 5.3 percent showed proficiency in math; of fifth graders, 21 percent were proficient in reading and 15 percent in math.

In the spring of 2001, school staff, in cooperation with district and union leaders, undertook a three-year program to restructure the school internally. By 2004, 75 percent of third graders demonstrated reading proficiency on the new Maryland State Assessment, and 67 percent demonstrated math proficiency. Fifth-grade students showed comparable gains: 54 percent demonstrated reading proficiency and 60 percent math proficiency. Similarly, the 2004 Comprehensive Test of Basic Skills (CTBS) scores for second graders were on par with those of some of the highest-performing schools in Montgomery County, showing increases of 26 percent to 70 percent.

During restructuring, the demographics of the student population remained substantially the same. The children at Broad Acres Elementary School came from all over the world, representing 31 countries and speaking 28 languages. The student population was 64 percent Hispanic; 23 percent African, West Indian, or African American; 13 percent Asian; and 1 percent White. While over 25 percent of the students received English language learner support, it was estimated that over 75 percent of our families spoke a language other than English in their homes. The mobility rate was about 30 percent, and almost 90 percent of the students received free and reduced-price meals. While demographics did not change during restructuring, the students at Broad Acres learned at consistently higher levels and sustained this achievement throughout the period. "We were doing the children of Broad Acres a disservice, and that's criminal," says Leleck, now the system's chief academic officer.

Bayewitz and his faculty worked to turn Broad Acres into the center of its community. There's a health clinic in the building. Teachers make home visits. A sign on Bayewitz's office wall says, "Student achievement will not be predictable by race."

"Yes, our kids have been through trauma—unbelievable stories," he says. "We recognize that and we sympathize, but it's no excuse for not learning."

He hands me a stack of essays that students wrote about their journeys to America. They tell of being chased across the border, of encounters with coyotes both human and animal. Whatever your beliefs about illegal immigration, these are children who were ordered onto trucks to travel to a place they could not imagine, for reasons they could not comprehend.

Now those children are learning: 81 percent met reading proficiency standards this year, up from 47 percent in 2003. Broad Acres did this without the reform tactics used in other districts—no young recruits from Teach for America, no cash for students who come to class, no linkage of teacher pay to test scores. Rather, the faculty gathers every Wednesday for hours of mentoring and brainstorming, creating plans for each child who is falling behind. In classrooms, bilingual or special education teachers slide in alongside the regular teacher, taking two or three children onto the floor to focus on computation or reading aloud.

The formula includes afterschool activities, arts and music, and a mental health team that swoops in to examine the family crisis that may lie behind a classroom outburst. But teachers say it's not extra budget lines that make the difference; it's the conviction that nothing will stand in the way of achievement. When a kindergartner keeps falling asleep in class, a teacher goes to see the parent. Problem identified: The family has one twin mattress for four children. Solution: The school gets the child a bed.

A boy arrived from North Africa last year and began acting out in kindergarten. "We couldn't keep him in a seat, couldn't talk to him," the principal says. "We had him evaluated and put him in Kim's class." That's Kim Burnim, the national Teacher of the Year in 2006. In many schools, the boy would be labeled "special ed" and shunted onto a separate track. But Burnim set up behavior markers and put peer pressure to work. "To stay here, where he wanted to be, he had to get in line with all the other ducks," she says. "We involve the other children; they take him under their wing and let him know we don't do disruptive things here." When I saw the boy, he moved easily from one activity to another, competing to finish his work and move on to the next bit of math fun.

Too often, schools desperate to boost test scores become grim factories in which children are force-fed rote skills. But at Broad Acres, teachers coach each other to keep kids engaged in rich material for its own sake. In Andrea Sutton's fifth-grade class, 16 kids sit on the floor, jumping up to explain to one another the roots of the American colonists' grievances with the British. The teacher's voice never rises above a stage whisper as she plies the class with questions that would fit nicely in a high school course.

"With all the pressure from No Child Left Behind, it's so easy to cut out history and science," Bayewitz says. "But these kids are going to need those complex skills in high school and college. And these kids are going to college."

Source: Condensed from "Working Together," by Marc Fisher, *Washington Post*, Thursday, January 8, 2009, p. B01. Used with permission.

Collaboration Between General and Special Educators Leads to a Reexamination of the "Pullout" Model

In most studies that explore ways to increase elementary student achievement through school reform, teacher collaboration typically appears among variables such as lower student-teacher ratios, increased per-pupil expenditures, and increased resources for teachers (Grissmer, Flanagan, Kawata, & Williamson, 2000). Collaboration between special and general educators is now viewed as being among the most important factors in the success of a school that is inclusive of all children. While more research is needed, many studies have demonstrated tentative links between collaboration and student achievement.

Some elementary-level special educators have indicated discomfort with their current "pullout" services and have begun redefining their roles and relationships with general educators (Thompson, Thurlow, Parson, & Barrow, 2000; Zigmond, 2003). In fact, there is a strong case for the instructional and social benefits of providing for the needs of all students in inclusive classrooms with differentiated instruction (Swartz, 2004).

A model practice referred to as "push-in" delivery of services (as opposed to pullout), in which special and general education teachers collaborate to provide services, is yielding benefits for students. Special teachers become more involved with the instruction that is delivered in general classrooms and, therefore, are perceived as integral members of the instructional team. Students benefit from the reduced stigma of identification as having "special needs"; they also benefit from better alignment of teaching strategies and cooperation among the various teachers they work with (Swartz, 2004). Not only does inclusive education for children with disabilities improve academic functioning, it also offers an opportunity for socialization with typical peers (without disabilities) in general education settings.

Whole School Collaboration Yields Student Achievement Gains: The Onward to Excellence Model

The general performance of students improves when schools use whole-school improvement approaches based on comprehensive professional collaboration. For example, the Onward to Excellence I and II (OTE) national model demonstration developed by the North Central Regional Educational Laboratory (NCREL; 2001a, 2001b) under contract with the U.S. Department of Education was designed to help school communities work together. Onward to Excellence has been operating for 20 years, and more than 1,000 schools have participated in the process. The model is characterized by several key elements: (1) collaborative decision making and professional learning communities, (2) shared leadership, and (3) continuous learning for improvement.

While it is difficult to measure fully the impact of complex whole-school reform processes, OTE schools have produced several outcomes. They have raised student achievement; established a common focus for all staff across grade levels, departments, and disciplines; helped teachers learn how to work together and support and trust each other through professional development; aligned teaching with state standards and standardized assessments; and involved parents and the community in the improvement work (Dorfman & Fisher, 2002; NCREL, 2001a, 2001b). Furthermore, two studies showed that OTE schools led to more teacher collaboration and research-based teacher practices and that the model was most effective in high-poverty districts (NCREL, 2004).

A Difficult Passage: Middle School Collaboration and Support Improve Students' Performance

Collaborative practices and supports for youth in middle school can have profound effects on their future success. The transition from elementary to middle school represents a major phenomenon in the life of the adolescent that requires additional attention and support. Research confirms what teachers and parents have known for decades—that a significant number of children show changes in academic performance, perceptions about school, and self-perceptions as they attempt to adjust to middle school. Closer collaboration among professionals in sending and receiving schools can impact student outcomes in several areas.

Academic Performance. Youth exhibit decreased academic performance and are at greatest risk for failure during their transition from eighth to ninth grade (Henderson & Raimondo, 2002; Hines, 2001; Kilgore et al., 2002; Mertens et al., 2007; RTI International, 2004; Sanders & Epstein, 2000; L. Wilson & Horch, 2004).

Grade Point Average. Students show a general decline in grade point average (GPA) in Grades 6 through 10, with the most dramatic drop in GPA at the transition point between Grades 6 and 7 (Mertens et al., 2007; Mullins & Irvin, 2000). Achievement scores are affected by the kinds of supports students receive in the transition year in middle school. For example, students who are grouped into interdisciplinary teams during their transition year perform significantly better on standardized achievement tests than students who are in departmentalized schools (McIntosh, Flannery, Sugai, Braun, & Cochrane, 2008; Mullins & Irvin).

Perceptions of School. Students' perceptions of their educational experiences generally influence their motivation to perform in school. When students have a history of failure in school, it is particularly difficult for them to stay motivated. When they believe that their poor performance is caused by factors out of their control, such as a disability, they are unlikely to see any reason to hope for an improvement (Mertens et al., 2007; Phelan et al., 1998; Sadowski, 2003).

Student Self-Perceptions. School transition affects the self-esteem of young adolescents. The lowest self-esteem ratings and highest self-consciousness ratings have been found in students between the ages of 12 and 14 (Buckroyd & Flitton, 2004; Linnenbrink & Pintrich, 2003; Simeonsson, McMillen, McMillen, & Lollar, 2002). Girls who made no school transition, instead remaining in a K–8 setting, maintained higher self-esteem ratings than girls who had made a school transition. The decline in self-esteem for boys and girls is magnified if significant life changes occur at the same time, such as onset of puberty, initiation of dating relationships, change of residence, or parental divorce (Cavanagh, Schiller, & Riegle-Crumb, 2006; H. Foster, Hagan, & Brooks-Gunn, 2009; Phelan et al., 1998; Sadowski, 2003).

In supportive interdisciplinary teams, students maintain their sense of academic competence, as well as their sense of perceived social acceptance, as they make the transition to middle school.

Professional Teaming in Middle School Improves Students' Performance

Most comprehensive school improvement models involving increased collaboration among teachers and other professionals have been implemented at the elementary school level. However, more recent research has shown that such collaboration to increase student achievement also works in middle school for students with and without disabilities (Hines, 2001). Students who participate in supportive transition activities and are placed in interdisciplinary teams make more successful transitions to middle school. Likewise, middle school educators claim that professional teaming helps students to maximize their learning (Hines, Roeser, Eccles, & Sameroff, 2000). The U.S. Office of Educational Research and Improvement (OERI) and Johns Hopkins University's Center for Social Organization of Schools developed a comprehensive school reform model oriented toward middle and secondary schools. A key component is the collaboration among teachers, students, and families. The boxed text provides a research-based example of school reorganization to promote collaboration among teachers.

SCHOOL REFORM FOR COLLABORATION IN THE MIDDLE SCHOOL

Innovative approaches to the school's organization facilitate teachers, students, and families developing strong bonds and close relationships. For example, some faculty remain with the same students for two or more years (called *looping*), and teacher teams share students and common planning time, during which they are provided training (called *semi-departmentalization*). Semi-departmentalization helps cut down class size, improves student-teacher bonds, and enables the teacher to connect subject matter more effectively across disciplines. There is evidence that the model can realize substantial gains in student performance while improving both student and staff morale. For example, in reading, students from one model school outgained comparison students by 5 scale score points, while students from the other model school outscored comparison students by 12 points. Both model schools continue to display outstanding and broad-based achievement gains in all years for which data are available.

Source: Balfantz, R. & MacIver, D. (2000). Johns Hopkins University, Center for Social Organization of Schools, 2000, by permission.

Teacher collaboration also affects teachers' expectations of students' abilities and students' expectations of themselves. Teachers who provide the majority of their services through team teaching or through consultation with general educators in standards-based environments expect a greater number of their students to meet high standards, work with more students on using accommodations, and discuss standards with more IEP teams than teachers at other grade levels who provided most or all of their services in separate special education classrooms and resource rooms (Thompson et al., 2000). Middle school students, their parents, and their teachers share the belief that middle-level students experience increased (1) self-confidence, (2) camaraderie, (3) support of the teachers, and (4) higher expectations and (5) avoid the low self-esteem that can result from placement in a special education setting (Hines, 2001).

Collaboration Improves Student Outcomes in Secondary and Post-Secondary School Years

Effective high schools are characterized by strong professional collaboration (McLaughlin & Talbert, 2001). Deshler and colleagues (2004), who have studied effectiveness of secondary education strategies for all students for over two decades, have concluded that collaboration is among the most important elements in building school capacity to improve education for all children. Schools build capacity to help students placed at risk and students with disabilities progress in general education by using a variety of group and team strategies, including teacher planning teams, critical friends groups, and advisory groups. For example, many schools use critical friends groups, which are small groups of teachers and administrators who work together over time to solve problems, critique work, and obtain support and feedback to improve their practices. Deschler and colleagues and others have concluded that it is the strength of the co-teaching relationships among teachers and the personal relationships with students that make the inclusion model work (see also Eick, Ware, & Jones, 2004).

DOES COLLABORATION PROMOTE STUDENT AND FAMILY SELF-DETERMINATION?

Over the past few decades, studies have confirmed the importance of family involvement in the development and educational progress of children and youth. A major research effort focused on families, the Harvard Family Research Project (HFRCP), develops and evaluates strategies to promote the well-being of children, youth, families, and their communities. Studies are centered on three areas that support children's learning and development—early childhood education, out-of-school time programming, and family and community support in education. Building on the assumption that schools cannot promote development of children and youth alone, HFRCP focuses national attention on complementary learning—the idea that a systemic approach, which integrates school and nonschool supports, can better ensure that all children have the skills they need to succeed. The following research findings demonstrate that the participation of parents and other family members in their children's schooling has broad positive effects for students.

When families are involved at school, not just at home, children perform better in school and stay in school longer. Several studies have provided qualitative evidence showing the positive effects of community involvement for families of a variety of ethnic backgrounds (Center for Equity and Excellence in Education, 2002; Crosnoe & Elder, 2004; Dorfman & Fisher, 2002; Eng et al., 2008; Ferguson, 2005; Frisco, Muller, & Frank, 2007; Guerra & Knox, 2008; Heard, 2007; Henderson & Mapp, 2002; Minke & Anderson, 2005). School–family–community partnerships typically involve community schools that are open to students, families, and community members before, during, and after school; provide a variety of opportunities and supports; and are operated by partnerships of school systems and community agencies.

Partnerships with families have been found to show improvements in the following student outcomes:

- Academic achievement
- School attendance
- Suspension rates
- Family involvement
- Family functioning
- Access to services
- Neighborhood safety (Allen, 2009; Dryfoos, 2002; Hill et al., 2004)

Recently, educational researchers have sought clearer correlations among professional collaboration, student self-determination, and student outcomes. While the special education literature contains many recommended strategies to promote self-determination, more research is needed to demonstrate that these strategies actually improve educational outcomes for children and youth placed at risk as well as those with disabilities (Wehmeyer, Field, Doren, Jones, & Mason, 2004). Currently, only 55 percent of schools offer self-advocacy or self-determination curriculum to students with disabilities (Wood, Karvonen, Test, Browder, & Algozzine, 2004).

Wehmeyer and colleagues (2004) conducted a comprehensive review of the literature on self-determination and found that while most studies lack a scientific research base, several studies have demonstrated a link between self-determination and improved educational outcomes for youth with disabilities. Their review yielded several important findings.

- Children who help choose school activities show enhanced motivation to perform those tasks and are more likely to achieve their goals.
- Students with higher self-determination scores in their final year of high school are more likely to have expressed a preference to live independently, have a savings or checking account, and be employed for pay.
- Instruction in self-determination increases participation and independence of students, including those placed at risk and those with disabilities. Self-determination skills are enhanced when students and families become active participants in the educational team and collaborative conferences (Field, Martin, Miller, Ward, & Wehmeyer, 1998; J. Martin & Marshall, 1995; Wehmeyer, 2007).
- Most studies of self-determination are focused on adolescents and adults; additional research is needed to examine the effects of self-determination on children ages 5 to 13 (Algozzine, Browder, Karvonen, Test, & Wood, 2001).

WHY IS IT IMPORTANT TO CELEBRATE OUR WORK AND RENEW OUR COMMITMENT?

Collaboration Makes Pioneers of Us All

As we read the litany of challenges and barriers to learning that children, families, and professionals face, it is easy for many of us to become discouraged. That discouragement usually arises from a sense that we are falling further behind as the requirements for student progress increase, the resources diminish, and the expectations for school staff expand. We are too small to attack a Goliath of obstacles that seems to grow every day, and we feel very alone in the task. But this is where we are . . . and it is where we must begin. We attack each new challenge not alone, but together, and we make a difference one student at a time. Each act of collaboration forces us to "see the world anew," rethink our traditional roles, and create new relationships with our peers that can help us work differently together on behalf of children and families. We are all pioneers on the frontier to improving educational outcomes for students. Therefore, we need more than ever to build and work in collaborative professional communities.

Effective change processes result in change in each of the professionals who participate in them. Collaborative work of compelling importance requires that professionals reexamine their conventional attitudes, beliefs, knowledge, and assumptions and be open to confronting new ideas. The process can be chaotic and uncomfortable at times, provoking thoughts and feelings of unnaturalness, frustration, vulnerability, and incompetence (Herasymowych, 1996). But it can also be exhilarating. Rewards or incentives for collaborative work and dedication to students are essential, but they do not necessarily need to be linked to student *academic* progress. Rather they can be awarded to teachers and professionals who inspire a group of students, show extraordinary dedication to a student against all odds, identify student talents, demonstrate peer collaboration and leadership, link others with external resources, or do innovative work with students or families. Here are some examples to consider.

- Nominations for awards of teachers and other school professionals who have made a noticeable impact on students and their community through their commitment to teaching and learning and support to students and families
- Special recognition for outstanding mentors to students, as mentoring programs require a considerable commitment of time, effort, and caring on the part of already busy people
- Modest salary differentials or stipends for collaborative leadership assignments
- Professional Growth Credit on certificate renewal, or as required for contract renewal or as required to move up on the salary schedule
- Release time to collaborate with peers on projects, mentor, conduct research, analyze student data, or participate in professional development
- Opportunity to participate in professional growth opportunities, such as presenting at conferences and meetings, and reimbursement for conference fees
- Special priority for courses taught
- Tuition reimbursement
- Recognition banquet or formal thank-you from the principal or district administrator
- Published open thank-you letters to the community in the local newspapers
- Small gifts, such as lapel pins, coffee mugs, "golden apple," or "school handbell," with the name of the mentor engraved
- Priority given to staff for budget support for instructional or student support materials (Sweeny, 2003)

Collaborate for Professional Development and Teacher Renewal

Continuing professional development is essential to renewal and advancement of staff expertise, morale, and commitment. A sound, coordinated plan for professional development combats discouragement and builds capacity for shared problem solving. Expertise in teaching and support roles comes from a process of sharing, attempting new ideas, reflecting on practice, and developing new approaches (California School Redesign Network, 2005).

Traditionally viewed as a series of one-shot training events, personnel development has come to involve much more creative kinds of activities that embed collaborative practices. Personnel development initiatives are now more likely to be designed to be cyclical (offered on a recurring basis) and some to be progressive (i.e., advanced training builds on previous training). In many initiatives, the training involves "collective participation," in which groups of personnel from the same school or district participate in the same training. Training is aligned with the actual work and goals of personnel and promotes active learning with opportunities for teachers to become engaged in analysis of their practices. As performance-based compensation becomes a more prevalent framework for teacher development, it must be part of a larger approach to improve teachers' working conditions and provide the professional supports teachers need to be successful in challenging classrooms (Raue, MacAllum, & Ristow, 2008).

Collaborate to Build Professional Communities

Traditional school structures often reinforce individual work and can actually contribute to competition and conflict (Beyerlein & Harris, 2003; Brownell, 2005), which undermines collaborative relationships. However, humans are social beings and naturally create relationships, networks, and communities. The successful leader/change agent looks for opportunities to harness this natural tendency to create communities and use it to address the important work of improving education for all children. He or she strives to create places, spaces, times, and opportunities for both formal and informal networking and community building.

Chapter 5 outlined four action-dimensions for collaboration. The fourth was *collaboration as building professional community*, which refers to the creative use of collaboration to connect school personnel with the larger external professional community. This process expands staff members' knowledge and skills by exposing them to the work of other schools and districts and to the expertise of others in the professional community. Examples of this form of collaboration and support include linking with professional associations, connecting teachers with national or regional resource centers, providing professional development, connecting with Web-based professional communities, and forming partnerships with universities to enhance the school's capacity to improve learning for all children (Kochhar-Bryant, 2008).

CLOSING: A CALL TO ACTION

Professionals working with our children and youth are extraordinarily challenged today. Their work must be recognized and rewarded—not only for their efforts to promote student academic achievement but for the many other aspects of development that *must be nurtured*. They must be recognized also for addressing the broader set of outcomes that surround the *whole child*—attending to the cognitive, social, emotional, physical, and talent development of children and youth from widely diverse backgrounds.

The future of our nation depends on the healthy development of our children—and the development of our children depends on the readiness and dedication of qualified professionals committed to working with all children. They appreciate diversity in their learners and understand that no dimension of development is outside their role or their concern. They appreciate diversity in their colleagues and accept that the work of building the future cannot be done in isolation but only in collaboration with all who share the common mission.

SUMMARY OF KEY POINTS

- Particular interest has been devoted to the benefits of collaboration and coordination in terms of improving the education and development of the whole child.
- Professional collaboration has become even more important in recent years because of its relevance to supporting academic achievement for all students, for which schools are newly accountable.

- A great deal of research has confirmed relationships between educational environments that address the needs of the whole child and student achievement.
- Over the past 30 years, a stream of research has addressed various ways to measure the well-being of children and youth and the construction of child well-being indices.
- Extensive research has confirmed the success of collaborative relationships among school professionals, professionals and parents, and school and community personnel.
- Professionals become less isolated, increase their effectiveness, and become more innovative when they collaborate.
- When school and community personnel collaborate, students and families are more likely to receive the related and supportive services they need to progress in general education. They are more likely to experience improved services at key transition points from early intervention to high school transition.

KEY TERMS AND PHRASES

- Cooperative communities
- Benefits and outcomes
- Communities of practice
- Evidence-based research
- Cultural influences
- Positive home–school relationships

- Self-determination outcomes
- Full-service schools model
- Community schools model
- School-based youth services model
- Indices of child well-being

References

Abrams, J. (2008). Habits of mind for the systems-savvy leader. In A. L. Costa & B. Kallick (Eds.), *Learning and leading with habits of mind: 16 essential characteristics for success* (pp. 291–306). Alexandria, VA: Association for Supervision and Curriculum Development.

Achilles, C. (1996). *Summary of recent class-size research with an emphasis on Tennessee's ProjectSTAR and its derivative research studies.* Nashville, TN: Center of Excellence for Research and Policy on Basic Skills.

Achilles, C. (1997). Small classes, big possibilities. *The School Administrator, 54,* 6–15.

Action for Healthy Kids. (2004). *The learning connection: The value of improving nutrition and physical activity in our schools.* Skokie, IL: Author. Retrieved December 20, 2009, from http://www .actionforhealthykids.org/resources/files/learning-connection.pdf

Action for Healthy Kids. (2008). *Progress or promises? What's working for and against healthy schools.* Skokie, IL: Author. Retrieved December 20, 2009, from http://www.a4hk.org/pdf/ Progress%20or%20Promises.pdf

Adelman, H. S., & Taylor, L. (2006a). School and community collaboration to promote a safe learning environment. *State Education Standard, 7*(1), 38–43.

Adelman, H. S., & Taylor, L. (2006b). *The school leader's guide to student learning supports: New directions for addressing barriers to learning.* Thousand Oaks, CA: Corwin.

Adelman, H. S., & Taylor, L. (2007a). Safe schools in the context of school improvement. In *Proceedings of persistently safe schools: The 2007 National Conference on Safe Schools.* Washington, DC: Hamilton Fish Institute on School and Community Violence, The George Washington University.

Adelman, H. S., & Taylor, L. (2007b). Systemic change and school improvement. *Journal of Educational and Psychological Consultation, 17,* 55–77.

Albus, D., & Thurlow, M. (2005). *Beyond subgroup reporting: English language learners with disabilities in 2002–2003 online state assessment reports* (ELLs with disabilities report 10). Minneapolis: National Center on Educational Outcomes, University of Minnesota. Retrieved December 20, 2009, from http://www.cehd.umn.edu/NCEO/OnlinePubs/ELLsDisReport10.html

Alcohol, Drug Abuse, and Mental Health Administration (ADAMHA) Reorganization Act of 1992, 42 U.S.C. § 300x *et seq.*

Algozzine, B., Browder, D., Karvonen, M., Test, D. W., & Wood, W. M. (2001). Effects of interventions to promote self-determination for individuals with disabilities. *Review of Educational Research, 71*(2), 219–277.

Allen, J. (2009). Effective home-school communication. *Family Involvement Network of Educators (FINE) Newsletter, 1*(1). Retrieved December 20, 2009, from http://www.hfrp.org/ family-involvement/publications-resources/effective-home-school-communication

Alliance for Excellent Education. (2004). *Alliance for Excellent Education commends NASSP report, Breaking Ranks II, for its hands-on approach* [Press release]. Retrieved December 20, 2009, from http://www.all4ed.org/press_room/press_releases/02182004

Alloy, L. B., Abramson, L. Y., Tashman, N., Berrebbi, D. S., Hogan, M. E., Whitehouse, W. G., et al. (2001). Developmental origins of cognitive vulnerability to depression: Parenting, cognitive, and inferential feedback styles of the parents of individuals at high and low cognitive risk for depression. *Cognitive Therapy and Research, 25,* 397–423.

Alspaugh, J. W. (1998). Achievement loss associated with the transition to middle school and high school. *The Journal of Educational Research, 92*(1), 20–25.

American Academy of Pediatrics, Committee on Children with Disabilities. (2001). Developmental surveillance and screening of infants and young children (RE0062). *Pediatrics, 108*(10), 192–196.

American School Counselor Association (ASCA). (2003). *The ASCA National Model: A framework for school counseling programs.* Alexandria, VA: Author.

American School Counselor Association (ASCA). (2004). *Ethical standards for school counselors.* Alexandria, VA: Author.

Americans for the Arts. (2009). *Americans for the Arts strategic plan: 2009–2011.* Washington, DC: Author.

Americans with Disabilities Act (ADA) of 1990, 42 U.S.C. § 12101 *et seq.* Retrieved December 20, 2009, from http://www.ada.gov/pubs/ada.htm

Anderson, A. R., Christenson, S. L., & Lehr, C. A. (2004). Promoting student engagement to enhance school completion: Information and strategies for educators. In A. S. Canter, L. Z. Paige, M. D. Roth, I. Romero, & S. A. Carroll, (Eds.), *Helping children at home and school II: Handouts for families and educators* (pp. S2-65–S2-68). Washington, DC: National Association of School Psychologists.

Anfara, V. A., & Andrews, P. G. (Eds.). (2003). *This we believe: Research and resources.* Washington, DC: National Middle School Association.

Annie E. Casey Foundation. (2009). *Taking results seriously for vulnerable children and families: The 20th annual kids count data book.* Washington, DC: Author.

Artiles, A. J. (1998). The dilemma of difference: Enriching the disproportionality discourse with theory and context. *Journal of Special Education, 32*(1), 32–36.

Artiles, A. J., & Ortiz, A. A. (2002). English language learners with special education needs: Contexts and possibilities. In A. J. Artiles & A. A. Ortiz (Eds.), *English language learners with special education needs: Identification, assessment, and instruction* (pp. 3–27). Washington, DC: Center for Applied Linguistics.

Assistance to States for the Education of Children with Disabilities Program and Preschool Grants for Children with Disabilities: Final Regulations, 34 C.F.R. § 300–301 (1992).

Association for Career and Technical Education (ACTE). (2005). *Summary of S. 250: Carl D. Perkins Career and Technical Education Improvement Act of 2005.* Alexandria, VA: Author.

Association for Supervision and Curriculum Development (ASCD). (2008). *Invest in the whole child: Educating our children in the 21st century.* Alexandria, VA: Author. Retrieved March 1, 2009, from http://www.siia.net

Atkins, M. S., Graczyk, P. A., Frazier, S. L., & Abdul-Adil, J. (2003). Toward a new model for promoting children's mental health: Accessible, effective, and sustainable school-based mental health services. *School Psychology Review, 32*(4), 503–514.

Aubusson, P., Steele, F., Dinham, S. K., & Brady, L. (2007). Action learning in teacher learning community formation: Informative or transformative? *Teacher Development, 11*(2), 133–148.

Bachrach, L. L. (1986). The challenge of service planning for chronic mental patients. *Community Health Journal, 22*(3), 170–174.

Baer, R., & Kochhar-Bryant, C. (2008). How can school collaboration and system coordination promote progress of high school students? In C. Kochhar-Bryant (Ed.), *Collaboration and system coordination for students with special needs: From early childhood to the postsecondary years.* Columbus, OH: Prentice Hall.

Baer, R., Simmons, T., & Flexer, R. (1996). Transition practice and policy compliance in Ohio: A survey of secondary special educators. *Career Development for Exceptional Individuals, 19*(1), 61–72

Balaban, N. (1995). Seeing the child, knowing the person. In W. Ayers (Ed.), *To become a teacher: Making a difference in children's lives* (pp. 49–57). New York: Teachers College Press.

Balfantz, R., & MacIver, D. (2000). Transforming high-poverty urban middle schools into strong learning institutions: Lessons from the first five years of the Talent Development Middle School. *Journal of Education for Students Placed at Risk (JESPAR), 5*(1), 1532–7671.

Balsano, A. B. (2005). Youth civic engagement in the United States: Understanding and addressing the impact of social impediments on positive youth and community development. *Applied Developmental Science, 9*(4), 188–201.

Banks, J., & McGee-Banks, C. A. (1992). *Multicultural education: Issues and perspectives* (2nd ed.). Boston: Allyn & Bacon.

Banks, R. (1997). *Bullying in schools: ERIC Digest.* Retrieved December 20, 2009, from http://www.ericdigests.org/1997-4/bullying.htm (ERIC Documentation Reproduction Service No. ED407154)

Barron-McKeagney, T., Woody, J. D., & D'Souza, H. J. (2002). Mentoring at-risk Latino children and their parents: Analysis of the parent-child relationship and family strength. *Families in Society: The Journal of Contemporary Human Service, 83*, 285–293.

Barros, R. M., Silver, E. J., & Stein, R. E. (2009). School recess and group classroom behavior. *Pediatrics, 123*(2), 431–436.

Barton, P. (2005). *One-third of a nation: Rising dropout rates and declining opportunities.* Princeton, NJ: Educational Testing Service. Retrieved December 20, 2009, from http://www.ets.org/Media/onethird.pdf

Basch, C. E. (2009, November). *Reducing educationally relevant health disparities: A missing link in school reforms to close the achievement gap of urban minority youth.* Paper presented at Comprehensive Educational Equity: Overcoming the Socioeconomic Barriers to School Success, Teachers College's Fourth Annual Symposium on Education Equity, New York.

Basch, C. E. (in press). *Healthier students are better learners.* New York: Teachers College Campaign for Educational Equity.

Bear, G. G. (2008). School-wide approaches to behavior problems. In B. Doll & J. A. Cummings (Eds.), *Transforming school mental health services: Population-based approaches to promoting the competency and wellness of children* (pp. 103–141). Thousand Oaks, CA: Corwin.

Bearman, P., Moody, J., Stovel, K., & Thalji, L. (2004). Social and sexual networks: The National Longitudinal Study of Adolescent Health. In M. Morris (Ed.), *Network epidemiology: A handbook for survey design and data collection* (pp. 201–237). New York: Oxford University Press.

Bechara, A., & Damasio, A. (2005). The somatic marker hyphothesis: A neural theory of economic decision making. *Games and Economic Behavior (52)*, 336–372.

Begley, S. (2000, Fall/Winter). Wired for thought. *Newsweek* (special issue), 25–30.

Benninga, J. S., Berkowitz, M. W., Kuehn, P., & Smith, K. (2006). Character and academics: What good schools do [Electronic version]. *Phi Delta Kappan, 87*(6), 448–452. Retrieved December 20, 2009, from http://www.pdkintl.org

Benson, P. L. (2007). Developmental assets: An overview of theory, research, and practice. In R. K. Silbereisen & R. M. Lerner (Eds.), *Approaches to positive youth development* (pp. 33–58). Thousand Oaks, CA: Sage.

Benson, P. L., Scales, P. C., Hamilton, S. F, & Sesma, A., Jr. (with Hong, K. L., & Roehlkepartain, E. C.). (2006a). Positive youth development so far: Core hypotheses and their implications for policy and practice. *Search Institute Insights & Evidence, 3*(1), 1–13.

Benson, P. L., Scales, P. C., Hamilton, S. F., & Sesma, A., Jr. (2006b). Positive youth development: Theory, research, and application. In W. W. Damon & R. M. Lerner (Eds.), *Handbook of child psychology, Vol. 1. Theoretical models of human development* (6th ed., pp. 894–941). New York: John Wiley.

Benz, M. R., Lindstrom, L., & Yovanoff, P. (2000). Improving graduation and employment outcomes of students with disabilities: Predictive factors and student perspectives. *Exceptional Children, 6*(4), 509–529.

Berkowitz, B. (2001). Studying the outcomes of community-based coalitions. *American Journal of Community Psychology, 29*(2), 213–227.

Berliner, D. C. (2009). *Poverty and potential: Out-of-school factors and school success.* Boulder, CO, & Tempe, AZ: Education and the Public Interest Center & Education Policy Research Unit. Retrieved December 20, 2009, from http://epicpolicy.org/publication/poverty-and-potential

Bernard, M. E., Stephanou, A., & Urbach, D. (2007). *ASG student social and emotional health report.* Oakleigh, Australia: Australian Scholarships Group. Retrieved December 20, 2009, from http://www.asg.com.au/Assets/Files/ASG_Student_Social_Emotional_Health_Report_Full.pdf

Bernhard, J. K., Freire, M., Pacini-Ketchabaw, V., & Villanueva, V. (1998). A Latin-American parent's group participates in their children's schooling: Parent involvement reconsidered. *Canadian Ethnic Studies, 30*(3), 77–99.

Berry, B., Johnson, D., & Montgomery, D. (2005). The power of teacher leadership. *Educational Leadership, 62*(5), 56–60.

Berry, M. A. (2002). *Healthy school environment and enhanced educational performance: The case of Charles Young Elementary School, Washington, DC.* Dalton, GA: Carpet and Rug Institute. Retrieved December 20, 2009, from http://www.carpet-rug.org/carpet-and-rug-industry/research-and-resources/scientific-research/charles-young.cfm

Beyerlein, M. M., & Harris, C. (2003). *Guiding the journey to collaborative work systems: A strategic design workbook.* San Francisco: Jossey-Bass.

Billig, S. (2001). Meeting the challenges of family involvement in the middle grades. *Middle Matters, 10*(2), 3–4.

Blair, C. (2003). *Self-regulation and school readiness.* Champaign, IL: ERIC Clearinghouse on Elementary and Early Childhood Education, Children's Research Center, University of Illinois.

Blank, M., & Berg, A. (2006). *All together now: Sharing responsibility for the whole child.* Alexandria, VA: Commission on the Whole Child, Association for Supervision and Curriculum Development. Retrieved December 20, 2009, from http://www.ascd.org/ASCD/pdf/sharingresponsibility.pdf

Blank, M. J., Melaville, A., & Shah, B. P. (2003). *Making the difference: Research and practice in community schools.* Washington, DC: Institute for Educational Leadership, Coalition for Community Schools. Retrieved December 20, 2009, from http://www.communityschools.org/CCSFullReport.pdf (ERIC Document Reproduction Service No. ED499103)

Blum, R. W., Beuhring, T., & Rinehart, P. M. (2000). *Protecting teens: Beyond race, income and family structure.* Minneapolis: University of Minnesota, Center for Adolescent Health. (ERIC Document Reproduction Service No. ED450075)

Bohn, A. P., & Sleeter, C. (2000). Multicultural education and the standards movement: A report from the field. *Phi Delta Kappan, 82*(2), 156–159.

Bohrnstedt, G. W., & Stecher, B. M. (Eds.). (2002). *What we have learned about class size reduction in California.* Sacramento: California Department of Education.

Boman, E., & Enmarker, I. (2004). Factors affecting pupils' noise annoyance in schools: The building and testing of models. *Environment and Behavior, 36*(2), 207–228.

Bonner-Tompkins, E. (2000, October). Well-being and school achievement: Using coordinated services to improve outcomes among students. *Gaining Ground Newsletter.* Washington, DC: Council of Chief State School Officers.

Boss, S. (1998). *Learning from the margins: The lessons of alternative schools.* Portland, OR: Northwest Regional Educational Laboratory.

Bostic, J. Q., & Miller, M. C. (2005). Teen Depression: When Should You Worry? *Newsweek,* April 25, 2005.

Bowman, D., Burdette, P., & Julianelle, P. (2008). *Homeless and special education administrative collaboration.* Alexandria, VA: National Association of State Directors of Special Education.

Bredekamp, V. S., & Copple, C. (1997). *Developmentally appropriate practice in early childhood programs* (Rev. ed.; N.A.E.Y.C. Series #234). Washington, DC: National Associations for the Education of Young Children.

Bremer, C. D., Kachgal, M., & Schoeller, K. (2003). Self-determination: Supporting successful transition. *Research to Practice Brief: Improving Secondary Education and Transition Services through Research, 2*(1). Minneapolis, MN: National Center on Secondary Education and Transition.

Brendtro, L. K., & Larson, S. J. (2006). *The resilience revolution: Discovering strengths in challenging kids.* Bloomington, IN: Solution Tree.

Brener, N. D., Weist, M., Adelman, H., Taylor, L., & Vernon-Smiley, M. (2007). Mental health and social services: Results from the School Health Policies and Programs Study 2006. *Journal of School Health, 77,* 486–499.

Brett, A., Smith, M., Price, E., & Huitt, W. (2003). Overview of the affective domain. *Educational Psychology Interactive.* Retrieved December 20, 2009, from the Valdosta State University Web site: http://chiron.valdosta.edu/whuitt/brilstar/chapters/affectdev.doc

Bridgeland, J. M., DiIulio, J. J., & Morison, K. B. (2006). *The silent epidemic: Perspectives of high school dropouts.* Washington, DC: Civic Enterprises & Peter D. Hart Research Associates. Retrieved December 20, 2009, from http://www.civicenterprises.net/pdfs/thesilentepidemic3-06.pdf

Bronfenbrenner, U. (1979). *The ecology of human development.* Cambridge, MA: Harvard University Press.

Bronfenbrenner, U. (1986). The ecology of the family as a context for human development: Research perspectives. *Developmental Psychology, 22,* 723–742.

Brookmeyer, K. A., Fanti, K. A., & Henrich, C. C. (2006). Schools, parents, and youth violence: A multilevel, ecological analysis. *Journal of Clinical Child and Adolescent Psychology, 35*(4), 504–514.

Brosse, A. L., Sheets, E. S., Lett, H. S., & Blumenthal, J. A. (2002). Exercise and the treatment of clinical depression in adults: Recent findings and future directions. *Sports Medicine, 32*(12), 741–760.

Brown, C. L. (2004). Reducing the over-referral of CLD students for language disabilities. *NABE Journal of Research and Practice, 2*(1), 225–243.

Brownell, M. T. (2005). High-quality teachers: How will leaders identify and support them? In B. Billingsley (Ed.), *Cultivating and keeping committed special educators: What principals and district leaders can do* (pp. 5–8). Thousand Oaks, CA: Corwin.

Buchanan, B. (2004). *Merge ahead: What mandated consolidation could mean for your district.* Washington, DC: The National School Boards Association.

Buckroyd, J., & Flitton, B. (2004). The measurement of self-concept in children with complex needs. *Emotional and Behavioural Difficulties, 9*(2), 131–139.

Burnham, J. J., & Jackson, C.M. (2000). School counselor roles: Discrepancies between actual practice and existing models. *Professional School Counseling, 4*(1), 41–49.

Burns, B. J., Costello, E. J., Angold, A., Tweed, D. L., Stangle, D. K., Farmer, E. M. Z., et al. (1995). Children's mental health service use across service sectors. *Health Affairs, 14,* 147–159.

Bush, T. (2007). Educational leadership and management: Theory, policy, and practice. *South African Journal of Education, 27*(3), 391–406.

Bush, T., & Glover, D. (2002). *School leadership: Concepts and evidence.* Nottingham, England: National College for School Leadership.

Butcher, L. M., & Plomin, R. (2008). The nature of nurture: A genomewide association scan for family chaos. *Behavioral Genetics, 38*(4), 361–371.

California Department of Education. (2005). *Getting results: Developing safe and healthy kids. Update 5: Student health, supportive schools, and academic success.* Sacramento: California Department of Education. Retrieved December 20, 2009, from http://www.cde.ca.gov/ls/he/at/gettingresults.asp

California School Redesign Network. (2005). *Collaborative planning and professional development.* Stanford, CA: Author.

Callahan, R. M., Wilkinson, L., Muller, C., & Frisco, M. (2009). ESL placement and schools: Effects on immigrant achievement. *Educational Policy, 23*(2), 355–384.

Canter, A. (2006). Problem solving and RTI: New roles for school psychologists. *Communiqué, 34*(5). Retrieved December 20, 2009, from http://www.nasponline.org/publications/cq/cq345rti.aspx

Carl D. Perkins Career and Technical Education Improvement Act of 2006, 20 U.S.C. § 2301 *et seq.* Retrieved December 20, 2009, from http://www.ed.gov/policy/sectech/leg/perkins/index.html

Carnegie Council on Adolescent Development. (1995). *Great transitions: Preparing adolescents for a new century.* Waldorf, MD: Author. (ERIC Document Reproduction Service No. ED388457)

Case, R., & Okamoto, Y. (with Griffin, S., McKeough, A., Bleiker, C., Henderson, B., & Stephenson, K. M.). (1996). The role of central conceptual structures in the development of children's thought. *Monographs of the Society for Research in Child Development, 61*(1–2).

Casey, B. J., Giedd, J. N., & Thomas, K. M. (2000). Structural and functional brain development and its relation to cognitive development. *Biological Psychology, 54,* 241–257.

Catron, T., & Weiss, B. (1994). The Vanderbilt School-Based Counseling Program: An interagency, primary-care model of mental health services. *Journal of Emotional and Behavioral Disorders, 2,* 247–253.

Cavanagh, S. E., Schiller, K., & Riegle-Crumb, C. (2006). Marital transitions, parenting, and schooling: Exploring the linkage between family structure history and adolescence. *Sociology of Education, 79,* 329–354.

Center for Equity and Excellence in Education. (2002). *Finding the family in comprehensive school reform models.* Arlington, VA: The George Washington University, Center for Equity and Excellence in Education.

Center for Equity and Excellence in Education. (2006). *State assessment policy and practice for English language learners: A national perspective.* Arlington, VA: The George Washington University, Center for Equity and Excellence in Education.

Center for Research on Education, Diversity & Excellence (CREDE). (2002). *Teacher-school-systemic integration for effective reform.* Retrieved December 20, 2009, from http://crede.berkeley .edu/research/tier/tier.html

Center for the Study and Prevention of Violence. (2006a). *Olweus Bullying Prevention Program (BPP).* Retrieved December 20, 2009, from http://www.colorado.edu/cspv/blueprints/ modelprograms/BPP.html

Center for the Study and Prevention of Violence. (2006b). (Updated from original source: Greenberg, M.T., Kusché, C. & Mihalic, S.F. [1998]. *Promoting alternative thinking strategies [PATHS]: Blueprints for violence prevention, book ten.* Blueprints for Violence Prevention Series [D.S. Elliott, Series Editor].) Boulder, CO: Center for the Study and Prevention of Violence, Institute of Behavioral Science, University of Colorado). *Promoting Alternative THinking Strategies (PATHS).* Retrieved December 20, 2009, from http://www.colorado.edu/cspv/ blueprints/modelprograms/PATHS.html

Center on Education Policy. (2006). *From the capital to the classroom: Year 4 of the No Child Left Behind Act.* Washington, DC: Author.

Centers for Disease Control and Prevention (CDC). (2006). *School health policies and programs study (SHPPS) 2006.* Atlanta, GA: Author.

Centers for Disease Control and Prevention (CDC). (2007). *2004 & 2005 national health interview survey* [Private data run]. Retrieved February 13, 2009, from http://www.cdc.gov/nchs/nhis.htm

Centers for Disease Control and Prevention (CDC). (2008). *Healthy youth! Coordinated school health program.* Retrieved December 20, 2009, from http://www.cdc.gov/HealthyYouth/CSHP/

Centre for Educational Research and Innovation. (1998). *Education policy analysis 1998.* Paris: Organisation for Economic Co-operation and Development.

Chaisson-Cardenas, J., & Moore, E. (2003). *What do you mean by diversity? Developing cultural competency skills across professional and community lines.* Iowa City: National Resource Center for Family Centered Practice, University of Iowa. Retrieved December 20, 2009, from http://www.uiowa.edu/~nrcfcp/dmcrc/conferences/Conf_Precid03/Session%201.3% 20Chaisson%20&%20Moore.pdf

Chicago Public Schools. (2007). *The Chicago Public Schools (CPS) Community Schools Initiative: Student and school outcomes.* Retrieved December 20, 2009, from http://communityschools .org/CCSDocuments/CPS%20Community%20Schools%20Initiative%20summary%208%2007 %20(2).pdf

Child Nutrition and Women, Infants and Children (WIC) Reauthorization Act of 2004, 42 U.S.C. § 1751.

Chomitz, V. R., Slining, M. M., McGowan, R. J., Mitchell, S. E., Dawson, G. F., & Hacker, K. A. (2009). Is there a relationship between physical fitness and academic achievement? Positive results from public school children in the northeastern United States. *Journal of School Health, 79*(1), 30–37.

Chrispeels, J., Strait, J., & Brown, J. (1999). The paradoxes of collaboration: What works? *Educational Leadership, 29*(2), 16–19.

Clark, D. L., & Astuto, T. A. (1994). Redirecting reform: Challenges to popular assumptions about teachers and students. *Phi Delta Kappan, 75*(7), 512–520.

Clements, M. A., Reynolds, A. J., & Hickey, E. (2004). Site-level predictors of children's school and social competence in the Chicago Child-Parent Centers. *Early Childhood Research Quarterly, 19*(2), 273–296.

Cobia, D. C., & Henderson, D. A. (2003). *Handbook of school counseling.* Upper Saddle River, NJ: Merrill Prentice Hall.

Cohen, E. (2004). Pockets of excellence: Implications for organizational change. In E. Cohen, C. M. Brody, & M. Sapon-Shevin (Eds.), *Teaching cooperative learning: The challenge for teacher education*. Albany: State University of New York Press.

Cole, S., Greenwald O'Brien, J., Gadd, G., Ristuccia, J., Wallace, L., & Gregory, M. (2005). *Helping traumatized children learn: Supportive school environments for children traumatized by family violence*. Boston: Massachusetts Advocates for Children. Retrived December 20, 2009, from http://www.massadvocates.org/publications/

Commission on the Whole Child. (2007). *The learning compact redefined: A call to action*. Alexandria, VA: Association for Supervision and Curriculum Development. Retrieved December 20, 2009, from http://www.ascd.org/ASCD/pdf/Whole%20Child/WCC%20Learning%20Compact.pdf

Committee for Economic Development. (2006). *Education for global leadership: The importance of international studies and foreign language education for U.S. economic and national security*. Washington, DC: Author.

Commonwealth of Pennsylvania Student Assistance Program Interagency Committee. (2004). *What is the student assistance program?* Retrieved December 20, 2009, from http://www.sap.state.pa.us

Community Foundations Leading Change (CFLeads). (2005). *Hampton, Virginia: A model of youth civic engagement*. Retrieved December 20, 2009, from http://www.cfleads.org/ccfy/civic/yce_model.htm

Conzemius, A., & O'Neill, J. (2001). *Building shared responsibility for student learning*. Alexandria, VA: Association for Supervision and Curriculum Development.

Cook, T. D., Murphy, R. F., & Hunt, H. D. (2000). Comer's School Development Program in Chicago: A theory-based evaluation. *American Educational Research Journal, 37*(2), 535–597.

Cooperrider, D. L. (2000). The "child" as agent of inquiry. In D. L. Cooperrider, P. F. Sorensen, Jr., D. Whitney, & T. F. Yaeger (Eds.), *Appreciative inquiry: Rethinking human organization toward a positive theory of change* (pp. 123–129). Champaign, IL: Stipes.

Corrigan, P. W., Watson A. C., Miller F. E. (2006). Blame, shame, and contamination: The impact of mental illness and drug dependence stigma on family members. *Journal of Family Psychology, 20*(2), 239–246.

Costa, A. L., & Kallick, B. (2000). *Habits of mind: A developmental series*. Alexandria, VA: Association for Supervision and Curriculum Development.

Council for Exceptional Children. (2001). Content standards for all beginning special education teachers. Arlington, VA: Author.

Council of State Governments. (2007). *School wellness policies: Legislator policy brief*. Lexington, KY: Healthy States Initiative. Retrieved December 20, 2009, from http://www.healthystates.csg.org/NR/rdonlyres/C87EB28D-B2F6-4399-B1BD-BC5617940019/0/SchoolWellnessSources.pdf

Crane, K., Gramlich, M. & Peterson, K. (2004). Putting interagency agreements into action. *Issue Brief, 3*(2). Minneapolis, MN: National Center on Secondary Education and Transition.

Crockett, J. B., & Kauffman, J. M. (1999). *The least restrictive environment: Its origins and interpretations in special education*. Mahwah, NJ: Lawrence Erlbaum Associates.

Cronin, J., Kingsbury, G. G., McCall, M. S., & Bowe, B. (2005). *The impact of the No Child Left Behind Act on student achievement and growth: 2005 edition*. Lake Oswego, OR: Northwest Evaluation Association.

Crosnoe, R., & Elder, G. H., Jr. (2004). Family dynamics, supportive relationships, and educational resilience during adolescence. *Journal of Family Issues, 25*(5), 571–602.

Crosnoe, R., Johnson, M. K., & Elder, G. H., Jr. (2004). School size and the interpersonal side of education: An examination of race/ethnicity and organizational context. *Social Science Quarterly, 85*(5), 1259–1274.

Cuban, L., & Usdan, M. (2002). *Powerful reforms with shallow roots: Getting good schools in 6 cities*. New York: Teachers College Press.

Cummins, J. (2001). Empowering minority students: A framework for intervention. *Harvard Educational Review, 71*(4), 656–676.

Curtis, W. J., & Cicchetti, D. (2003). Moving research on resilience into the 21st century: Theoretical and methodological considerations in examining the biological contributors to resilience. *Development and Psychopathology, 15,* 773–810.

Curtis, W. J., & Cicchetti, D. (2007a). Emotion and resilience: A multi-level investigation of hemispheric electroencephalogram asymmetry and emotion regulation in maltreated and non-maltreated children. *Development and Psychopathology, 19*(3), 811–840.

Curtis, W. J., & Cicchetti, D. (2007b). Multilevel perspectives on pathways to resilient functioning. *Development and Psychopathology, 19*(3), 627–629.

Cushman, K. (1998). Teacher renewal: Essential in a time of change. *Horace, 14*(4).

Dahl, S. (1998, June). *Communications and culture transformation: Cultural diversity, globalization and cultural convergence.* Project presented to the European University, Barcelona, Spain. Retrieved December 20, 2009, from http://www.stephweb.com/capstone/capstone.shtml

Daisey, J. M., Angell, W. J., & Apte, M. G. (2003). Indoor air quality, ventilation, and health symptoms in schools: An analysis of exciting information. *Indoor Air, 13*, 53–64.

Damasio, A. R. (2005). The neurobiological grounding of human values. In J. P. Changeux, A. R. Damasio, W. Singer, & Y. Christen (Eds.), *Neurobiology of human values* (pp. 47–56). London: Springer Verlag.

Damasio, H. (2005). Disorders of social conduct following damage to prefrontal cortices. In J. P. Changeux, A. R. Damasio, W. Singer, & Y. Christen (Eds.), *Neurobiology of human values* (pp. 37–46). London: Springer Verlag.

Dance, J. (2001). Shadows, mentors, and surrogate fathers: Effective schooling as critical pedagogy for inner-city boys. *Sociological Focus, 34*(4), 399–415.

Darling-Hammond, L., & Youngs, P. (2002). Defining "highly qualified teachers": What does "scientifically-based research" actually tell us? *Educational Researcher, 31*(9), 13–25.

Davis, K. D., Taylor, K. S., Hutchison, W. D., Dostrovsky, J. O., McAndrews, M. P., Richter, E. O., et al. (2005). Human anterior cingulate cortex neurons encode cognitive and emotional demands. *The Journal of Neuroscience, 25*(37), 8402–8406.

De Bellis, M. D. (2005). The psychobiology of neglect. *Child Maltreated, 10*(2), 150–172.

Deci, E. L., & Ryan, R. M. (2006). An overview of self-determination theory: An organismic-dialectic perspective. In *Handbook of self-determination research* (pp. 3–36). Rochester, NY: University of Rochester Press.

Deci, E. L., & Ryan, R. M. (2008). Facilitating optimal motivation and psychological well-being across life's domains. *Canadian Psychology, 49*(1), 14–23.

Derzon, J. H., Wilson, S. J., & Cunningham, C. A. (1999). *The effectiveness of school-based interventions for preventing and reducing violence.* Nashville, TN: Center for Evaluation Research and Methodology, Vanderbilt University.

Deshler, D. D. (2005). Adolescents with learning disabilities: Unique challenges and reasons for hope. *Learning Disability Quarterly, 28*(2), 122–124.

Deshler, D. D., Schumaker, J. B., & Woodruff, S. K. (2004). Improving literacy skills of at-risk adolescents: A schoolwide response. In D. S. Strickland & D. E. Alvermann (Eds.), *Bridging the literacy achievement gap Grades 4–1* (pp. 86–104). New York: Teachers College Press.

Dettmer, P., Dyck, N., & Thurston, L. P. (2005). *Consultation, collaboration, and teamwork for students with special needs* (5th ed.). Boston: Allyn & Bacon.

Dewey, J. (2006). *The school and society.* Whitefish, MT: Kessinger. (Original work published 1899)

Dodge, K. A., Dishion, T. J., & Lansford, J. E. (2006). *Deviant peer influences in programs for youth.* New York: Guilford Press.

Dodge, T., & Jaccard, J. (2006). The effect of high school sports participation on the use of performance-enhancing substances in young adulthood. *Journal of Adolescent Health, 39*(3), 367–373.

Doll, B., & Cummings, J. (2008). Why population-based services are essential for school mental health and how to make them happen in your school. In B. Doll & J. Cummings (Eds.), *Transforming school mental health services: Population-based approaches to promoting the competency and wellness of children* (pp. 1–20). Thousand Oaks, CA: Corwin.

Doll, B., Sands, D., Wehmeyer, M. L., & Palmer, S. (1996). Promoting the development and acquisition of self-determined behavior. In D. J. Sands & M. L. Wehmeyer (Eds.), *Self-determination across the life span: Independence and choice for people with disabilities* (pp. 65–90). Baltimore: Paul H. Brookes.

Dorfman, D., & Fisher, A. (2002). *Building relationships for student success: School-family-community partnerships and student achievement in the Northwest.* Portland, OR: Northwest Regional Education Laboratory.

Downer, J. T., Rimm-Kaufman, S. E., & Pianta, R. C. (2007). How do classroom conditions and children's risk for school problems contribute to children's engagement in learning? *School Psychology Review, 36,* 413–432.

Driscoll, A. K., Russell, S. T., & Crockett, L. J. (2008). Parenting style and youth outcomes across immigrant generation. *Journal of Family Issues, 29,* 185–209.

Dryfoos, J. G. (2002). *Evaluation of community schools: Findings to date.* Washington, DC: Coalition for Community Schools, Institute for Educational Leadership.

DuBois, D. L., Holloway, B. E., Valentine, J. C., & Cooper, H. (2002). Effectiveness of mentoring programs for youth: A meta-analytic review. *American Journal of Community Psychology, 30,* 157–198.

DuFour, R. (2003). Leading edge: "Collaboration lite" puts student achievement on a starvation diet. *Journal of Staff Development, 24*(3), 1–3.

DuFour, R. (2004). What is a "professional learning community"? *Educational Leadership, 61*(8), 6–11.

Dumais, S. A. (2006). *After-school activities and students' mathematics achievement: Differences by gender, race, and socioeconomic status.* Paper presented at the annual meeting of the American Sociological Association, Montreal, Canada. Retrieved December 20, 2009, from http://www .allacademic.com/meta/p103727_index.html

Dunst, C., & Bruder, M. (2002). Valued outcomes of service coordination, early intervention, and natural environments. *Exceptional Children, 68*(3), 361–375.

Eccles, J. S., Barber, B. L., Stone, M., & Hunt, J. (2003). Extracurricular activities and adolescent development. *Journal of Social Issues, 59*(4), 865–889.

Education Commission of the States. (2007). *Student support and remediation: State requires individual learning plans for at-risk students.* Denver, CO: Author. Retrieved December 20, 2009, from http://mb2.ecs.org/reports/Report.aspx?id=1544

Educational Policy Reform Research Institute. (2004). *Ensuring accountability for all children in an era of standards-based reform: Alternate achievement standards* (Policy symposium proceedings, February 4–6, Arlington, VA). College Park, MD: Educational Policy Reform Research Institute. (ERIC Document Reproduction Service No. ED484251)

Eick, C. J., Ware, F. N., & Jones, M. T. (2004). Coteaching in a secondary science methods course: Learning through a coteaching model that supports early teacher practice. *Journal of Science Teacher Education, 15*(3), 197–209.

Eisenman, L. T. (2001). Conceptualizing the contribution of career-oriented schooling to self-determination. *Career Development for Exceptional Individuals, 24,* 3–17.

Eisenman, L. T., & Chamberlin, M. (2001). Implementing self-determination activities: Lessons from schools. *Remedial and Special Education, 22,* 138–147.

Elders, M. J. (2002, March). *Keynote address.* 57th Annual Conference of the Association for Supervision and Curriculum Development, San Antonio, TX.

Elias, M. J. (2001, Winter). Middle school transition: It's harder than you think; Making transition to middle school successful. *Middle Matters,* 1–2.

Elias, M. J. (2004). Strategies to infuse social and emotional learning into academics. In J. E. Zins, R. P. Weissberg, M. C. Wang, & H. J. Walberg (Eds.), *Building academic success on social and emotional learning. What does the research say?* (pp. 113–134). New York: Teachers College Press.

Eng, S., Kanitar, K., Cleveland, H. H., Herbert, R., Fischer, J. L., & Wiersma, J. D. (2008). School achievement differences among Chinese and Filipino American students: Acculturation and the family. *Educational Psychology, 28*(5), 535–550.

Epstein, M. H., Rudolph, S., & Epstein, A. A. (2000). Using strength-based assessment in transition planning. *Teaching Exceptional Children, 32*(6), 50–54.

Essex, M. J., Klein, M. H., Cho, E., & Kalin, N. H. (2002). Neural systems of positive affect: Relevance to understanding child and adolescent depression? *Development and Psychopathology, 17,* 827–850.

Ettling, D. (2002, January 31). The praxis of sustaining transformative change. *Teachers College Record.* Retrieved December 20, 2009, from http://www.tcrecord.org

ExpectMore.gov. (2008). *Detailed information on the Children's Mental Health Services Assessment.* Retrieved December 20, 2009, from http://www.whitehouse.gov/omb/expectmore/detail/10000298.2002.html

Fagan, W. T. (2001). *The literacy maze: Practice without policy. The Morning Watch: Educational and Social Analysis, 29,* 1–2. Retrieved December 20, 2009, from http://www.mun.ca/educ/faculty/mwatch/fall21.htm

Fairbanks, S., Sugai, G., Guardino, D., & Lathrop, M. (2007). Response to Intervention: Examining classroom behavior support in second grade. *Exceptional Children, 73,* 288–310.

Farmer, T. W., Quinn, M. M., Hussey, W., & Holahan, T. (2001). The development of disruptive behavioral disorders and correlated constraints: Implications for intervention. *Behavioral Disorders, 26,* 117–130.

Federal Interagency Forum on Child and Family Statistics. (2009). *America's children: Key national indicators of well-being, 2009.* Retrieved December 20, 2009, from http://www.childstats.gov/americaschildren

Feldman, A. F., & Matjasko, J. L. (2007). Portfolios and profiles of adolescent school-based extracurricular activity participation. *Journal of Adolescence, 30,* 313–332.

Ferguson, C. (2005). *Reaching out to diverse populations: What can schools do to foster family-school connections? A strategy brief of the National Center for Family and Community Connections with Schools.* Austin, TX: Southwest Educational Development Laboratory. (ERIC Document Reproduction Service No. ED486468)

Fidler, P. (2001). *The impact of class size reduction on student achievement.* Los Angeles: Los Angeles Unified School District, Program Evaluation and Research Branch. (ERIC Document Reproduction Service No. ED474386)

Field, S., Hoffman, A., & Spezia, S. (1998). *Self-determination strategies for adolescents in transition.* Austin, TX: Pro-Ed.

Field, S., Martin, J., Miller, R., Ward, M., & Wehmeyer, M. (1998). *A practical guide to promoting self-determination.* Reston, VA: Council for Exceptional Children.

Finn, J. D. (1998). *Class size and students at risk: What is known? What is next?* Washington, DC: National Institute on the Education of At-Risk Students, Office of Educational Research and Improvement, U.S. Department of Education.

Finn, J. D. (2002). Class-size reduction in grades K–3. In A. Molnar (Ed.), *School reform proposals: The research evidence* (pp. 15–24). Tempe: Education Policy Research Unit, Arizona State University.

Fisher, M. (2009). Working together. *Washington Post,* January 8, p. B01. Retrieved December 20, 2009, from http://www.washingtonpost.com/wp-dyn/content/article/2009/01/07/AR2009010703485.html

Fixsen, D. L., Blasé, K. A., Horner, R., & Sugai, G. (2009). *Scaling-up brief,* No. 1. Chapel Hill: FPG Child Development Institute, The University of North Carolina at Chapel Hill. Retrieved December 20, 2009, from http://www.fpg.unc.edu/~sisep/docs/SISEP_Brief_1_ScalingUp_2009.pdf

Flowers, N., Mertens, S., & Mulhall, P. (1999). The impact of teaming: Five research-based outcomes of teaming. *Middle School Journal, 31*(2), 57–60.

Foster, H., Hagan, J., & Brooks-Gunn, J. (2009). Growing up fast: Stress exposure and subjective "weathering" in emerging adulthood. *Journal of Health and Social Behavior, 49*(2), 162–177.

Foster, S., Rollefson, M., Doksum, T., Noonan, D., & Robinson, G. (2005). *School mental health services in the United States, 2002–2003* (DHHS Pub. No. [SMA] 05–4068). Rockville, MD: Center for Mental Health Services, Substance Abuse and Mental Health Services Administration.

Fowler, S., Donegan, M., Lueke, B., Hadden, S., & Phillips, B. (2000). Evaluating community collaboration in writing anteragency agreements on the age 3 transition. *Exceptional Children, 67*(1), 35–50.

Fredericks, J. A., Blumenfeld, P. C., & Paris, A. H. (2004). Student engagement: Potential of the concept, state of the evidence. *Review of Educational Research, 74*(1), 59–109.

Fredericks, L. (2003). *Social and emotional learning, service-learning, and educational leadership.* Chicago: Collaborative for Academic, Social, and Emotional Learning (CASEL). Retrieved December 20, 2009, from http://www.casel.org/pub/reports.php

Freiberg, H. J., Connell, M. L., & Lorentz, J. (2001). Effects of Consistency Management® on student mathematics achievement in seven Chapter I elementary schools. *Journal of Education for Students Placed at Risk, 6*(3), 249–270.

Friedman, K. A., Leone, P. E., & Friedman, P. (1999). Strengths-based assessment of children with SED: Consistency of reporting by teachers and parents. *Journal of Child and Family Studies, 8,* 169–180.

Friend, M., & Cook, L. (2009). *Interactions: Collaboration skills for school professionals* (6th ed.). Columbus, OH: Prentice Hall.

Frisco, M. L., Muller, C., & Frank, K. A. (2007). Family structure change and adolescents' school performance: A propensity score approach. *Journal of Marriage and Family, 69,* 721–741.

Frumkin, H. (2006). Introduction: Safe and healthy school environments. In H. Frumkin, R. J. Geller, & I. L. Rubin (with J. Nodvin) (Eds.), *Safe and healthy school environments* (pp. 3–10). New York: Oxford University Press.

Fullan, M. (1999). *Change forces: The sequel.* New York: Routledge Falmer.

Garcia, E. (2005). *NCLR Escalera Project: Taking steps to success.* Washington, DC: National Council for La Raza, Division of Workforce and Economic Development.

Garringer, M. (2003). *Foundations of successful youth mentoring: A guidebook for program development.* Washington, DC: Hamilton Fish Institute on School and Community Violence, The George Washington University.

Gastic, B. (2005). *Safety net: Examining school-based efforts to improve student safety.* University of North Carolina.

Gee, L. (2006). Human-centered design guidelines. In D. G. Oblinger (Ed.), *Learning spaces* (pp. 10.1–10.13). Washington, DC: Educause. Retrieved December 20, 2009, from http://www.educause.edu/LearningSpaces/10569

Geenan, S., Powers, L. E., & Lopez-Vasquez, A. (2001). Multicultural aspects of parent involvement in transition. *Exceptional Children, 67*(2), 265–282.

Giedd, J. N. (2004). Structural magnetic resonance imaging of the adolescent brain. *Annals of the New York Academy of Science, 1021,* 77–85. Retrieved December 20, 2009, from http://intramural.nimh.nih.gov/research/pubs/giedd05.pdf

George, P. S., & Lawrence, G. (1982). *Handbook for middle school teaching.* Glenview, IL: Scott Foresman.

German, S., Martin, J., Marshall, L., & Sale, H. (2000). Promoting self-determination: Using "Take Action" to teach goal attainment. *Career Development for Exceptional Individuals, 23*(1), 27–38.

Glatthorn, A. A., & Jailall, J. M. (2008). *The principal as curriculum leader: Shaping what is taught and tested* (3rd ed.). Thousand Oaks, CA: Corwin.

Glover, R. (2003). Keys to successful school collaboration. *Excerpt in Education Update, 5*(6), Feb. 20, 2003 (2–3).

Gogtay, N., Ordonez, A., Herman, D. H., Hayashi, K. M., Greenstein, D., Vaituzis, C., et al. (2007). Dynamic mapping of cortical development before and after the onset of pediatric bipolar illness. *Journal of Child Psychology & Psychiatry, 48*(9), 852–862.

Goldenberg, C. (2008, Summer). Teaching English language learners: What the research does—and does not—say. *American Educator,* 8–23, 42–43. Retrieved December 20, 2009, from http://www.aft.org/pubs-reports/american_educator/issues/summer08/goldenberg.pdf

Goleman, D. (1995). *Emotional intelligence.* New York: Bantam Books.

Gordon, D. T. (2002). Fuel for reform: The importance of trust in changing schools; Are good social relationships key to school improvement? *Harvard Education Letter, 18*(4), 1–4. (ERIC Document Reproduction Service No. ED474556)

Gorman, J. C., & Balter, L. (1997). Culturally sensitive parent education: A critical review of quantitative research. *Review of Educational Research 67*(3), 339–370.

Goswami, U. (2006). Neuroscience and education: From research to practice? *Nature Reviews Neuroscience, 7,* 406–411.

Gottfredson, D. C., & Bauer, E. L. (2007). Interventions to prevent youth violence. In L. S. Doll, S. E. Bonzo, D. A. Sleet, & J. A. Mercy (Eds.), *Handbook on injury and violence prevention*. New York: Springer.

Gottfredson, G. D., & Gottfredson, D. C. (2007). School violence. In D. Flannery, A. Vazonsyi, & I. Waldman (Eds.), *The Cambridge handbook of violent behavior*. New York: Cambridge University Press.

Gottfredson, G. D., Gottfredson, D. C., Payne, A. A., Gottfredson, N. C. (2005). School climate predictors of school disorder: Results from a national study of delinquency prevention in schools. *Journal of Research in Crime and Delinquency, 42*(4), 412–444.

Greenberg, M. T., Weissberg, R. P., Utne O'Brien, M., Zins, J. E., Fredericks, L., Resnik, H., et al. (2003). Enhancing school-based prevention and youth development through coordinated social, emotional, and academic learning. *American Psychologist, 58*(6/7), 466–474.

Greene, G., & Kochhar-Bryant, C. A. (2009). Transition of culturally and linguistically diverse youth with disabilities. In C. A. Kochhar-Bryant & G. Greene, *Pathways to successful transition for youth with disabilities: A developmental process* (2nd ed.). Englewood Cliffs, NJ: Prentice Hall-Merrill Education.

Greenwood, C. R., Horton, B. T., & Utley, C. A. (2002). Academic engagement: Current perspectives on research and practice. *School Psychology Review, 31*(3), 328–349.

Grissmer, D. W., Flanagan, A., Kawata, J., & Williamson, S. (2000). *Improving student achievement: What state NAEP scores tell us*. Santa Monica, CA: RAND.

Guerra, N. G., & Knox, L. (2008). How culture impacts the dissemination and implementation of innovation: A case study of the Families and Schools Together program (FAST) for preventing violence with immigrant Latino youth. *American Journal of Community Psychology, 41*, 304–313.

Guetzloe, E. (2003). *Depression and disability in children and adolescents: ERIC digest*. Retrieved December 20, 2009, from http://www.ericdigests.org/2005-1/depression.htm (ERIC Document Reproduction Service No. ED482340)

Guilamo-Ramos, V., Litardo, H., & Jaccard, J. (2005). Prevention programs for reducing adolescent problem behaviors: Implications of the co-occurrence of problem behaviors in adolescence. *Journal of Adolescent Health, 36*(1), 82–86.

Gumenyuk, V., Korzyukov, O., Alho, K., Escera, C, & Näätänen, R. (2003). Effects of auditory distraction on electrophysiological brain activity and performance in children aged 8–13 years. *Psychophysiology, 41*(1), 30–36.

Gun-Free Schools Act of 1994, 20 U.S.C. § 8921 *et seq.*

Gunnar, M. R., & Fisher, P. A. (2006). Bringing basic research on early experience and stress neurobiology to bear on preventive interventions for neglected and maltreated children. *Development and Psychopathology, 18*, 651–677.

Hagborg, W. J., (1998). An investigation of a brief measure of school membership. *Adolescence, 33*(130), 461–468.

Hagebak, B. (1992). *Getting local agencies to cooperate: A grass roots primer for the human services*. Baltimore: University Park Press.

Hair, E., & Moore, K. A. (2007). *Disconnected youth: The influence of family, programs, peers, and communities on becoming disconnected*. Washington, DC: Child Trends.

Hall, G., & Hord, S. (2001). *Implementing change: Patterns, principles and potholes*. Needham Heights, MA: Allyn & Bacon.

Hallfors, D., Waller, M., Bauer, D., Ford, C., & Halpern, C. (2005). Which comes first in adolescence—sex and drugs or depression? *American Journal of Preventive Medicine, 29*(3), 163–170.

Hargreaves, A., Earl, L., Moore, S., & Manning, S. (2001). *Learning to change: Teaching beyond subjects and standards*. San Francisco: Jossey-Bass.

Harner, D. P. (1974). Effects of thermal environment on learning skills. *The Educational Facility Planner, 12*, 4–6.

Harry, B. (2002). Trends and issues in serving culturally diverse families of children with disabilities. *The Journal of Special Education 36*(3), 131–138.

Harry, B., & Klinger, J. (2007). Discarding the Deficit Model. *Educational Leadership, 64*, 5, pp. 16–21.

Hart, D., Zafft, C., & Zimbrich, K. (2001). Creating access to postsecondary education for all students. *The Journal for Vocational Special Needs Education, 23*(2), 19–30.

Haugaard, J. J. (2000). *Problematic behaviors during adolescence.* New York: McGraw-Hill.

Hauser, M. (2006). *Moral minds: How nature designed our universal sense of right and wrong.* New York: HarperCollins.

Heard, H. E. (2007). The family structure trajectory and adolescent school performance. *Journal of Family Issues, 28*(3), 319–354.

Heckman, J. J., & Rubinstein, Y. (2001). The importance of noncognitive skills: Lessons from the GED testing program. *The American Economic Review, 91*(2), 145–154.

Henderson, A. T., & Mapp, K. L. (2002). *A new wave of evidence: The impact of school, family and community connections on student achievement.* Austin, TX: Southwest Educational Development Laboratory.

Henderson, A. T., & Raimondo, B. (2002). Every child counts: Citizens tackle school district's achievement gap. *Middle Ground Magazine, 5*(4).

Herasymowych, M. (1996). Building learning organizations: Managing change means managing learning. *Infomine, 3*(3).

Herrera, C., Grossman, J. B., Kauh, T. J., Feldman, A. F., & McMaken, J. (with Jucovy, L. Z.). (2007). *Making a difference in schools: The Big Brothers Big Sisters school-based mentoring impact study.* Philadelphia: Public/Private Ventures. Retrieved December 20, 2009, from http://www.ppv .org/ppv/publications.asp

Herrera, C., Sipe, C. L., & McClanahan, W. S. (with Arbreton, A. J. A., & Pepper, S. K.). (2000). *Mentoring school-age children: Relationship development in community-based and school-based programs.* Philadelphia: Public/Private Ventures. Retrieved December 20, 2009, from http://www .ppv.org/ppv/publications.asp

Heslin, K. C., Casey, R., Shaheen, M. A., Cardenas, F., & Baker, R. S. (2006). Racial and ethnic differences in unmet need for vision care among children with special health care needs. *Archives of Ophthalmology, 124*(6), 895–902.

Higgins, S., Hall, E., Wall, K., Woolner, P., & McCaughey Higgins, C. (2005). *The impact of school environments: A literature review.* Newcastle upon Tyne, England: The Centre for Learning and Teaching School of Education, Communication and Language Science, University of Newcastle.

High Plains Educational Cooperative. (2005, March/April). *The role of the school psychologist in the High Plains Educational Cooperative's Responsiveness to Intervention model.* Paper presented at the National Association of School Psychologists Annual Convention, Atlanta, GA. Retrieved December 20, 2009, from http://www.nasponline.org/conventions/2005resources/Role% 20of%20SP%20High%20Plains.pdf

Hill, N., Castellino, D. R., Lansford, J. E., Nowlin, P., Dodge, K. A., Bates, J. E., et al. (2004). Parent academic involvement as related to school behavior, achievement, and aspirations: Demographic variations across adolescence. *Child Development, 75*, 1491–1509.

Himmelman, A. (1996). Collaboration and the three T's: Time, trust and turf constraints. *Health Systems Leader, 3*(10), 13–16.

Hinde, E. (2003, August 3). Reflections on reform: A former teacher looks at school change and the factors that shape it. *Teachers College Record.* Accessed December 20, 2009, from http://www .tcrecord.org

Hines, R. A. (2001). *Inclusion in middle schools: ERIC digest.* Retrieved December 20, 2009, from http://www.ericdigests.org/2002-3/inclusion.htm (ERIC Document Reproduction Service No. ED459000)

Hoagwood, K., & Erwin, H. D. (1997). Effectiveness of school-based mental health services for children: A 10-year research review. *Journal of Child and Family Studies, 6*(4), 435–451.

Hoagwood, K., & Johnson, J. (2003). School psychology: A public health framework. *Journal of School Psychology, 41*, 3–21.

Hodgkinson, H. (2006). *The whole child in a fractured world.* Alexandria, VA; Commission on the Whole Child, convened by the Association for Supervision and Curriculum Development. Retrieved December 20, 2009, from http://www.ascd.org/ASCD/pdf/fracturedworld.pdf

Hodgkinson, H. L. (2003). *Leaving too many children behind: A demographer's view on the tragic neglect of American's youngest children.* Washington DC: Institute for Educational Leadership.

Hofferth, S. L., Reid, L., & Mott, F. L. (2001). The effects of early childbearing on schooling over time. *Family Planning Perspectives, 33*(6). Retrieved December 20, 2009, from http://www.guttmacher.org/pubs/journals/3325901.html

Horner, R. H., Sugai, G., Todd, A. W., & Lewis-Palmer, T. (2005). Schoolwide behavior support. In L. M. Bambara & L. Kern (Eds.), *Individualized supports for students with problem behaviors: Designing positive behavior plans* (pp. 359–390). New York: Guilford Press.

Hough, D. L. (2003). *Research, rhetoric, and reality: A study of studies addressing NMSA's 21st-century research agenda.* Columbus, OH: National Middle School Association.

Howard, G. R. (1993). Whites in multicultural education: Rethinking our role. *Phi Delta Kappan, 75*(1), 36–41.

Huang, L., Stroul, B., Friedman, R. Mrazek, P., Friesen, B., Pires, S., et al. (2005). Transforming mental health care for children and their families. *The American Psychologist, 60*(6), 615–627.

Huffman, T. (2003). A comparison of personal assessments of the college experience among reservation and non-reservation American Indian students. *Journal of American Indian Education, 42*(2), 1–16.

Hunley, S. (2008). Preparing learning space to increase engagement. In A.Thomas & J. Grimes (Eds.), *Best practices in school psychology V* (pp. 813–826). Bethesda, MD: National Association of School Psychologists.

Huttenlocher, P. R. (2002). *Neural plasticity: The effects of environment on the development of the cerebral cortex.* Cambridge, MA: Harvard University Press.

Immordino-Yang, M. H. (2008). Strange lessons. *New Scientist, 199*(2664), 44–45.

Immordino-Yang, M. H., & Damasio, A. (2007). We feel, therefore we learn: Relevance of affective and social neuroscience to education. *Mind, Brain, and Education, 1*(1), 3–10.

Individuals with Disabilities Education Act (IDEA) of 2004, 20 U.S.C. § 1400 *et seq.*

Irvin, L. K., Horner, R. H., Ingram, K., Todd, A. W., Sugai, G., Sampson, N. K., et al. (2006). Using office discipline referral data for decision making about student behavior in elementary and middle schools: An empirical evaluation of validity. *Journal of Positive Behavior Interventions, 8*, 10–23.

Izzo, M., Hertzfeld, J., Simmons-Reed, E., & Aaron, J. (2001). Promising practices: Improving the quality of higher education for students with disabilities. *Disability Studies Quarterly, 21*(1). Retrieved December 20, 2009, from http://www.dsq-sds.org/article/viewFile/251/252

Jackson, A. W., & Davis, G. A. (2000). *Turning points 2000: Educating adolescents in the 21st century; A report of Carnegie Corporation of New York.* New York: Teachers College Press.

Jackson, T. L. (2003, December). Secondary transition coordinators at the state level. *Quick Turn Around.* Retrieved December 20, 2009, from http://www.projectforum.org/docs/secondary_transition.pdf

Jehl, J., & Kirst, M. W. (1992). Getting ready to provide school-linked services: What schools must do. *The Future of Children: School-Linked Services, 2*(1), 95–106.

Jenkins, J. M., & Ball, S. (2000). Distinguishing between negative emotions: Children understanding of the social regulatory aspects of emotion. *Cognition and Emotion, 14*(2), 261–282.

Jeynes, W. (2002). *Divorce, family structure, and the academic success of children.* Binghamton, NY: Haworth Press.

John-Steiner, V., Weber, R. J., & Minnis, M. (1998). The challenge of studying collaboration. *American Educational Research Journal, 35*(4), 773–783.

Johnson, A. W. (1998). *An evaluation of the long-term impacts of Sponsor-a-Scholar: Final report to Commonwealth Fund.* Princeton, NJ: Mathematica Policy Research, Retrieved January 20, 2009, from http://www.solutionsforamerica.org

Johnson, D. R., Thurlow, M. L., & Stout, K. E. (2007). *Revisiting graduation requirements and diploma options for youth with disabilities: A national study* (Technical report 49). Minneapolis: University of Minnesota, National Center on Educational Outcomes.

Johnston, L. D., O'Malley, P. M., Bachman, J. G., & Schulenberg, J. E. (2009). *Monitoring the Future national results on adolescent drug use: Overview of key findings, 2008* (NIH Pub. No. 09-7401). Bethesda, MD: National Institute on Drug Abuse.

Johnston, M. (1997) *Contradictions in collaboration: New thinking on school-university partnerships.* New York: Teacher College Press.

Kalyanpur, M., & Harry, B. (1999). *Culture in special education: Building reciprocal family-professional relationships.* Baltimore: Paul H. Brookes.

Kam, C. M., Greenberg, M. T., & Kusche, C. A. (2007). Sustained effects of the PATHS curriculum on the social and psychological adjustment of children in special education. *Journal of Emotional and Behavioral Disorders, 12*(2), 66–78.

Kauffman, D. L. (1980). *Systems one: An introduction to systems thinking.* Minneapolis, MN: Future Systems.

Kaufman, J., Yang, B. Z., Douglas-Palumberi, H., Houshyar, S., Lipschitz, D., & Krystal, J. H. (2004). Social supports and serotonin transporter gene moderate depression in maltreated children. *Proceedings of the National Academy of Sciences of the USA, 101,* 17316–17421.

Kay, K. (2009). Middle schools preparing young people for 21st century life and work. *Middle School Journal, 40*(5), 41–45.

Kemple, J. (2004). *Career academies: Impacts on labor market outcomes and educational attainment.* New York: Manpower Demonstration Research (MCRC). (ERIC Document Reproduction Service No. ED484616)

Kendziora, K., Bruns, E., Osher, D., Pacchiona, D., & Mejia, B. (2001). *Systems of care: Promising practices in children's mental health 2001 series, Vol 1. Wrap-around: Stories from the field.* Washington, D.C.: Center for Effective Collaboration and Practice, American Institutes for Research. Retrieved December 20, 2009, from http://cecp.air.org/AIR_Monograph.pdf

Kennedy, E. M. (2007, January). Keynote address to the Center for American Progress event "Supporting Student Learning: Massachusetts Style," Washington, DC.

Kerckhoff, A. C. (2002). The transition from school to work. In J. T. Mortimer & R. Larson (Eds.), *The changing adolescent experience: Societal trends and the transition* (pp. 52–87). New York: Cambridge University Press.

Kilgore, K., Griffin, C. C., Sindelar, P. T., & Webb, R. B. (2001). Restructuring for inclusion: A story of middle school renewal (part I). *Middle School Journal, 33*(2), 44–51.

Kilgore, K., Griffin, C. C., Sindelar, P. T., & Webb, R. B. (2002). Restructuring for inclusion: Changing teaching practices (part II). *Middle School Journal, 33*(3), 7–13.

Kirst, M., & Jehl, J. (1995). *Getting ready to provide school-linked, integrated services.* Oak Brook, IL: North Central Regional Educational Laboratory.

Kleiner, B., Porch, R., & Farris, E. (2002). *Public alternative schools and programs for students at risk of education failure: 2000–01; Statistical analysis report* (NCES 2002-004). Washington, DC: National Center for Education Statistics, U.S. Department of Education.

Klinger, J., Hoover, J., & Baca, L. (2008). *Why do English language learners struggle with reading? Distinguishing language acquisition from learning disabilities.* Thousand Oaks, CA: Corwin.

Knight, S. L., & Boudah, D. (2003). Using participatory research and development to impact student outcomes. In D. Wiseman & S. Knight (Eds.), *The impact of school-university collaboration on K–12 student outcomes* (pp. 131–165). Washington DC: American Association of Colleges of Teacher Education.

Kochhar, C. A., & Erickson, M. (1993). *Partnerships for the 21st century: Developing business-education partnerships for school improvement.* Rockville, MD: Aspen.

Kochhar-Bryant, C. (2002). Profiling success in alternative education. *Review of Alternative Education, 1*(2).

Kochhar-Bryant, C. (2008). *Collaboration and system coordination for students with special needs: From early childhood to the postsecondary years.* Columbus, OH: Prentice Hall.

Kochhar-Bryant, C., & Bassett, D. (2003). Challenge and promise in aligning transition and standards-based education. In C. A. Kochhar-Bryant & D. S. Bassett (Eds.), *Aligning transition and standards-based education: Issues and strategies* (pp. 1–24). Arlington, VA: Council for Exceptional Children.

Kochhar-Bryant, C., & Stephenson, J. (2007, April). *Exploring the relationship between state discipline policies and exclusionary educational practices for adolescents.* Paper presented at the American Educational Research Association Conference, Chicago.

Kofman, F., & Senge, P. (1993). Communities of commitment: The heart of learning organizations. *Organizational Dynamics, 22*(2), 5–23.

Kohler, P. D. (2002). *Taxonomy for transition programming: Worksheet for interagency collaboration practices.* Kalamazoo: Department of Educational Studies, Western Michigan University.

Koller, E. (2007). *Developing a social neuroscientific understanding of youth behaviors: Basic understanding.* Retrieved December 20, 2009, from http://gwired.gwu.edu/hamfish/merlin-cgi/p/downloadFile/d/19149/n/off/other/1/name/018pdf/

Kozleski, E. (2005, February). *The disproportionate representation of culturally and linguistically diverse students in special education* [Transcript]. Teleconference of the National Center on Secondary Education and Transition (NCSET). Retrieved December 20, 2009, from http://www.ncset.org/teleconferences/transcripts/2005_02.asp

Kumashiro, K. (2001). Posts' perspectives on anti-oppressive education in social studies, English, mathematics, and science classrooms. *Educational Researcher, 30*(3), 3–12.

Kuo, F. E., & Faber-Taylor, A. (2004). A potential natural treatment for attention-deficit/hyperactivity disorder: Evidence from a national study. *American Journal of Public Health, 94*(9), 1580–1586.

Lambert, L. (2003). *Leadership capacity for lasting school improvement.* Alexandria, VA: Association for Supervision and Curriculum Development.

Lambie, G. W., & Williamson, L. L. (2004). *The challenge to change from guidance counseling to professional school counseling: A historical proposition.* Retrieved December 20, 2009, from http://findarticles.com/p/articles/mi_m0KOC/is_2_8/ai_n8580063

Lange, C. M., & Sletten, S. J. (2002). *Alternative education: A brief history and research synthesis.* Alexandria, VA: Project FORUM, National Association of State Directors of Special Education. (ERIC Document Reproduction Service No. ED462809)

Learning First Alliance. (2001). *Every child learning: Safe and supportive schools.* Washington, DC: Author. (ERIC Document Reproduction No. ED461919)

Lehr, C. A., Lang, C. & Lanners, E. (2004). *Alternative schools: Findings from a national survey of the states* (Research Report 2). Minneapolis: Institute on Community Integration, University of Minnesota.

Lenroot, R. K., & Giedd, J. N. (2006). Brain development in children and adolescents: Insights from anatomical magnetic resonance imaging. *Neuroscience & Biobehavioral Reviews, 30*(6), 718–729.

Levine, C. (1998). A lasting collaboration is more than a two-step dance. *The School Administrator, 55*(6). Retrieved December 20, 2009, from http://findarticles.com/p/articles/mi_m0JSD/is_6_55/ai_77196382/

Levine, P., & Wagner, M. (2005). *The transition to adulthood for the special education population* (Policy Brief Issue No. 24). Philadelphia: MacArthur Foundation Research Network on Transitions to Adulthood and Public Policy.

Lewis, M. D., Lamm, C., Segalowitz, S. J., Stieben, J., & Zelazo, P. D. (2006). Neurophysiological correlates of emotion regulation in children and adolescents. *Journal of Cognitive Neuroscience, 18*(3), 430–443.

Lewis, C., Watson, M., & Schaps, E. (1999). Recapturing education's full mission: Educating for social, ethical, and intellectual development. In C. M. Reigeluth (Ed.), *Instructional design theories and models: A new paradigm of instructional theory* (pp. 511–536). Mahwah, NJ: Lawrence Erlbaum Associates.

Li, R. & Associates. (2004). *National Symposium on Learning Disabilities in English Language Learners, Washington, D.C., October 14–15, 2003: Symposium summary.* Washington DC: U.S. Department of Education and U.S. Department of Health and Human Services. Retrieved December 20, 2009, from http://www.nichd.nih.gov/publications/pubs/upload/ELL_summary.pdf

Lindsay, J. (2004). *The Hmong in America: A story of tragedy and hope.* Retrieved December 20, 2009, from http://www.jefflindsay.com/Hmong_tragedy.html

Linnenbrink, E. A., & Pintrich, P. R. (2003). The role of self-efficacy in student engagement and learning in the classroom. *Reading and Writing Quarterly: Overcoming Learning Difficulties, 19*(2), 119–137.

Lippman, L., Atienza, A., Rivers, A., & Keith, J. (2008). *Developmental perspective on college & workplace readiness.* Washington, DC: Child Trends.

Little, P. (2009). *Supporting student outcomes through expanded learning opportunities.* Cambridge, MA: Harvard Family Research Project.

Little, P., Wimer, C., & Weiss, H. B. (2008). *After-school programs in the 21st century: Their potential and what it takes to achieve it.* Cambridge, MA: Harvard Family Research Project.

López, G. (2001). The value of hard work: Lessons on parent involvement from an (im)migrant household. *Harvard Education Review, 71*(3), 416–437.

Lucas, R. E., & Baird, B. M. (2004). Extraversion and emotional reactivity. *Journal of Personality and Social Psychology, 86*(3), 473–485.

Luthar, S. S., & Brown, P. J. (2007). Maximizing resilience through diverse levels of inquiry: Prevailing paradigms, possibilities, and priorities for the future. *Development and Psychopathology, 19,* 931–955.

Lynch, E. W. (1997). Developing cross-cultural competence. In E. W. Lynch & M. J. Hanson (Eds.), *Developing cross-cultural competence: A guide for working with children and families* (pp. 47–90). Baltimore: Paul H. Brookes.

Maddison, R., Vander Hoorn, S., Jiang, Y., Ni Mhurchu, C., Exeter, D., Dorey, E., et al. (2009). The environment and physical activity: The influence of psychosocial, perceived and built environmental factors. *International Journal of Behavioral Nutrition and Physical Activity, 6.* Retrieved December 20, 2009, from http://www.ijbnpa.org/content/pdf/1479-5868-6-19.pdf

Mager, R. F. (1984). *Preparing instructional objectives* (2nd ed.). Belmont, CA: David S. Lake.

Marin, P., & Brown, B. (2008). The school environment and adolescent well-being: Beyond academics. *Child Trends Research Brief.* Washington, DC: National Adolescent Health Information Center. Retrieved December 20, 2009, from http://www.childtrends.org/Files/Child_Trends-2008_11_14_RB_SchoolEnviron.pdf

Martin, D., Martin, M., Gibson, S., & Wilkins, J. (2007). Increasing prosocial behavior and academic achievement among adolescent African-American males. *Adolescence, 42*(168), 689–698.

Martin, G. N. (1996). Olfactory remediation: Current evidence and possible applications. *Social Science and Medicine, 43,* 63–70.

Martin, J. E., & Marshall, L. H. (1995). ChoiceMaker: A comprehensive self-determination transition program. *Intervention in School and Clinic, 30*(3), 147–156.

Martin, J. E., Marshall, L. H., & De Pry, R. (2002). Participatory decision-making: Innovative practices that increase student self-determination. In R. Flexer, T. Simmons, P. Luft, & R. Barr (Eds.), *Planning transition across the life span* (pp. 304–332). Columbus, OH: Merrill.

Maslow, A. (1954). *Motivation and personality.* New York: Harper.

Masten, A. S. (2007). Resilience in developing systems: Progress and promise as the fourth wave rises. *Development and Psychopathology, 19,* 921–930.

Mauro, T. (n.d.). *What is a 504 plan?* Retrieved December 20, 2009, from http://specialchildren.about.com/od/504s/f/504faq1.htm

McCardle, P., Mele-McCarthy, J., Cutting, J., Leos, K, & D'Emilio, T. (2005). Learning disabilities in English language learners: Identifying the issues. *Learning Disabilities Research & Practice, 20*(1), 1–5.

McCloskey, M.. (2007). The whole child. *InfoBrief,* No. 51. Alexandria, VA: Association for Supervision and Curriculum Development.

McCollum, D. (2006). Child maltreatment and brain development. *Minnesota Medicine, 89*(3), 48–51.

McIntosh, K., Flannery, K. B., Sugai, G., Braun, D., & Cochrane, K. L. (2008). Relationships between academics and problem behavior in the transition from middle school to high school. *Journal of Positive Behavior Interventions, 10*(4), 243–255.

McLaughlin, M. W., & Talbert, J. E. (2001). *Professional communities and the work of high school teaching.* Chicago: University of Chicago Press.

McLeod, B. (1996). *School reform and student diversity: Exemplary schooling for language minority students* (NCBE Resource Collection Series No. 4). Washington, DC: National Clearinghouse for English Language Acquisition & Language.

McLeod, P. (2005). *Instructional strategies for English learners with disabilities.* Washington, DC: Council of Chief State School Officers.

Meier, A. M. (2007). Adolescent first sex and subsequent mental health. *American Journal of Sociology, 112*(6), 1811–1847.

Melaville, A., Blank, M. J., & Berg, A. (2006). *Community and family engagement: Principals share what works*. Washington, DC: Coalition for Community Schools, Institute for Educational Leadership.

Menard, C. B., Bandeen-Roche, K. J., Chilcoat, H. D. (2004). Epidemiology of multiple childhood traumatic events: Child abuse, parental psychopathology, and other family-level stressors. *Social Psychiatry and Psychiatric Epidemiology, 39*(11), 857–865.

Menard, S., Grotpeter, J., Gianola, D., O'Neal, M. (2008). *Evaluation of bully-proofing in your school: Final report*. Washington, DC: U.S. Department of Justice. Retrieved December 20, 2009, from http://www.ncjrs.gov/pdffiles1/nij/grants/221078.pdf

Mennuti, R. B., & Christner, R. W. (2009). School-based mental health: Training school psychologists for comprehensive service delivery. In E. García-Vázquez, T. D. Crespi, & C. A. Riccio (Eds.), *Handbook of education, training, and supervision of school psychologists in school and community: Vol. 1. Foundations of professional practice* (pp. 235–258). New York: Routledge.

Merriam-Webster's Collegiate Dictionary (11th ed.). (2003). Springfield, MA: Merriam-Webster.

Mertens, S. B., Anfara, V. A.,Jr., & Caskey, M. M. (Eds.). (2007). *The young adolescent and the middle school*. Charlotte, NC: Information Age.

Michaels, C. A., (1994). Transition, adolescence, and learning disabilities. In C. A. Michaels (Ed.), *Transition strategies for persons with learning disabilities* (pp. 1–2). San Diego, CA: Singular.

Midobuche, E. (2001). More than empty footprints in the sand: Educating immigrant children. *Harvard Educational Review, 71*(3), 529–535.

Midura, D. W., & Glover, D. R. (2003). *Essentials of team building: Principles and practices*. Champaign, IL: Human Kinetics.

Miller, R. (n.d.). *Holistic education: A brief introduction*. Retrieved December 20, 2009, from http://www.educationrevolution.org/holisticintro.html

Miller, R. (2005). Philosophical sources of holistic education. *Değerler Eğitimi Dergisi [Journal of Values Education]*, 3(10).

Miller, R. (2008). *The self-organizing revolution: Common principles of the educational alternatives movement*. Brandon, VT: Psychology Press.

Minke, K. M., & Anderson, K. J. (2005) Family-school collaboration and positive behavior support. *Journal of Positive Behavior Interventions, 7*(3), 181–185.

Minnesota System of Interagency Coordination Communication Project (2003, fall). Service coordination: What's it all about? *Newsletter of the Minnesota System of Interagency Coordination*. Minneapolis, MN: University of Minnesota, Institute on Community Integration.

Montiel-Overall, P. (2005). *Toward a theory of collaboration for teachers and librarians*. Chicago: American Library Association.

Mulhall, P. F. (2007). Health promoting, high performing middle level schools: The interrelationships and integration of health and education for young adolescent success and well-being. In. S. B. Mertens, V. A. Anfara Jr., & M. M. Caskey (Eds.), *The young adolescent and the middle school* (pp. 1–26). Charlotte, NC: Information Age.

Mullins, E. R., & Irvin, J. L. (2000). What research says: Transition into middle school. *Middle School Journal, 31*(3), 57–61.

Muñoz, K. A., Krebs-Smith, S. M., Ballard-Barbash, R., Cleveland, L. E. (1997). Food intakes of U.S. children and adolescents compared with recommendations. *Pediatrics, 100*(3), 323–329.

National Association for Sports and Physical Education. (2001). *New study supports physically fit kids perform better academically*. Retrieved January 14, 2007, from http://www.aahperd.org

National Association for the Education of Young Children (NAEYC). (2009). *Developmentally appropriate practice in early childhood programs serving children from birth through age 8*. Washington, DC: Author.

National Association of School Psychologists (NASP). (2008). *Helping children cope in unsettling times: The economic crisis tips for parents and teachers*. Bethesda, MD: Author.

National Center for Early Development and Learning. (2005). *Section 619 profile* (13th ed.). Chapel Hill, NC: FPG Child Development Institute.

National Center for Education Statistics. (2000). *Condition of America's public school facilities.* Washington, DC: U.S. Department of Education. Retrieved December 20, 2009, from http://nces.ed.gov/pubsearch/pubsinfo.asp?pubid=2000032

National Center for Health Education. (2005). *Growing Healthy®: Coordinated school health education.* Retrieved December 20, 2009, from http://www.nche.org/growinghealthy_coordinated schoolhealth.htm

National Center on Education, Disability and Juvenile Justice (EDJJ). (n.d.). *Transition planning and services.* College Park: University of Maryland. Retrieved December 20, 2009, from http://www.edjj.org/focus/TransitionAfterCare/transition.html

National Center on Outcomes Research. (2001). *Practice guidance for delivery outcomes in service coordination.* Towson, MD: Author.

National Center on Secondary Education and Transition (NCSET). (2002). Youth with disabilities and the Workforce Investment Act of 1998. *NCSET Policy Update, 1*(2).

National Clearinghouse for English Language Acquisition. (2005). *Biennial report to Congress on the implementation of Title III, Part A of ESEA.* Washington, DC: The George Washington University.

National Education Association. (2009). *Comprehensive curriculum.* Retrieved December 20, 2009, from http://www.nea.org/home/12957.htm

National Governors Association. (2003). *Issue brief: Preventing obesity in youth through school-based efforts.* Washington DC: Author. Retrieved December 20, 2009, from http://www.nga.org/Files/pdf/022603PREVENTING.pdf

National Institute on Alcohol Abuse and Alcoholism. (2004/2005). Alcohol development in youth—A multidisciplinary overview [Entire issue]. *Alcohol Research & Health, 28*(3). Retrieved December 20, 2009, from http://pubs.niaaa.nih.gov/publications/arh283/toc28-3.htm

National Middle School Association (NMSA). (1995). *This we believe: Developmentally responsive middle level schools.* Columbus, OH: Author.

National Middle School Association (NMSA). (1999). *NMSA research summary #8: Grade 5 in the middle school.* Retrieved December 20, 2009, from http://www.ncmsa.net/ressum8.htm

National Middle School Association (NMSA). (2002). *Supporting students in their transition to middle school: Position paper jointly adopted by the National Middle School Association and the National Association of Elementary School Principals.* Westerville, OH: Author.

National Middle School Association (NMSA) Research Committee. (2003). An adult advocate for every student. In *This we believe: Successful schools for young adolescents* (pp. 16–17). Westerville, OH: National Middle School Association.

National Task Force on Community Leadership. (2008). *Framework for community leadership for a community foundation.* Retrieved December 20, 2009, from http://www.cfleads.org/community_leadership/frameworks.php

National Youth Development Information Center. (n.d.-a). *What is youth development? Youth development.* Retrieved December 20, 2009, from http://www.nydic.org/nydic/programming/whatis/development.htm

National Youth Development Information Center. (n.d.-b). *What is youth development? Youth development critical tasks, competencies or assets.* Retrieved December 20, 2009, from http://www.nydic.org/nydic/programming/whatis/tasks.htm

Neuman, S. B. (2009). *Changing the odds for children at risk: Seven essential principles of educational programs that break the cycle of poverty.* Santa Barbara, CA: Praeger.

Nieto, S. (2000). Placing equity front and center: Some thoughts on transforming teacher. *Journal of Teacher Education, 51*(3), 180–187.

No Child Left Behind Act of 2001, 20 U.S.C. § 6301 *et seq.* Retrieved December 20, 2009, from http://www.ed.gov/policy/elsec/leg/esea02/index.html

Noddings, N. (2005). *The challenge to care in schools* (2nd ed.). New York: Teachers College Press.

North Central Regional Educational Laboratory (NCREL). (2001a). *Re-engineering schools: Getting started.* Chicago: Author.

North Central Regional Educational Laboratory (NCREL). (2001b). *Smaller learning communities.* Chicago: Author.

North Central Regional Education Laboratory (NCREL). (2004). *Promising school-linked services initiatives.* Retrieved May 11, 2005, from http://www.ncrel.org

Nye, B., Hedges, L. V., & Konstantopoulos, S. (2004). Do minorities experience larger lasting benefits from small classes? *Journal of Educational Research, 98*(2), 94–100.

Obiakor, F. E., Utley, C. A., Smith, R., & Harris-Obiakor, P. (2002). The comprehensive support model for culturally diverse exceptional learners: Intervention in an age of change. *Intervention in School and Clinic, 38*, 14–27.

Obiakor, F. E., & Wilder, L. K. (2003). Disproportionate representation in special education. *Principal Leadership, 4*(2), 17–21.

O'Hara, M. (2006). In search of the next enlightenment? The challenge for education in uncertain times. *Journal of Transformative Education, 4*(2), 105–117.

Olson, L. (2007). What does "ready" mean? *Education Week, 26*(40), 7–8, 10–12.

Olweus, D., Limber, S., & Mihalic, S. F. (1999). *Blueprints for violence prevention: Vol. 9. Bullying prevention program.* Boulder, CO: Center for the Study and Prevention of Violence.

Orfield, G., Losen, D., Wald, J., & Swanson, C., (2004). *Losing our future: How minority youth are being left behind by the graduation rate crisis.* Cambridge, MA: The Civil Rights Project at Harvard University.

Ortiz, D. (2004). *NCLB & IDEA 2004: A reexamination of the "Highly Qualified Teacher" definition & a consideration of the impact in the field of special education.* Unpublished paper, George Washington University.

Osguthorpe, R. T., & Patterson, R. S. (1998). *Balancing the tensions of change: Eight keys to collaborative educational renewal.* Thousand Oaks, CA: Corwin.

Osher, D., & Fleischman, S. (2005). Research matters: Positive culture in urban schools. *Educational Leadership, 62*(6), 84–85.

Osher, D., Sprague, J., Weissberg, R. P., Axelrod, J., Keenan, S., Kendziora, K., et al. (2007). A comprehensive approach to promoting social, emotional, and academic growth in contemporary schools. In A. Thomas & J. Grimes, J. (Eds.), *Best practices in school psychology* (5th ed., Vol. 4, pp. 1263–1278). Bethesda, MD: National Association of School Psychologists.

Pally, R. (2007). The predicting brain: Unconscious repetition, conscious reflection, and therapeutic change. *The International Journal of Psychoanalysis, 88*(4), 861–881.

Partnership for 21st Century Skills. (2009). *21st century skills, education and competitiveness: A resource and policy guide.* Tucson, AZ: Author.

Patton, J., & Trainor, A. (2003). Utilizing applied academics to enhance curricular reform in secondary education. In C. A. Kochhar-Bryant & D. S. Bassett (Eds.), *Aligning transition and standards-based education: Issues and strategies.* Arlington, VA: Council for Exceptional Children.

Peek, M. E., Cargill, A., & Huang, E. S. (2007). Diabetes health disparities: A systematic review of health care interventions. *Medical Care Research and Review, 64*(5S), 101S–156S.

Pellegrini, A. D. (2005). *Recess: Its role in education and development.* Mahwah, NJ: Lawrence Erlbaum.

Pennsylvania Training and Technical Assistance Network (PATTAN). (2009). Advisory panel on least restrictive environment. Retrieved December 20, 2009, from http://www.pattan.net/partners/BureauDirectorsAdvisoryPanelonLeastRestrictiveEnvironmentPractices.aspx

Pennsylvania Truancy Task Force. (n.d.). *Pennsylvania truancy toolkit: 10 strategies to improve attendance.* Retrieved December 20, 2009, from http://www.patruancytoolkit.info/index.cfm

Perez, M. A., & Pinzon, H. L. (1997). Latino families: Partners for success in school settings. *Journal of School Health, 67*(5), 182–185.

Peter F. Drucker Foundation for Nonprofit Management. (2002). *Meeting the collaboration challenge workbook: Developing strategic alliances between nonprofit organizations and businesses.* San Francisco: Jossey-Bass.

Petrill, S. A., Pike, A., Price, T. S., & Plomin, R. (2004). Chaos in the home and socioeconomic status are associated with cognitive development in early childhood: Environmental risks identified in a genetic design. *Intelligence, 32*(5), 445–460.

Phelan, P., Davidson, A., & Yu, H. (1998). *Adolescents' worlds: Negotiating family, peers, and school.* New York: Teachers College Press.

Phelan, P., Yu, H. C., & Davidson, A. L. (1994). Navigating the psychosocial pressures of adolescence: The voices and experiences of high school youth. *American Educational Research Journal, 31*(2), 415–447.

Pianta, R. C., LaParo, K. M., Payne, C., Cox, M. J., & Bradley, R. (2002). The relation of kindergarten classroom environment to teacher, family, and school characteristics and child outcomes. *Elementary School Journal, 102*(3), 225–238.

Pinkerton, D. (2004). *Preparing children with disabilities for school.* Orange, CA: Child Development Institute.

Plutchik, R. (2001). The nature of emotions. *American Scientist, 89*, 34–350.

Pounder, D. G. (1999). Opportunities and challenges of school collaboration. *University Council for Education Administration Review, 40*(3), 1–3, 9–10.

Pugach, M. C., & Johnson, L. J. (1999). *Collaborative practitioners, collaborative schools.* Denver: Love.

Pugach, M. C., & Warger, C. L. (2001). Curriculum matters: Raising expectations for students with disabilities. *Remedial and Special Education, 22*, 194–196.

Pulliam, J. D., & Van Patten, J. J. (1999). *History of education in America* (7th ed.). Upper Saddle River, NJ: Prentice-Hall.

Physical & Health Education Canada (PHE Canada). (2009). *Quality School Health.* Retrieved December 20, 2009, from http://www.cahperd.ca/eng/health/about_qsh.cfm

Ratner, C. (2004). Genes and psychology in the news. *New Ideas in Psychology, 22*(1), 29–47.

Raue, K., MacAllum, K., & Ristow, L. (2008). *Building systems to recognize teachers of excellence: Lessons from the Ohio Teacher Incentive Fund* (Issue Paper #2). Columbus: Ohio Teacher Incentive Fund.

Raver, C. C., Garner, P. W., & Smith-Donald, R. (2007). The roles of emotion regulation and emotion knowledge for children's academic readiness: Are the links causal? In R. C. Pianta, M. J. Cox, & K. L. Snow (Eds.), *School readiness and the transition to kindergarten in the era of accountability* (pp. 121–147). Baltimore: Paul H. Brookes.

Raywid, M. A. (1993). Finding time for collaboration. *Educational Leadership, 51*(1), 30–34.

Raywid, M. A. (1998). The journey of the alternative schools movement: Where it's been and where it's going. *The High School Magazine, 6*(2) 10–14.

Redd, Z., Brooks, J., & McGarvey, A. M. (2002). Educating American youth: What makes a difference? *Child Trends Research Brief.* Washington, DC: Child Trends. Retrieved December 20, 2009, from http://www.childtrends.org/what_works/youth_development/education/Child_Trends-2002_08_01_RB_K4.pdf

Rehabilitation Act of 1973, 29 U.S.C. § 793 *et seq.*

Research and Training Center on Service Coordination. (2001). *Data report: Service coordination policies and models.* Farmington, CT: Research and Training Center on Service Coordination, Division of Child and Family Studies, University of Connecticut Health Center.

Resnick, M. D., Ireland, M., & Borowsky, I. (2004). Youth violence perpetration: What protects? What predicts? Findings from the National Longitudinal Study of Adolescent Health. *Journal of Health Economics, 35*(5), 424–433.

Response Ability. (2005). *Promoting resilience and wellbeing.* Retrieved December 20, 2009, from http://www.responseability.org/client_images/30334.pdf

Riehl, C. J. (2000). The principal's role in creating inclusive schools for diverse students: A review of normative, empirical, and critical literature on the practice of educational administration. *Review of Educational Research, 70*(1), 55–81.

Ritchie, S. Maxwell, K., & Clifford, R. M. (2007). FirstSchool: A new vision for education. In R. Pianta, M .J. Cox, & K. L. Snow (Eds.), *School readiness and the transition to kindergarten in the era of accountability* (pp. 85–96). Baltimore: Paul H. Brookes.

Rodriguez, C., & Bernard, A. (2007). *The effects of looping on perceived values and academic achievement.* Alexandria, VA: Education Research Service.

Roehlkepartain, E. C., & Scales, P. C. (2007). *Developmental assets: A framework for enriching service-learning.* Scotts Valley, CA: National Service-Learning Clearinghouse.

Roeser, R. W., Eccles, J. S., & Sameroff, A. J. (2000). School as a context of early adolescents' academic and social-emotional development: a summary of research findings. *The Elementary School Journal, 100*(5), 443–471.

Rose, L. C., & Gallup, A. M. (2006). *38th annual Phi Delta Kappa/Gallup poll of the public's attitudes toward the public schools*. Bloomington, IN: Phi Delta Kappa.

Rosman, E., McCarthy, J., Woolverton, M. (2001). *Interagency coordination*. Washington, DC: Georgetown Child Development Center.

Rossi, P. H., Lipsey, M. W., Freeman, H. E. (2003). *Evaluation: A systematic approach* (7th ed.). Thousand Oaks, CA: Sage.

Roth, J. L., & Brooks-Gunn, J. (2003). What exactly is a youth development program? Answers from research and practice. *Applied Developmental Science, 7,* 92–109.

RTI International. (2004). *Annual report*. Research Triangle, NC: Author.

Ruiz-de-Velasco, J., & Fix, M. (with Clewell, B. C.). (2000). *Overlooked & underserved: Immigrant students in U.S. secondary schools*. Washington, DC: Urban Institute Press. Retrieved December 20, 2009, from http://www.urban.org/UploadedPDF/overlooked.pdf (ERIC Document Service Reproduction No. ED449275)

Rumberger, R. W. (2004). Why students drop out of school. In G. Orfield (Ed.), *Dropouts in America: Confronting the graduation rate crisis* (pp. 131–155). Cambridge, MA: Harvard Education Press.

Sadowski, M. (2003). Introduction: Why identity matters at school. In M. Sadowski, (Ed.), *Adolescents at school: Perspectives on youth, identity, and education* (pp. 1–7). Cambridge, MA: Harvard Education.

Safe and Drug-Free Schools and Communities Act of 1994, 20 U.S.C. § 7111 *et seq.*

Sagawa, S. (2003). Service as a strategy for youth development. In A. Lewis (Ed.), *Shaping the future of American youth: Youth policy in the 21st century* (pp. 35–40). Washington, DC: American Youth Policy Forum. Retrieved December 20, 2009, from http://sagawajospin.com/shaping_future_youth.pdf

Salend, S. J., Garrick Duhaney, L. M., & Montgomery, W. (2002). A comprehensive approach to identifying and addressing issues of disproportionate representation. *Remedial and Special Education, 23*(5), 289–300.

Salovey P., & Grewal D. (2005) The science of emotional intelligence. *Current Directions in Psychological Science, 14*(6), 281–285.

Sanchez, J., Stuckey, M. E., & Morris, R. (1998). Distance learning in Indian country: Becoming the spider on the web. *Journal of American Indian Education, 37*(3), 1–17.

Sanders, M. G., & Epstein, J. L. (2000). Building school-family-community partnerships in middle and high schools. In M. G. Sanders (Ed.), *Schooling students placed at risk: Research , policy, and practice in the education of poor and minority adolescents* (pp. 339–361). NJ: Lawrence Erlbaum.

Santiago, E., Ferrara, J., & Blank, M. (2008). A full-service school fulfills its promise. *Educational Leadership, 65*(7), 44–47.

Schiraldi, V., & Ziedenberg, J. (2001). *Schools and suspensions: Self-reported crime and the growing use of suspensions*. Washington, DC: Justice Policy Institute.

Schneider, M. (2002). *Do school facilities affect academic outcomes?* Washington, DC: National Clearinghouse for Educational Facilities. Retrieved December 20, 2009, from http://www.edfacilities.org/pubs/outcomes.pdf

School Health Policies and Programs Study (SHPPS) 2006 [Special issue]. (2007). *Journal of School Health, 77*(8).

Scott, C. (2008). *A call to restructure restructuring: Lessons from the No Child Left Behind Act in five states*. Washington DC: Center on Education Policy.

Seaburn, D. B., Lorenz, A. D., Gunn, B., Gawinski, L. B., & Maukson, L. B. (2003). *Models of collaboration: A guide for mental health professionals working with health care practitioners*. New York: Basic Books.

Search Institute. (2007). *40 developmental assets for adolescents*. Minneapolis, MN: Author. Retrieved December 20, 2009, from http://www.search-institute.org/content/40-developmental-assets-adolescents-ages-12-18

Seltzer, M. M., Greenberg, J. S., Floyd, F. J., & Hong, J. (2004). The trajectory of development in adolescents and adults with autism. *Mental Retardation and Developmental Disabilities Research Reviews, 10,* 234–247.

Senge, P. M. (1994). *The fifth discipline: The art & practice of the learning organization*. New York: Doubleday.

Sharpe, M. N., & Hawes, M. E. (2003). Collaboration between general and special education: Making it work. *Issue Brief, 2*(1). Minneapolis: National Center for Secondary Education and Transition, University of Minnesota. (ERIC Document Reproduction Service No. ED481548)

Silk, J. S. , Vanderbilt-Adriance, E., Shaw, D. S., Forbes, E. E., Whalen, D. J, Ryan, N. D., et al. (2007). Resilience among children and adolescents at risk for depression: Mediation and moderation across social and neurobiological contexts. *Development and Psychopathology, 19*, 841–865.

Simeonsson, R. J., McMillen, B. J., McMillen, J. S., & Lollar, D. (2002, November). *Risk behaviors among middle school students with and without disabilities: The North Carolina Middle School YRBS.* Paper presented at the 130th Annual Meeting of the American Public Health Association, Philadelphia.

Skiba, R. J., & Knesting, K. (2002). Zero tolerance, zero evidence: An analysis of school disciplinary practice. In R .J. Skiba & G. G. Noam (Eds.), *Zero tolerance: Can suspension and expulsion keep schools safe?* (New directions for youth development, no. 92) (pp. 17–43). San Francisco: Jossey-Bass.

Slater, L. (2004). Collaboration: A framework for school improvement. *International Electronic Journal for Leadership in Learning, 8*(5). Retrieved December 20, 2009, from http://www.ucalgary .ca/iejll/vol8/Slater

Society for Neuroscience. (2003a, February). Child abuse and the brain. *Brain Briefings.* Washington, DC: Author. Retrieved December 20, 2009, from http://www.sfn.org/baw/SfNResources/ files/Child%20Abuse%20and%20the%20Brain.pdf

Society for Neuroscience. (2003b, March). Diet and the brain. *Brain Briefings.* Washington, DC: Author. Retrieved December 20, 2009, from http://www.sfn.org/baw/SfNResources/files/ Diet%20and%20the%20Brain.pdf

Soodak, L. C., & Erwin, E. J. (2000). Valued member or tolerated participant: Parent's experiences in inclusive early childhood settings. *Journal of the Association for Persons with Severe Handicaps, 25*(1), 29–41.

Southern Governors' Association. (2004). *New traditions: Options for rural high school excellence.* Washington, DC: Author. Retrieved December 20, 2009, from http://www.southerngovernors .org/Portals/0/PDFDocuments/SGANewTraditions.pdf

Speas, C. (2003). *Class-size reduction program evaluation, 2001–2002: A report to the North Carolina Department of Public Instruction.* Raleigh, NC: Wake County Public School System, Department of Evaluation and Research.

Staub, E. (1992). *The roots of evil: The origins of genocide and other group violence.* Cambridge, England: Cambridge University Press.

Stegelin, D. (2004). Early childhood education. In F. P. Schargel & J. Smink (Eds.), *Helping students graduate: A strategic approach to dropout prevention* (pp. 115–123). Larchmont, NY: Eye on Education.

Stephens, R. D., & Arnette, J. L. (2000). *From the courthouse to the schoolhouse: Making successful transitions* (OJJDP Juvenile Justice Bulletin NCJ 178900). Washington, DC: Office of Juvenile Justice and Delinquency Prevention.

Stonehill, R. M., Little, P. M., Ross, L., Neergaard, L., Harrison, L., & Deich, S. (2009). *Enhancing school reform through expanded learning.* Naperville, IL: Learning Point Associates.

Stranges, E., Merrill, C. T., & Steiner, C. A. (2008). Hospital stays for asthma for children, 2006. *Healthcare Cost and Utilization Project (HCUP) Statistical Brief #58.* Rockville, MD: Agency for Healthcare Research and Quality. Retrieved December 20, 2009, from http://www.hcup-us.ahrq.gov/reports/statbriefs/sb58.pdf

Stuhlman, M., Hamre, B., & Pianta, R. (2002). Building supportive relationships with adolescents. *Middle Matters, 11*(3), 1–3.

Stump, C. S., & Hagie, C. (2003). *The pilot year: Lessons learned from a first-year inclusion program.* Manuscript in preparation.

Substance Abuse and Mental Health Services Administration (SAMHSA), Center for Mental Health Services. (2004). *Comprehensive community mental health services program for children and their families.* Retrieved December 20, 2009, from http://mentalhealth.samhsa.gov/ publications/allpubs/Ca-0013/default.asp

Substance Abuse and Mental Health Services Administration (SAMHSA), Office of Applied Studies. (2006). *National household survey on drug abuse: Main findings, selected years, 1982 through*

2001; and National Survey on Drug Use and Health, 2002 through 2005. Retrieved December 20, 2009, from http://www.oas.samhsa.gov/p0000016.htm

Substance Abuse and Mental Health Services Administration (SAMHSA), Office of Applied Studies. (2007). *2006 National Survey on Drug Use & Health: Detailed tables.* Retrieved December 20, 2009, from http://oas.samhsa.gov/NSDUH/2k6NSDUH/tabs/TOC.htm

Sugai, G. (2007). Promoting behavioral success in schools: Commentary on exemplary practices. *Psychology in the Schools, 44*(1), 113–118.

Sugai, G., & Horner, R. (2006). A promising approach for expanding and sustaining the implementation of school-wide positive behavior support. *School Psychology Review, 35,* 245–259.

Sugai, G., Horner, R. H., & Gresham, F. (2001). Behaviorally effective school environments. In M. R. Shinn, G. Stoner, & H. M. Walker (Eds.), *Interventions for academic and behavior problems: Preventive and remedial approaches* (pp. 315–350). Silver Spring, MD: National Association of School Psychologists.

Sussman, T. (2000). Interagency collaboration and welfare reform. *Welfare Information Network Issue Note, 4*(1). (ERIC Document Reproduction Service No. ED451410)

Swaim, S. (2003, Winter). What middle schools should and can be. *Middle Matters, 4,* 4–6.

Swanson, C. (2008). *Cities in crisis: A special analytic report on high school graduation.* Bethesda, MD: Editorial Projects in Education.

Swartz, S. (2004). *Working together: A collaborative model for the delivery of special services in general classrooms.* San Bernardino, CA: Foundation for Comprehensive Early Literacy Learning. Retrieved December 20, 2009, from http://www.stanswartz.com/collaboration.html

Swearer, S. M., Espelage, D. L., Love, K. B., & Kingsbury, W. (2008). School-wide approaches to intervention for school aggression and bullying. In B. Doll & J. A. Cummings (Eds.), *Transforming school mental health services: Population-based approaches to promoting the competencies and wellness of children* (pp. 187–212). Thousand Oaks, CA: Corwin.

Sweeny, B. (2003). *Mentoring incentives.* Retrieved December 20, 2009, from http://www.mentoring-association.org/MembersOnly/K12/RecognIdeas.html

Swick, K. J., Boutte, G., & Van Scoy, I. (1999). Families and schools: Building multicultural values together. In *Annual Editions: Multicultural Education, 98/99.* Guilford, CT: Dushkin. (Reprinted from *Childhood Education, 72*(2), 75–79, 1995)

Takanishi, R. (1997). Education for healthy futures: Health promotion and life skills training. In R. Takanishi & D. A. Hamburg (Eds.), *Preparing adolescents for the twenty-first century: Challenges facing Europe and the United States* (pp. 108–121). New York: Cambridge University Press.

Tanner, C., K., & Morris, R. F. (2002). School physical environment and teacher and student morale: Is there a connection? *School Business Affairs, 68,* 4–8.

Thompson, A. E., & Kaplan, C.A. (1999). Emotionally abused children presenting to child psychiatry clinics. *Child Abuse and Neglect, 23*(2), 191–196.

Thompson, S., Thurlow, M., Parson, L., & Barrow, S. (2000). *Initial perceptions of educators as they work toward including students with disabilities in Minnesota's high standards* (Minnesota Report 25). Minneapolis: National Center on Educational Outcomes, University of Minnesota.

Tierney, J. P., Grossman, J. B. (with Resch N. L.). (2000). *Making a difference: An impact study of Big Brothers/Big Sisters (re-issue of 1995 study).* Philadelphia: Public/Private Ventures. Retrieved January 20, 2009, from http://www.ppv.org/ppv/publications.asp

Tindle, K., Leconte, P., Buchanan, L., & Taymans, J. M. (2005). Transition planning: Community mapping as a tool for teachers and students. *Research to Practice Brief, 4*(1). Minneapolis, MN: National Center on Secondary Education and Transition. (ERIC Document Reproduction Service No. ED495871)

Tobin, T. J., & Sugai, G. (2005). Preventing problem behaviors: Primary, secondary, and tertiary level prevention interventions for young children. *Journal of Early Intensive Behavior Intervention, 2*(3), 115–124.

Trail, K. (2000). Taking the lead: The role of the principal in school reform. *CSRD Connections, 1*(4), 1–9. (ERIC Document Reproduction Service No. ED451604)

Turnbull, H. R., III, Turnbull, A. P., Wehmeyer, M. L., & Park, J. (2003). A quality of life framework for special education outcomes. *Remedial and Special Education, 24,* 67–74.

University of Central Florida. (2004). *Curriculum module series for building teacher preparation capacity through partnerships with families.* Orlando: University of Central Florida.

University of Illinois at Urbana-Champaign. (2009, March 26). Social skills, extracurricular activities in high school pay off later in life. *ScienceDaily.* Retrieved December 20, 2009, from http://www.sciencedaily.com/releases/2009/03/090325132536.htm

Urdan, T., & Klein, S. (1999). Early adolescence: A review of the literature. In *Collected papers from the OERI [Office of Educational Research and Improvement] Conference on Adolescence: Designing developmentally appropriate middle schools* (pp. 19–52). Reston, VA: National Association of Secondary School Principals.

U.S. Department of Education. (2000). *A blueprint for progress in American education.* Washington, DC: National Educational Research Policy and Priorities Board, U.S. Department of Education. Retrieved December 20, 2009, from http://www.ed.gov/offices/OERI/NERPPB/blueprintforprogress.pdf

U.S. Department of Education. (2001). *Guidance concerning state and local responsibilities under the Gun-Free Schools Act.* Washington, DC: Author.

U.S. Department of Education. (2002). *A new era: Revitalizing special education for children and their families; Report of the President's Commission on Excellence in Special Education.* Jessup, MD: ED Pubs.

U.S. Department of Education. (2003). *When schools stay open late: The national evaluation of the 21st-century learning centers program; First year findings.* Washington, DC: Author. Retrieved December 20, 2009, from http://www.ed.gov/pubs/21cent/firstyear/

U.S. Department of Education. (2004). *Early implementation of supplemental educational services under the No Child Left Behind Act: Year one report.* Washington, DC: Author.

U.S. Department of Education. (2008a). *The biennial report to Congress on the implementation of the Title III state formula grant program: School years 2004–06.* Washington, DC: Office of English Language Acquisition, Language Enhancement, and Academic Achievement for Limited English Proficient Students, U.S. Department of Education. Retrieved December 20, 2009, from http://www.ed.gov/about/offices/list/oela/title3biennial0406.pdf

U.S. Department of Education. (2008b). *2008 Safe Schools/Healthy Students Initiative grants.* Retrieved December 20, 2009, from http://www.sshs.samhsa.gov/Announcements/2008 Announcement.aspx

U.S. Department of Education. (2009). *Language minority school-aged children.* Washington, DC: National Center on Education Statistics. Retrieved December 20, 2009, from http://nces.ed.gov/programs/coe/2009/section1/indicator08.asp

U.S. Department of Health and Human Services (DHHS). (2005). *Dietary guidelines for Americans: 2005.* Washington, DC: Author.

U.S. Department of Health and Human Services (DHHS). (2007). *Child maltreatment 2005.* Washington, DC: Government Printing Office.

U.S. Department of Justice, Bureau of Justice Statistics. (2004). *National Crime Victimization Survey (NCVS).* Federal Bureau of Investigation, Uniform Crime Reporting Program, Supplementary Homicide Reports.

U.S. Department of Justice, Bureau of Justice Statistics. (2005). *Indicators of School Crime and Safety.* Retrieved March 9, 2010 from http://bjs.ojp.usdoj.gov/index.cfm?ty=pbdetail&iid=455

U.S. General Accountability Office (GAO). (2003). *Child welfare and juvenile justice: Federal agencies could play a stronger rule in helping states reduce the number of children placed solely to obtain mental health services* (GAO-03-397). Washington, DC: Government Printing Office.

U.S. General Accountability Office (GAO). (2004). *Special education: Additional assistance and better coordination needed among education offices to help states meet the NCLBA teacher requirements* (GAO-04-659). Washington, DC: Author.

U.S. General Accountability Office (GAO). (2007). *African American children in foster care: Additional HHS assistance needed to help states reduce the proportion in care* (GAO-07-816). Washington, DC: Author. Retrieved December 20, 2009, from http://www.gao.gov/new.items/d07816.pdf

U.S. Office of Management and Budget (OMB). (2009). *Detailed information on the Childrens Mental Health Services Assessment.* Retrieved December 20, 2009, from http://www.whitehouse.gov/omb/expectmore/detail/10000298.2002.html

Valencia, R. B., & Black, M.S. (2002). Mexican Americans don't value education!—On the basis of the myth, mythmaking, and debunking. *Journal of Latinos and Education, 1*(2), 81–103.

Valentine, J. W., Clark, D. C., Hackman, D. G., & Petzko, V. N. (2002). *A national study of leadership in middle level schools, Vol 1. A national study of middle-level leaders and school programs.* Reston, VA: National Association of Secondary School Principals.

Valle, J., & Aponte, E. (2002). IDEA and collaboration: A Bakhtinian perspective on parent and professional discourse. *Journal of Learning Disabilities 35*(5), 469–479.

Vanderbleek, L. M. (2004). Engaging families in school-based mental health treatment. *Journal of Mental Health Counseling, 26*(3), 211–224.

Vaughn, S., Bos, C. S., & Schumm, J. S. (2003). *Teaching exceptional, diverse, and at-risk students in the general education classroom* (3rd ed.). Boston: Allyn & Bacon.

Veltkamp, L. J., & Lawson, A. (2008). Impact of trauma in school violence on the victim and the perpetrator: A mental health perspective. In T. Miller (Ed.), *School violence and primary prevention.* New York: Springer.

Villa, R., & Thousand, J. (1999). *Restructuring for caring and effective education: Piecing the puzzle together.* Baltimore: Paul H. Brookes.

Volkow, N. (2005). Confronting the rise in abuse of prescription drugs. *National Institute on Drug Abuse, 19*(5), 3. Retrieved December 20, 2009, from http://www.drugabuse.gov/NIDA _Notes/NNVol19N5/Index.html

Volpe, R., Batra, A., Bomio, S., & Costin, D. (1999). *Third generation school-linked services for at risk children.* Toronto, Canada: Laidlaw Research Centre, Institute of Child Study.

von Bertalanffy, L. (1976). *General system theory: Foundations, development, applications* (rev. ed.). New York: George Braziller. (Original work published 1968)

Wald, P., & Castleberry, M. (2000). *Educators as learners: Creating a professional learning community in your school.* Alexandria, VA: Association for Supervision and Curriculum Development.

Wandry, D., & Pleet, A. (2003). *The role of families in secondary transition: A practitioner's facilitation guide.* Arlington, VA: Division on Career Development & Transition, The Council for Exceptional Children.

Wasburn-Moses, L. (2005). Roles and responsibilities of secondary special education teachers in an age of reform. *Remedial and Special Education, 26*(3), 151–158.

Waterman, R. (2006). *Breaking down barriers, creating space: A guidebook for increasing collaboration between schools and the parents of English language learners.* Denver: Colorado Department of Education.

Waterman, R., & Harry, B. (2008). *Building collaboration between schools and parents of English language learners: Transcending barriers, creating opportunities.* Tempe, AZ: National Center for Culturally Responsive Education Systems.

Watt, T. T. (2003). Are small schools and private schools better for adolescents' emotional adjustment? *Sociology of Education, 76,* 344–367.

Waxman, H. C., Lee, Y.-H., & MacNeil, A. (2008). Principals' strategies for successfully closing the achievement caps in their schools. *Academic Leadership, 6*(3). Retrieved December 20, 2009, from http://www.academicleadership.org/emprical_research/483.shtml

Wehlage, G. G., Rutter, R. A., Smith, G. A., Lesko, N., & Fernandez, R. R. (1989). *Reducing the risk: Schools as communities of support.* Philadelphia: Falmer Press.

Wehmeyer, M. L. (2007). *Promoting self-determination in students with developmental disabilities.* K. R. Harris & S. Graham (Series Eds.), *What works for special-needs learners.* New York: Guilford Press.

Wehmeyer, M. L., Abery, B., Mithaug, D. E., Powers, L. E., & Stancliffe, R. J. (2003). *Theory in self-determination: Foundations for educational practice.* Springfield, IL: Charles C Thomas.

Wehmeyer, M. L., Field, S., Doren, B., Jones, B., & Mason, C. (2004), Self-determination and student involvement in standards-based reform. *Exceptional Children, 70,* 413–425.

Weissbourd, R. (1996). *The vulnerable child: What really hurts America's children and what we can do about it.* New York: Addison-Wesley.

Wenger, E. C. (1998, June). Communities of practice: Learning as a social system. *Systems Thinker.* Retrieved December 20, 2009, from http://www.co-i-l.com/coil/knowledge-garden/cop/ lss.shtml

Wenger, E. C. (2006). *Communities of practice: A brief introduction.* Retrieved December 20, 2009, from http://www.ewenger.com/theory/

Wenger, E. C., McDermott, R., & Snyder, W. M. (2002). *Cultivating communities of practice: A guide to managing knowledge.* Boston: Harvard Business School Press.

Wenger, E. C., & Snyder, W. M. (2000, January–February). Communities of practice: The organizational frontier. *Harvard Business Review*, 139–145.

Werner, E. E. (2004). Journeys from childhood to midlife: Risk, resilience, and recovery. *Pediatrics, 114*(2), 492.

Wertheimer, R., & Atienza, A. (2006). *Vulnerable youth: Recent trends; A report to the Annie E. Casey Foundation.* Washington, DC: Child Trends. Retrieved December 20, 2009, from http://www.aecf.org/upload/publicationfiles/da3622h1249.pdf

Wheatley, M. J., & Kellner-Rogers, M. (1999). *A simpler way* (paperback ed.). San Francisco: Berrett-Koehler.

Whelley, T., Hart, D., & Zafft, C. (2002). *Coordination and management of services and supports for individuals with disabilities from secondary to postsecondary education and employment.* Retrieved December 20, 2009, from http://www.ncset.hawaii.edu/institutes/dec2002/papers/pdf/whelley%20coordP.pdf

White House Conference on Children and Youth. (1930). *Children's charter, White House conference on child health and protection.* College Park, MD: U.S. Children's Bureau Files, National Archives.

White, D. L., & Kochhar-Bryant, C. A. (2005, September). *Foundation for alternative education. Hamilton Fish Institute Reports and Essays Serial.* Washington, DC: Hamilton Fish Institute, George Washington University.

White, D. L., & Kochhar-Bryant, C. A. (2007). Status and contemporary issues in alternative education. *Hamilton Fish Institute Reports and Essays Serial.* Washington, DC: Hamilton Fish Institute on School and Community Violence, The George Washington University.

Whiting, G. (2006). From at risk to at promise: Developing scholar identities among black males. *The Journal of Secondary Gifted Education, 17*(4), 222–229.

Wiggins, J., & McTighe, J. (2005). *Understanding by design* (2nd exp. ed.) Alexandria, VA: Association for Supervision and Curriculum Development.

Wills, J., & Luecking, R. (2004). Making the connections: Growing and supporting new organizations; Intermediaries. *InfoBrief,* No. 8. Washington, DC: National Collaborative on Workforce and Disability for Youth.

Wilson, D. B., Gottfredson, D. C., & Najaka, S. S. (2001). School-based prevention of problem behaviors: A meta-analysis. *Journal of Quantitative Criminology, 17,* 247–272.

Wilson, L. M., & Horch, H. W. (2004). Implications of brain research for teaching young adolescents. *Middle School Journal, 34*(1), 57–61.

Wood, F. (2007). *Handbook of research in emotional and behavioral disorders.* New York: Guilford Press.

Wood, W., Karvonen, M., Test, D., Browder, D., & Algozzine, B. (2004). Self-determination skills in IEP planning. *Teaching Exceptional Children, 36*(3), 8–16.

Workforce Investment Act of 1998, 29 U.S.C. 2801 *et seq.* Retrieved December 20, 2009, from http://www.doleta.gov/usworkforce/wia/wialaw.txt

Wynne, E., & Walberg, H. (1995). The virtues of intimacy in education. *Educational Leadership, 5,* 53–54.

Wyon, D. P., Anderson, I. B., & Lundqvist, G. R. (1991). The effects of moderate heat stress on mental performance. *Scandinavian Journal of Work, Environment, and Health, 5,* 352–361.

Yates, J. R., & Ortiz, A. (1998). Issues of culture and diversity affecting educators with disabilities: A change in demography is reshaping America. In R. J. Anderson, C. E. Keller, & J. M. Karp (Eds.), *Enhancing diversity: Educators with disabilities in the education enterprise.* Washington, DC: Gallaudet University Press.

Yazzie-Mintz, E. (2007). *Voices of students on engagement: A report on the 2006 High School Survey of Student Engagement.* Bloomington: Indiana University Center for Evaluation and Education Policy. Retrieved December 20, 2009, from http://ceep.indiana.edu/hsse/pdf/HSSSE_2006_Report.pdf

Zaff, J., & Michelsen, E. (2002). Encouraging civic engagement: How teens are (or are not) becoming responsible citizens. *Child Trends Research Brief.* Washington, DC: Child Trends. Retrieved December 20, 2009, from http://www.childtrends.org/Files//Child_Trends-2002_10_01_RB_CivicEngagement.pdf

Zehler, A. M., Fleischman, H. L., Hopstock, P. J., Pendzick, M. L., & Stephenson, T. G. (2003). *Descriptive study of services to LEP students and LEP students with disabilities: No. 4. Special topic report: Findings on special education LEP students.* Arlington, VA: Development Associates.

Zehr, M. A. (2003). Culture clash. *Education Week, 22*(21), 26–30.

Zemke, R. (1999). Maybe problem-solving is the problem. Don't fix that company. *Training, 36*(6), 26–33.

Zigmond, N. (2003). Searching for the most effective service delivery model for students with learning disabilities. In H. L. Swanson, K. R. Harris, & S. Graham (Eds.), *Handbook of learning disabilities* (pp. 110–122). New York: Guilford Press.

Zimmerman, B. J. (2002). Becoming a self-regulated learner: An overview. *Theory into Practice, 41*(2), 64–70.

Zins, J., Weissberg, R., Wang, M., & Walberg, H. (Eds.) (2004). *Building academic success on social and emotional learning: What does the research say?* New York: Teachers College Press.

Zionts, L. T., Zionts, P., Harrison, S., & Bellinger, O. (2003). Urban African American families' perceptions of cultural sensitivity within the special education system. *Focus on Autism and Other Developmental Disabilities, 18*(1), 41–50.

Index

CORWIN

A SAGE Company

The Corwin logo—a raven striding across an open book—represents the union of courage and learning. Corwin is committed to improving education for all learners by publishing books and other professional development resources for those serving the field of PreK–12 education. By providing practical, hands-on materials, Corwin continues to carry out the promise of its motto: **"Helping Educators Do Their Work Better."**

NSDC's purpose: Every educator engages in effective professional learning every day so every student achieves.